Global Developments in Healthcare and Medical Tourism

Sudip Paul
North-Eastern Hill University, India

Sharad Kumar Kulshreshtha
North-Eastern Hill University, India

A volume in the Advances in Hospitality, Tourism, and the Services Industry (AHTSI) Book Series

IGI Global
DISSEMINATOR OF KNOWLEDGE

Published in the United States of America by
IGI Global
Medical Information Science Reference (an imprint of IGI Global)
701 E. Chocolate Avenue
Hershey PA, USA 17033
Tel: 717-533-8845
Fax: 717-533-8661
E-mail: cust@igi-global.com
Web site: http://www.igi-global.com

Library of Congress Cataloging-in-Publication Data

Names: Paul, Sudip, 1984- editor. | Kulshreshtha, Sharad Kumar, 1978- editor.
Title: Global developments in healthcare and medical tourism / Sudip Paul and Sharad Kumar Kulshreshtha, editors.
Description: Hershey, PA : Medical Information Science Reference (an imprint of IGI Global), [2020] | Includes bibliographical references.
Identifiers: LCCN 2019009087| ISBN 9781522597872 (hardcover) | ISBN 9781522597889 (ebook)
Subjects: | MESH: Medical Tourism--trends | Delivery of Health Care--trends | Internationality
Classification: LCC RA793.5 | NLM W 81 | DDC 362.1--dc23 LC record available at https://lccn.loc.gov/2019009087

This book is published in the IGI Global book series Advances in Hospitality, Tourism, and the Services Industry (AHTSI) (ISSN: 2475-6547; eISSN: 2475-6555)

British Cataloguing in Publication Data
A Cataloguing in Publication record for this book is available from the British Library.

Advances in Hospitality, Tourism, and the Services Industry (AHTSI) Book Series

ISSN:2475-6547
EISSN:2475-6555

Editor-in-Chief: Maximiliano Korstanje, University of Palermo, Argentina

MISSION

Globally, the hospitality, travel, tourism, and services industries generate a significant percentage of revenue and represent a large portion of the business world. Even in tough economic times, these industries thrive as individuals continue to spend on leisure and recreation activities as well as services.

The Advances in Hospitality, Tourism, and the Services Industry (AHTSI) book series offers diverse publications relating to the management, promotion, and profitability of the leisure, recreation, and services industries. Highlighting current research pertaining to various topics within the realm of hospitality, travel, tourism, and services management, the titles found within the AHTSI book series are pertinent to the research and professional needs of managers, business practitioners, researchers, and upper-level students studying in the field.

COVERAGE

- Casino Management
- Food and Beverage Management
- Cruise Marketing and Sales
- Hotel management
- Sustainable Tourism
- Service Training
- Health and Wellness Tourism
- Leisure & Business Travel
- Destination Marketing and Management
- Service Design

IGI Global is currently accepting manuscripts for publication within this series. To submit a proposal for a volume in this series, please contact our Acquisition Editors at Acquisitions@igi-global.com or visit: http://www.igi-global.com/publish/.

The Advances in Hospitality, Tourism, and the Services Industry (AHTSI) Book Series (ISSN 2475-6547) is published by IGI Global, 701 E. Chocolate Avenue, Hershey, PA 17033-1240, USA, www.igi-global.com. This series is composed of titles available for purchase individually; each title is edited to be contextually exclusive from any other title within the series. For pricing and ordering information please visit http://www.igi-global.com/book-series/advances-hospitality-tourism-services-industry/121014. Postmaster: Send all address changes to above address.

Titles in this Series

For a list of additional titles in this series, please visit:
https://www.igi-global.com/book-series/advances-hospitality-tourism-services-industry/121014

Strategic Business Models to Support Demand, Supply, and Destination Management in the Tourism and Hospitality Industry
Luisa Cagica Carvalho (Institute Polytechnic of Setúbal, Portugal & University of Évora, Portugal) Lurdes Calisto (University of Évora, Portugal) and Nuno Gustavo (Escola Superior de Hotelaria e Turismo do Estoril, Portugal)
Business Science Reference • copyright 2020 • 357pp • H/C (ISBN: 9781522599364) • US $245.00 (our price)

Impact of Risk Perception Theory and Terrorism on Tourism Security Emerging Research and Opportunities
Maximiliano E. Korstanje (University of Palermo, Argentina)
Business Science Reference • copyright 2020 • 144pp • H/C (ISBN: 9781799800705) • US $175.00 (our price)

Translation and Communication in the Promotion of Business Tourism Emerging Research and Opportunities
Elena Alcalde Penalver (University of Alcalá, Spain) and Alexandra Santamaría Urbieta (University of Alcalá, Spain)
Business Science Reference • copyright 2020 • 186pp • H/C (ISBN: 9781799801429) • US $165.00 (our price)

Cultural Tourism in the Wake of Web Innovation Emerging Research and Opportunities
J. Scott McDonald (University of Texas at El Paso, USA) John R. Bennett Jr. (Valdosta State University, USA) Keith A. Merwin (Merwin & Associates, USA) and Gerald A. Merwin Jr. (Valdosta State University, USA)
Business Science Reference • copyright 2019 • 139pp • H/C (ISBN: 9781522583950) • US $165.00 (our price)

For an entire list of titles in this series, please visit:
https://www.igi-global.com/book-series/advances-hospitality-tourism-services-industry/121014

IGI Global
DISSEMINATOR OF KNOWLEDGE

701 East Chocolate Avenue, Hershey, PA 17033, USA
Tel: 717-533-8845 x100 • Fax: 717-533-8661
E-Mail: cust@igi-global.com • www.igi-global.com

Table of Contents

Detailed Table of Contents

share experiences their families, friends, and new people. Travelling also gives them a positive attitude as makes them feel good about themselves and gives them a sense of hope. Travelling is not about avoiding social conflict within their families or communities nor treating themselves alone to not be a burden to their families.

Vishakhapatnam is a coastal city of Andhra Pradesh, one of the commercial hubs of Andhra Pradesh and very near to the south part of Odisha. The city has many super specialty hospitals and is home to various tourist destinations. People of Southern Odisha do not have good medical facilities always rush to Visakhapatnam for even small treatments. Southern Odisha comprises of the following districts: Gajapati, Rayagada, Koraput, Nabrangpur, Malkangiri, and Ganjam. These districts are still deprived of basic medical facilities, and traveling to Visakhapatnam is more suitable than to the capital of Odisha (Bhubaneswar) due to distance. The methodology of this chapter is based on secondary sources such as a published book, journals, reports, articles, newspapers, and online sources. In this chapter, a descriptive method is employed. Primary data was collected from the people staying in various hospitals in Vishakhapatnam for medical purposes.

The European Directive 2011/24/EU establishes the rules for the access to cross-border healthcare to ensure the mobility of patients and promote cooperation between the different Member States. This study aims to understand its impact and the role that medical tourism can play in the healthcare context in Portugal. On the one hand, it makes a reflection on the challenges arising from its adoption, and, on the other hand, it discusses the possible impacts of its implementation, specifically in two sub-regions of the Central Region, and the role of medical tourism in light of the views of health policymakers and other local and regional stakeholders. The attractive conditions of Portugal translate into a potential destination for medical tourism; however, the transposition of the Directive reveals several weaknesses. Only through the design of a strategic plan of action, necessarily collective, participative, and accountable, that lists the supply, the potential demand, and priority options for the country and for each region, it is possible to effectively develop medical tourism.

Preface

"Increased domestic spending is essential for achieving universal health coverage and the health-related Sustainable Development Goals." – TedrosAdhanom Ghebreyesus, Director-General, World Health Organization

This book as per the title 'Global Developments in Healthcare and Medical Tourism' focuses on the recent developments in healthcare and medical tourism in the global context. Each chapter of this book addresses its relevance and significance in a very systematic manner and highlights the scope of healthcare and medical tourism in the 21st century. The global scenario of healthcare sector is changing as well as transforming rapidly due to its cutting edge research & development, advancement of technology for the better cure and care of human beings. This book also covers the trends of recent growth in field of medical tourism worldwide specially Asia and Middle East. Every chapter of this book acts as a direction towards inclusive and universal health support system so patient can move anywhere in the world for quality health and wellbeing. There is an old proverb 'Health is Wealth'. Healthy nations are more energetic, efficient, economically empowered, enterprising, in terms of growth and development and to shape better future their countries. Every nation must try his best to provide accessible, affordable, assured, advanced, and all time quality and inclusive healthcare of their people. Health, happiness and wellness are a fundamental human right and every nation should firm to achieve universal healthcare and the Sustainable Development Goals. Healthcare services are the most prior areas worldwide in terms of quality services and affordable cost of service delivery. Globally, the healthcare stakeholders are striving to develop an ecosystem to shape the future of healthcare and establish a sustainable smart health community. Healthcare service providers are very much emphasizing arduous healthcare business management, quality oriented operational efficiency, and best smart healthcare solutions. All these actions indicate quality healthcare, costs minimization, lessening margins, with the emerging healthcare service models with cashless and health insurances. This sector is fostering investment through establishing new public-private partnership for developing better health services tomorrow. There is an incredible opportunity to change the trajectory of health and healthcare in low- and middle-income countries. According to the United Nations Organization, the world population is projected to reach 8.5 billion in 2030, and to increase further to 9.7 billion in 2050 and 11.2 billion by 2100. Additional healthcare resources and service innovation is needed globally to deliver the long-term care and chronic disease management services required by a rapidly increasing senior population. There is a global report which is published by Price Water Cooper's on 'Emerging Trends in Healthcare' indicates that the demographic shifts and societal changes are intensifying pressures on health systems and demanding new directions in the delivery of healthcare. In this context, the Sustainable Development Goals focuses through SDG-4 will emphasis on "Ensure Healthy Lives and Promote Well-Being for all at all Ages", for achieving universal health.

Asia is an emerging healthcare destination due its population base. As per the UNO, sixty-one per cent of the global population lives in Asia i.e., 4.7 billion. China with 1.44 billion people and India 1.39 billion people remain the two largest countries of the world, both with more than 1 billion people, representing 19 and 18 per cent of the world's population, respectively. Recently in Government of India has launched *'Ayushman Bharat'* is National Health Protection Scheme, which will cover over 10 crore poor and vulnerable families (approximately 50 crore beneficiaries) providing coverage upto 5 lakh rupees per family per year for secondary and tertiary care hospitalization. As per the report from 'Deloitte-2019 Global Healthcare Outlook-Shaping Future', "Global health care expenditures are expected to continue to rise as spending is projected to increase at an annual rate of 5.4 percent between 2017-2022, from USD $7.724 trillion to USD $10.059 trillion". Middle East and North Africa (MENA) is a key market, such as Saudi Arabia, UAE, Turkey, and Egypt, will continue to invest greater resources into healthcare expenditure.

Smart healthcare is an innovative technology enabled healthcare solution which is transforming healthcare and medical space globally. The advanced technological solution i.e., big data, cloud computing, internet of medical things, artificial intelligence, block chain etc. are some pro-technological applications which have recently adopted by healthcare sector for delivering quality healthcare experience. Medical tourism is the fastest growing phenomenon through the world. The people are searching world class medical care with affordable budget and quality cure for the various treatments like orthopedic surgery, oncology, cancer cosmetic surgery, cardiovascular, cardiology dental surgery, neurology and neurosurgery treatments, fertility/IVF etc. The western countries have always be most preferred destination for medical tourists due most advance technology and high-end research, well monitored quality care for medical procedures, quick response for medical care but quite costly affair for developing and third world nations. In these western countries are U.S.A., France, Germany, U.K., Costa Rica, Israel, Mexico, Turkey etc. International accreditations for medical care play vital role for the growth and development as well as to develop global medical tourism market network for developing trust and brand of hospital chains throughout the world. The Joint Commission International (JCI) which is US-based Joint Commission launched its international affiliate agency in 1999, develop for accreditation standards best and uniform global healthcare.

South Asian countries are investing in healthcare and medical sector. These countries are developing medical tourism as a niche tourism product as an USP of the destination. Singapore, Thailand, Malaysia, India, South Korea, Japan and Australia are some leading medical tourism destinations. The many countries have bring reform to promote medical tourism their governments have taken initiative to implement good healthcare policies by the making of ease of doing medical tourism deliver instant Visas for medical purpose, promoting wellness tourism through spas and wellness centres and Ayurveda, naturopathy, yoga, meditation, traditional therapeutic massages for rejuvenating tourist experience. In India, there is a committed National Medical and Wellness Tourism Board in India that facilitates and promotes medical tourism which covers modern medical sciences and the ancient healthcare practices. In spite of there is a separate Ministry for Ayurveda, Yoga, Unani, Siddha and Homeopathy which is well known as (AYUSH) for promotion of ancient healthcare therapies and traditional medicines. Wellness tourism practices are also more popularizing after the UN Declaration of International Yoga Day which observe June 21 every year since 2015. The corporate sector are now offering incentive-based wellness programs with luxury and retreats which are collaborated by five star luxury hotels chains, spa resorts and hospitals. In USA and Europe majority of the companies provide workplace wellness programs for their employees for mental and physical fitness.

The rapid growth of medical tourism has mobiles the stakeholders to tap the healthcare and medical tourism opportunities by developing new business models and patient centric services, exploring new medical detonations. These stakeholders are tour operators and travel agencies, visa facilitation centre, air charter companies running air ambulance services, hotels, wellness centres, medical equipment companies, healthcare consultancies and health Insurance companies, medical tourism professionals, employees, clients, suppliers, marketing collaborators, medical tourism associations, etc. The future of healthcare and medical tourism is very perspective. The rapid growing population and challenging health issues due lifestyle disorder, stress, pollution, and climate changes are some adverse cause of effects on human life. In this context for getting quality care and mental and physical rejuvenation through wellness and advance medical care always will be a supportive holistic system for society in future. The cutting edge technology, digital healthcare system, involvement of artificial intelligence, virtual and augmented realities will give new paradigm to this sector globally.

Chapter 1 of this book signifies the role of India as an emerging wellness and medical tourism destination and the changing outlook of government policy, promotion of wellness and medical tourism to attract global tourists by developing wellness centres, luxurious health spas and resorts and world-class medical infrastructure for quality healthcare, innovative marketing and in economy cost treatments with the team of multi-specialist doctors. Chapter 2 there is focuses on key considerations for stakeholders of medical tourism which substantiate the approaches of holistic stakeholders to evolve and involve with the pace the growth of medical tourism with the comprehensive Investigation of significant deliberations. Chapter 3 is identifying the major obstructions of dental Implants for Indian patients by Out Patient Department with rapidly growing dental issues, lack of implant facility every hospital s and clinics, less numbers of dentists, cost of treatment, dental medical equipment, quality care and dental care awareness in India. Chapter 4 focuses on transformation of Dubai as a world-class healthcare and medical tourism destination. In this context the strategic indicators like vision of government for quality healthcare, new health policy growth in urban investment and infrastructure etc. are developing Dubai as a medical tourism hub. Chapter 5 defines about various travel motivations of cancer patients to cure this critical disease. There are many countries that have specialized and advanced cancer care in range and quality of cutting edge treatment options, best cancer diagnostic centres, sophistication of innovative research practices. Chapter 6 emphasis on various aspects and reasons of growth in medical tourism in Visakhapatnam specially people from South Odisha which is a state of eastern part of India where the advance medical facilities are very less and costly. Chapter 7 reflects about the European health and medical destination with perspectives for medical tourism developments in Portugal's Central Region is focusing on the practices of healthcare stakeholders and theirs perceptions towards medical tourism in Portugal. Chapter 8 discloses about alcohol consumption in Turkey which is most important tourist destination. Ankara, Istanbul, and Antalya are the most visited cities. Alcohol consumption in population aged 15 years and older consumption is very high and impacts on health determines in Turkey through Multinomial Probit Model. Chapter 9 focusses on the most universal disease happened due to changing lifestyle and work culture directly link to increase the level of mental and physical stress, fatigues which responsible change in efficiency and psychological behavior. This chapter tries to justify and correlates the effects of stress management and healthcare issues. Chapter 10 explain about Kerala a coastal state of southern India best known its traditional and indigenous wellness practices called 'Ayurveda' and hub of wellness tourism. This chapter highlights the study of green and sustainable marketing practices in the selected Ayurvedic Resorts of Kerala. Chapter 11 emphases on the joint collaborations reflect the networks among various medical tourism suppliers worldwide. This collaborative is essential efficient for medical tourism service supply chain operations for accessible global healthcare services for everyone. Chapter 12 reveals about healing and rejuvenation traditional wellness therapies of God own country 'Kerala' which is an emerging wellness tourism destination in India and Asia. The Ministry of Tourism and Ministry of AYUSH, Government of India is promoting the 'Wellness' as an USP of destination Kerala. Chapter 13 focuses on advance medical technology based on HRV-A Powerful Tool in Medical Diagnosis which is used for measure of variation in time between each heartbeat. This variation is controlled by promotive part of the nervous system called automatic nervous system. It is to be considered a robust technology for better cure of diseases. Chapter 14 highlights the prospects and challenges of medical tourism on the evidences based study of Manipur which is north eastern state of India sharing international border with Myanmar. Recently, there is rise of healthcare and medical tourism and tourists are moving from Manipur as well as Myanmar for better health services and diagnosis. Chapter 15 justify about the United Arab Emirates as an emerging medical tourism destination which reveals about the emerging medical tourism and healthcare trends, Healthcare policy of UAE, Investment in healthcare and Medical tourism, Government initiatives, public-private partnership, and key initiatives to achieving sustainable development goals.

Finally, this book will very much helpful for the scholars, researchers, academicians, and health and medical tourism practitioners. The wide coverages of in-depth discussion and outcomes of these chapters will be more potential to develop better understanding about cutting-edge information of healthcare and medical tourism globally. Readers of this book will definitely enlighten and to insights the best contemporary practices of medical tourism worldwide.

Chapter 1
Emerging Trends of Wellness and Medical Tourism in India

Anita Medhekar
https://orcid.org/0000-0002-6791-4056
Central Queensland University, Australia

ABSTRACT

India is a leading health tourism destination attracting patients as medical tourists from all over the world. Health tourism is a provision of private healthcare in collaboration with the government and the tourism sector. India has a competitive advantage over other countries engaged in health tourism in combining traditional Ayurveda, Yoga, Unani, Siddhi, and Homeopathy (AYUSH) with allopathic medicine and complex high end of medical surgeries such as cancer, cardiac, and hip and knee replacements. This chapter will identify the factors driving the growing economic importance of wellness and medical tourism to India, opportunities, and challenges in developing India as a global healthcare destination.

INTRODUCTION

Developing country as India is a leading health tourism destination attracting patients for wellness tourism and medical tourism from all over the world. India has a competitive advantage over other countries engaged in medical tourism, in combining wellness type of traditional medicine such as Ayurveda, Yoga, Unani, Siddhi and Homeopathy (AYUSH) with modern allopathic medicine and complex high-end of medical surgeries such as cancer, cardiac and hip and knee replacements. Medical tourism is provision of cost effective elective and complex surgeries in collaboration with the government, private medical hospitals and the tourism industry for patients

DOI: 10.4018/978-1-5225-9787-2.ch001

seeking diagnostic, elective, cosmetic, dental and reproductive treatments, along with having a holiday for rest and recovery at an attractive destination (Brotman, 2010; Gupta, 2008; Medhekar & Ali, 2012; Singh, 2008; Sultana, Haque, Momen, & Yasmin, 2014).

Global travel for healthcare tourism phenomenon is driven by globalisation, privatisation and outsourcing of healthcare and internet communication technologies (Horowitz & Rosensweig, 2007; Runnels & Tuner, 2011; Smith, Chanda, & Viroj, 2009). Developing countries such as Thailand, India, Malaysia, South Africa, Brazil, and South Korea, are popular destinations for outsourcing medical treatment overseas such as dental, eye, cancer, orthopaedic and cardiac due to world class hospitals and highly skilled and overseas trained medical professionals (Awadzi & Panda, 2006; Baliga, 2006; Bookman & Bookman, 2007; Connell, 2013; Dasgupta & Dasgupta, 2014). In 2009, India ranked second after Thailand as a healthcare destination in number of medical tourist arrivals (IMT, 2009).

Medical tourism is an economic activity that involves trade in healthcare related services from the medical and tourism sectors of the economy (Bookman & Bookman, 2007). Jones and McCullough (2007) have described medical tourism as "international economics in action" (p. 1077) as patients seek first world quality and state-of-the-art medical technology and innovative surgical procedures in developing countries at an affordable prices (Crooks et al., 2011; Medhekar, Wong & Hall, 2014; Turner, 2007). Potential patients as wellness or medical tourists search for information on the internet websites of private hospitals, medical tourism facilitators and government health tourism portals before they make a decision to travel abroad for treatment (Lunt, Hardey, & Mannion, 2010; Medhekar & Newby, 2013; Moghavvemi et al., 2017). The main objective of the health tourists is to improve their health, wellbeing and quality of life.

According to Connell (2006), "India is capitalizing on its low costs and highly trained doctors to appeal to these medical tourists" (p.1), besides promoting thousands of years old attractions of heritage and cultural tourism. The success of health tourism sector can be quantified by number of inbound wellness and tourists travelling on medical visa (M-visa) and amount of foreign exchange revenue generated. Health tourists not only spend on healthcare related goods and services, but also spend on local travel, accommodation, sightseeing, shopping and hospitality sector.

The number of overseas patients granted with medical visa, for medical tourism to India is on the rise. Foreign patients as medical tourists visiting India is growing at the rate of 30% a year since 2012. In 2012, nearly 1,71,021 medical visas were issued which increased to 2,36, 898, in 2013 and 2,01,333 in 2016 to 361,060 in 2017 (IMTJ, 2017a, 2017b). The medical visas issued by the Indian Embassy in Oman is on the rise by 100% from 5255 M-visas and 3,902 medical attendant visas in 2015, rising to 11,613 M-visa and 8,491 medical attendant visas in 2016 (IHCO,

2017), indicating India as a choice of healthcare destination for medical treatment for patients from neighbouring countries.

This chapter is structured as follows. The first introductory section of the chapter introduces the growing economic importance and significance of medical tourism to India. Section 2 provides the literature review on medical tourism in general and India in particular. Section 3 discusses the role of the Indian government in supporting the development and promotion of health tourism. Section 4, evaluates the challenges and opportunities of sustainable development of India as a global healthcare destination with the aim to also benefit the local population in terms of availability of affordable, accessible, and accredited (AAAA) healthcare. Section 5 provides managerial and policy implications for the government, private hospitals/ medical and tourism sectors of the economy to develop and promote wellness and medical tourism. The final section, provides conclusion and future research directions to advance the knowledge in the field of wellness and medical tourism.

LITERATURE REVIEW

Health conscious consumers are travelling abroad for Health Tourism to improve their health and quality of life. Health care tourism from the supply-side is defined by Goodrich and Goodrich (1987), as an "attempt on the part of a tourist facility or destination to attract tourist by deliberately promoting its health-care services and facilities, in addition to its regular tourist amenities" (p. 217). These services according to them may include medical examination at the hotel, special diet, herbal wraps, hydrotherapy, spas, Turkish baths and acupuncture. In early medical literature, medical tourism was about a medical specialist travelling for the purpose of delivering healthcare to the people (Morgan, 2007). According to Medhekar et al. (2014), under the umbrella of health tourism there are two main macro branches –wellness and medical tourism as shown in Figure 1, having various micro-niche types of treatment speciality in India.

Wellness Tourism

Traditionally western countries like USA, Germany, Austria and France including Thailand only considered spa, massage and hot-water springs as part of wellness or alternative/traditional treatments (Chen, Chang, & Wu, 2013, Costa, Quintela, & Mendes, 2015; Garcia-Altes, 2005; Henderson, 2003; Smith & Puczko, 2009; Smith & Puczko, 2014). India provides excellence in their own niche areas of wellness-tourism due to natural endowment (hot-water springs, natural oils, and herbal plants medicine) and medial tourism super-surgical speciality based on state-of-the-art

Figure 1. Health tourism typology
Source: Developed for this paper & adapted from Medhekar et al. (2014)

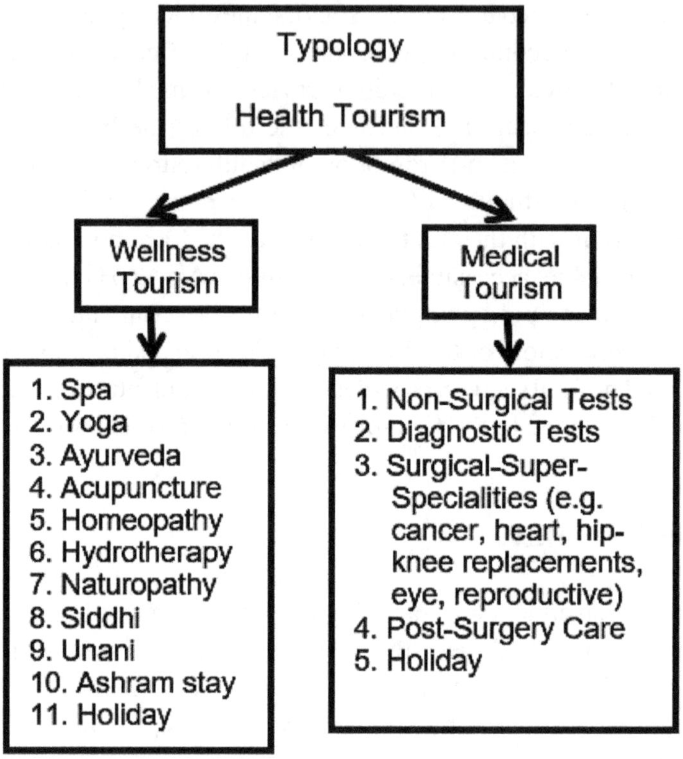

diagnostic and surgical procedures, innovative drugs, medical technology, and human-resource expertise in medical surgeries (Medhekar et al., 2014). Indian wellness sector which includes traditional yoga, herbal plants and Ayurveda medicines, are integral part of Indian way of life. Traditional medicine/therapy under wellness tourism, is the fastest growing niche segment of health travel and leisure industry.

In case of wellness type of travel, a patient first chooses the facility which specialises in a particular type of wellness therapy such as Yoga, Ayurveda, herbal therapy and then the destination, India or Thailand. The tourism industries have capitalised on the wellness and medical specialities provided by a particular medical and wellness facility, and based on its location, market and promote these destinations touristic attractions, along with medical tourism. Heung and Kucukusta (2013) studied the development of wellness tourism in China, exploring the emerging wellness industry related factors that support its development depends on resources, touristic attractions, policy and planning, development, management and marketing based on model of sustainable wellness development (Sheldon & Park, 2008).

In a developing country as India, wellness treatment goes beyond spa and message. Wellness tourism service providers include wellness travel agents, 1 to 5 star hotels, Yoga and Ayurvedic resorts and Spa facilities. It includes staying in a wellness resort or Ashram with natural surroundings, and adopting a simple vegetarian and spiritual life style, learning about local traditional Ayurvedic herbal medicines, detox treatment, oils, message, yoga, diet and leaning to cook and eat vegetarian food based on individual diagnostic health requirements.

Wellness is an integral part of Indian daily life practiced in traditional Yoga, Ayurveda and herbal medicine. The Indian ministry of tourism in 2011 provided guideline for accreditation of wellness centres developed by National Board for Accreditation of Hospitals & Healthcare Services (NBAH) in consultation with AYUSH – Ayurveda, Yoga, Unani, Herbal, Spa, and Siddhi (GOI, 2018b) to harness the traditional AYUSH medicine sector. These can be categorised as micro-niche wellness types of treatments. The Ministry of Tourism has set up a National Medical and Wellness Tourism Board (NMWTB) and Marketing Development Assistance (MDA) scheme to support the matters relating to capacity building, monitoring, regulating, and facilitating the marketing and promotion of India as a destination for medical and wellness tourism (Business Standard, 2016). The accreditation of wellness centres is essential for credibility and market development of traditional medicine driven by NBAH, AYUSH, and ministry of tourism, state governments and other stakeholders of the wellness tourism sector.

Medical Tourism

Medical tourism industry report by Edelhelt (2008) considers medical travel where a "patient travelling to another country for more affordable care, or care that is of higher quality or more accessible" (p. 10). Smith and Puczko (2009) are of the opinion that, beyond wellness tourism such as spa and hot-water spring, medical tourism is an extreme form of medical surgeries where patients from developed countries, are travelling to developing countries, with the aim to improve their health and wellbeing. Whereas Johnston et al, (2010) placed emphasis on the aim of travel and considers medical tourism as "patients leaving their country of residence outside of established cross-border care arrangements made with the intent of accessing medical care, often surgery abroad" (p. 1).

In case of medical tourism different types of micro-niche treatments are super-specialities of high-end surgeries such as cardiac, cancer, cosmetic, dental, eye, hip/knee replacement, plastic surgery, organ transplant, brain, neurosurgery, reproductive and gender-reassignment. Figure 2 provides the key nine source countries of medical tourists who travelled to India on medical visa in 2014. Bangladesh is topping the list followed by Afghanistan and so on.

Figure 2. Source countries of medical tourists to India
Source: FICCI-GOI (2016)

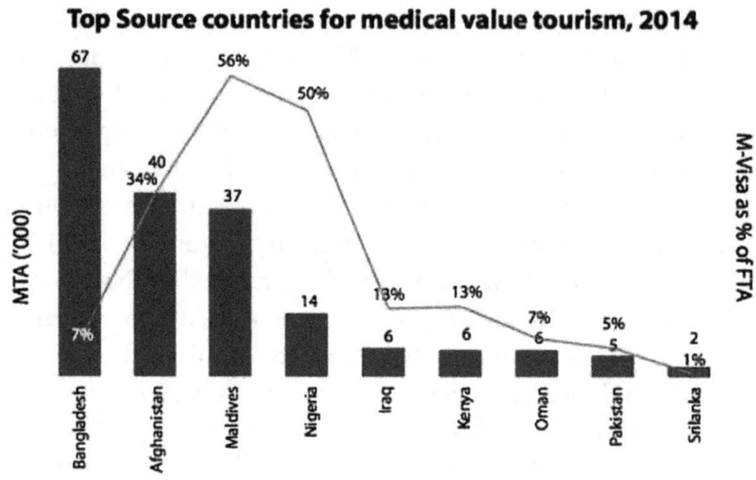

Various push factors motivate foreign patients to travel from home-country to an overseas host-country for medical treatment. Such as, rising healthcare costs and health insurance costs at home, uninsured or underinsured procedures, long waiting time for surgery, non-availability of certain surgical procedures due to ethical or regulatory reasons, less developed country, high disposable income, ease of travel, ageing population in developed countries and informed decision-making process (Bookman & Bookman, 2007; Lunt et al., 2010; Turner, 2007; Lunt & Mannion, 2014). Patients as medical tourists travel to seek second opinion on diagnostic tests and for undertaking complex surgeries such as heart, cancer, eye surgery, dental procedures, cosmetic, reproductive treatment and, hip or knee replacements and may engage in touristic activities if health permits.

Furthermore, host-country pull factors include, affordable first world Joint Commission International (JCI) accredited quality of medical treatment/surgery with less or no waiting time, pre and post-surgery care, privacy and confidentiality, physicians qualifications, state-of-the-art hospital facilities and services, patient safety with positive healthcare outcome and an attractive destination for tourism (Medhekar & Newby, 2013; Medhekar et al., 2014). A qualitative study by thematic analysis of interview findings with inbound actual medical tourists to India, from the demand side ranked the pull-factors in ascending order, as important factors that influence the decision to travel abroad for medical treatment/surgery. The factors were — less surgery waiting-time for, healthcare quality and accreditation, staff/ surgeons expertise, healthcare information, hospital facilities and services, patient-safety, medical travel-risk, surgical costs and holiday opportunity (Medhekar, Wong, & Hall, 2019).

Another recent empirical survey finding by Collins, Medhekar, Wong, and Cobanoglu (2019) on outbound medical travel from the US citizens from 541 post-travel US medical tourist responses, concludes that foreign patients when choosing a country for medical treatment considered four factors, such as attractiveness of tourism destination, medical tourism costs, country environment and high quality of medical and tourism facilities and services. The highest number of outbound US patients in their study travelled to India (175), followed by China (66), Thailand (57), Mexico (19), and Turkey (16), and the rest were distributed across other countries. This study also indicates that India is the preferred choice of destination for high-end of medical treatment/surgery due to the four main factors mentioned in their study.

Joint Commission International (JCI) has accredited 38 healthcare facilities, diagnostic clinics and hospitals in India, until February 2019 (JCI, 2019). The JCI accreditation is renewed every three years, and declined if quality assurance standards are not maintained by the medical facilities, hospitals and diagnostic clinics. India not only has world class healthcare facilities and highly qualified wellness and medical professionals but also has the advantage of English language along with cultural familiarity with South Asian languages, food, and music, to attract large number of medical travellers from neighbouring Afghanistan, Pakistan, Nepal, Bangladesh, SriLanka, Burma, Maldives and sub-Saharan African countries including expatriate Indians and diaspora (Medhekar & Ali, 2012; Medhekar & Haq, 2015).

ROLE OF INDIAN GOVERNMENT IN DEVELOPING HEALTHCARE TOURISM

The Rao governments, 9th Five Year Plan (1997-2002) 'New Economic Policy' reforms of the 1990s, aimed to provide alternative private finance initiatives and privatise healthcare by opening up public sector for private corporate investments and public-private partnerships (Medhekar, 2012). This led to the cuts in public sector expenditure in health and commodification of healthcare services. The 'New Economic Policy Reforms' also led to the acceptance of economic policy advocated by World Health Organisation's Commission of Macroeconomics and Health, that investment in health was the pathway to economic development for developing countries (WHO, 2001; Basu & Nundy, 2008) such as India.

These macroeconomic reforms in healthcare led to public private partnerships in healthcare provision by opening up healthcare sector to foreigners, and an important source of foreign exchange earnings through trade in healthcare services. The central governments 10th five year plan 2002-2007, clearly outlined in its National Health

Policy to achieve acceptable, accessible, affordable and sustainable standard of health system. This can be achieved through utilisation of private sector resources to solve public health issues, finance health by liberalising insurance sector and redefine the state's role of being the provider as well as the financer of healthcare services, through public and private partnerships (GOI, 2003).

For India, tourism is one of the largest foreign exchange earners especially since the development and promotion of wellness and medical tourism sectors. The Government of India's 2002, National Tourism Policy highlights seven objectives for sustainable tourism development, in terms of welcome, information, facilitation, safety, cooperation, infrastructure development and cleanliness, which can be applied in context of health tourism (MOT-GOI, 2018). The various tourism campaigns by the government of India such as 2002 the "Incredible India" campaign, "India: The Global Health Destination" and the 2008 "Guest is like God" (in Sanskrit 'Athiti Devo Bhava') have been successful in attracting in-bound tourists to India (MOT, 2012).

The government of India announced in the 10th five-year plan (2002-2007) to promote India as a world class "Global Healthcare Destination" providing affordable quality of super-surgical specialities with less waiting time, along with wellness type of traditional treatments (CII & McKinsey, 2002; Deloitte, 2008; MTI-2005). It has played a key role in providing subsidies and export promotion measures to develop medical tourism in India. For example, acquiring prime land for private hospital construction at a subsidised rate, introduction of M-Visa and medical-escort visa, medical tourism is eligible for all fiscal incentives related to export earnings, 100% foreign direct investment in medical tourism facilities, increased depreciation allowance from 25% to 40% on used medical machinery and equipment and reduced import duties on medical technology (Chinai & Goswami, 2008; GOI, 2003; Medhekar & Ali, 2012).

A joint study in 2002 (CII & McKinsey, 2002) outlined enormous opportunities and potential growth for this sector. In 2005, an estimated 150,000 medical tourists travelled to India and this was expected to increase by 15% each year. By the end of 2012 the industry was predicted to grow by $US 2 billion. The number of foreign patients as medical tourists visiting India currently is growing at the rate of 30 per cent a year (CII & Mckinsey, 2002; FICCI, 2008; Gupta, 2008; MOT, 2005). It is projected by the Federation of Indian Chambers of Commerce and Industry (FICCI) that the health-care market in India will generate around US$ 2.2 billion by year 2012, that is 5.2% of gross domestic product (GDP) by 2012, to US$ 3 billion by 2013, to between US$ 50 billion and US$ 69 billion, or 6.2% and 8.5% of GDP by 2020 from healthcare (Chinai & Goswami, 2007; Deloitte, 2008; FICCI, 2008). The main sources of inbound medical tourist to India are from Bangladesh, Middle East, UK, USA, Canada, Africa and other developing countries (Singh, 2008; Gupta, 2004; Medhekar, 2014; RNCOS, 2010).

According to the India Ministry of Tourism, recently most of the inbound medical tourists arrive from the neighbouring developing countries of Afghanistan, Bangladesh, Nepal, Pakistan, SriLanka, Oman, Yemen, Uzbekistan, Iraq, Maldives, Kenya, Tanzania, and Nigeria and issue of M-visa and MX-visa has increased since 2015. The government of India has introduced a national healthcare tourism portal to market and provide valuable information to the potential wellness and medical tourist regarding accredited (JCI, NABH & NABL) medical providers and types of medical procedures, surgical-speciality and wellness types available, location and language capabilities before making a decision to travel to India for treatment. Nearly 99 super-speciality hospitals, 16 wellness and rejuvenation centres and 28 Ayurveda and alternative medicine hospitals and resorts are listed on the government website (http://www.indiahealthcaretourism.com/).

The Government of India has taken the following measures to develop, provide incentives and promoted India in 2002 campaign as an 'Incredible India: Global Healthcare Destination' to the world (GOI, 2003; MOT-GOI, 2018; Medhekar & Ali, 2012; MOT 2012).

1. Introduction of M-Visa in 2003, allowing multiple entries and valid for a year and second year is extended, based on physicians recommendation from a hospital where treatment is undertaken. Emergency- Visa on Arrival (VoA) for medical reasons also provides three months stay for medical purposes. Two Medical Escort / Attendant Visa (MX) for accompanying blood related family members is allowed, whose validity is for same period as patient's medical visa.
2. Since 2003 Medical Tourism (MT) is legally an "export" and deemed eligible for all fiscal incentives extended to export earnings wellness and medical tourism related goods and services.
3. Incentives for 100% foreign direct investment in medical infrastructure facilities, medical research and development initiatives and diagnostic machinery.
4. Lower import duties on state-of-the-art medical technology, life-saving medical equipment and diagnostic machinery as inbound medical travel is categorised as an export industry.
5. Increased depreciation allowances from 25% up to 40%, on used medical machinery and diagnostic equipment.
6. Providing prime land at subsidised rates to build private hospitals and health infrastructure to treat foreign patients (Gupta, 2008), with the promise of providing free health care for certain number of domestic poor patients as their corporate social responsibility.
7. Joint Commission International accreditation and certification of 17 hospitals and three (3) medical facilities in 2010. This has since increased to 38 hospitals

(JCI, 2019) including certification by the National Accreditation Board for Hospitals and Healthcare Providers (Anon, 2009).

8. Organizing medical tourism trade fairs, exhibitions, and conferences in developed and developing countries in partnership with private corporate hospitals, medical schools, tourism sector and medical tour facilitators to promote inbound wellness and medical tourism to India.
    - To reduce bureaucratic delays and expedite visas on arrival (VoA) scheme for health and medical tourists was introduced in 2010 for 5 countries Finland, Japan, Luxembourg, New Zealand and Singapore. In 2011, VoA has been extended to Cambodia, Indonesia, Vietnam, Philippines, Laos and Myanmar and since then to most of the countries. A total number of 7,662 VOA's were issued during January-July 2012 as compared to 6,594 VoA during corresponding period of 2011 registering a positive growth of 16.2 per cent (The Hindu, 2012) which is on the rise.
9. Different state governments have taken independent measures to promote medical tourism. For example: Kerala promoted as "Gods Own Country", is known for various wellness packages incorporating traditional AYUSH spiritual philosophy and therapy. Gujarat government has developed an integrated medical tourism circuit policy connecting super-speciality hospitals with heritage and cultural tourism. The current Modi governments "Look East Policy " for the seven East Indian states, is also focussing on developing private hospitals to attract medical tourists from neighbouring countries to East of the border - Burma and Bangladesh for medical tourism. Further, Karnataka state is focussing more on developing tele-medicine, billing and disease coding technology. Similarly in Maharashtra, the state government in collaboration with the Federation of Indian Chambers of Commerce and Industry (FICCI) has launched Medical Tourism Council of Maharashtra (MTCM) (Medhekar, 2013).
10. Government in 2009, has provided monetary schemes under Market Development Assistance (MDA) to private wellness centres and medical hospitals including medical travel facilitators accredited by JCI, NBAH and AYUSH for national and global participation and promotional activities in wellness and medical trade fairs, events, and conferences approved by the niche tourism division of Indian Government Ministry of Tourism. Further, assistance to wellness tourism service providers for capacity building in AYUSH related traditional medicines and therapy.

Government of India Ministry of Tourism website (GOI, 2018a), reported that India stands out amongst the other Asian destination for medical tourism as the medical tourism stakeholders seek to deliver value in healthcare in terms of high-quality and efficiency in low input-cost such as medical /nonmedical labour cost, medicines and surgical costs. Aim is to provide values in medical travel with less waiting time, JCI accreditation, besides world class medical facilities, diagnostic clinics, experienced surgeons, and quality of nursing care. The Incredible India 2.0 campaign objective was to promote India as an attractive destination for spiritual, wellness and medical tourism (MOT, 2012). Government's services exports promotions council, developed healthcare tourism portal which provides detail information to the potential wellness and medical tourists regarding approximate costs of treatment, 578-NBAH accredited hospital location, and accommodation and medical-visa requirements.

This has none-the-less given rise to dual healthcare system in India. Public hospitals are for the domestic lower middle class and poor population. Whereas, world class private hospitals are for the affluent domestic population, expatriate foreigners, Indian diaspora and overseas patients (Medhekar et al., 2019). Modi government in 2018 has proposed to introduce health reforms such as national health insurance scheme for the millions of domestic poor patients living below poverty line, to provide equitable access to those who cannot afford healthcare.

CHALLENGES FOR WELLNESS AND MEDICAL TOURISM

There are numerous challenges that wellness resorts and private hospitals treating foreign patients have to face, due to competition from other accredited private hospitals within the country, and from popular super-specialty medical hospitals at overseas destinations.

1. Competition: Traditional healthcare treatments Ayurveda, Yoga, Unani, Herbal, Naturopathy etc. complements the modern allopathic treatment which gives India a comparative advantage over other countries to provide a holistic healthcare package. However, India faces competition from Thailand, Malaysia, Dubai and Singapore in terms of very high quality of tourism and health infrastructure, as well as an attractive, safe, clean and a reputable destination not only for wellness and medical travel, but also for tourism attractions.
2. Patient Safety and Security: Challenge of safety and security of the medical tourists within the country and in the hospital is very important. Within the country relates to safety from road accident, theft of personal belongings, terrorism, caught in a natural disasters such as earthquake and tsunami, political coup and physical attack. Hospital safety relates to patient safety issues such

as safety from medication errors, clinical errors, hospital virus and theft of personal belongings within the hospital.

3. Quality Accreditation: Challenge of maintaining accreditation of private wellness centers/resorts and hospitals by international accrediting bodies as JCI and national accreditation by NBAH is necessary to ensure world class quality in healthcare tourism services to attract inbound foreign patients.
4. Qualified Medical Professionals: Challenge to ensure supply of wellness and medical professionals such as nurses, and specialist surgeons to meet the future demand for such services. This needs accredited medical schools in collaboration with foreign universities graduating highly trained doctors, surgeons, nurses, para-medical and allied-healthcare professionals for the wellness and medical tourism industry.
5. Qualified Non-Medical Staff: Challenge to ensure supply of medical tourism related non-medical staff such as hospital management, human resource managers, security staff, accountants, foreign language interpreters, dieticians, yoga instructors, personal nursing attendants, and staff with medical literacy for medical hotels and medical-travel facilitators catering to health tourists.
6. Medical Legal and Ethical Issues: Medical legal and ethical regulation should be up-to-date and adhered to by the medical tourism healthcare providers at all levels of patient safety by the hospital, to protect the patient and organ donor to uphold the reputation of the Indian private hospital and medical professionals.
7. Challenge of Public Hygiene: Poor and neglected public hygiene has a negative impact on public health within the hospital and in the country related to virus, flue, super-bug, cleanliness, eliminate sensitive medical waste and garbage on street and provide clean washroom facilities for the tourists.
8. Challenge of Country Infrastructure for the Health Tourist: India needs world class tourism infrastructure such as wheel chair access, lifts, airport, hotels, roads, safe and efficient local transport services and safe food and drinking water facility as in Thailand, Malaysia and Singapore.
9. Challenge of Attracting Patients from Crossborder: Challenge of maintaining peace in South Asia, and attracting crossborder patients from South Asian Association for Regional Cooperation (SAARC) countries for wellness and super-specialist treatment/surgery and providing VoA for medical reasons and promoting peace, cooperation and health-diplomacy between India, Pakistan and Bangladesh besides other SAARC nations.
10. Challenge of Healthcare Equity: A developing country like India has a dual healthcare system, where on one hand it is treating foreign patients in high-end of surgical super-specialty, in world class healthcare facilities. On the other hand, there are millions of poor people in India living in urban as well as rural areas who do not have access to affordable primary healthcare or even

medicines. The issue is about healthcare availability, affordability, and access to accredited quality (AAAA) of healthcare for the domestic poor and lower middle class population.

POLICY IMPLICATIONS

1. Corporate private hospitals are for the domestic Indian medical tourists as well as overseas patients who have the ability to pay. The public system is for the poor and lower middle class population. The Indian government assumes that by providing subsidies and incentives to support the development of medical tourism industry, will automatically take care of affordable access and equity related issues to healthcare facilities and services for the domestic population. In reality, studies have shown that private hospitals have refused basic treatment to poor patients, despite of agreeing with the government to provide free treatment to a certain number of the domestic poor patients or adopt a slum or orphanage, in return of government subsidies and support to private hospitals for developing medical tourism business.
2. It is essential that promotional information regarding health tourism should be truthful and credible. The key stakeholders, such as specialist private hospitals, diagnostic clinics, wellness and medical travel facilitators, government at state and central level, ministries of tourism, transport and health, airline industry, hotels and hospitality industry and tour-operators in the tourism industry, are all playing a role in marketing and promoting Indian medical expertise and traditional wellness and modern medical treatment/surgeries to the world. There is always an aspect of lure of opportunities of tourism and sightseeing involved, besides highlighting the information related to cost of treatment, patient privacy, safety, less or no waiting list and quality of healthcare facilities, pre-post nursing care and medical professionals skills and experiences by the medical-tour facilitators, government promotional trade fairs and tourism campaigns.
3. Private medical hospitals and wellness centers/resorts treating foreign patients have to maintain and enhance quality for accreditation purposes and focus on patient safety, less waiting time, world class healthcare facility, appointing qualified and experienced medical and non-medical staff, medical precision, competitive and affordable pricing. The healthcare service providers should not compromise quality of healthcare service delivery to patients, which can ruin the reputation of the healthcare service provider, physician, medical-travel facilitator and the country.

4. Indian government has to recognise the economic benefits that flow from international trade in healthcare services, employment opportunism in wellness, medical and tourism sectors including allied healthcare and interpreting services and attract medical tourist. Government has initiated various supportive health tourism capacity and skill building and policy initiatives to meet the future demand and increase market share in the region from promoting their affordable and international JCI and NBAH accredited quality of medical facilities, wellness centers and super-specialties to attract foreign patients.
5. Similarly, marketing initiatives to attract foreign direct investment in health infrastructure, health research, trade fairs and shows, quality accreditation by JCI, government sponsored and updated health information portals with working links, should provide names of approved hospital, promoting niche specialist surgeries such as, dental, cosmetic, cancer, bariatric and hip replacements. Further, other Pull-factors are surgery waiting list, affordable quality of nursing care, English speaking overseas educated medical staff, not only to promote country's healthcare competitiveness, but also to achieve healthcare competency in wellness and medical sector with its world class qualified staff and state-of-the-art medical hospitals, diagnostic clinics and wellness facilities. Likewise, corporate private hospitals for example: Apollo group, Wockhardt, Asian Heart and Fortis group in India take their own initiative to develop websites to market and promote their healthcare facilities, super-surgical speciality, physicians, quality of care, patient testimonials, blogs and arrange online appointment and chat with a consultant specialists regarding health issues in real time.
6. The growth of health tourism industry is driven by dissemination of information via the internet and social medical tools (Lunt et al., 2010). Corporate private hospitals treating foreign patients, medical travel facilitators and tourism industry is capitalising on the demand for super-speciality or niche medical surgery and using various online platforms to promote and attracts medical patients from abroad. Patients are using internal information from previous experience and from friends and relatives word of mouth (WOM), and external sources of information (brochures, medical trade fairs, media, government health travel portals, hospital website, patient testimonials, advertising tourism campaigns and health travel facilitators websites) to make a decision to travel abroad for wellness and medical treatment. These internet portals are patient centric, regarding not just destination and hospital, but also type of treatment, surgeon, post-surgery care, and other healthcare services (Medhekar & Newby, 2013). With advanced internet communication and technology, patients as medical tourists with complex health problems also search the internet, for online communities with similar health issues such as cancer, reproductive, organ transplants through patient blogs, testimonials, to know about others experiences

of offshore surgery, hospital, quality of treatment, specialist surgeon and pre/post-surgery care.

7. Outsourcing of public health support services, despite the benefits to foreign medical tourists, can also impose an increase operational, financial and transaction costs related to health tourism related services (Carruth & Carruth, 2010). Therefore government regulation is necessary to find a balance between costs and benefits to domestic and foreign patients of developing and supporting health tourism, and maintain equity in access, availability, affordability and providing accredited quality of healthcare services to domestic population including value in medical travel to foreigners.
8. Finally public-private-partnerships are essential between the key stakeholders from the medical and tourism sectors of the economy in order to identify clear health related public policy guidelines on responsibility and operations, transparency, regulation, evaluation mechanism, and sustained financial support for NGO and commitment for healthcare service delivery, through partnerships from government policy makers to ensure equity in access, quality and values for money in healthcare service delivery to locals and foreigners. Overall the benefits from partnerships and collaboration outweigh the costs in terms of world class quality of healthcare, diagnostic clines, traditional wellness resorts, for improving health and wellness of domestic and foreign patients the long run. Ruckert and Labonté (2014) in their paper discuss the global health partnerships and health diplomacy, where neo-liberal private interest are to be more embedded within the shrinking public sector to influence national and global health policy to achieve good affordable quality of equitable access to affordable quality of health for all people.

CONCLUSION

Health tourism to India has grown exponentially in the last decade driven by private sector super-speciality hospitals and Ayurvedic hospitals. It has many advantages over other Asian competitors such as affordable cost, English language specking medical and non-medical professionals, highly skilled and overseas qualified medical staff, availability of advanced surgical super-speciality, and state-of-the-art medical diagnostic technology. The government of India has introduced a national healthcare tourism portal to market and provide valuable information to the potential wellness and medical tourist before making a decision to travel to India for treatment. Future research could focus on interviews with healthcare service providers at wellness resorts and private hospitals treating foreign patients, followed by a survey from actual wellness and medical tourists in India. Another area could be to interview the medical travel facilitators to find out the services they provide to the outbound medical tourist from India and inbound wellness and medical tourists to India.

REFERENCES

Al-Amin, M., Makarem, S. C., & Pradhan, R. (2011). Hospital ability to attract international patients: A conceptual framework. *International Journal of Pharmaceutical and Healthcare Marketing*, *5*(3), 205–221. doi:10.1108/17506121111172211

Awadzi, W., & Panda, D. (2006). Medical tourism: Globalization and the marketing of medical services. *Journal of Hospitality and Tourism*, *11*(1), 75–81.

Baliga, H. (2006). Medical Tourism is the new wave of outsourcing from India. *India Daily*, *21*(4), 16–19.

Bookman, M. Z., & Bookman, K. R. (2007). *Medical tourism in developing countries*. New York: Palgrave MacMillan. doi:10.1057/9780230605657

Brotman, B. A. (2010). Medical tourism private hospitals: Focus India. *Journal of Health Care Finance*, *37*(1), 45–50. PMID:20973373

Business Standard. (2016). *The foreign tourists who visited India for medical purpose during 2012, 2013, and 2014*. Retrieved from http://www.business-standard.com/article/news-cm/the-116042500714_1.html

Carruth, P. J., & Carruth, A. K. (2010). The financial and cost accounting implications of medical tourism. *International Business and Economics Research Journal*, *9*(8), 135–140.

Chen, K.-H., Chang, F.-H., & Wu, C. (2013). Investigating the wellness tourism factors in hot springs hotel customer service. *International Journal of Contemporary Hospitality Management*, *25*(7), 1092–1114. doi:10.1108/IJCHM-06-2012-0086

Chinai, R., & Goswami, R. (2007). Medical visas mark growth of Indian medical tourism. *Bulletin of the World Health Organization*, *85*(3), 164–165. doi:10.2471/BLT.07.010307 PMID:17486202

CII & McKinsey. (2002). *Healthcare in India: The road ahead*. New Delhi: Confederation of Indian Industries & McKinsey & Company.

Collins, A., Medhekar, A., Wong, H. Y., & Cobanoglu, C. (2019). Factors influencing outbound medical travel from the USA. *Tourism Review*, *74*(3), 463–479. doi:10.1108/TR-06-2018-0083

Connell, J. (2006). Medical tourism: Sea, sun, sand and … surgery. *Tourism Management, 26*(6), 1093–1100. doi:10.1016/j.tourman.2005.11.005

Connell, J. (2013). Contemporary medical tourism: Conceptualisation, culture and commodification. *Tourism Management, 34*, 1–13. doi:10.1016/j.tourman.2012.05.009

Costa, C., Quintela, J., & Mendes, J. (2015). Health and Wellness Tourism: A Strategic Plan for Tourism and Thermalism Valorization of São Pedro do Sul. In M. Peris - Ortiz & J. Á. García (Eds.), Health and wellness tourism. Emergence of a new market segment (pp. 77-99). Heidelberg, Germany: Springer. doi:10.1007/978-3-319-11490-3_2

Crooks, V. A., Turner, L., Snyder, J., Johnston, R., & Kingsbury, P. (2011). Promoting medical tourism in India: Messages, images, and the marketing of international patient travel. *Social Science & Medicine, 72*(5), 726–732. doi:10.1016/j.socscimed.2010.12.022 PMID:21310519

Dasgupta, S., & Dasgupta, D. (2014). *Globalisation and transnational surrogacy in India: Outsourcing life*. Plymouth, UK: Lexington Books.

Deloitte. (2008). *Medical Tourism: Consumers in Search of Value*. Deloitte Centre for Health Solutions.

Edelhelt, J. (2008). Defining medical tourism or not? *Medical Tourism Magazine, 5*, 9–10.

FICCI. (2008). New Delhi: Fostering Quality Healthcare for All. Federation of Indian Chamber of Commerce & Ernst and Young.

Garcia-Altes, A. (2005). The development of health tourism services. *Annals of Tourism Research, 32*(1), 262–266. doi:10.1016/j.annals.2004.05.007

Goodrich, J., & Goodrich, G. (1987). Health-care tourism- an exploratory study. *Tourism Management, 8*(3), 217–222. doi:10.1016/0261-5177(87)90053-7

Government of India (GOI). (2003). *Health Sector in India*. New Delhi: GOI, Budget Papers.

Government of India (GOI). (2018a). *India: Healthcare Tourism*. Retrieved from http://www.indiahealthcaretourism.com/

Government of India (GOI). (2018b). *Wellness and Medial Tourism*. Retrieved from http://tourism.gov.in/wellness-medical-tourism

Gupta, A. (2008). Medical Tourism India: Winners & losers. *Indian Journal of Medical Ethics*, *5*(1), 4–5. PMID:18630244

Henderson, J. (2003). Healthcare tourism in South- East Asia. *Tourism Review International*, *3*, 271–290.

Heung, V., & Kucukusta, D. (2013). Wellness tourism in China, resources, development and marketing. *International Journal of Tourism Research*, *15*(4), 346–359. doi:10.1002/jtr.1880

Horowitz, M. D., & Rosensweig, J. A. (2007). Medical Tourism-Health Care in the Global Economy. *Physician Executive*, *33*(6), 24–31. PMID:18092615

Indian Hgh Commission Oman (IHCO). (2017). *Medical visas issued to Omani citizens*. Retrieved from https://www.morevisas.com/immigration-news-article/medical-visas-issued-to-omani-citizens-for-india-rise-100/4993/

Indian Medical Tourism (IMT). (2009). *India Ranks 2nd in Med-Tourism*. Retrieved from www.medicaltourism.org/consortium.jsp?sect=con

International Medical Tourism Journal (IMTJ). (2017a, May). *Medical & wellness tourism board for India*. Retrieved from https://www.imtj.com/news/medical-wellness-tourism-board-india/

International Medical Tourism Journal (IMTJ). (2017b, July). *India medical tourism statistics released*. Retrieved from https://www.imtj.com/news/india-medical-tourism-statistics-released

JCI. (2019). *Joint Commission International Accreditation Standards for Hospitals*. Retrieved from http://www.jointcommissioninternational.org/about-jci/jci-accredited-or

Johnston, R., Crooks, V., Snyder, J., & Kingsbury, P. (2010). What is known about the effects of medical tourism in destination and departure countries? A scoping review. *International Journal for Equity in Health*, *9*(1), 24. doi:10.1186/1475-9276-9-24 PMID:21047433

Lunt, N., Hardey, M., & Mannion, R. (2010). Nip, Tuck and Click: Medical Tourism and the Emergence of Web-Based Health Information. *The Open Medical Informatics Journal*, *4*(4), 1–11. doi:10.2174/1874431101004010001 PMID:20517465

Lunt, N., & Mannion, R. (2014). Patient mobility in the global marketplace: A multidisciplinary perspective. *International Journal of Health Policy and Management*, *2*(4), 155–157. doi:10.15171/ijhpm.2014.47 PMID:24847479

Medhekar, A. (2012). Managing the Growth of Medical Tourism in India by Public-Private-Partnerships. In K. Roy & S. Kar (Eds.), *Development Management in the 21st Century, Readings in World Development* (pp. 59–72). New York: Nova.

Medhekar, A. (2013). Maharashtra Medically Yours: A Global Player in Medical Tourism. *Bi-Annual Journal. Cosmos*, *3*(V), 38–53.

Medhekar, A. (2014). Public-Private Partnerships for Inclusive Development: Role of Private Corporate Sector in Provision of Healthcare Services. Procedia - Social and Behavioral Sciences Journal, 157, 33-44.

Medhekar, A., & Ali, M. M. (2012). A Cross-Border Trade in Healthcare services: Bangladesh to India. *The Business and Management Review*, *2*(1), 1–13.

Medhekar, A., & Haq, F. (2015). Halal Branding of medical Tourism: case of Indian hospitals. In H. El-Gohary & R. Eid (Eds.), *Emerging Research in Islamic Marketing and Tourism in the Global Economy* (pp. 160–189). IGI Global Publishing. doi:10.4018/978-1-4666-6272-8.ch008

Medhekar, A., & Newby, L. (2013). Information Search to Travel Abroad for Medical Treatment: An Empirical Study. *Proceedings of International Conference on Healthcare Systems and Global Business Issues*, 77-96.

Medhekar, A., Wong, H. Y., & Hall, J. (2014). Medical tourism: A theoretical framework for an innovation in global healthcare provision. In A. Goyal (Ed.), *Innovations in services marketing and management: Strategies for emerging economies* (pp. 148–169). Hershey, PA: IGI Global. doi:10.4018/978-1-4666-4671-1.ch009

Medhekar, A., Wong, H. Y., & Hall, J. (2019). Factors influencing inbound medical travel to India. *Journal of Health Organization and Management*, *33*(2), 155–172. doi:10.1108/JHOM-08-2018-0234 PMID:30950309

Ministry of Tourism Government of India (MOT-GOI). (2018). *Wellness & Medical Tourism*. Retrieved from http://tourism.gov.in/wellness-medical-tourism

Ministry of Tourism (MOT). (2012). *Incredible India Theme Brochures- Government of India*. Retrieved from http://tourism.gov.in/tourism

Moghavvemi, S., Ormond, M., Musa, G., Isa, C. R., & Chandy, J. (2017). Connecting with prospective medical tourists online: A cross-sectional analysis of private hospital websites promoting medical tourism in India, Malaysia and Thailand. *Tourism Management*, *58*(Feb), 154–163. doi:10.1016/j.tourman.2016.10.010

Morgan, M. A. (2007). Another view of "humanitarian ventures" and "fistula tourism". *International Urogynecology Journal and Pelvic Floor Dysfunction*, *18*(6), 705–707. doi:10.100700192-007-0309-9 PMID:17252312

RNCOS. (2010). *Booming Medical Tourism in India. Tourism Industry Research Solutions*. New Delhi: RNCOS E-Services.

Ruckert, R., & Labonté, R. (2014). Public-private-partnerships in global health: The good, the bad and the ugly. *Third World Quarterly*, *35*(9), 1598–1614. doi:10.1080/01436597.2014.970870

Runnels, V., & Turner, L. (2011). Bioethics and transnational medical travel: India, "medical tourism", and the globalisation of healthcare. *Indian Journal of Medical Ethics*, *8*(1), 42–44. PMID:22106599

Sheldon, P.J. & Park, S.Y. (2008). Sustainable wellness tourism: Governance and Entrepreneurship Issues. *Acta turis-tca, 20*(2), 151-172.

Shetty, P. (2010). Medical tourism booms in India, but at what cost? *Lancet*, *37*(6), 671–672. doi:10.1016/S0140-6736(10)61320-7 PMID:20879077

Singh, P. K. (2008). *Medical Tourism*. New Delhi, India: Kanishka Publishers.

Smith, M., & Puczko, L. (2009). *Health and Wellness Tourism*. Oxford, UK: Elsevier.

Smith, M., & Puczko, L. (2014). *Spa, Wellness and Medical Travel (2nd ed.)*. London: Routledge.

Smith, R., Chanda, R., & Viroj, T. (2009). Trade in health-related services. *Lancet*, *373*(9663), 593–601. doi:10.1016/S0140-6736(08)61778-X PMID:19167053

Sultana, S., Haque, A., Momen, A., & Yasmin, F. (2014). Factors affecting the attractiveness of medical tourism destination: An empirical study on India. *Iranian Journal of Public Health*, *43*(7), 867–876. PMID:25909055

Turner, L. (2007). First World Healthcare at Third World Prices: Globalisation, Bioethics and Medical Tourism. *Biosocieties*, *2*(3), 303–325. doi:10.1017/S1745855207005765

Voigt, C., & Laing, J. H. (2010). Journey into Parenthood: Commodification of Reproduction as a New Tourism Niche Market. *Journal of Travel & Tourism Marketing*, *27*(3), 252–268. doi:10.1080/10548401003744685

World Health Organisation. (2001). *Macroeconomics and Health: Investing in Health for Economic Development. Report of the Commission on Macroeconomics and Health*. Geneva: WHO.

ADDITIONAL READING

Cohen, G. (2017). Medical tourism, medical migration, & global justice: Implications for biosecurity in globalised world. *Medical Law Review*, *25*(2), 200–222. doi:10.1093/medlaw/fwx013 PMID:28402562

Hazarika, I. (2010). Medical tourism: Its potential impact on the health workforce and health system in India. Asia-Pacific action on human resources for health. *Health Policy and Planning*, *25*(2), 248–251. doi:10.1093/heapol/czp050 PMID:19926658

Jackson, E., Millbank, J., Karpin, I., & Stuhmcke, A. (2017). Learning from cross-border reproduction. *Medical Law Review*, *25*(1), 23–46. PMID:28073821

Junio, M. M. V., Kim, J. H., & Lee, T. J. (2017). Competitiveness attributes of a medical tourism destination: The case of South Korea with importance-performance analysis. *Journal of Travel & Tourism Marketing*, *34*(4), 444–460. doi:10.1080/10548408.2016.1182454

Kasper, H., & Reddy, S. (2017). Spaces of connectivity: The formation of medical travel destination in Delhi national capital region (India). *Asia Pacific Viewpoint*, *58*(2), 228–241. doi:10.1111/apv.12159

Reddy, S., & Qadeer, I. (2010). Medical tourism in India: Progress or Predicament? *Economic and Political Weekly*, *XLV*(20), 69–75.

Robinson, M., & Novelli, M. (2005). *Niche tourism: An introduction*. In *Contemporary issues, trends and cases* (pp. 1–14). Oxford, UK: Elsevier.

Turner, L. (2011). Quality in health care and globalisation of health services: Accreditation and regulatory oversight of medical tourism companies. *Journal Quality in HealthCare*, *23*(1), 1–7. doi:10.1093/intqhc/mzq078 PMID:21148210

KEY TERMS AND DEFINITIONS

Medical Travel/Tourism: Travelling for medical treatment/surgery is an activity where a patient travels within the country or overseas to purchase a medical product or healthcare service such as cancer surgery, cosmetic, dental, eye surgery, hip and knee replacement, and engages in some touristic activity, shopping, and sightseeing if health permits.

Wellness Travel/Tourism: Travelling for wellness tourism is an activity where a person travels within the country or overseas to purchase a wellness product, traditional medicine or wellness service Ayurveda, Yoga, Unani, Siddhi, and Homeopathy (AYUSH), at a wellness/rejuvenation resort/centre to heal one's body, mind and spirit, and engages in some touristic activity, shopping, and sightseeing if health permits.

Chapter 2
Considerations for Stakeholders of Medical Tourism:
A Comprehensive Examination

Nitya Saxena
National Center of Excellence for SAM Management (NCoE), Lady Hardinge Medical College, New Delhi, India

ABSTRACT

Several countries are competing for a higher share in the billion dollar medical tourism market, which is expected to reach USD 28 billion by 2024. The situation is as interesting as it can get. A whole new economy has prospered around medical tourism with various stakeholders including patients, hospitals, insurers, medical tourism facilitators, and the government. The concerns of these stakeholders ought to be diverse but should not be diverging for the industry to function appropriately. The motive of this chapter is to review the economy around medical tourism from stakeholder perspectives and enlist the factors to consider while designing business policies.

INTRODUCTION

Medical tourism is a phenomenon and not a policy-driven consequence. With several countries competing for a higher share in $100 billion market, the situation is as interesting as it can get. Even though the phenomenon of medical tourism is centuries old, the world has witnessed a trend reversal. In earlier times it was the

DOI: 10.4018/978-1-5225-9787-2.ch002

rich from the developing countries that used to travel to the developed world in order to seek quality care. But now, it is the not so rich people from the developed world who are now willing to seek care in low and middle-income countries like Thailand, Malaysia, and India.

Over-reliance of United States' on the private sector for care substantially increased the cost. While in the United Kingdom, the health system tilted towards socialist approach post World War II (Richmond et al, 1996) and solely relied on public provision of healthcare. Both systems faced unintended consequences and resulted in a high cost in the US and long waiting time in the UK. Meanwhile, second and third world countries were recovering post-de-colonization. Their health system was not in good shape even for their own citizens leave aside foreign patients. Over time, the effects of liberalization and globalization spilled over to various sectors including health. And with increased global migration, developing countries gained access to opportunities in the developed world.

The global education system enabled medical practitioners to be trained in a developed country which empowered the workforce in a developing country to have international standard medical services. Close proximity due to international migration further helped to build the trust between the citizen of developed countries and the workforce of the less industrialized world. At that point, it was difficult to determine the consequences of such an exchange on healthcare. With the passage of time, second and third world countries ramped up their health system to match their quality with that of developed at a cheaper cost. Simultaneously, rich countries faced issues with insurance coverage, long waiting in their health system. As per 2011 estimates, 15 percent of the US population was uninsured. Europe achieved almost 100 percent coverage under NHS (except Greece, Bulgaria, and Cypress) (Gilbert, 2015) but patients faced long waiting time. Under these circumstances, the boundaries of health care seeking expanded, the flow of patients reversed, and 'healthcare' joined the commodity list of the international market place.

A whole new economy prospered around medical tourism with various stakeholders including patients, hospitals, insurers, medical tourism facilitators and the government. The prime focus of this chapter is to discuss the concerns and considerations of these stakeholders while transacting in the medical tourism market. The chapter sequentially discusses the (1) stakeholder's purpose, power, and position, (2) theories of medical tourism followed by (3) Enabling factors of medical tourism and its framework; (4) Medical tourism disparities and (5) Future of medical tourism.

WHO ARE STAKEHOLDERS OF MEDICAL TOURISM: DEFINITION AND PERSPECTIVES?

- **Patients:** The chapter focuses on patients traveling from developed countries to developing countries to seek medical care. They are the centre of the medical tourism industry and hence what matters to them is what matters the most to the industry to grow. Hence, they constitute the core of medical tourism framework and the industry is knit around their requirements. Main concerns of patients can be quality, cost, ease of follow up, the environment of the destination country and others which is discussed in great detail in this chapter.
- **Hospital Owners:** Mostly the countries involved in medical tourism have a dual system of health care with private/corporate hospitals and public hospitals. While public hospitals primarily cater to citizens (locals), it is the large corporate hospitals that are engaged in medical tourism. An interesting scenario has emerged because of this dual system that has divided resource availability for local versus foreign patient for human resource and budget availability. Since quality hospitals are an essential pre-requisite of medical tourism, hospital owners are unarguably an important stakeholder.
- **Government (Destination and Originating Country):** The destination country of medical tourism stands to gain substantially in monetary terms and each country is competing for a larger share in $100 billion (estimate 2016-17) industry. These countries are striving to increase their attractiveness as a destination and are an important stakeholder. Additionally, medical tourism is surrounded by the debate of providing care to the foreign patient at the cost of a local citizen. The challenge for them is to strike a balance between the provision of care for the foreign patient and the local poor.
    - On the other hand, the government of the originating country is worried about the annual increase in medical tourism to other low-middle income countries. Developed economies like the USA and the United Kingdom are dealing with different limitations and challenges. In US healthcare cost containment has become incrementally difficult while in the UK there is a long waiting queue for a non-emergency medical condition. Given these challenges, medical tourism can either be considered as a solution or a problem that needs a solution. Since their taxpayers are forced to opt for overseas treatment, medical tourism is largely seen in a negative light. At times patients return and acquire foreign infection or other medical complication and incur a heavy financial loss. Implicitly government is to be blamed for such consequences as they failed to provide access to the required care. Government of the country of origin

emerges as a stakeholder who aims to deter medical tourism through policy reforms.

- **Insurance Companies**: With cross border insurance transactions it is an opportunity as well as a challenge for insurance companies to rebuild their offerings. At present, there are only one or two players that are willing to reimburse the treatment cost of medical service availed in a foreign country. In 2006, a study reported an annual saving of $1.4 billion if one in ten patient of low-risk surgery opts for treatment abroad (Mattoo & Rathindran, 2006). The estimate needs an update but it backs up the argument to engage in medical tourism product offering for insurance companies. With the phenomenon catching up, insurance companies may explore international collaborations and setup claim settlement mechanism and international monitoring body.
- **Medical Tourism Facilitators:** A new stream of the profession has come into being with the growth of the medical tourism industry. These organizations/ individuals provide ancillary services in the medical tourism process. MTF's specialized and differentiate their services for a specific country, hospital, and type of treatment (Gan and Frederick, 2011). Primarily they are the information keepers for patient and business developers for hospitals and countries. They are the stakeholders of quality, reliable and transparent medical tourism experience.

GROUNDING MEDICAL TOURISM: A THEORETICAL PERSPECTIVE

Boundaries of Medical Tourism

Akin to the phenomena, the boundary and definition of medical tourism are equally hazy. To seek medical care, patients may travel within the country (domestic tourism) or outside (international tourism) for treatment. They may travel for leisure services like massage/spa as well as for medical/surgical intervention. Tourist may fall ill during a vacation and seek emergency care in the destination. Expatriates may prefer treatment in their home country contributing to international travel for treatment. Or they may also get treated in their country of current residence and still be counted as a medical tourist. All these tourism can be accounted for as medical tourism or maybe not depending on the country norms. Early literature in the field did not differentiate between wellness tourism and medical tourism until Smith and Puczko (2009) in their book provided a clear differentiation. They clubbed wellness tourism and medical tourism under a broader term health tourism and confined the boundary of medical tourism to any medical, surgical or dental intervention. Further,

Mckinsey report (2008) proposes the exclusion of expatriates as medical tourists who are treated in the country of current residence and also exclude emergency cases of tourists. Connell (2006, p. 1094) defines "*medical tourism as a niche that has emerged from the rapid growth of what has become an industry, where people travel often long distances to overseas countries to obtain medical, dental and surgical care while simultaneously being holidaymakers*". This chapter has used Connell definition of medical tourism to evaluate the phenomena. To reaffirm, international patients seeking care overseas barring expatriates seeking care in the current country of residence and emergency cases should be accounted for as a medical tourist.

Placement of Medical Tourism in the Globalization Framework

Globalization has catalyzed the evolution of health sectors through spill over and exchange of knowledge, resources, technology, and institutional practices. Advances in health Industry has contributed significantly towards economic development through increased production of goods and services. Figure 1 depicts the conceptual framework proposed by WHO for the placement of medical tourism in relation to other constructs of the health system and globalization. The process of globalization has led to technological change, privatization, resource re-allocation, and global competition. To facilitate this process there is a conforming restructuring in institutional governance, structure, and policy. A similar reorganization is reflected in the health system in resource allocation, healthcare costing, and pricing, insurance, and individual risk factors. In nutshell, global governance institutions and medical tourism co-evolved through the restructuring of the private sector in terms of quality and cost thus providing more choices for the end consumer.

Theories of the Medical Tourism Market

Various existing theories can be combined to understand the phenomena of medical tourism. Are theories helpful for stakeholders? Theories are useful to elucidate the phenomenon and design policies accordingly. However, not foolproof, a brief knowledge of them can be beneficial for the business/ government who wants to boost their medical tourism.

Health is often debated for its belonging either to economic or social goods. Health system has many anomalies that cause a market failure like moral hazard, asymmetric information, supply-induced demand, and others. Over time there is consensus over the fact that health cannot be called a pure economic good as healthcare market requires significant government interventions to function properly.

However, medical tourism presents an interesting leg of the healthcare industry which reinstates the point that demand for healthcare is inelastic and can take people

Figure 1. Theoretical framework of medical tourism in a global setting
Source: World Health Organization

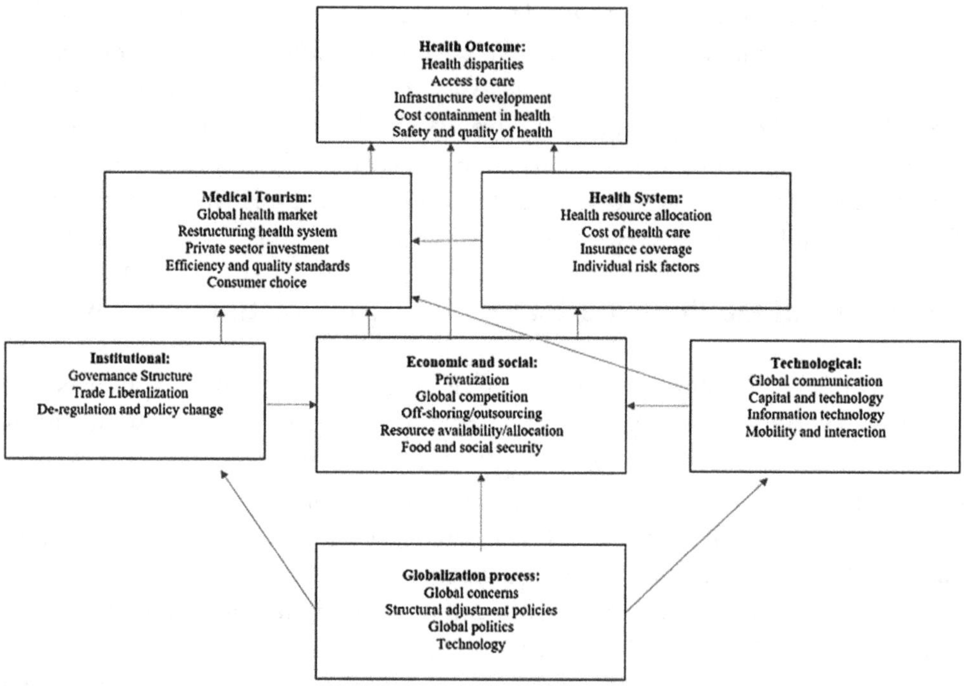

to distant places. Interestingly, unlike healthcare market, health tourism has given rise to near perfect market conditions. Let's evaluate the medical tourism market for the characteristics of a perfectly competitive market.

- A competitive market has a *large number of buyers and sellers.* With the convergence of the global market, patients have the option to choose from a large number of healthcare providers either located in the far south or next country neighbor. Similarly, for business operating in medical tourism, there are patients from rich as well as not so rich regions. In 2016-17, the medical tourism industry was valued at $100 billion which provides an ambitious market for sellers (Medical Tourism Association Report, 2016). With CAGR of 8.8% between 2018 – 2024, the industry is expected to touch near perfect competition.
- *Identical or Homogeneity of the Product:* In a perfectly competitive market, the product being sold is near identical in nature that is buyer can purchase the product from any of the sellers. This criterion is easy to fulfill in the product market but in the service industry often the service is not identical.

Medical tourism is predominantly a service industry that offers a variety of surgeries, dental procedures and hence it is difficult to have unique service across all healthcare providers and in fact differentiation in service is primary selling proposition. However, homogeneity can be achieved in technical quality for which Medical Tourism Association, an international body, provides required training and accreditation. As on today, Thailand has 65 internationally accredited hospitals followed by India (38), Singapore (22), Malaysia (13), Mexico(7) and Costa Rica (2). Such an attempt is likely to bring homogeneity in the technical quality of health care providers (Joint Commission International, 2019). The homogenous product criteria are valid and can be fulfilled for only for technical quality and low middle-income countries (LMIC) countries are on the march for it.

- Free Entry and Exit of Firms: In medical tourism, concerned firms are health care providers, medical tourism facilitators (MTF), and insurance firms. Substantial capital and resource investment are required to enter the market and maintain the edge. For hospitals, they need to train doctors and paramedical officers, invest in medical equipment and set up business ties with insurance companies and MTF. Insurance firms need to develop profitable products, international collaboration and seek a large subscription base. Medical tourism, however, can be considered as an extended business for hospitals and insurance companies but for MTFs, the stakes are high. Hence there exist a mix of such firms for whom entry and exit barriers are high for some it is low.
- Perfect Knowledge of the Market: Medical Tourism Facilitators (MTF) who provide ancillary services to a patient are the knowledge keepers. These organizations maintain tie-up with private hospitals, procure information of complete chain of the medical procedure and provide it to medical tourists. It is difficult to say if the knowledge provided is perfect because MTFs are more like marketing firms that are hired by private hospitals to stay in business. However, they do have the incentive to stay ethical in their approach to have a sustainable business. The moderating role of facilitator in medical tourism is quite significant (Mohamad et al, 2012). In a survey, results showed that 61% of the respondents stated facilitators role was very important in making their choices and decision to pursue their treatment in different countries (Jagyasi, 2010a), 27% stated moderately important and only 10% respondents regarded facilitator as optional (Jagyasi,2010a). Their role in the industry as knowledge providers has given rise to a competitive market.
- Absence of Price Control: The question here is whether sellers are price takers or price setters. Health care is known to have the most opaque pricing system especially in LMIC where insurance system is not well established.

> But in medical tourism, the cost is the main driving force in deciding the destination and hence it is determined in a competitive fashion. In information documents of medical tourism, it is not uncommon to see price comparatives of different surgery across different providers. Hence even though hospitals may still hold price control for the domestic market, but for international patients, they are forced to offer competitive prices.

There are other factors that determine the competitiveness of a market like free mobility of factors of production which is not suitable to evaluate a service industry. It can be concluded that the market of medical tourism is not perfectly competitive, but it is progressing towards one increasingly.

Another theoretical parallel can be drawn from the economic theory of pull and push factor to explain the demand and supply of medical tourism (Dunn, 1977). Pull factors focus on demand-side factors which are consumer-focused i.e. socio-economic profile (age, gender, income) and health-related factors(insurance coverage, the severity of disease). Pull factors focus on medical tourism offerings (i.e. supply side) medical facility, country environment, etc. Based on this theory, an index of medical tourism is developed by Fetscherin and Stephano (2016) discussed in the framework section.

ENABLING FACTORS OF MEDICAL TOURISM: A REAL-WORLD ASSESSMENT OF THE COMPLEX PHENOMENA

As discussed previously, the world has witnessed a trend reversal in the directional flow of medical tourist. Over the years many Asian countries and few others emerged as a favorite destination for medical tourism. Most of the patient traffic arises from developed economies like the United States, the United Kingdom. However, there are parts of the world like South Africa and the Middle East who opt for medical tourism in the absence of quality care in the home country. Extensive Medical tourism is just the tip of the ice-berg and needs assessment for underlying causes.

High cost and long waiting time are often cited as a major reason to travel for medical reasons. An American citizen opts for an offshore treatment because of insurance deficit. A middle-class American is either uninsured or has inadequate coverage for the essential procedure (Lancaster 2004; Horowitz 2007). Another category of patients looks overseas for cosmetic surgeries or fertility treatments that are not covered under insurance.

In the United Kingdom, multiple research and news articles dates to mid-'90s and early 20's that flags the issue of long waiting queue under National Health System (NHS) (Newton et al. 1995; Richmond et al 1996; Martin et al 2003). Long waiting queues for elected procedures made patients either opt for private treatment locally or travel to other countries.

These supply-side issues push up the demand for medical tourism and the pursuit for the destination begins. The decision of destination is highly variable and is difficult to fit in a single framework. For example, the patient may place the quality considerations above the cost if the disease in concern has high stakes with low success rates. Singapore, for example, has developed a niche for high-end specialized treatments like stem cell therapy and neuro-surgery and is not a low-cost destination.

If the disease in concern carries low risk with a high success rate, the decision-making process becomes more liberal and other factors enter the zone of decision making. Culture of the destination country can be a comforting factor as the paramedical staff and other caregivers in a hospital spend maximum time with the patient. For this reason, patients originating from UAE may choose a country like Malaysia over others owing to low cultural difference.

Other basic parameters can be safety, corruption, language, tourism attractiveness of the host country. Interestingly, legal aspects can also enable medical tourism. Demand for abortions and euthanasia depicts a classical example of medical tourism to Northern Australia and Switzerland where these procedures are legal. These factors may not be a major concern, but they do carry some weight in the decision making.

Often, the type of surgery overrides all the above-mentioned factors. For example, India provides an apt destination for knee replacement surgery and cardiac procedures with a near perfect balance of quality and cost while Singapore is a preferred destination for stem cell therapy irrespective of the cost. As discussed, Singapore with 22 internationally accredited hospitals, focuses on quality alone. It has developed ties with health insurance companies in Japan to provide high-quality medical services. Mexico specializes in dental and orthopedics and Germany for stem cell and oncology. Thailand has 65 internationally accredited hospitals and specializes in cosmetic and dental surgery. Thailand clearly wants to take advantage of foreign tourist it attracts and extends the profit to medical tourism. There is apparent variability among decision makers and across countries in functioning their medical tourism.

Given multiple factors contribute to decision making, how can the relative importance of each factor be determined? The confusing net of all these factors has provided an apt platform for researchers to indulge in relative weights calculation. Knowledge of relative importance should be of interest to stakeholders in designing an attractive offering. A detail discussion on this aspect awaits in the section frameworks for stakeholders.

FRAMEWORK FOR STAKEHOLDERS

The complete process of medical tourism can be better understood in different dimensions. The first dimension is the choice of destination or country; the second dimension is medical tourism capability of that country and the third dimension is an organization of ancillary services around medical tourism. With these dimensions, Fetscherin and Stephano (2016) developed a comprehensive scale to measure medical tourism – Medical Tourism Index. "*The Medical Tourism Index measures the attractiveness of a country as a medical tourism destination in terms of the overall country environment; healthcare costs and tourism attractiveness, and quality of medical facilities and services*".

The scale, in its framework, gives weights to (1) overall countries environment, (2) attractiveness as a tourist destination, (3) medical tourism cost and (4) facility and services. A country's environment can be appealing if it has low corruption, culturally similar to the patient's country, familiar language, stable economy, safe for travelers and a stable exchange rate. Under tourist destination, weights are given as per attractiveness as a tourist destination, richness in cultural heritage/ natural attraction sites and good weather. Parameters for cost considered travel cost, accommodation cost, treatment and ancillary service cost. Under facility and service weights are measured for quality or doctors and hospitals, state-of-the-art medical equipment and international certifications. The study determined weights to be 34% for the country's environment, 16% for a tourism destination, 16% for medical tourism cost and 34% for Facility and Services.

The framework is among the first line of comprehensive work but with certain limitations. It did not consider the type of surgery as it makes the assessment difficult. But in practice, type of surgery may supersede all other parameters in decision making. The sample used is representative of the USA alone which needs validation for other countries. The respondents are the general public and not the patients engaged in medical tourism. In the future, one can expect a more inclusive scale to understand the drift of medical tourism. Stakeholders are suggested and expected to support the development of such scales by provision of accurate data and pre & post surveys.

MEDICAL TOURISM AND RELATED DISPARITIES

Issue of Access to Local Poor Population and Not So Rich Foreign Patients

Unlike other sectors, medical tourism is debated to grow at the cost of the local vulnerable section of the society who cannot afford healthcare. Large corporate hospitals attract efficient workforce for the treatment of foreign patients thus leaving the less efficient workforce for its own citizens. Inadequate doctor to patient ratio supports the argument and pose a real challenge for the government of destination countries. There is a visible movement of medical resources from public to private hospitals to gain better career prospects. Containment of this issue is an enormous challenge for the government. As a stakeholder, it is essential to address this subject time and again to ensure not to grow medical tourism by footing over the country's poor. However, it is essential to validate the argument empirically. There is a need for separate record keeping for medical tourism in healthcare accounts to understand the inflow of patients and reallocation of local resources. As literature points out, destination countries will need to use at least part of the revenues from increased inflows of foreign patients to ensure improved health care access for their own poorer citizens (Mattoo and Rathindran,2006).

On the other hand, the government of the country of origin is concerned about the shortcomings of their healthcare system. The outflow of patients indicates that the public health system is inadequate and/or private hospitals are inaccessible and taxpayers contribution is not justified. Hence, the government is not likely to support the phenomena of medical tourism for long. Government of developed worked are now actively engaged in policy corrections. They may consider fixing quota on the number of patients seeking overseas care. But healthcare is a sensitive issue which cannot be denied on any grounds given that WHO counts it among the basic human right. A sustainable solution needs to be devised in agreement with all the stakeholders.

Commercial Surrogacy

Commercial surrogacy grew at a fast pace and so the ethical issues around it. Usually, the surrogate mothers belong to low middle-income countries. The power distance between the surrogate mother and client is immense. This gives rise to several ethical issues around social and health wellness of surrogate mother. Major concerns are remuneration, the robustness of informed consent, quality of surrogate care, exploitation of the poor and custody rights (if the baby develops medical complications) (See Deonandan, Green and Van Beinum, 2012). A list of countries has pulled the plug from commercial surrogacy including Thailand in 2015 and India in 2018. Ukraine, Russia, and Georgia still have not enacted laws to ban surrogacy. Stakeholders should not be a part of any ethical conflict that can harm their business.

Organ Donation

Transplantation centers in destination countries propped up to facilitate organ trafficking from poor locals (Commercial living donors) to resource-rich medical tourist. The United Network for Organ Sharing (UNOS), defines transplant tourism as 'the purchase of a transplanted organ abroad that includes access to an organ while bypassing laws, rules, or processes of any or all countries involved'. As a stakeholder of the destination country, it is essential to have an ethical protocol for donor selection in order to hedge poor from this dangerous exploitation. The long-term aim should be to attain national-self sufficiency in organ donation. For this purpose, Insurance companies are placed perfectly to stay vigilant and flag this issue in the country of origin. A denial of an insurance claim if found guilty can act as a deterrent for such practices.

FUTURE OF MEDICAL TOURISM

Medical tourism is here to stay as long as each country's health system remains unique and dissimilar from one another. An important factor that can strengthen the reach of medical tourism is technology. With the advent of high-speed internet and telemedicine technology, it is possible to bring down the cost of overseas care drastically. Additionally, pre-consultation or post- surgery follow up using digital health opens multiple channels of access which will increase the patient's trust. A study determined that perception-expectation gap is significantly reduced in those medical tourists who have undergone telemedicine prior to their medical treatment (George &Henthorne,2009). However, in the same study, they found that customer satisfaction was not significantly higher than the patients who have not undergone telemedicine. The first result indicates that patients carry an expectation based on their perception from the experience. With the help of telemedicine, patients gain prior exposure to the type of facility, equipment, and doctor. This exposure let them recalibrate their expectation and the quality of care they are likely to get. On the other hand, the second result of the study indicates their disappointment with the level of service they received vs the expectation set by prior- telemedicine consultation. Here take away for stakeholders is that having a telemedicine setup is good to generate initial traction but to gain the business continuity they should match the promised level of service offered during teleconsultation.

For the government of the destination country, telemedicine can put a bandage on the issue of access to poor citizens. The government may impose subsidy on telemedicine for private hospitals if they use the same facility to consult the local poor. In the future, the government may find a way to channelize funds from medical tourism to enhance access to the local poor.

Future collaboration: In this shrinking world it is difficult to imagine any profession in silos. With the penetration of technology in medicine, a substantial contribution is required from biomedical engineer, information technology support, Data security engineers, legal advisers, and insurance product developers (actuarial scientist).

CONCLUSION

Medical Tourism has converged the stand-alone health system across countries into one. The ancient phenomenon has grown substantially in the past two decades and has observed a trend reversal. The inflow of foreign patients in low- and middle-income countries has grown many fold. So much so that several countries are competing to be a preferred medical tourism destination. With an annual estimated growth of 8.8%, it is inevitable to engage in the discussion of growth factors. These growth factors are of immense interest for stakeholders of the industry. The patient is the primary stakeholder who generates the demand to seek overseas care. The other two stakeholders, hospital and medical tourism facilitators (MTF) respond to these demands and try to provide a comprehensive experience of high-quality medical service bundled with a vacation. The service can either be self-financed or reimbursed by an insurance company. At present, there are only a few insurance companies that offer overseas care reimbursement. However, the role of the insurance company is likely to emerge in coming years as an important stakeholder. In the whole process of medical tourism, the government of both countries (origin and destination) acts as a regulator and time to time restructure policies accordingly. The interplay of these five stakeholders and their concerns formed the core of this chapter.

Based on various definitions proposed in the past, the chapter confined the analysis to international patients seeking care overseas barring expatriates seeking care in the current country of residence and emergency cases. Though health is a social sector with various market failures, medical tourism has emerged as a globally competitive health market with minimal failures. Further, the push and pull factors of economics are employed by Fetscherin and Stephano (2016) to develop a framework that considers the relative importance of the country environment, attractiveness as a tourism destination, medical tourism cost, and ancillary Facility and Services.

The liberal exchange of cross country patients has given rise to disparities as well. LMIC are often faced with resource constraint and medical tourism has been blamed to pull limited resources from poor locals. To better understand the issue, there is a need for separate record keeping for medical tourism in healthcare accounts to understand the inflow of patients and reallocation of local resources. Commercial surrogacy and organ donation (turned into trafficking) are some serious issues that have caught the attention of international bodies in the age of medical tourism. These disparities require constant vigilance and monitoring which cannot be left on private firms and hospitals engaged in the service. An international arrangement is called for to generate empirical evidence and make policy corrections.

Even with disparities, the benefits of medical tourism cannot be denied. And with the introduction of digital interventions like telemedicine, the growth, reach and acceptance of medical tourism will continue to grow.

REFERENCES

Dann, G. M. (1977). Anomie, ego-enhancement and tourism. *Annals of Tourism Research*, *4*(4), 184–194. doi:10.1016/0160-7383(77)90037-8

Deonandan, R., Green, S., & Van Beinum, A. (2012). Ethical concerns for maternal surrogacy and reproductive tourism. *Journal of Medical Ethics*, *38*(12), 742–745. doi:10.1136/medethics-2012-100551 PMID:23047836

Fetscherin, M., & Stephano, R. M. (2016). The medical tourism index: Scale development and validation. *Tourism Management*, *52*, 539–556. doi:10.1016/j.tourman.2015.08.010

Gan, L. L., & Frederick, J. R. (2011). Medical tourism facilitators: Patterns of service differentiation. *Journal of Vacation Marketing*, *17*(3), 165–183. doi:10.1177/1356766711409181

George, B. P., & Henthorne, T. L. (2009). The incorporation of telemedicine with medical tourism: A study of consequences. *Journal of Hospitality Marketing & Management*, *18*(5), 512–522. doi:10.1080/19368620902950097

Horowitz, M. D., Rosensweig, J. A., & Jones, C. A. (2007). Medical tourism: Globalization of the healthcare marketplace. *Medscape General Medicine*, *9*(4), 33. PMID:18311383

Joint Commission International. (2019). *JCI accredited organizations*. Retrieved from https://www.jointcommissioninternational.org/about-jci/jci-accredited-organizations/?c=India&a=Hospital%20Program

Lancaster, J. (2004). Surgeries, side trips for medical tourists. *Washington Post, 21*.

Martin, R. M., Sterne, J. A., Gunnell, D., Ebrahim, S., Smith, G. D., & Frankel, S. (2003). NHS waiting lists and evidence of national or local failure: Analysis of health service data. *BMJ (Clinical Research Ed.), 326*(7382), 188. doi:10.1136/bmj.326.7382.188 PMID:12543833

Mattoo, A., & Rathindran, R. (2006). How health insurance inhibits trade in health care. *Health Affairs, 25*(2), 358–368. doi:10.1377/hlthaff.25.2.358 PMID:16522578

Mohamad, W. N., Omar, A., & Haron, M. S. (2012). The moderating effect of medical travel facilitators in medical tourism. *Procedia: Social and Behavioral Sciences, 65*, 358–363. doi:10.1016/j.sbspro.2012.11.134

Newton, J. N., Henderson, J., & Goldacre, M. J. (1995). Waiting list dynamics and the impact of earmarked funding. *BMJ (Clinical Research Ed.), 311*(7008), 783–785. doi:10.1136/bmj.311.7008.783 PMID:7580440

Richmond, C. (1996). NHS waiting list have been a boon for private medicine in the UK. *CMAJ: Canadian Medical Association Journal, 154*(3), 378. PMID:8564909

Zion Market Research. (2018). Retrieved on 30/04/2019 from https://www.globenewswire.com/news-release/2018/06/25/1528923/0/en/Global-Medical-Tourism-Market-Expected-to-Reach-USD-28-0-Billion-by-2024-Zion-Market-Research.html

ADDITIONAL READING

Gilbert (2015). The Uninsured Across the OECD Countries and U.S. States. Retrieved from http://theincidentaleconomist.com/wordpress/wp-content/uploads/2015/06/OECD-Uninsured.pdf 2015

Jagyasi, P. (2010). *Medical Tourism: Research & Survey Report*. Dr Prem.

Medical Tourism Association. (2019). Retrieved from https://www.medicaltourismassociation.com/en/index.html

Mohamad, W. N., Omar, A., & Haron, M. S. (2012). The moderating effect of medical travel facilitators in medical tourism. *Procedia: Social and Behavioral Sciences, 65*, 358–363. doi:10.1016/j.sbspro.2012.11.134

Tarlow, P. (2007). Dark tourism–the appealing 'dark'side of tourism and more. In *Niche tourism* (pp. 61–72). Routledge.

Chapter 3
Priortizing Barriers of Dental Implants for Patients Attending OPD

Madhuri Pradhan
KIIT University, India

Suchismita Satapathy
https://orcid.org/0000-0002-4805-1793
KIIT University, India

B. B. Nayak
KIIT University, India

ABSTRACT

Carelessness, bad habits, genetics, and age are the most important factors for tooth decay. Many dental problems, including decay, can easily be fixed by dental implants. In this chapter, an effort is taken to prioritize the barriers of dental implants by multi-criteria decision-making techniques like Promethee.

INTRODUCTION

A dental implant is a titanium post (like a tooth root) that is surgically positioned into the jawbone beneath the gum line that allows your dentist to mount replacement teeth or a bridge into that area. An implant doesn't come loose like a denture can. Dental implants also benefit general oral health because they do not have to be anchored to other teeth, like bridges. Because implants fuse to your jawbone, they provide stable support for artificial teeth. Dentures and bridges mounted to implants won't slip or

DOI: 10.4018/978-1-5225-9787-2.ch003

shift in your mouth an especially important benefit when eating and speaking. This secure fit helps the dentures and bridges as well as individual crowns placed over implants feel more natural than conventional bridges or dentures.

But, For some people, ordinary bridges and dentures are usually not comfortable, due to sore spots, poor ridges or gagging. In addition, ordinary bridges must be joined to teeth on either side of the space left by the missing tooth.In implants no adjacent teeth need to be prepared or ground down to hold your new replacement tooth/teeth in place. But implants need to have healthy gums and adequate bone to support the implant. Implants are usually more expensive than other methods of tooth replacement. There are two methods of implants Endosteal implants and subperiosteal implants.

Although dental implant is a very useful technique still dental implant failurerate is also very high. Dental implant failures can take place for several reasons. It may be Short-term failures which can be described as a failure to heal in the bone, a process called "osseointegration. The short-term failures can be treated by removing the implant, repairing the surgical site with a bone graft and allowing it to heal before attempting to place another fixture. Since bone heals much more slowly than soft tissue, this process can take several months. Long-term dental implant failure presents an entirely different set of challenges. They can occur after the implant has healed and become integrated in the bone, and after an implant has been restored. The most common long-term failure (and unfortunately the most difficult kind to treat) is called peri-implantitis. Peri-implantitis is a chronic infection in the gum and ultimately the bone that supports the implant. It may be likened to the periodontal disease process affecting teeth, since both result in the loss of the supporting structure (bone) around a fixed part. Symptoms may include discomfort and pus or bleeding from the gums. The main cause of patients avoiding dentists are fear of pain, time and availability, financial reason. Many people do not fond of visiting doctors.

BACKGROUND

Bandyopadhyay et.al.(2017) have studied to assess oral hygiene-related knowledge and practices among engineering students of Bhubaneswar city and also to evaluate the concepts about the side effects of tobacco usage among those students. Kubota et.al(2016) have highlighted the destruction of periodontal tissue by smoking and the unfavorable clinical course of periodontal disease in patients with a cigarette smoking habit. The present study demonstrates that periodontal disease models are useful for elucidating the pathogenesis of cigarette smoking-related periodontal diseases. Jhu et.al (2003) have studied and found that children in India and china where 71.6% and 73.6% respectively had a regular dental visit every 6 months.

Gopinath v (2010) has carried out to assess the oral hygiene practices and habits among practicing general dentists. Revathi et al (2017) have focused on degradation mechanisms such as corrosion, tribocorrosion and wear condition of the material. And explored on the evaluation of surface treatment to improve wear and corrosion performance of material. And on surface modification technique such as coating method. Liu et al (2017) have found binary ti alloys, in particular to ti—zr,ti–ag, ti–cu,ti–au, etc. with the alloying components has a high potential as implant materials due to good mechanical performance without compromising the biological behaviour compare to cp-ti. Gepreel et al. (2012) have explored β-type ti alloys composing mainly of low cost common metals such as mn, sn or fe, that show high strength, low young's modulus and exhibit good mechanical properties, biocompatibility and non toxic . Correa et al.(2013) have explained about mechanical properties which were assessed with measure of hardness and elastic modulus and addition of zirconium increase density of the material compared to cpti. Medvedev et.al (2015) have found the effect of surface treatment and mechanical properties of the implant. Bicudoa et.al (2016) have focused on analysis of the mechanical behaviour of different type implants subjected to fatigue test on different substrates. Greger et al. (2010) investigated the titanium and its alloys which show tremendously a success substance for the fabrication of dental and orthopaedic implants, because of their favorable combination of properties like low elastic modulus, low weight, greater strength to weight ratio, very excessive corrosion resistance and remarkable popular biocompatibility. Saini et al. (2015) it was observed that in present day dental implant have recently started to expand and make use of the advantages of biotechnology in health care and gaining popularity among the patients and in the medical field. Jahan and Edwards worked on amalgam tooth filling and a hip joint prosthesis material selection problem (2013). This study is the first study on material selection for dental implant with MCDM. Jahan and Edwards worked on amalgam tooth filling and a hip joint prosthesis material selection problem (2013). This study is the first study on material selection for dental implant with MCDM. Şenyiğit and Demirel (2018) have selected the best material to be used in implant design is chromium cobalt according to the Entropy based Simple Additive Weighting and Analytic Hierarchy Process methods.

Research Methodology

To find problems of dental patients a standard questionare is designed by literature review and expert analysis and a cross-sectional questionnaire study was carried out in OPD of Dental Colleges to find several dental problems faced by patients and frequency of visit. One hundred and fifty patients participated in this study. The patients were asked to answer a questionnaire on dental problems faced within last 5 years

.Likert scale of 1to 5 is used to collect data .1= Totally disagree,2=disagree,,3=no opinion,4=agree,5=totally agree. To find Barriers and customer satisfaction of Dental implants a questionnaire survey of 150 patients was conducted including experts opinion and literature survey. Experts are selected consisting of 5 experts of medical college,10 dental surgeons,6 academicians .Same Likert scale 1 to 5 is used. 1=Totally disagree,2=disagree,,3=no opinion,4=agree,5=totally agree. Then Promethee-II is implemented to find most important barriers that discards dental implants. Then dental implantation is measured by measuring customer satisfaction in successive implantation.

RESULT DISCUSSION

It was observed from the Table.1,that in dental implants no of Patients are maximum in percentage (96.05%), then Bleeding Due to irregular brushing habit 95%.So more extensive study is essential for study on dental implants. Table 1 shows Dental problems of patients.

Dental implants are artificial tooth roots that provide a permanent base for fixed, replacement teeth. Compared to dentures, bridges and crowns, dental implants are a popular and effective long-term solution for people who suffer from missing teeth, failing teeth or chronic dental problems. Although patient suffering and doctors suggesting for dental implants are more in number compared to others still it is not preferred by patients .Still patients afraid of implants due to fear and try to avoid it. In India still it is not popular. Patients have many questions about cost, effectiveness, durability procedure etc. So an effort was taken to find barriers that hindering the dental implants in India. Then Promethee-II is implemented to find most important barriers that discards dental implants.

Promethee-II

The PROMETHEE II method allows one to establish a complete ranking between possible movements based on outranking relations.

Procedure of Promethee-II:

Normalization of Decision matrix using the following equation:

$R_{ij} = [X_{ij}\text{-min}(X_{ij})]/[\max(X_{ij})\text{-min}(X_{ij})]$ (i=1, 2..n;j=1,2..m)

where X_{ij} is the performance measure of ith factor with respect to j^{th} criterion.

Computation of evaluative differences of ith factor with respect to other factors.

This step involved the calculation of differences in criteria values between different factors pair-wise.

Calculation of preference function Pj (i, i′) using the following equation:

Preference Functions Values:

$P(i, i') = 0$ If $R_i \leq R_{i'}$

Table 1. Dental problems of patients visiting OPD

Cause for visit to OPD	Number of Patient(%)
dental problem faced due to cavity	126 (86.88)
Pain due to toothache	111 (77.08)
Use of drugs and tabaco decays tooth and cause of hanging teeth	120 (83.33)
Chocolates &sweets creates tooth problem	14 (9.72)
Half broken teeth	09 (6.25)
Fall down and accidents	16 (11.11)
Mouth cancer	28 (20.05)
Diabetics	13 (9.02)
Bleeding Due to irregular brushing habit	138 (95.83)
Drinking habits	129 (89.58)
Age problem	07 (4.25)
Mouth smell	06(3.11)
Dental implants	141(96.05)
Regular check up	11 (8.62)
For shaping teeth	108 (90.83)
Root canal	121 (83.58)

$P(i, i') = (R_i - R_{i'})$ If $R_i > R_{i'}$

$R_1 - R_2 = 0$

$R_1 - R_3 = 0.076923$

.

.

$R_9 - R_7 = 0.538462$

$R_9 - R_8 = 0$

Aggregated Preference Function Values:

$\Pi (i, i') = [\, WxP\left(i,i'\right)]/ W$. ere W = 3)

$(P_{11} - P_{12})*W = 0$

$(P_{11} - P_{13})*W = 0$

.

.

Ranking Matrix:

$$\varphi+ (i) = \frac{1}{n-1}\sum_{i'=1}^{n}\Pi\left(i,i'\right) (i \neq i')$$

$$\varphi- (i) = \frac{1}{n-1}\sum_{i'=1}^{n}\Pi\left(i',i\right) (i \neq i')$$

$$\Phi^{+} = (\Pi_{.2} + \Pi_{.3} .. \Pi_{.9})/8 = 1.307694$$

$$\Phi^{-} = (\Pi_{.1} + \Pi_{.1} .. \Pi_{.1})/8 = 1.076922$$

$$\Phi = \Phi^{+} - \Phi^{-} = 0.230772$$

Ranking is done according to the value of Φ. Table 2 to 5 is useful to calculate agreegate preference function. Table 2 shows input weights of barriers.

Table 3 shows normalized value of barriersof dental implants.

Table 4 shows preference function of barriers.

Table 5 gives aggregated preference functions of matrix.

Table 6 shows ranking of barriers of dental implants

After ranking it is found that, Strength of material used in implantation and its durability is the most important barrier ranked first, Technical design for proper implantation ranked second and Suitable Material selection for implantation is ranked third. It shows that these are the cause of patients not preferring dental implantation. So to avoid these barriers suitable technology, suitable materials and

Table 2. Input weights assigned for Barriers

	Barriers	Averaged Value
A	Mental preparedness for replace of teeth	3.28
B	Technical design for proper implantation	3.72
C	Fear of surgery& pain	3.12
D	Success in implantations and lasting	3.68
E	Strength of material used in implantation and its durability	3.88
F	Lack of knowledge and education.	3.28
G	Not got clear information from dentist	3.2
H	Suitable Material selection for implantation	3.84
I	High cost	3.32
J	Not clear about procedure	3.68

Table 3. Normalized value of barriers

	Barriers	Normalized Value
A	Mental preparedness for replace of teeth	0.210
B	Technical design for proper implantation	0.789
C	Fear of surgery& pain	0
D	Success in implantations and lasting	0.736
E	Strength of material used in implantation and its durability	1
F	Lack of knowledge and education.	.210
G	Not got clear information from dentist	0.105
H	Suitable Material selection for implantation	0.947
I	High cost	0.263
J	Not clear about procedure	0.736

design aspects must be consider which can make artificial implants not only look natural but it can function long term also like natural teeth. The selection of the implant materials, their generation system, manufacturing method, age-long durability, biocompatibility with medical principle and professional dental field of study are therefore essential. Today precision investment casting manufacturing generation process of dental implant produced many defects and faults due to imperfect castings and their mechanical properties cannot close to the standard. The implant made by this process cannot exactly measure the elastic modulus (2). Materials, for example, metal alloys and ceramics are broadly utilized for the manufacture of dental implant. Ceramic production either make up the whole implants or can be connected as a covering onto the metallic core. A perfect implant should be higher strength character, biocompatibility, fatigue nature and fracture toughness characteristics and capable to withstand the reactive environment that exposed within the human body (3). Several types of metallic material are used for implant, among them the stainless steel has been limited due to its bad fatigue strength and galvanic corrosion.

CONCLUSION

Dental implants have been gaining importance in the field of dentistry. The implant insertion in missing teeth has become choice of both patients and dentists. Though it is nowadays considered preferred management for edentulous area, complications and failures are not uncommon. Still by avoiding barriers the implant technology can be popular among patients. Dental implants are quite common in today's life.

Table 4. Preference function value of barriers

Barrier Pairs	Values
AB	0
AC	0.210526
AD	0
AE	0
AF	0
AG	0.105263
AH	0
AI	0
AJ	0
BA	0.578948
BC	0.789474
BD	0.052632
BE	0
BF	0.578948
BG	0.684211
BH	0
BI	0.526316
BJ	0.052632
CA	0
CB	0
CD	0
CE	0
CF	0
CG	0
CH	0
CI	0
CJ	0
DA	0.526316
DB	0
DC	0.736842
DE	0
DF	0.526316
DG	0.631579
DH	0

continued on following page

Table 4. Continued

Barrier Pairs	Values
DI	0.473684
DJ	0
EA	0.789474
EB	0.210526
EC	1
ED	0.263158
EF	0.789474
EG	0.894737
EH	0.052632
EI	0.736842
EJ	0.263158
FA	0
FB	0
FC	0.210526
FD	0
FE	0
FG	0.105263
FH	0
FI	0
FJ	0
GA	0
GB	0
GC	0.105263
GD	0
GE	0
GF	0
GH	0
GI	0
GJ	0
HA	0.736842
HB	0.157894
HC	0.947368

continued on following page

Table 4. Continued

Barrier Pairs	Values
HD	0.210526
HE	0
HF	0.736842
HG	0.842105
HI	0.68421
HJ	0.210526
IA	0.052632
IB	0
IC	0.263158
ID	0
IE	0
IF	0.052632
IG	0.157895
IH	0
IJ	0
JA	0.526316
JB	0
JC	0.736842
JD	0
JE	0
JF	0.526316
JG	0.631579
JH	0
JI	0.473684

The successful implant leads to patient as well as dentist satisfaction. However, risk factors, such as diabetes, periodontitis, bruxism, and smoking have deleterious effects on survival rate of dental implants. Counseling the diabetic patients regarding the habits and oral hygiene is necessary to improve the success rates of implants.

Table 5. Aggregated preference functions matrix

	A	B	C	D	E	F	G	H	I	J
A	0	0	0.211	0	0	0	0.105	0	0	0
B	0.579	0	0.789	0.053	0	0.579	0.684	0	0.526	0.053
C	0	0	0	0	0	0	0	0	0	0
D	0.526	0	0.737	0	0	0.526	0.632	0	0.474	0
E	0.789	0.211	1	0.263	0	0.789	0.895	0.053	0.737	0.263
F	0	0	0.211	0	0	0	0.105	0	0	0
G	0	0	0.105	0	0	0	0	0	0	0
H	0.737	0.158	0.947	0.211	0	0.737	0.842	0	0.684	0.211
I	0.053	0	0.263	0	0	0.053	0.158	0	0	0
J	0.526	0	0.737	0	0	0.526	0.632	0	0.474	0

Table 6. Ranking table

Barriers	Φ+	Φ-	Φ(Total)	Ranks
A	0.315789	3.210528	-2.894739	7
B	3.263161	0.36842	2.894741	3(3rd)
C	0	4.999999	-4.999999	10
D	2.894737	0.526316	2.368421	4
E	5.000001	0	5.000001	1(ist)
F	0.315789	3.210528	-2.894739	8
G	0.105263	4.052632	-3.947369	9
H	4.526313	0.052632	4.473681	2(2nd)
I	0.526317	2.894736	-2.368419	6
J	2.894737	0.526316	2.368421	5

REFERENCES

Bandyopadhyay, A., Bhuyan, L., Panda, A., & Kailash, C. (2017, June). Assessment of Oral Hygiene Knowledge, Practices, and Concepts of Tobacco Usage among Engineering Students in Bhubaneswar, Odisha, India. *The Journal of Contemporary Dental Practice*, *18*(6), 1–6. PMID:28621268

Bicudo, P., Reis, J., Deus, A. M., Reis, L., & Vaz, M. F. (2016). Mechanical behaviour of dental implants. *Procedia Structural Integrity*, *1*, 26–33. doi:10.1016/j.prostr.2016.02.005

Correa, D. R. N., Vicente, F. B., Donato, T. A. G., Arana-Chavez, V. E., Buzalaf, M. A. R., & Grandini, C. R. (2014). The effect of the solute on the structure, selected mechanical properties, and biocompatibility of Ti–Zr system alloys for dental applications. *Materials Science and Engineering C*, *34*, 354–359. doi:10.1016/j.msec.2013.09.032 PMID:24268269

Gepreel, M. A. H., & Niinomi, M. (2013). Biocompatibility of Ti-alloys for long-term implantation. *Journal of the Mechanical Behavior of Biomedical Materials*, *20*, 407–415. doi:10.1016/j.jmbbm.2012.11.014 PMID:23507261

Gopinath, V. (2010, April-June). Oral hygiene practices and habits amongdental professionals in Chennai. *Indian Journal of Dental Research*, *21*(2), 195–200. doi:10.4103/0970-9290.66636 PMID:20657087

Greger, M., Widomská, M., & Kander, L. (2010). Mechanical properties of ultra-fine grain titanium. *Journal of Achievements in Materials and Manufacturing Engineering*, *40*(1), 33–40.

Jahan, A., & Edwards, K. L. (2013). Weighting of dependent and target-based criteria for optimal decision-making in materials selection process: Biomedical applications. *Materials & Design*, *49*, 1000–1008. doi:10.1016/j.matdes.2013.02.064

Kubota, M., Yanagita, M., Mori, K., Hasegawa, S., Yamashita, M., Yamada, S., ... Murakami, S. (2016, May). The effects of cigarettesmoke condensate and nicotine on periodontal tissue in a periodontitismodel mouse. *PLoS One*, *11*(5), e0155594. doi:10.1371/journal.pone.0155594 PMID:27203240

Liu, X., Chen, S., Tsoi, J. K., & Matinlinna, J. P. (2017). Binary titanium alloys as dental implant materials—a review. *Regenerative Biomaterials, 4*(5), 315-323.

Medvedev, A. E., Molotnikov, A., Lapovok, R., Zeller, R., Berner, S., Habersetzer, P., & Dalla Torre, F. (2016). Microstructure and mechanical properties of Ti–15Zr alloy used as dental implant material. *Journal of the Mechanical Behavior of Biomedical Materials*, *62*, 384–398. doi:10.1016/j.jmbbm.2016.05.008 PMID:27258932

Revathi, A., Borrás, A. D., Muñoz, A. I., Richard, C., & Manivasagam, G. (2017). Degradation mechanisms and future challenges of titanium and its alloys for dental implant applications in oral environment. *Materials Science and Engineering C, 76*, 1354–1368. doi:10.1016/j.msec.2017.02.159 PMID:28482503

Saini, M., Singh, Y., Arora, P., Arora, V., & Jain, K. (2015). Implant biomaterials: A comprehensive review. *World Journal of Clinical Cases: WJCC, 3*(1), 52. doi:10.12998/wjcc.v3.i1.52 PMID:25610850

Şenyiğit, E., & Demirel, B. (2018). The selection of material in dental implant with entropy based simple additive weighting and analytic hierarchy process methods. *Sigma J Eng & Nat Sci, 36*(3), 731–740.

Zhu, L., Petersen, P. E., Wang, H. Y., Bian, J. Y., & Zhang, B. X. (2003, October). Oral healthknowledge, attitudes and behaviour of children and adolescentsin China. *International Dental Journal, 53*(5), 289–298. doi:10.1111/j.1875-595X.2003.tb00762.x PMID:14560803

KEY TERMS AND DEFINITIONS

Dental Implants: Metal posts or frames that are surgically positioned into the jawbone beneath your gums.

Endosteal Implants: These are surgically implanted directly into the jawbone. Once the surrounding gum tissue has healed, a second surgery is needed to connect a post to the original implant. Finally, an artificial tooth (or teeth) is attached to the post-individually, or grouped on a bridge or denture.

Promethee: The Preference Ranking Organization Method for Enrichment of Evaluations and its descriptive complement geometrical analysis for interactive aid are better known as the Promethee.

Subperiosteal Implants: These consist of a metal frame that is fitted onto the jawbone just below the gum tissue. As the gums heal, the frame becomes fixed to the jawbone. Posts, which are attached to the frame, protrude through the gums. As with endosteal implants, artificial teeth are then mounted to the posts.

APPENDIX

Table 7. Barriers of dental implants

1	Mental preparedness for replace of teeth	1	2	3	4	5
2	High cost					
3	Fear of surgery& future					
4	Not clear about procedure					
5	Not got clear information from dentist					
6	Lack of knowledge and education.					
7	Suitable Material selection for implantation					
8	Technical design for proper implantation					
9	Strength of material used in implantation and its durability					

Chapter 4
Strategic Indicators of the Role of Government in Developing Dubai as a Medical Tourism Hub

Farooq Haq
https://orcid.org/0000-0002-1620-9226
Canadian University Dubai, Dubai, UAE

Anita Medhekar
https://orcid.org/0000-0002-6791-4056
CQUniversity, Australia

ABSTRACT

Medical tourism is a growing phenomenon in the Middle East. Dubai is strategically located to competitively attract patients from Islamic backgrounds given the cultural congruence with the Middle Eastern countries for medical tourism. Dubai is famous for its shopping, sightseeing, desert safaris, state-of-the art tourism facilities, and as a melting pot for Eastern and Western civilizations. The government of United Arab Emirates is playing a key role to support the development of Dubai as a medical tourism hub of the Middle East and diversify the oil-based economy in an innovative way. It is developing various niche tourism products and services embedded in the non-oil sectors of the economy by applying the five strategic indicators required to study the role of governments in planning and supporting sustainable tourism.

DOI: 10.4018/978-1-5225-9787-2.ch004

INTRODUCTION

Dubai is famous for its luxury shopping, sightseeing, recreation facilities, state-of-the art tourism facilities, financial capital of middle east, global property market, and an attractive medical travel destination. The main economy of United Arab Emirates (UAE) is production and export of oil, natural gas, services sector -shipping, finance, luxury real estate, shopping and tourism (Alhosani & Zaidan, 2014; Ballentyne, 2015; Sharpley, 2008; Zaidan, 2016). Tourism plays a key role in Dubai's economy, with nearly 10 million people visiting Dubai every year in Emirates region. Nearly 10 million inbound tourists visit Dubai every year, with a domestic population of 9.4 million (MTI, 2019). In terms of geography, Dubai is strategically located to attract patients from Islamic backgrounds given the cultural familiarity with the Middle Eastern countries (Haq & Medhekar, 2015). Dubai is considered as "New York/Las Vegas/Miami rolled into one" (Bagaeen, 2007, p. 173).

Dubai is already a popular tourist destination and known as the melting pot of eastern and western civilisations (Alhosani & Zaidan, 2014; Ballantyne, 2015; Henderson, 2014; Inhorn, 2016; Khan & Alam, 2014). It is also known as "A star in the East" (Balakrishnan, 2008). According to Alhosani and Zaidan (2014), the travel and tourism sector is projected to grow, annually at 4.1% and create 245,000 employment opportunities by 2023. Dubai is like Singapore, which is the hub of finance, tourism, luxury shopping, and an attractive medical tourism destination of the Middle East (Henderson, 2007).

Medical tourism is a growing phenomenon in the Middle East. The number of people from neighbouring countries and Europe, are travelling in-bound to Dubai in the UAE, for medical treatment, diagnostic tests and complex surgery. Medical travel/tourism is on the rise due to high quality of medicals services, use of high-tech medical technology, and is emerging and considered as a medical tourism hub (Al-Harbi, 2018). People are travelling for second opinion for diagnostic tests and specialist surgeries such as cosmetic, infertility treatments, dental, orthopaedic and cardiac. Global patients as medical tourists are very well informed. They make an informed decision and travel crossborder or long distances between continents to developing countries such as Thailand, India, Malaysia, Turkey, South Africa, Brazil, Mexico, Egypt and Dubai, which are global healthcare destinations for medical treatment and complex surgeries (Bookman & Bookman, 2007; Connell, 2013; Deloitte, 2008; Horowitz & Rosensweig, 2007; Lunt & Mannion, 2014; Manaf et al., 2015; Medhekar & Ali, 2012; Omar et al., 2015; Sag & Zengul, 2018; Sandberg, 2017).

There are numerous economic opportunities and challenges to develop Dubai's Healthcare City as a global medical tourism hub of the Middle East along with diversifying its non-oil sector of the economy (Mansfeld & Winckler, 2007; Medhekar & Haq, 2016; Oxford Business Group, 2017; Sag & Zengul, 2018). Given the geographical location, warm climate, tourism destination and a transit gateway to Europe, Africa and Asia, Dubai has a major competitive advantage in developing and promoting its first-class Joint Commission International (JCI) accredited health tourism facilities to diversify the tourism economy (Mansfeld & Winckler, 2007). There are until 2019-July, many healthcare organisations, hospitals and diagnostic clinics accredited by JCI all over the world. In UAE 210; Singapore 21; Malaysia 13, Saudi Arabia 104, and India 37- have been accredited by JCI with the gold seal of standard approval as foreign patients look for JCI accreditation when choosing a hospital for medical treatment/surgery (JCI, 2019).

Tourism related opportunities for developing and promoting Dubai as a global hub for Medical Tourism are not studied sufficiently, which is a gap to be covered in this chapter. The purpose of this chapter is to: (i) Examine the significance of medical tourism development in Dubai as a Middle Eastern hub for medical travel/tourism. (ii) Apply the five strategic indicators to study the role of Dubai Government in supporting the planning and development of global medical tourism hub in Dubai. (iii) Propose a public-private partnership (PPPs) framework that could be adopted by Dubai Health Authority (DHA) to develop and promote Dubai as a "Global as well as Halal Medical Tourism" hub of the Middle East.

This chapter is structured as follows. The first section of the chapter introduces the growing economic importance and significance of medical tourism in Dubai. Section 2 provides the literature review on medical tourism. Section 3 provides the healthcare vision and values of the Dubai Government in developing public and private healthcare and medical tourism, with respect to the five strategic indicators for sustainable development provided by Nwosu and Onah (2016) and Birkic, Pilija, and Sebrek (2014)- (i) vision and values and implementation and control, (ii) long-term orientation, (iii) physical and economics analysis, (iv) supply capabilities and evaluation of alternatives, and (v) stakeholders' participation. Section 4 identifies challenges and opportunities of developing Dubai as a global medical tourism hub. Section 5, proposes and recommends public-private partnerships between key stakeholders to plan, develop, and promote Dubai as a global medical tourism hub and policy implications. Final section 6 covers conclusion and future research directions to advance the knowledge in the field of global healthcare.

LITERATURE REVIEW

Carrera and Bridges (2006) were the first to conceptualise, distinguish and clearly define the two terms health tourism and medical tourism. "Health tourism is defined as the organised travel outside one's local environment for the maintenance, enhancement or restoration of the individual wellbeing in mind and body". Medical tourism...is defined as "the organised travel outside one's natural healthcare jurisdiction for the enhancement or restoration of the individual's health through medical intervention" (Carrera & Bridges 2006, p.449).

Therefore, medical travel is about travelling within the country from remote or regional areas if treatment is not available to capital cities, called domestic medical travel (Haq & Medhekar, 2015). Due to globalisation, people travel cross border to neighbouring countries or long distances across oceans to another country for seeking medical treatment and surgery is known as international medical travel or medical tourism. This includes surgeries such as heart, cancer, cardiac, cosmetic, reproductive, dental and hip and knee replacements (Runnels & Turner, 2011; Turner, 2007).

Medical Tourism

There is extant multidisciplinary literature on the growing global phenomenon of medical tourism from different perspectives (Chuang et al. 2014; Majeed & Lu, 2017; Lunt, Horsfall, & Hanefeld, 2016; Adam, Snyder, Crooks, & Johnston, 2015; Connell, 2015; Smith, Álvarez, & Chanda, 2011; Lunt & Carrera, 2010; Manaf et al., 2015; Medhekar, Wong, & Hall, 2019). In the last decade, travelling abroad has become "safe, fast, and inexpensive enough to support the resort hospitals that comprise the backbone of the medical tourism service industry" (Burkett, 2007, p.226). Deloitte (2008) health report has identified that pull-factors such as low cost, JCI accredited quality of care, surgeons expertise, and shorter waiting time/ list for surgeries as the key drivers for medical travel. Patients as medical tourists are travelling from developed to developing countries for complex surgeries, as Cotton, Henry, and Hasek (2014), calls medical travel as low-cost and high-quality medical technology innovations in developing countries as "value innovation or cost-efficient innovation" (p. 1). Medical travel is influenced not just by the need to improve once health but also by social, economic, political, exchange rate, tourism opportunities, climate, language and cultural factors (Collins, Medhekar, Wong, & Cobanoglu, 2019; Medhekar et al., 2019; Whittaker & Chee, 2016).

Medical tourism is possible due to globalisation, digitisation, international trade and privatisation of healthcare (Ghose, 2010). "Internet is altering how people consume healthcare, the way in which they obtain information and the manner in which they evaluate {treatment} alternatives" (Miller & West, 2008, p.245). Few empirical studies such as Lunt, Hardey, and Mannion (2010) assert that, "A key driver in the medical tourism phenomenon is the platform provided by the internet for gaining access to healthcare information and advertising" (p.1). Sag and Zengul (2018) surveyed 288 patients and found that medical tourists who travelled to Turkey had different health behaviours based on their geographical region of residence contributing to the medical tourist's behaviour and market segmentation.

Quantitative survey of 541 United States actual medical tourists as participant by Collins et al. (2019) found that American medical patient, some of them diaspora, travelled abroad to top five destinations of India, China, Thailand, Mexico and Turkey based on attractiveness of tourism destination, country related factors, medical tourism costs and facilities and services provided by the healthcare service provider.

Dubai is also a popular destination for medical treatment in niche areas of cosmetic, dental and reproductive treatment. The number of overseas patients from the Middle East and European countries visiting Dubai for medical travel is on the rise. Dubai being a hub for air-travel transit also faces competition from other countries such as Turkey, Saudi Arabia, South Africa, India, Singapore, and Thailand (Connell, 2015; Finch, 2014; JCI, 2019; Medhekar et al., 2019; Omar et al., 2015; Sag & Zengul, 2018). According to the Medical Tourism Index {MTI} (2019) survey, Dubai's global ranking is 16th as a medical tourism destination and overall MTI score is 67.54, '*destination environment*' it is ranked 18th with a score of (61.71); and ranked 22nd for '*medical tourism industry*', with a score of 68.42; followed by 10th position in the '*quality of facilities and services', with a score of 72.49.*

Hence, the UAE-Dubai Government can adopt the approach from Thailand, India, or Singapore for developing Dubai as a Middle Eastern global hub for medical tourists. The former Crown Prince Sheikh Mohammed Bin Rashid Al Maktoum and the current ruler of Dubai set out a strategic vision for the UAE tourism planning and development to diversify the non-oil sector of the economy and laid the foundation for the development of tourism in Dubai in the early 1980s. Dubai is already the star tourism destination of the Middle East offering diverse tourism opportunities and now on its way to become the Middle-Eastern hub of medical tourism.

DUBAI GOVERNMENT HEALTHCARE

UAE has a public system which caters to all needs of domestic patients and private healthcare, which treats domestic as well as foreign patients or medical tourists. Dubai Healthcare City, covering 20 million square feet area and attracts major healthcare partners from American corporations, pharmaceutical, medical equipment and medical device companies. It is projected that by 2020, Dubai will have medical equipment and 34 pharmaceutical plants. Dubai Healthcare Authority (DHA) has two healthcare free economic trade zone, which attracts inbound healthcare tourists looking for wellness and medical treatment (MTI, 2019).

Vision and Values

The UAE government's Vision - 2021, is to provide access to affordable and available first-class universal healthcare to all its citizens. According to Vision-2021 "the UAE [will]... invest continuously to build world- class healthcare infrastructure, expertise and services in order to fulfill citizens' growing needs and expectations" (The UAE Healthcare Sector, 2014). According to Dubai Health Authority (DHA, 2018) government is taking all necessary steps to put Dubai on the global healthcare map as one of the top five medical tourism destinations in the world, to attract foreign patients providing highly accredited international quality of treatment. Now DHA aims to attract approximately 500,000 medial tourists by 2020, by upgrading and building medical capabilities such as state-of-the-art medical facilities, technology, and medical professional's expertise, healthcare services, patient safety, medical complaint procedure, patients' rights and responsibilities before they travel, and positive patient experience (Hotelier-Middle East, 2018).

International patients in 2007-08, travelled for cosmetic, plastic surgery, dental, infertility, eyes, dental, sports medicine, reconstructive surgery, bariatric, and orthopaedic (Ballentyne, 2008) which are popular treatments even in 2018, given the medical professional expertise. The government in United Arab Emirates have made all efforts to invest in excellent healthcare infrastructure facilities, Dubai healthcare city and meet all national and international healthcare accreditation requirements by JCI. UAE healthcare vision for 2021 states that "the UAE [will]... invest continuously to build world- class healthcare infrastructure, expertise and services in order to fulfil citizens' growing needs and expectations" (The UAE Healthcare Sector, 2014).

Government has also developed various e-health smart phone applications systems and integrated digital online comprehensive gateways for medical tourists for taking an appointment with the hospital, make all other travel, and visa arrangements. It is a popular destination for high end of surgeries specialising in opthomology, dental, dermatology, reproductive, plastic surgery, preventative medicine and sports medicine (IMTJ, 2017; Inhorn, Shrivastav, & Patrizio, 2014). Various medical tourism packages are offered by the Government of Dubai Health Authority website to cater to patients' healthcare and tourism needs (https://www.dxh.ae/about-us/about-dxh/).

UAE's world first medical tourism portal provides online one-stop-shop— a live chat with a medical consultant, and various tabs with drop down menus related to directories of assistant, plan your trip, supporting services, which include police and ambulance, newsroom and health travelogue all on one e-portal. Dubai Health Authority has also collaborated with The Health Bank to drive the development and growth of medical tourism and provide tailor-made preventative and wellness related health management solutions on the online portal (IMTJ, 2017).

Long Term Orientation

The long-term orientation of the Dubai Government is the diversification of its economy and moving into non-oil-based industries, where tourism is the obvious option (Inhorn, 2016; Zaidan, 2016; Henderson, 2014). In recent years, medical tourism has been recognised a non-natural based and heavily technology and infrastructure dependent tourism product that suits the resources and capabilities of Dubai's economy (Dominic, 2016; Haq & Medhekar, 2015).

The long-term orientation for tourism planning for any government can be based on various conceptual medical tourism models that have been proposed from demand and supply side for developing countries (Bookman & Bookman, 2007). Whereas Heung, Kucukusta, and Song (2010), integrated demand and supply model was in context of Hong Kong. Caballero-Danell and Mugomba (2007) proposed a medical tourism model from marketing and distribution channel perspective, which include factors of branding, infrastructure, legal, market, product, operators, communication channels, social, and customer benefits. KO (2011) conceptualised medical tourism systems model of four components medical tourists, generating regions of medical tourists, destination regions, and medical tourism industries. Medhekar and Newby (2012) have proposed an Information Search Model of Medical Treatment Abroad, as potential medical tourists search for internal (personal experience) and external information (internet, print, media, family, friends, doctor, medical tours operator, health insurance provider) before they make the decision to travel abroad for treatment.

Al-Amin, Makarem, and Pradhan's (2011) conceptual framework included, surgical costs, JCI quality and surgeons experience that influence hospitals ability to attract foreign patients (hospitals exports performance), and healthcare internationalisation. Haq and Medhekar (2015) proposed a Culturally Sensitive Muslim Typology to market Indian medical tourism to Muslim patient in an Islamic way, in other words Halal branding of medical tourism, which can be adopted by Dubai. Khan et al. (2017) proposed a conceptual model for medical tourism push factors and risk faced by medical tourists in developed and developing regions.

Physical and Economic Analysis

The next strategic indicator applied for the Dubai Government's initiative to develop medical tourism is the physical and economic analysis. This applies the five strategic indicators required to study the role of governments in planning and supporting sustainable tourism identified by Nwosu and Onah (2016) and Birkic, Pilija, and Sebrek (2014). The five strategic indicators adopted to study the role of Dubai Government steering Dubai to be the global medical tourism hub have been recognised as: long term orientation based on supply capability and evaluation of alternatives; physical and economic analysis; stakeholders' participation; vision and values and implementation and control. These indicators can be studied and applied in case of Dubai with respect to the example of medical tourism from the top three global medical tourism destinations of Thailand, India, and Singapore (Colleen et al., 2019; Khan et al., 2017; Medhekar, 2013; Medhekar et al., 2019; Nutworadee, 2015; Wongkit and McKercher 2013). Further, Medhekar et al. (2019) qualitative interview with 24-inbound medical tourists to India generated the following themes and considered information search, cost home versus overseas, waiting time for surgery, medical travel-risk, patent safety, hospital employee's expertise, hospital quality accreditation facilities and services as factors influencing their decision to travel abroad for medical treatment/surgery.

Focussing on empirical studies related to Thailand, which is the top global medical tourism destination for the last two decades, Wongkit and McKercher (2013) proposed medical tourists typology for Thailand concludes that the decision-making process to travel is based on availability of medical facilities, procedure and medical professionals' expertise. Medical tourists are motivated to seek various types of surgeries and travel abroad to improve their health and wellbeing. For example from cosmetic and dental to enhance their appearance, reproductive to fulfill their desire to become parents to cure of complex diseases and health issues such as cancer, heart, orthopaedic, organ transplant and hip replacements. This is influences by type of treatment available, surgical procedures demanded by the patient, hospital and physician's reputation, accreditation quality and destination attractiveness (Bostan & Yalcin, 2016; Nutworadee, 2015).

Medical tourists to Thailand in particular are — medical focussed; seeking cosmetic surgery, and tourism focussed; engaging in traditional types, overall health check-up and dental-care (Kanittinsuttitong, 2015). Total volume and characteristics of patients travelling from the UK to Thailand in 2010, was studied by Noree et al. (2014). Data was collected from five major hospitals electronic records from Thailand. They concluded that 104,830 patients who travelled from different countries to Thailand for elective surgery, their main motivation was costs savings (less than 500US$) on elective surgery and 60% of these patients were UK nationals.

Supply Capability and Evaluation of Alternatives

Since medical tourism does not rely on natural resources and could be developed effectively by strong investment in technology and infrastructure (Zaidan, 2016; Sharpley, 2008), the government of Dubai can fulfil this requirement by attracting skilled migrant expertise in medical and tourism sectors of the economy. Overseas patients also prefer cultural familiarity with language and food, and therefore Dubai can attract many affluent medical travellers from the Islamic countries (Haq

& Medhekar, 2015; Stephenson, 2014). Government of UAE, Ministry of Health provided universal healthcare for all the citizens of Dubai and take responsibility for healthcare facilities accreditation, health regulation, and medical staffing (Inhorn, 2016).

There is public healthcare for emirates citizens and private sector health provision for expatriates and foreigners as medical tourists. According to CEO of Al Zahra Hospital, Mohaymen Abdelghany, Dubai, "Medical tourism is an important sector for us and it is set to grow considerably as Dubai positions itself as a regional and international centre" with the goal of increasing international medical tourists to 500,000 by 2020 (Oxford Business Group, 2017). Dubai is not only a popular regional tourism transit hub between Africa and Europe but also aims to become a Middle Eastern medical travel/ tourism hub due to its low cost, state-of-the-art medical technology, JCI accreditation, multi-lingual highly trained overseas-educated human resources and no surgery-waiting period.

Evaluation of Alternatives for Healthcare Dubai

Healthcare in Dubai is a combination of public and private system. Public sector provides comprehensive healthcare to all citizens. Private healthcare sector on the other hand caters to expatriates and medical tourist, in state-of-the-art medical facilities and medical technology and high quality of medical services with experienced surgeons. Dubai Healthcare city established in 2006 is the first free trade economic zone for wellness and medical centres followed by second being established under DHA. Government public health expenditure is growing to solve the serious lifestyle related health problems such as diabetes, heart problem and obesity. Investing in quality private healthcare for treating foreign patients is not possible without government support for promotion and investment in country infrastructure (Medhekar, 2014). The UAE government has developed the Dubai healthcare city in 2002 and is strategically promoting medical tourism to expatriate workers and cross border patients from the member countries of Gulf Cooperation Council (GCC).

Healthcare in UAE, Patient are looking for affordable coat, availability of treatment, less waiting time, privacy and confidentiality, pre and post-surgery care and over and above quality of medical procedures with positive healthcare outcomes where hospitals have JCI accreditation (JCI, 2019). In United Arad Emirates, JCI has accredited 210 private healthcare facilities/organisations, diagnostic clinics and hospitals in UAE, which is the highest in the world followed by 107 each in the kingdom of Saudi Arabia and China. This is followed by accreditation of hospitals and clinics in Brazil (63), Thailand (67), Turkey (43), and India (37). The JCI accreditation is renewed every three years or rejected if quality assurance standards are not maintained. This helps to ensure patient safety standards in context of hospital hygiene, medication and surgical errors and providing high quality of healthcare services.

Stakeholder Participation

To implement the vision of the rulers, Dubai government must establish public-private-partnerships with the key stakeholders servicing the health and tourism industry and provide business friendly environment to attract foreign direct investment, highly skilled expatriate workers, state-of-the-art tourism infrastructure, to diversify, modernise and stabilise the economy by supporting the development of health tourism. This can also save millions of dollars, as complex state-of-the-art medical facilities and expertise will be available in UAE, for its citizens health and wellbeing (Dominic, 2016; Medhekar & Haq, 2016; WHO, 2015).

Increasing medical and health insurance costs and long waiting-list in developed countries, due to which global medical tourism is now a billion-dollar industry. Since 2017 to 2022, inbound medical travel spending in UAE is expected to grow 9.6% with increased demand for complex lifesaving procedures and cosmetic surgeries. Etihad Airways is promoting medical travel to UAE by supporting foreign tourists in two steps. (i) Providing health evaluation service, where the medical tourists will be examined by Etihad airlines one of the 12 doctors on duty with Fit–to-Fly" status within one day. (ii) Pick up service from home or hotel to airport, boarding and accompanied to the destination by a qualified nurse in aviation and transport medicine, is the need of medical travellers to have a safe and hassle-free medical travel (Silva, 2019).

Lessons from Thailand, Singapore, and India

Dubai has many lessons to learn from Thailand, Singapore and the Indian government who has fully supported the development and promotion of their countries as medical tourism destinations. Globally, Singapore was ranked in second position after Thailand as a medical tourism destination in 2008. However, in 2009, India was placed second and Singapore in third position in terms of number of medical tourists, revenue and affordable surgery cost (IMT, 2009; Medhekar, 2014).

Currently large number of Middle Eastern and European tourist's travel to Thailand for medical treatment related to cosmetic, dental and reproductive treatment, along with tourism opportunities. The famous state-of-the-art private hospitals for example are Bumrungrad, Bangkok Hospital, Paolo Memorial Hospital, Phuket Plastic Surgery Clinic, and Bangkok Adventist Hospital. Development and growth of medical tourism has been a long-term government strategy in Thailand in cooperation with private hospitals to establish the country as the "health tourism hub of Asia", since the Asian financial crisis of 1997. It is in collaboration with the Thailand Ministries of Public Health and Commerce with the internationally accredited private hospitals such as Bumrungrad Hospital, which is the largest private hospital in terms of number of beds (Rerkrujipimol & Assenov, 2011). On one hand, Thailand attracted foreign medical tourists who were coming mainly for tourism attractions along with seeking traditional treatments like spa, herbal medicine, massage including cosmetic and gender change surgeries (Pocock & Phua, 2011).

The Government of Thailand has taken the following measures to develop and promote Thailand as a world class Medical Tourism Hub of Asia along with traditional therapies of Thai spa and massage (Tourism Authority of Thailand, 2002).

- The tourism industry in Thailand is very well established with many attractions.
- Country infrastructure is in place to accommodate medical tourists.
- Government has provided tax holidays to businesses involved in medical tourism industry.
- Encouraged land ownership rights for foreign investors to build hospitals.
- Hospitals in Thailand provide personal care to the patients- language interpreters and special international wings.
- Many Thailand hospitals are JCI accredited and adhere to ISO standards.
- Doctors and surgeons are well trained and qualified from the US and UK.
- Organising medical trade fairs, seminars and exhibitions overseas by the private hospitals in collaboration with the Ministry of Public Health, Tourism Authority, Foreign Affairs and Department of Export Promotion.
- Law and regulation regarding ethical adverting must be followed by TV-media, internet and print to promote medical tourism to foreigners.

Singapore on the other hand is a top destination for tourism, shopping, conferences, financial and business capital of South-East Asia. It is now a third most popular health tourism destination which includes wellness tourism and medical tourism. Singapore is Asia's medical tourism hub and specialises in high-end complex surgeries with all its public and private 21 hospitals are JCI accredited (Asia's Medical Tourism, 2012; Pocock & Phua, 2011; Woodman, 2007). The Government of Singapore from the beginning has adopted an innovative product development and diversified tourism strategy of Singapore Brand, to attract overseas tourists from all over the world.

The Singapore government works in partnership with Ministry of Health and Tourism, the Economic Development Board, International Enterprise Singapore, and Singapore Tourism Board to provide wellness and medical tourism packages which are of affordable quality and at state-of-the-art JCI accredited medical hospitals (Asia's Medical Tourism, 2012; Woodman, 2007). Singapore's costs may be higher than India and Thailand, however, it attracts affluent patients from Asia and Europe for complex surgeries. The famous hospitals are Alexandra Hospital, National University Hospital, Changi General Hospital and Singapore National Cancer Centre, Raffles Hospital, and Thompson Medical Centre.

The Singapore Government has taken the following measures to develop and promote Singapore brand of medical tourism, which is focussing on high-end of surgeries and medical tourism experience.

- Singapore tourism industry is dynamic, innovative and well established.
- Government is directly involved in marketing and promoting Singapore medical tourism hospitals and has sponsored patient beyond borders Singapore edition.
- All 21 hospitals are having JCI accredited quality gold seal of approval.
- It specializes in high-tech complex surgeries such as cancer, heart, cosmetic and became famous for successful surgery separating conjoined twins.
- It has also well-established pharmaceutical, medical technology and biomedical-research laboratories.
- Highly qualified and overseas educated medical and non-medical professionals.
- Singapore government provides tax breaks for investment in health and medical related infrastructure facilities, medical equipment and technology.

In case of India, like Thailand it is not only a popular tourism destination but also medical travel destination along with wellness tourism which includes yoga, Ayurveda and herbal therapies. The development, growth and promotion of medical tourism as a niche tourism segment was recognised by the Indian government since the beginning of this century (Brotman, 2010; Chinai & Goswami, 2007; IMT, 2009; Medhekar, 2013). Medical tourism is basically provision of affordable private care to patients who are uninsured or underinsured, long waiting list for surgery, and if treatment is not available in their country due to regulation (Bookman & Bookman, 2007; Burns, 2015; Kasper & Reddy, 2017; Pande, 2010; Reddy & Qadeer, 2010; Sultana, Haque, Momen, & Yasmin, 2017; Turner, 2007). Popular corporate private hospitals such as Apollo Group of Hospitals, Wockhardt, Jahangir, Max Healthcare India, Fortis Group of Hospitals, Asian Heart, and Fortis-Escorts Heart Institute, provide state-of the art healthcare facilities and JCI accredited quality of medical facilities and surgeons expertise.

In 2003, budget speech, and the in the 10th five-year plan (2002-2007), Indian government called for India to be a "Global Health Destination" (Government of India, 2008; Kasper & Reddy, 2017; Medhekar, 2014). Government has taken the following measures to develop and promote wellness and medical tourism to India.'

- Introduction of medical-visa, medical escort-visa and medical-visa on arrival.
- Medical tourism is considered as an export of healthcare services which is eligible for all export related fiscal incentives, extended to other export income.
- Lowering import duties on life saving medical dices and medicines.
- 100% incentives for foreign direct investment in medical tourism related investments in medical facilities, infrastructure, research and development.
- Nearly 40% depreciation rate on medical equipment and machinery.
- Encouraging JCI accredited hospitals and medical facilities.
- Having medical tourism trade fairs, exhibitions, and conferences in overseas locations to promote medical travel to India. For example, Global health destination campaign in 2002 and 2008.
- Central government encouraging different states to promote their medical tourism super speciality.

OPPORTUNITIES AND CHALLENGES

Opportunities

Developing Dubai as a healthcare destination, like Thailand, Singapore and India, with full support from the government can provide numerous opportunities for the health, tourism, hospitality, pharmaceutical, research and development, trade, and other allied healthcare areas, contributing to the economic development of the country. A country cannot just depend on export of oil and gas for its development. It must diversify the economy in service sectors such as international finance, banking, construction, education, pharmaceuticals and health, which is sustainable and attract educated and highly skilled local and migrant workers to drive the economy.

In 2012, nearly 107,000 foreign medical tourists travelled to UAE for medical treatment, generating foreign exchange revenue of 625 million Dirhams (Kannan, 2014). In 2016, nearly 326,000 foreign patients visited Dubai for medical treatment due to affordable quality, cultural preference and convenience to travel cross border (Dominic, 2016; Stephenson, 2014). The CEO of The Medical Tourism Association mentioned that "The experience isn't just in the hospital… attractions in Dubai/Abu Dhabi provide a perfect environment because when medical tourists come to a country, they bring their spouse or family members and can spend several weeks in the area." Further, like the India's first halal hospital certified by Saudi Arabia and Malaysian halal authorities in Hyderabad, catering to patients from Islamic background and countries (Haq & Medhekar, 2015). Dubai can also develop certified halal medical hospital catering for the patients sensitive to their religious/cultural practices along with patients/medical tourists belonging to other cultural orientation to attract Islamic tourists and compete with India, Indonesia and Malaysia.

Challenges

1. *Skilled Human Resource:* developing a healthcare destination of the Middle East requires highly skilled human resources from medical and non-medical background to support health tourism industry. Such as medical professionals-physicians, surgeons nurses, allied healthcare, pharmaceuticals, medical technology, hospitality and hotel management staff, interpreters with multiple language skills, architects and civil engineers.
2. *Competition from JCI accredited medical hospitals from other Arab and Middle Eastern countries:* UAE has to ensure high quality of healthcare service delivery, state-of-the-art medical facilities and pre and post-surgery care to retain and attract medical tourists from the Middle Eastern countries and beyond. Dubai-UAE with (195) medical hospitals and clinics accredited by JCI in the Middle East, faces competition based on JCI accredited hospitals which are preferred by foreigners mainly from Saudi Arabia (107), Israel (32), Qatar (15), Egypt (10), Jordon (9), Oman (6) and Lebanon (5) (JCI, 2019).
3. *Travel documentation and medical-Visa processing:* Government needs to introduce like India, medical visa and medical escort visa for easy processing and travel arrangements to save time for the potential patients who need urgent treatment and surgery.
4. *All-inclusive excellent healthcare for local citizens:* With the development of health tourism, it is essential that same level of medical facilities at an affordable cost is made available for all the local citizens.
5. *Reduce outbound medical travel from UAE:* The challenge is how to build trust amongst the wealthy UAE citizens and the government officials that they can trust their countries healthcare system for medical treatment and surgery. This will reduce the government costs of outbound medical travel, as the wealthy UAE citizens will use JCI accredited hospitals in Dubai.
6. *Challenge of maintaining and enhancing health services quality*: It is a challenge to enhance the quality of healthcare services, patient safety, and zero tolerance for medication and clinical errors for maintaining JCI accreditation, which is renewed every two years and discontinued if international healthcare quality standard are not met.

To meet the opportunities and overcome the challenges in sustainable development of Dubai as a healthcare destination of the Middle East it is necessary to have strategic public-private partnerships between the key stakeholders. Dubai Healthcare

Experience Program has launched a comprehensive package of specialist medicals services for foreign patients with 26 six public and private hospitals, in partnership with Department of Tourism, Commerce and Marketing (DTCM), Directorate of Residency and Foreigners Affairs, and private sector medical tourism related businesses along with Patient Protection Plan and Patient Bill of Rights (Medhekar & Haq, 2016). The strategic public-private partnerships with various stakeholders will be the key to success towards developing and promoting Dubai as a global medical tourism hub.

For example, Zulekha Healthcare Group aims to lead the UAE's healthcare digital transformation and support the UAE Vision 2021 by providing state-of-the-art world-class healthcare technology and lead in artificial intelligence use of stemcell therapies in the medical tourism to provide high quality of healthcare services to domestic and international patients. Zulekha Hospital has collaborated with a health-tech company Okadoc, facilitating real-time doctors' appointments rescheduling or cancelation of appointments anytime from anywhere to enhance patient experiences. This will assist patients to manage their bookings online, find doctors by location, expertise, availability and spoken language view detailed doctor's profile, and receive appointment reminders, without any human intervention (Trade Arabia Business News, 2019).

RECOMMENDATIONS AND POLICY IMPLICTIONS

Government of Dubai has taken various initiatives to reach the goal of being a healthcare destination, in terms of research and development in healthcare, quality accreditation, infrastructure investments in health and tourism facilities, continuous collaboration with public and private healthcare providers and global health tourism marketing campaigns and trade fairs. Due to UAE governments positive vision and polices, it is considered the best and safe country for tourism amongst the middle eastern countries. Dubai has an attractive destination image, positive economic environment and low level of corruption, which makes it an attractive destination for potential medical tourists when making a choice to travel abroad for wellness or medical tourism. To be competitive and provide first world quality in healthcare. Dubai still must have affordable costs, provide positive patient experience and be culturally sensitive not just to patients from middle eastern countries with Arabic culture, but also to patients or medical tourists from other cultures.

Dubai Health Authority along with Emirates Holidays of Emirates airlines have formed partnerships to provide tailor made wellness and medical tourism packages targeting tourists from the Middle East and Saudi Arabia. These packages include return flights, three to four day stay in a hotel for health and wellness facilities along with best of Dubai sightseeing, recreation and shopping arrangements. These packages also include accommodation arrangements with Palm Dubai retreat, Medina Jumeirah, Raaya Wellness Retreat, to provide health and wellness programs. It-DHA has also entered into partnerships with US medical hospitals to bring in advanced medical technologies, and high standards in medical practice. The top medical school such as John Hopkins University operates 466- bed Al-Taiwan hospital. Further, Cleveland clinic in partnership with Mubadala Healthcare jointly operates a 360-bed hospital. Furthermore, partnerships are also formed with US and UK pharmaceuticals and medical equipment sector to bring in the best of medical technology and pharmacy to UAE, which is expected to grow to 25 billion Dirhams by 2025.

Based on the above discuss it is suggested that healthcare providers should establish and maintain strategic partnerships with the following stakeholders for developing and promoting Dubai as a 'Medical Tourism Hub of the Middle East'.

1. Healthcare industry – including local public and private hospitals and international healthcare service providers in Dubai.
2. Tourism Industry – The tourism and hospitality sectors must work in collaboration with the airlines and the hospitals to transport and provide accommodation to the foreign patients as medical tourists. They also have to provide wheel chair access, interpreting services, travel desk, including twenty four seven doctors and nurses on board, pharmacy and ambulance service in case of an emergency. Medical Hotels need to cater to the dietary requirements of the patients in case of heart and diabetes related issues.
3. Airlines – the top local airlines such as Emirates and Etihad are already very supportive and could be used more tactically to enhance the medical tourism growth.
4. Medical Market – All local and global medicine, pharmaceutical and medical device, lifesaving medicine, blood and organ supply, manufacturers and sellers could join the medical tourism drive by providing exclusive services for patients traveling to Dubai for medical treatment/surgery.
5. Real Estate and Builders – The real estate developers could play a significant role in building places, hotels and motels with special facilities for medical tourists and their family members.
6. Technology and Digitisation – As discussed, the trend towards use of technology in medical services long with digitization of the distribution services is required. The vision of e-governance also maps with the digitalization of medical tourism and e-providers can play a critical part in this marriage of success.

CONCLUSION

Inbound medical tourism to Dubai is on the rise and expected to reach 500,000 by 2021, as reported by the Dubai Health Authority. It is taking all the steps to develop wellness, medical and cosmetic treatment and promote Dubai as the preferred healthcare destination of the Middle East, offering world medical treatment supported by state-of-the-art medical technologies, no waiting lists, and post-surgery care. All these medical tourism services have JCI accreditation to ensure international healthcare quality of medical facilities, diagnostic clinics, medical laboratories, surgeries, medical professionals' qualifications and patient safety.

This paper presented an analysis of the five strategic indicators that highlight the role of Dubai Government to be a medical tourism hub. The analysis of these indicators presents the long-term orientation based on supply capability, reflecting upon the diversification of UAE economy and establishing Dubai as the global medical tourism hub; relying upon all types of tourists visiting for medical treatments. The government has to focus its vision and values for a better society and sustainable economy by attracting and retaining medical tourists. All relevant alternatives linked with opportunities and challenges were evaluated in this paper with a strategic concentration on probing the physical and economic capacity. The outstanding solution was the stakeholders' participation that is suggested to be crafted as public private partnerships with healthcare, real estate, airlines, medicine and digitalization.

An empirical study based on findings of the five strategic indicators is the obvious future study. A qualitative in-depth interview conducted with suppliers, medical tourism facilitators/operators and providers of the strategic partners will open a way towards the successful process of public private partnerships. A quantitative survey with actual Dubai-inbound foreign medical tourists could be undertaken to know their medical tourism experience in Dubai-UAE and identify the factors that motivated them to travel to Dubai for medical treatment/tourism. Further, the information gathered from medical tourism healthcare providers and the actual medical tourists can be utilized to improve the setting and communication of products and services associated with the medical tourism in Dubai.

REFERENCES

Adam, K., Snyder, J., Crooks, V. A., & Johnston, R. (2015). Tourism discourse and medical tourists' motivations to travel. *Tourism Review*, *70*(2), 85–96. doi:10.1108/TR-04-2014-0015

Al-Amin, M., Makarem, S. C., & Pradhan, R. (2011). Hospital ability to attract international patients: A conceptual framework. *International Journal of Pharmaceutical and Healthcare Marketing*, *5*(3), 205–221. doi:10.1108/17506121111172211

Al-Harbi, M. H. (2018). *How UAE became a medical tourism hub*. Retrieved from https://gulfnews.com/opinion/op-eds/how-uae-became-a-medical-tourism-hub-1.2239792

Alhosani, N., & Zaidan, E. (2014). Shopping Tourism and Destination Development: Dubai as a Case Study. *Arab World Geographer*, *17*(1), 66–81.

Asia's Medical Tourism. (2012). *Truly A Leading Medical Tourism Hub*. Retrieved from asiasmedicaltourism.com/medical-tourism/medical-tourism-singapore

Bagaeen, S. (2007). Brand Dubai: The Instant city; or the instantly recognizable city. *International Planning Studies*, *1*(2), 173–197. doi:10.1080/13563470701486372

Balakrishnan, M. S. (2008). Dubai- A star in the East. *Journal of Place Management and Development*, *1*(1), 62–91.

Ballentyne, B. (2015). Huge opportunity for health tourism. *Middle East Economic Digest*, *59*(6), 1–3.

Birkic, D., Pilija, I. C., & Sebrek, J. K. (2014). T*he role of local government in planning of sustainable tourism of coastal destination.* Faculty of Tourism and Hospitality Management in Opatija. Biennial International Congress. Retrieved from https://search.proquest.com/docview/1658462265?accountid=33975

Bookman, M. Z., & Bookman, K. R. (2007). *Medical tourism in developing countries*. New York: Palgrave MacMillan. doi:10.1057/9780230605657

Bostan, S., & Yalcin, B. (2016). Factors, affecting the medical destination selection of health tourists. *The Journal of International Social Research*, *9*(43), 1729–1735. doi:10.17719/jisr.20164317741

Brotman, B. A. (2010). Medical Tourism Private Hospitals: Focus India. *Journal of Health Care Finance*, *37*(1), 45–50. PMID:20973373

Burkett, L. (2007). Medical Tourism: Concerns, benefits and the American perspective. *The Journal of Legal Medicine*, *28*, 223-245.

Burns, R. L. (2015). Medical tourism opportunities and challenges: Illustration from US-India trade. *International Journal of Healthcare Management*, *8*(1), 15–26. doi:10.1179/2047971914Y.0000000091

Caballero-Danell, S., & Mugomba, C. (2007). *Medical tourism and its entrepreneurial opportunities: A conceptual framework for entry into the industry (Unpublished master's thesis)*. University of Gothenburg. Retrieved from http://gupea.ub.gu.se/dspace/handle/ 2077/4671

Carrera, P. M., & Bridges, J. P. (2006). Globalisation and healthcare: Understanding health and medical tourism, Expert Review of Pharmacoeconomics & Outcomes Research. *Future Drugs*, *7*(1), 447–445.

Chinai, R., & Goswami, R. (2007). Medical visas mark growth of Indian medical tourism. *Bulletin of the World Health Organization*, *85*(3), 164–165. doi:10.2471/BLT.07.010307 PMID:17486202

Chuang, T. C., Liu, J. S., Lu, L. Y., & Lee, Y. (2014). The main paths of medical tourism, from transplantation to beautification. *Tourism Management*, *45*(1), 49–58. doi:10.1016/j.tourman.2014.03.016

Collins, A., Medhekar, A., Wong, H. Y., & Cobanoglu, C. (2019). Factors influencing outbound medical travel from the USA. *Tourism Review*, *74*(3), 463–479. doi:10.1108/TR-06-2018-0083

Connell, J. (2013). Contemporary medical tourism: Conceptualisation, culture and commodification. *Tourism Management*, *34*, 1–13. doi:10.1016/j.tourman.2012.05.009

Connell, J. (2015). From medical tourism to transnational health care? An epilogue for the future. *Social Science & Medicine*, *124*, 398–401. doi:10.1016/j.socscimed.2014.11.015 PMID:25467883

Cotton, M., Henry, A., & Hasek, L. (2014). Value innovation: An important aspect of global surgical care. *Globalization and Health*, *10*(1), 1–5. doi:10.1186/1744-8603-10-1 PMID:24393237

Dasgupta, S., & Dasgupta, D. (2014). *Globalisation and transnational surrogacy in India: Outsourcing life*. Plymouth, UK: Lexington Books.

Deloitte. (2008). *Medical Tourism: Consumers in Search of Value*. Deloitte Centre for Health Solutions.

Dominic, D. (2016). Medical tourism holds promising potential for UAE. *Middle East Economic Digest*, *60*(2), 1–5.

Dubai Health Authority. (2018). Retrieved from https://www.dxh.ae/about-us/about-dxh/

Finch, S. (2014). Thailand top destination for medical tourists. *Canadian Medical Association Journal, 186*(1), E1–E2. doi:10.1503/cmaj.109-4655 PMID:24246587

Ghose, K. (2010). Hospitality in and out of the hospitals. Creating and maintaining brand equity for medical tourism destination brands. *Romanian Journal of Marketing, 5*(1), 114–131.

Government of India (GOI). (2003). *Health Sector in India, Government of India, 2003 Budget Papers*. New Delhi: GOI.

Haq, F., & Medhekar, A. (2015). Halal Branding of Medical Tourism: case of Indian hospitals. In H. El-Gohary & R. Eid (Eds.), *Emerging Research in Islamic Marketing and Tourism in the Global Economy* (pp. 160–189). IGI Global.

Henderson, J. C. (2007). Destination Development. *Journal of Travel & Tourism Marketing, 20*(3-4), 33–45. doi:10.1300/J073v20n03_03

Henderson, J. C. (2014). Global Gulf Cities and Tourism: A Review of Abu Dhabi, Doha and Dubai. *Tourism Recreation Research, 39*(1), 107–114. doi:10.1080/02508281.2014.11081329

Heung, V., Kucukusta, D., & Song, H. (2010). A Conceptual Model of Medical Tourism: Implications for Future Research. *Journal of Travel & Tourism Marketing, 27*(3), 236–251. doi:10.1080/10548401003744677

Horowitz, M. D., & Rosensweig, J. A. (2007). Medical Tourism-Health Care in the Global Economy. *Physician Executive, 33*(6), 24–31. PMID:18092615

Hotelier Middle East. (2018). *Dubai on track to attract medical tourists*. Retrieved from http://www.hoteliermiddleeast.com/32871-dubai-on-track-to-attract-500000-medical-tourists-by-2020/

IMTJ. (2017). Dubai Health Authority Partners to Drive Medical Tourism. *International Medical Travel Journal*. Retrieved from https://www.imtj.com/news/dubai-health-authority-partners-drive-medical-tourism/

Indian Medical Tourism (IMT). (2009). *India Ranks 2nd in Med-Tourism*. Available: www.medicaltourism.org/consortium.jsp?sect=con

Inhorn, M. C. (2016). Cosmopolitan conceptions in global Dubai? The Emiratization of IVF and its Consequences. *Reproductive Biomedicine Society, 2*, 24–31. doi:10.1016/j.rbms.2016.04.004 PMID:29892713

Inhorn, M. C., Shrivastav, P., & Patrizio, P. (2012). Assisted reproductive technologies and fertility "tourism": Examples from global Dubai and the Ivy League. *Medical Anthropology*, *31*(3), 249–265. doi:10.1080/01459740.2011.596495 PMID:22540317

JCI. (2019). *Joint Commission International Accreditation Standards for Hospitals*. Retrieved from https://www.jointcommissioninternational.org/about-jci/jci-accredited-organizations/?c=United%20Arab%20Emirates

Kanittinsuttitong, N. (2015). Motivation and Decision on Medical Tourism Service in Thailand. *ASEAN Journal of Management & Innovation*, *2*(2), 24–36.

KannanP. (2014). Retrieved from http://www.thenational.ae/uae/tourism/dubai-reveals-master-plan-for-500-000-medical-tourists-a-year

Kasper, H., & Reddy, S. (2017). Spaces of connectivity: The formation of medical travel destination in Delhi national capital region (India). *Asia Pacific Viewpoint*, *58*(2), 228–241. doi:10.1111/apv.12159

Khan, M. J., Chelliah, S., Haron, M. S., & Ahmed, S. (2017). Push factors, risks, and types of visit intentions of international medical travellers-A conceptual model. *International Journal of Healthcare Management*, *10*(2), 115–121. doi:10.1080/20479700.2017.1304345

Khan, S., & Alam, S. (2014). Kingdom of Saudi Arabia: A potential destination for medical tourism. *Journal of Taibah University Medical Sciences*, *9*(4), 257–262. doi:10.1016/j.jtumed.2014.01.007

KO, T.G. (2011). Medical Tourism System Model. *International Journal of Tourism Sciences*, *11*(1), 18–51.

Lunt, N., & Carrera, P. (2010). Medical tourism: Assessing the evidence on treatment abroad. *Maturitas*, *66*(1), 27–32. doi:10.1016/j.maturitas.2010.01.017 PMID:20185254

Lunt, N., Hardey, M., & Mannion, R. (2010). Nip, Tuck and Click: Medical Tourism and the Emergence of Web-Based Health Information. *The Open Medical Informatics Journal*, *4*(4), 1–11. doi:10.2174/1874431101004010001 PMID:20517465

Lunt, N., Horsfall, D., & Hanefeld, J. (2016). Medical tourism: A snapshot of evidence on treatment abroad. *Maturitas*, *88*, 37–44. doi:10.1016/j.maturitas.2016.03.001 PMID:27105695

Lunt, N., & Mannion, R. (2014). Patient mobility in the global marketplace: A multidisciplinary perspective. *International Journal of Health Policy and Management*, *2*(4), 155–157. doi:10.15171/ijhpm.2014.47 PMID:24847479

Majeed, S., & Lu, C. (2017). *Changing Preferences, Moving Places and Third-Party Administrators: A Scoping Review of Medical Tourism Trends (1990-2016).* Almatourism. doi:10.6092/issn.2036-5195/6675

Manaf, N. H. A., Hussain, H., Kassim, P. N. J., Alavi, R., & Dahari, Z. (2015). Medical tourism service quality: Finally, some empirical findings. *Total Quality Management & Business Excellence*, *26*(9/10), 1017–1028. doi:10.1080/14783363.2015.1068597

Mansfeld, Y., & Winckler, O. (2007). The tourism industry as an alternative for the GCC oil-based rentier economies. *Tourism Economics*, *13*(3), 333–360. doi:10.5367/000000007781497728

Medhekar, A. (2013). Indian Government Policy to Support Trade in Medical Tourism Services. In *Proceedings of the 7th International Conference on Healthcare Systems and Global Business Issues*, (pp. 205-218). Jaipur, India: JNU Press.

Medhekar, A. (2014). Government Policy Initiatives for Developing Sustainable Medical Tourism Industry. *GSTF- Journal on Business Review*, *3*(3), 95-105.

Medhekar, A., & Ali, M. M. (2012). A Cross-Border Trade in Healthcare services: Bangladesh to India. *The Business and Management Review*, *2*(1), 1–13.

Medhekar, A., & Haq, F. (2016). Medical Tourism Development in Dubai: Managing Challenges and Opportunities. *Global Journal of Business and Social Science Review*, *4*(4), 20–28.

Medhekar, A., & Newby, L. (2012). Information Search for Medical Treatment Abroad. *Journal of Applied Global Research*, *5*(3), 53–72.

Medhekar, A., Wong, H. Y., & Hall, J. E. (2019). Factors influencing inbound medical travel to India. *Journal of Health Organization and Management*, *33*(2), 155–172. doi:10.1108/JHOM-08-2018-0234 PMID:30950309

Medical Tourism Index (MTI). (2019). *Medical Tourism: Dubai Global Ranking*. Retrieved from https://www.medicaltourismindex.com/destination/dubai/

Miller, E., & West, D. (2008). Characteristics associated with use of public and private web sites as sources of health care information. *Medical Care*, *45*(3), 245–251. doi:10.1097/01.mlr.0000244509.60556.49 PMID:17304082

Noree, T., Hanefelf, J., & Smith, R. (2014). UK medical tourists in Thailand: They are not who you think they are. *Globalization and Health*, *10*(29), 1–7. PMID:24885204

Nutworadee, K. (2015). Motivation and Decision on Medical Tourism Service in Thailand. *ASEAN Journal of Management & Innovation*, *2*(2), 24–36.

Nwosu, B., & Onah, G. (2016). The role of government in driving human capital development in the tourism industry in Nigeria. *Worldwide Hospitality and Tourism Themes*, *8*(2), 221–234. doi:10.1108/WHATT-11-2015-0047

Omar, F., Hassan, N., Hussain, H., Mana, S., & Awad, O. (2015). Travel Health, Gaps in Knowledge, Attitudes, and Practices among Dubai Travellers, Dubai, UAE. *International Journal of Preventive Medicine Research*, *1*(3), 126–131.

Oxford Business Group. (2017). *Medical Tourism Grows in Dubai*. Retrieved from https://oxfordbusinessgroup.com/analysis/healthy-returns-medical-tourism-segment-

Pande, A. (2010). Commercial Surrogacy in India: Manufacturing the perfect mother worker. *Signs (Chicago, Ill.)*, *35*(4), 969–992. doi:10.1086/651043

Pocock, S. N., & Phua, H. K. (2011). Medical tourism and policy implications for health systems: A conceptual framework from a comparative study of Thailand, Singapore and Malaysia. *Globalization and Health*, *7*(1), 12. doi:10.1186/1744-8603-7-12 PMID:21539751

Reddy, S., & Qadeer, I. (2010). Medical Tourism in India: Progress or Predicament? *Economic and Political Weekly*, *XLV*(20), 69–75.

Rerkrujipimol, J., & Assenov, I. (2011). Marketing Strategies for Promoting Medical Tourism in Thailand. *Journal ofTourism. Hospitality & Culinary Arts*, *3*(2), 95–105.

RNCOS. (2010). *Tourism Industry: Booming Medical Tourism in India, Industry Research Solutions*. New Delhi: RNCOS E-Services Pvt Ltd.

Runnels, V., & Turner, L. (2011). Bioethics and transnational medical travel: India, 'medical tourism', and the globalisation of healthcare. *Indian Journal of Medical Ethics*, *8*(1), 42–44. PMID:22106599

Sag, I., & Zengul, F.D. (2018). Why do medical tourists choose Turkey as a medical tourism destination? *Journal of Hospitality and Tourism Insight*. doi:10.1108/JHTI-05-2018-0031

Sandberg, D. S. (2017). Medical tourism: An emerging global healthcare industry. *International Journal of Healthcare Management*, *10*(4), 281–288. doi:10.1080/20479700.2017.1296213

Sharpley, R. (2008). Planning for Tourism: The Case of Dubai. *Tourism and Hospitality Planning & Development*, *5*(1), 13–30. doi:10.1080/14790530801936429

Silva, V. (2019). *Up and About: Etihad Offers Services to Passengers with Pre-Existing Medical Conditions*. Retrieved from https://apex.aero/2019/01/16/caring-passengers-preexisting-conditions

Smith, R., Álvarez, M. M., & Chanda, R. (2011). Medical tourism: A review of the literature and analysis of a role for bi-lateral trade. *Health Policy (Amsterdam)*, *103*(2-3), 276–282. doi:10.1016/j.healthpol.2011.06.009 PMID:21767892

Stephenson, M. L. (2014). Deciphering 'Islamic hospitality': Developments, Challenges and Opportunities. *Tourism Management*, *40*, 155–164. doi:10.1016/j.tourman.2013.05.002

Stephenson, M. L. (2014). Tourism, development and 'destination Dubai: Cultural dilemmas and future challenges. *Current Issues in Tourism*, *17*(8), 723–738. doi:10.1080/13683500.2012.754411

Sultana, S., Haque, A., Momen, A., & Yasmin, F. (2014). Factors affecting the attractiveness of medical tourism destination: An Empirical Study on India- Review Article. *Iranian Journal of Public Health*, *43*(7), 867–876. PMID:25909055

The United Arab Emirates Healthcare Sector. (2014). Retrieved from http://usuaebusiness.org/content/up-loads/2014/06/HealthcareReport.pdf

Tourism Authority of Thailand. (2002). *Health Tourism – The Rising Star: Strategies for Success, Thailand as a Center of Excellent Health of Asia*. Available at: http://www.tatnews.org/common/print.asp?id=1983

Trade Arabia Business News. (2019). *Zulekha opens extended facility in Dubai*. Retrieved from http://www.tradearabia.com/news/HEAL_350315.html

Turner, L. (2007). From Durham to Delhi: 'medical tourism' and the global economy. In J. Cohen-Kohler & M. Seaton (Eds.), *Comparative program on health and society* (pp. 109–131). Toronto: University of Toronto.

Whittaker, A., & Chee, H. L. (2016). 'Flexible bio-citizenship' and international medical travel: Transnational mobilities for care in Asia. *International Sociology*, *31*(3), 286–304. doi:10.1177/0268580916629623

Wongkit, M., & McKercher, B. (2013). Towards a typology of medical tourists: A case study of Thailand. *Tourism Management*, *38*, 4–12. doi:10.1016/j.tourman.2013.02.003

Woodman, J. (2007). *Singapore: Patients Beyond Borders: Singapore Edition*. Singapore: Healthy Travel Media.

World Health Organisation (WHO). (2015). *UAE Health Strategy*. Retrieved from http://www.who.int/countryfocus/cooperation_strategy/_en.pdf

Zaidan, E. A. (2016). Tourism shopping and new urban entertainment: A case study of Dubai. *Journal of Vacation Marketing*, *22*(1), 29–41. doi:10.1177/1356766715589426

ADDITIONAL READING

Cohen, G. (2017). Medical tourism, medical migration, & global justice: Implications for biosecurity in globalised world. *Medical Law Review*, *25*(2), 200–222. doi:10.1093/medlaw/fwx013 PMID:28402562

Jackson, E., Millbank, J., Karpin, I., & Stuhmcke, A. (2017). Learning from cross-border reproduction. *Medical Law Review*, *25*(1), 23–46. PMID:28073821

Junio, M. M. V., Kim, J. H., & Lee, T. J. (2017). Competitiveness attributes of a medical tourism destination: The case of South Korea with importance-performance analysis. *Journal of Travel & Tourism Marketing*, *34*(4), 444–460. doi:10.1080/10548408.2016.1182454

Kasper, H., & Reddy, S. (2017). Spaces of connectivity: The formation of medical travel destination in Delhi national capital region (India). *Asia Pacific Viewpoint*, *58*(2), 228–241. doi:10.1111/apv.12159

Turner, L. (2011). Quality in health care and globalisation of health services: Accreditation and regulatory oversight of medical tourism companies. *Journal of Quality in Health Care*, *23*(1), 1–7. doi:10.1093/intqhc/mzq078 PMID:21148210

KEY TERMS AND DEFINITIONS

Halal Tourism: Due to cultural sensitivities, people from Islamic background prefer to visit a country for tourism or medical purposes that is familiar and complies with their religious beliefs, customs and tradition, which applies to food, medication, and spiritual rituals.

Medical Tourism: Medical tourism is a phenomenon, where people travel abroad for medical treatment and surgery to improve their health and quality of life.

Public-Private Partnerships: The partnership between private organizations and various governmental departments to achieve a common goal.

Chapter 5
Travel Motivations of Cancer Patients

Sharon Mendoza Dreisbach
https://orcid.org/0000-0002-1141-4423
Skyline University College, UAE

Mohit Vij
https://orcid.org/0000-0002-2351-7040
Skyline University College, UAE

Jeconiah Louis Dreisbach
https://orcid.org/0000-0002-3761-9267
Asian Institute of Management, Philippines

ABSTRACT

Affordable travel costs and technological advances in medical procedures have enabled an increased number of patients visiting medical tourist destinations. Distances are not a barrier to treatment anymore. Moreover, medical studies also mention that travelling in itself can be part of the patient's treatment affecting positively on their condition. This study aims at examining the travel motivations and factors of female breast cancer patients and survivors by applying Iso-Ahola's motivation theory. The theory sorted travel motivations in four categories: personal escaping, interpersonal escaping, personal seeking, and interpersonal seeking. Descriptive analysis of the data obtained from the survey showed that patients travel to create share experiences their families, friends, and new people. Travelling also gives them a positive attitude as makes them feel good about themselves and gives them a sense of hope. Travelling is not about avoiding social conflict within their families or communities nor treating themselves alone to not be a burden to their families.

DOI: 10.4018/978-1-5225-9787-2.ch005

INTRODUCTION

Recent past has witnessed an increase in breast cancer cases as well as community initiatives towards generating an awareness resulting in support through various types of funding for the breast cancer patients. There will be an increase in the medical tourism in Asia led by growth of cancer cases (Global Cancer Diagnostics Market, 2018-2027), Affordable air travel and fast-developing technology assisting tourists with illnesses makes it relatively easier for them, their guardians, and their healthcare providers to travel even to countries far from their origin to seek further medical treatment. Increased international travel is seen in cancer patients undergoing therapy and soon after therapy has been done (Mikati, Taur, Seo, & Shah, 2013). Hunter-Jones (2006) found that taking a holiday off is a way to transcend over and recover from cancer treatment. Travel is also considered by post-cancer patients as a therapeutic opportunity to escape from the stress that they experienced while undergoing cancer treatment. Travel's intrinsic benefit in speeding up the rehabilitating process decreased treatment time for the serious illnesses of patients. Georgetown University Hospital cancer researchers, studied the travel patterns of patients who underwent major cancer surgeries on their lungs, esophagus, liver, pancreas, and gastric and colorectal sections. It was found that the senior citizens (patients) travel the farthest compared to the patients that are in the age bracket of 18-50 years (Smith et al., 2015). For purposes of clinical trials and seeking for the best treatment their illness, cancer patients from the United Kingdom were found to be willing to travel long distances to contribute to research development in cancer studies (Moorcraft et al., 2016). Patients would go as far as to donating tissue samples for researching biopsies. On the other hand, British patients in the outlying islands of the country are having a hard time travelling and seeking immediate treatment due to the advanced stages of their cancer diagnosis (Turner et al., 2017). In Asia, however, patients are less likely to participate in clinical trials for breast cancer studies. Hong Kong Chinese breast cancer survivors' psychological situation affected their willingness to take part in such studies, pointing out that it is "somewhat distressing", and some have been diagnosed with clinical depression and anxiety (Lee, 2016). Singaporean researchers meanwhile studied the barriers of clinical trial participation among Chinese, Malay, and Indian patients of varying breast cancer stages (Lee, Ow, Lie, & Dent, 2016). Women willing to join the clinical trials expressed interest in knowing the best therapy for their illness, having a cost-effective profile, and they also have trust in the doctors and local healthcare system. Those who are unwilling expressed barriers such as having previous bad experiences with doctors, trials, and drugs and having conservative attitude towards risk-taking. Malay patients expressed that the possibility 'fatality' of the procedure acted as a barrier in taking part in the clinical trials.

Kotton (2013) emphasized that clinicians and travel medicine specialists should educate their patients about the importance of prevention through pre-travel medical care and providing a detailed travel history to know what possible illness are going to be prevented. There are even manuals/guides available for medical professionals to minimize the potential risks and dangers that the patient may face during the travels (Perdue & Noble, 2007). Eventually, a number of initiatives have been taken by airlines and hospitality sector towards sponsoring travel and stay for breast cancer patients as part of their community services. Qatar Airways, American Airlines, Delta Airlines and Etihad Airways are among the airlines who are quite active in this regard. A number of hotels all over the world also support the initiative.

Although a lot has been published about medical tourism in particular, it is often looked into from the lenses of the tourism suppliers as an extension of tourist product or community service. Little attention has been paid towards understanding the travel motivations and decision making of the end-user that is the patient itself. In the previous studies, motivations that are commonly cited include unmet health-care needs in home territories, avoiding waiting times for care and low costs (Johnston, Crooks, Snyder, & Kingsbury, 2010). However, not much has been deliberated based on the established travel motivation theories/models (Ramirez de Arellano, 2007; Connell, 2011), particularly from the psychological aspects of the breast cancer patients.

This study aims at investigating the role of tourism and travel discourses influencing the decision-making of breast cancer patients through applying an established travel motivation model. The study is unique from two perspectives. Firstly, it studies the travel motivations of a specific set of population which are breast cancer patients. Though the aviation and hospitality sector has taken up variety of initiatives for breast cancer patients, yet there are no confirmed evidences of these initiatives' relevancy and appropriateness. Secondly the study is one of its kind being conducted in United Arab Emirates (UAE) which after being an established luxury tourist destination, has also entered into realm of medical tourism. The study bring forth insights on travel motivations of breast cancer patients which are helpful to the tourism and hospitality sector for developing meaningful strategies striking a balance between their marketing and corporate social responsibility initiatives.

TRAVEL PATTERNS OF CANCER PATIENTS

Cancer patients are considered to be immunocompromised travellers (Shah, 2016). This means that they have a high risk of acquiring travel-related illnesses due to the weakness of their immune system. However, immunocompromised patients were found travelling to high-risk destinations with limited or inadequate travel preparations on the special care that they will be require (Bialy et al., 2015). In a particular study tracing the travel destinations of patients from the Memorial Sloan-Kettering Cancer Centre, the world's leading institution in cancer treatment, it was found that its patients travelled for tourism and visiting family and friends in areas where there is a high risk of yellow fever and malaria (Mikati, Taur, Seo, & Shah, 2010). As a reaction to the study of Mikati et al., Kotton (2013) emphasized that clinicians and travel medicine specialists should educate their patients about the importance of prevention through pre-travel medical care and providing a detailed travel history to know what possible illness are going to be prevented. Despite this, researchers in cancer medicine have developed vaccines that improved the quality of life of cancer patients, allowing them increased mobility and ability to travel overseas. Increased international travel is seen in cancer patients undergoing therapy and soon after therapy has been done (Mikati, Taur, Seo, & Shah, 2013). Hunter-Jones (2006) found that taking a holiday off is a way to transcend over and recover from cancer treatment. Travel was considered by post-cancer patients as a therapeutic opportunity to escape from the stress that they experienced while undergoing cancer treatment. Travel's intrinsic benefit in speeding up the rehabilitating process decreased treatment time for the serious illnesses of patients. In a study of American senior citizen colon cancer patients aged 60 to 80 years old, it found out that the said aged bracket travels long distances of beyond 50 miles from their homes, with patients along the 60-69-year-old age bracket traveling the farthest (Massarweh et al., 2014). Reasons for travelling include further treatment for other illnesses and leisure. Georgetown University Hospital cancer researchers, meanwhile, traced the travel patterns of patients who underwent major cancer surgeries on their lungs, esophagus, liver, pancreas, and gastric and colorectal sections. It was found that the senior citizens (patients) travel the farthest compared to the patients that are in the age bracket of 18-50 years (Smith et al., 2015). For purposes of clinical trials and seeking for the best treatment their illness, cancer patients from the United Kingdom were found to be willing to travel long distances to contribute to research development in cancer studies (Moorcraft et al., 2016). Patients would go as far as to donating tissue samples for researching biopsies. On the other hand, British patients in the outlying islands of the country are having a hard time travelling and seeking immediate treatment due to the advanced stages of their cancer diagnosis (Turner et al., 2017). In Asia, however, patients are less likely to participate in clinical trials for breast cancer studies. Hong Kong Chinese breast cancer survivors' psychological situation affected their willingness to take part in such studies, pointing out that it is "somewhat distressing", and some have been diagnosed with clinical depression and anxiety (Lee, 2016). Singaporean researchers meanwhile studied the barriers of clinical trial participation among Chinese, Malay, and Indian patients of varying breast cancer stages (Lee, Ow, Lie, & Dent, 2016). Women willing to join the clinical trials expressed interest in knowing the best therapy for their illness, having a cost-effective profile, and they also have trust in the doctors and local healthcare system. Those who are unwilling expressed barriers such as having previous bad experiences with doctors, trials, and drugs and having conservative attitude towards risk-taking. Malay patients expressed that the possibility 'fatality' of the procedure acted as a barrier in taking part in the clinical trials.

Due to the limited literature on the travel motivations and preferences of medical tourists from the United Arab Emirates (UAE) and the Philippines, this comparative study would contribute to the said discourses in tourism research. The findings will be helpful for the service providers to consider travel related needs and requirements for the breast cancer patients as a motivation leading to faster recovery and also for the tourism and hospitality practitioners to conceptualize appropriate and relevant services leading to better marketing strategies and positioning themselves in this context.

TRAVEL MOTIVATIONS OF EMIRATIS AND FILIPINOS

The United Arab Emirates (UAE) and the Philippines are in two different positions when it comes to the travel priorities of its citizens. Due to the improved economic situation of the Philippines during the Aquino administration, the Filipinos became one of the top-spending tourists in the world with an estimate of US $9.9 billion of international spending in 2015 (De Guzman, 2016). This trend is not seen to continue, however, due to the declining state of the economy during the Duterte administration. UAE, meanwhile, is establishing itself as a centre of medical tourism in the Middle East. The Dubai medical tourism industry alone generated an income of more than AED 1.4 billion in 2016 (Dubai Health Authority, 2017) through its Dubai Health Experience (DXH) program launched in 2016 by Sheikh Hamdan bin Mohammed bin Rashid Al Maktoum, Crown Prince of Dubai and Chairman of the Executive Council. The emirate 326,649 international medical tourists in 2016, 37% of which came from Asia, 31% came from the nearby GCC member-states, 15% coming from Europe, and 17% came from various parts of the world. The said program eased visa application procedures for potential medical tourists to encourage them to come to the country (Khaleej Times, 2017). To increase the number of medical tourists in the UAE by 2020, the DHA will be focusing on development and upgrading of eye and cancer care services (Gulf News, 2018).

Although there is an abundance of travel motivations related publications, limited literature is available on the travel motivations of Emiratis (UAE citizens) and Filipinos (Philippines citizens). A 2011 study on the points of view of UAE citizens travelling to the State of Victoria in Australia found that the travel motivations of the former in travelling to the said territory was to spend time on holidays with their families, relax, and do shopping (Michael, Armstrong, Badran, & King, 2011). In a separate study examining the push and pull travel motivations of Emiratis to Australia for a holiday, it was found that Emiratis were motivated to travel to Australia in three factors: (1) physical; (2) interpersonal; and (3) fun needs (Michael, Wien, & Reisinger, 2017). Emiratis mainly left their country during holidays for the purpose of being exposed to new environments and cultures, however, they ought to contact and be with fellow Emiratis upon arriving in Australia. Being in Australia also meant breaking the gender roles of the traditional Islamic culture of the UAE. A respondent mentioned that her father, while in Australia, helped her mother in cooking and doing household chores, a task that he would not do when in UAE. Another respondent also expressed that it was fun for them to wear Western clothing, and not *"shaila and abhaya"* which are traditional wear for Emirati women in UAE. It gave them a sense of freedom. Filipino millennial in the age group 18 to 34, meanwhile, were more likely to travel than their elders (Saavedra, 2015). Filipino millennial tend to travel to a particular destinations with booming industry and culture and also got influenced from the destinations featured movies and/or a place where award shows and concerts happen. Moreover, 78% of the millennial seek adventurous and thrilling vacations like safaris and swimming with sharks. The elder travellers only visit places that are seen in notable travel publications or websites. However, no particular studies were conducted to look into the travel motivations of medical tourists from the said two countries.

THEORETICAL FRAMEWORK

Although a number of travel/tourism related motivation models are presented in the past (Yousaf, Amin, & Santos, 2018), the models proposed by Crompton (1979) and Iso-Ahola (1982) base on social-psychological aspects explaining the motivational factors and corresponding behaviours in the context of tourism. Iso-Ahola's motivation theory's in comparison to Crompton fits better in our case as the major tenets in this theory revolves around "escaping and seeking" (Biswas, 2008; Snepenger, King, Marshal, & Uysal,2006). This theory proposes a four-dimensional structure for analysing the travel motivations of tourists: (1) personal escaping; (2) interpersonal escaping; (3) personal seeking; and (4) interpersonal seeking. This theory sees that there is a "psychological benefit of tourist experiences stems from an interaction between escaping routine or stressful environments and seeking opportunities for intrinsic rewards" (Dunn Ross & Iso-Ahola, 1991).

Another reason for using this theory is that the four motivational dimensions developed by Iso-Ahola have been utilized in numerous studies (Spenenger et al,

2006; Miswas, 2008) earlier. For the purpose of this study, the researcher expanded the 12-item motivational dimensions and developed a 16-item specific situational dimension for cancer patients to freely relate their experiences while travelling (table). The additional dimensions were discussed and approved by the oncologists having significant experience with the breast cancer patients.

Personal Seeking

1. I travel because it makes me feel good about myself.
2. By travelling I feel like a winner.
3. When I think myself as a traveler, I see a different person who is experiencing new things.
4. Travelling gives me a sense of hope/quality of life.

Interpersonal Seeking

5. Travelling gives me an opportunity to engage in activities and meet new people.
6. I travel to meet my friends and family.
7. I wish to travel so that I be with who share similar interests.

Personal Escaping

8. I travel to change my environment and lifestyle.
9. Travelling helps in avoiding stress at work/home.
10. I travel because it helps in avoiding the economic stress relating to unexpected expenses for treatment.
11. I travel because it helps me do my other treatment not covered by the insurance.
12. Travelling helps me to cope up on new environment.
13. I travel to have another option for my treatment that is within my capacity to pay.

Interpersonal Escaping

14. I travel to avoid social conflict within my family and the community.
15. Travelling helps me to feel not sick.
16. I travel for treatment by myself not to burden other family members.

METHODOLOGY

This study aims at examining the travel motivations of breast cancer patients. To know the travel frequencies and motivations of the said patients, the researchers used a structured questionnaire based on Iso Aloha motivation model as discussed above. The respondents were undergoing pre or post-cancer treatment in a hospital in Abu Dhabi, United Arab Emirates and in General Santos City, Philippines. Approval from the hospital authorities was taken before collecting the data from the patients. The method of data collection was by non-probability convenience sampling. Only respondents who were willing to answer the survey were given the link to the survey.

A total of thirty-nine (39) respondents (31 from the UAE and 8 from the Philippines) answered the electronic survey done by the researcher. Table 1 shows the demographic characteristics of the respondents from the United Arab Emirates and the Philippines, respectively.

Table 1 indicates that 41.03% of the respondents currently have or had Stage 2 breast cancer. Those with or had Stage 3 breast cancer followed with 30.77% of the total respondents. A majority of the respondents (64.1%) are currently undergoing treatment for their illness, married (64.1%), female (94.87%), and college graduates (82.05%). The mean age of the respondents is 46, with a standard deviation of 8.6. Most of the respondents from both countries were Filipinos (76.92%), followed by Emiratis (7.69%), and the rest were of different nationalities from North America, South Asia, and Africa.

FINDINGS AND ANALYSIS

As mentioned earlier, the researcher has developed a comprehensive 16-item survey to know the travel motivations of breast cancer patients based on Iso-Ahola's motivational theory. This section will discuss the results of the survey conducted. Table 2 shows the analysis of travel motivation factors of breast cancer patients from Abu Dhabi, United Arab Emirates and General Santos City, Philippines.

A comparative analysis in table 2 shows that the two leading travel motivations of the respondents differ from both countries. The more diversified respondents, in terms of nationalities, from the United Arab Emirates had personal seeking as a primary motivation to travel. Personal seeking factors involve personal and individualistic motivations such as feeling good about themselves, breaking personal expectations and feeling a winner, and having a sense of hope. Respondents from the Philippines, meanwhile, travel mainly to connect with people. In interpersonal travel motivations, the Filipinos show interest in having shared experiences with new people and with those who they already knew, such as their families and friends.

Table 1. Demographic characteristics of the respondents

Variable	Category	United Arab Emirates (n=31)		The Philippines (n=8)	
		Frequency	%	Frequency	%
Stage of Breast Cancer	No specific stage	4	12.9	0	0
	Stage 1	1	3.23	1	12.5
	Stage 2	12	38.71	4	50
	Stage 3	9	29.03	3	37.5
	Stage 4	5	16.13	0	0
Treatment Status	On-going treatment	22	70.97	3	37.5
	Complete remission (cancer-free)	9	29.03	5	62.5
Civil Status	Single	10	32.26	1	12.5
	Married	20	64.52	5	62.5
	Divorced	1	3.23	2	25
Gender	Female	29	93.55	8	100
	Male	2	6.45	0	0
Age Bracket	30-39	9	29.03	1	12.5
	40-49	13	41.94	3	37.5
	50-59	7	22.58	4	50
	60-69	2	6.45	0	0
Educational Attainment	Secondary/High School Level	3	9.68	0	0
	Associate's degree	1	3.23	0	0
	College undergraduate	1	3.23	0	0
	College graduate	24	77.42	8	100
	Master's degree	1	3.23	0	0
	Doctorate degree	1	3.23	0	0
Nationality	Canadian	1	3.23	0	0
	Emirati	3	9.68	0	0
	Filipino	22	70.97	8	100
	Indian	1	3.23	0	0
	Pakistani	1	3.23	0	0
	South African	1	3.23	0	0
	Sri Lankan	1	3.23	0	0
	Sudanese	1	3.23	0	0

Table 2. Analysis of travel motivation factors

Travel Motivations	Total		UAE		PH	
	Mean	Rank	Mean	Rank	Mean	Rank
Personal Seeking	**4.471**	**1**	**4.411**	**2**	**4.531**	**1**
Gives me a sense of hope/quality of life.	4.427	3	4.354	3	4.5	2
I see a different person who's experiencing new things.	4.379	4	4.258	4	4.5	2
Makes me feel good about myself.	4.586	1	4.548	1	4.625	1
I feel like a winner.	4.492	2	4.484	2	4.5	2
Interpersonal Seeking	**4.298**	**2**	**4.43**	**1**	**4.167**	**2**
Gives me an opportunity to engage in activities and meet new people.	4.508	1	4.516	1	4.5	1
Meet my family and friends.	4.195	2	4.516	3	3.875	3
I will be with people who share similar interests.	4.191	3	4.258	2	4.125	2
Personal Escaping	**3.691**	**3**	**3.736**	**3**	**3.646**	**3**
Change my environment and lifestyle.	4.286	2	4.322	2	4.25	1
Helps in avoiding stress at work/home.	4.32	1	4.516	1	4.125	2
Avoids the economic stress relating to unexpected expenses for treatment.	3.346	4	3.193	4	3.5	4
Helps me do other treatment not covered by my insurance.	3.08	6	3.161	5	3	6
Cope up on new environment.	3.969	3	4.064	3	3.875	3
Another option for my treatment that is within my capacity to pay.	3.143	5	3.161	5	3.125	5
Interpersonal Escaping	**3.35**	**4**	**3.408**	**4**	**3.292**	**4**
Avoid social conflict within my family and the community.	2.887	3	2.774	3	3	2
Helps me not to feel sick.	4.143	1	4.161	1	4.125	1
Treatment by myself not to burden other family members.	3.02	2	3.29	2	2.75	3

Respondents from both countries, however, are consistent in expressing that mixed feelings with regards to the items on personal and interpersonal escaping. All agree that travelling helps them avoid stress as it introduces new environments and lifestyles. It was only the respondents from the UAE that agreed to the factor that travelling could help them cope up. It is also notable that the respondents expressed the factor that travelling helps them not to feel sick. Travelling, for them, is not about avoiding social conflict within their families or communities nor treating themselves alone to not be a burden to their families.

One way ANOVA test was used to examine the differences in the groups. Table 3 shows the travel motivations with respect to the marital status. The respondents who are married are likely not to travel because their spouse and other family members are already with them while having their treatments. Most of the respondents who are married and working have insurance that covers the treatment of the cancer, while the respondents who are married and not working are dependents of their husband insurance which also covers the treatments for cancer. In comparison to UAE, the respondents from Philippines prefer to travel in order to have more time with the family and friends (table 4).

Table 5 shows responses on travel motivation with respect to the stages of breast cancer. Traveling was favoured mostly by patients in stage 1 to 3.

Table 3. ANOVA results of travel motivation with respect to marital status

	Sum of Squares	df	Mean Square	F	Sig.
I travel because it makes me feel good about myself.	0.978	2	0.489	1.216	0.31
By travelling, I feel like a winner.	2.663	2	1.332	1.76	0.189
When I think myself as a traveller, I see a different person who's experiencing new things.	1.052	2	0.526	1.058	0.359
Travelling gives me a sense of hope/quality of life.	1.21	2	0.605	1.423	0.256
Travelling gives me an opportunity to engage in activities and meet new people.	0.98	2	0.49	1.6	0.218
I travel to meet my friends and family.	3.074	2	1.537	2.1	0.14
I wish to travel so that I be with people who share similar interests.	6.25	2	3.125	3.377	0.047
I travel to change my environment and lifestyle.	3.263	2	1.632	1.723	0.195
Travelling helps in avoiding stress at work/home.	0.744	2	0.372	0.453	0.64
I travel because it helps in avoiding the economic stress relating to unexpected expenses for treatment.	6.899	2	3.45	3.426	0.045
I travel because it helps me do my other treatment not covered by the insurance.	0.817	2	0.409	0.317	0.73
Travelling helps me to cope up on new environment.	4.707	2	2.353	2.778	0.078
I travel to have another option for my treatment that is within my capacity to pay.	3.365	2	1.682	1.341	0.276
I travel to avoid social conflict within my family and the community.	2.45	2	1.225	0.854	0.436
Travelling helps me to feel not sick.	0.445	2	0.222	0.263	0.77

Table 4. ANOVA results of travel motivation with respect to the living country

	Sum of Squares	df	Mean Square	F	Sig.
I travel because it makes me feel good about myself.	0.097	1	0.097	0.233	0.632
By travelling, I feel like a winner.	0.329	1	0.329	0.409	0.527
When I think myself as a traveller, I see a different person who's experiencing new things.	0.016	1	0.016	0.03	0.863
Travelling gives me a sense of hope/quality of life.	0.001	1	0.001	0.003	0.956
Travelling gives me an opportunity to engage in activities and meet new people.	0.016	1	0.016	0.048	0.829
I travel to meet my friends and family.	3.595	1	3.595	5.19	0.03
I wish to travel so that I be with people who share similar interests.	0.275	1	0.275	0.253	0.618
I travel to change my environment and lifestyle.	0.131	1	0.131	0.129	0.722
Travelling helps in avoiding stress at work/home.	0.637	1	0.637	0.797	0.379
I travel because it helps in avoiding the economic stress relating to unexpected expenses for treatment.	0.996	1	0.996	0.859	0.361
I travel because it helps me do my other treatment not covered by the insurance.	0.069	1	0.069	0.054	0.818
Travelling helps me to cope up on new environment.	0.008	1	0.008	0.008	0.93
I travel to have another option for my treatment that is within my capacity to pay.	0	1	0	0	0.991
I travel to avoid social conflict within my family and the community.	0.275	1	0.275	0.188	0.667
Travelling helps me to feel not sick.	0.004	1	0.004	0.005	0.946

"Traveling makes me feel good about myself because it gives me hope and positivity about life."

"I want to prove that cancer is not a hindrance for any patient or survivor to see the beauty of the world."

"When I feel good about myself it strengthen me more to overcome and get-through with the different treatments. That makes my recovery much faster and easier".

However, respondents in stage 4 were unlikely to consider traveling because of their ongoing treatment. Stage 4 condition means that the cancer have metastasized to other parts of the body. In that condition, the cancer cannot be cured and but it can be only treated with aggressive systematic therapy. Subsequently, respondents

Table 5. Patient response with respect to cancer stage - ANOVA Table

	Sum of Squares	df	Mean Square	F	Sig.
I travel because it makes me feel good about myself.	3.657	3	1.219	3.737	0.022
By travelling, I feel like a winner.	2.755	3	0.918	1.179	0.334
When I think myself as a traveller, I see a different person who's experiencing new things.	3.358	3	1.119	2.561	0.074
Travelling gives me a sense of hope/quality of life.	1.98	3	0.66	1.597	0.211
Travelling gives me an opportunity to engage in activities and meet new people.	0.069	3	0.023	0.066	0.978
I travel to meet my friends and family.	2.48	3	0.827	1.065	0.379
I wish to travel so that I be with people who share similar interests.	1.049	3	0.35	0.31	0.818
I travel to change my environment and lifestyle.	8.966	3	2.989	3.791	0.02
Travelling helps in avoiding stress at work/home.	2.417	3	0.806	1.015	0.4
I travel because it helps in avoiding the economic stress relating to unexpected expenses for treatment.	2.142	3	0.714	0.595	0.623
I travel because it helps me do my other treatment not covered by the insurance.	0.265	3	0.088	0.065	0.978
Travelling helps me to cope up on new environment.	7.358	3	2.453	3.116	0.041
I travel to have another option for my treatment that is within my capacity to pay.	2.657	3	0.886	0.671	0.577
I travel to avoid social conflict within my family and the community.	8.549	3	2.85	2.227	0.106
Travelling helps me to feel not sick.	0.338	3	0.113	0.129	0.942

who were still having an on-going treatment were most likely not to travel. Many of them would preferred to be with their family as it would help them to have more comfort and the sense of peace during treatment (table 6).

CONCLUSION

A comprehensive 16-item survey was conducted to 39 breast cancer patients on their travel motivations. Utilizing the four-dimensional structure of the motivational theory by Iso-Ahola to measure and analyse the travel motivations of the said respondents, this study found that breast cancer patients travel to create connections with people, whether it be with their families and friends, or to meet new people and have new

Table 6. Patient response with respect to Treatment status - ANOVA Table

	Sum of Squares	df	Mean Square	F	Sig.
I travel because it makes me feel good about myself.	0.279	1	0.279	0.679	0.416
By travelling, I feel like a winner.	1.564	1	1.564	2.039	0.163
When I think myself as a traveller, I see a different person who's experiencing new things.	2.344	1	2.344	5.31	0.028
Travelling gives me a sense of hope/quality of life.	1.331	1	1.331	3.263	0.08
Travelling gives me an opportunity to engage in activities and meet new people.	1.071	1	1.071	3.648	0.065
I travel to meet my friends and family.	0.002	1	0.002	0.002	0.962
I wish to travel so that I be with people who share similar interests.	1.257	1	1.257	1.195	0.283
I travel to change my environment and lifestyle.	2.246	1	2.246	2.367	0.134
Travelling helps in avoiding stress at work/home.	0.82	1	0.82	1.033	0.317
I travel because it helps in avoiding the economic stress relating to unexpected expenses for treatment.	0.782	1	0.782	0.67	0.419
I travel because it helps me do my other treatment not covered by the insurance.	0.142	1	0.142	0.112	0.74
Travelling helps me to cope up on new environment.	0.378	1	0.378	0.395	0.534
I travel to have another option for my treatment that is within my capacity to pay.	0.763	1	0.763	0.588	0.449
I travel to avoid social conflict within my family and the community.	13.281	1	13.281	12.626	0.001
Travelling helps me to feel not sick.	0.159	1	0.159	0.192	0.664

experiences. Travelling also gives them a positive attitude as makes them feel good about themselves, gives them a sense of hope, feel like a winner, and see new and different things. Varying responses were obtained on the items about personal and interpersonal escaping. The respondents agree that by travelling, it gives them a change of environment and lifestyle, helps avoid stress at work or at home, and copes them up as they are introduced to a new environment. Close responses were received on items about avoiding economic stress, helping them do treatment not covered by their insurance, and it gives them another option for their treatment that is within their capacity to pay. Travelling, meanwhile, helps the breast cancer patients feel not sick. However, they do not agree that travelling can help them avoid social conflict within their families and communities. A simple majority of the respondents cannot say for certain if travelling removes the burden of treatment from their families. Data obtained from this study transcends geographical regions as respondents come from various nationalities, backgrounds, and generations. This will hopefully shed light on the travelling interests and motivations of the medical tourists, and, in turn, will be utilized in improving health tourism services. The results should be considered while developing appropriate and relevant societal marketing campaign by the airlines/hospitality sector. Travel motivations for breast cancer patients are found to differ from various perspectives, which in return would help the practitioners to segment market (within the breast cancer patients) and facilitate them as per their requirement.

LIMITATIONS

The study was based on an established motivation model and the data was collected through a structured questionnaire framed after reviewing relevant and significant literature. However, the sample size remains a limitation of the current study. Although an effort was made to contact several patients through their doctors/hospitals, not many of them gave their consent for the survey. However, the patients who actually participated in the survey were forthcoming and responsive.

ACKNOWLEDGMENT

The authors are thankful to Dr Mohanad Diab, Head of Department–Medical Oncology, practicing at NMC Royal Hospital, DIP, Dubai; NMC Royal Hospital, Khalifa City, Abu Dhabi and NMC Speciality Hospital, Abu Dhabi, for his diligent support to the authors during all the stages of the study. The first author of this research was diagnosed with Stage 3 breast cancer and while being treated at various hospitals, she interacted with other patients with inclination to travel. This led to the conception of the idea for this study.

REFERENCES

Bialy, C., Horne, K., Dendle, C., Kanellis, J., Littlejohn, G., Ratnam, I., & Woolley, I. (2015). International travel in the immunocompromised patient: A cross-sectional survey of travel advice in 254 consecutive patients. *Internal Medicine Journal, 45*(6), 618–623. doi:10.1111/imj.12753 PMID:25827660

Biswas, M. (2008). *Confirmatory factor analysis of Iso-Ahola's motivational theory. An Application of structural equation modelling*. Paper presented at the Conference on Tourism in India - Challenge Ahead, Kozhikode, India.

De Guzman, L. E. P. (2016). Filipinos among World's Biggest Spenders on Travel. *Business World*. Retrieved from http://www.bworldonline.com/

Dubai Health Authority. (2017). *Dubai Medical Tourism Industry Generated More than AED 1.4billion for the Emirate in 2016*. Retrieved from https://www.dha.gov.ae/

Dunn Ross, E. L., & Iso-Ahola, S. E. (1991). Sightseeing tourists' motivation and satisfaction. *Annals of Tourism Research, 18*(2), 226–237. doi:10.1016/0160-7383(91)90006-W

Global cancer diagnostics market 2018-2027: Prevalence of cancer cases, government initiatives for funding and awareness about cancer and growing medical tourism in Asia. (2018, Nov 26). NASDAQ OMX's News Release Distribution Channel.

Gulf News. (2018). *Dubai Health Authority Focuses on Eye and Cancer Care Services*. Retrieved from https://gulfnews.com/

Hunter-Jones, P. (2006). Managing Cancer: The Role of Holiday Taking. *Journal of Travel Medicine, 10*(3), 170–176. doi:10.2310/7060.2003.35762 PMID:12757692

Iso-Ahola, S. E. (1982). Toward a Social Psychological Theory of Tourism Motivation: A Rejoinder. *Annals of Tourism Research, 9*(2), 256–262. doi:10.1016/0160-7383(82)90049-4

Johnston, R., Crooks, V. A., Snyder, J., & Kingsbury, P. (2010). What is known about the effects of medical tourism in destination and departure countries? A scoping review. *International Journal for Equity in Health, 9*(24). doi:10.1186/1475-9276-9-24 PMID:21047433

Khaleej Times. (2017). *Dubai to promote medical tourism by easing visa procedures*. Retrieved from https://www.khaleejtimes.com/

Kotton, C. N. (2013). Safe Travels! After Cancer Treatment. *Journal of Travel Medicine, 20*(2), 69–70. doi:10.1111/jtm.12014 PMID:23464711

Lee, G. E. (2016). Factors Associated with Willingness to Participate in Clinical Trials among Diverse Asian Patients with Breast Cancer. *European Journal of Cancer*, *60*, 1–19. doi:10.1016/j.ejca.2016.03.030 PMID:27038842

Lee, G. E., Ow, M., Lie, D., & Dent, R. (2016). Barriers and Facilitators for Clinical Trial Participation among Diverse Asian Patients with Breast Cancer: A Qualitative Study. *BMC Women's Health*, *16*(43). doi:10.118612905-016-0319-1 PMID:27449505

Massarweh, N. N., Chiang, Y.-J., Xing, Y., Chang, G. J., Haynes, A. B., You, Y. N., ... Cormier, J. N. (2014). Association Between Travel Distance and Metastatic Disease at Diagnosis Among Patients With Colon Cancer. *Journal of Clinical Oncology*, *32*(9), 942–948. doi:10.1200/JCO.2013.52.3845 PMID:24516014

Michael, I., Armstrong, A., Badran, B., & King, B. (2011). Dubai Outbound Tourism: An Exploratory Study of Emiratis and Expatriates. *Journal of Vacation Marketing*, *17*(1), 83–91. doi:10.1177/1356766710391448

Michael, N., Wien, C., & Reisinger, Y. (2017). Push and Pull Escape Travel Motivations of Emirati Nationals to Australia. *International Journal of Culture, Tourism and Hospitality Research*, *11*(3), 274–296. doi:10.1108/IJCTHR-04-2016-0039

Mikati, T., Taur, Y., Seo, S. K., & Shah, M. K. (2010). International Travel Patterns for Patients Diagnosed with Cancer. *Abstracts of the 48th Annual Meeting of IDSA*. Retrieved from https://idsa.confex.com/

Mikati, T., Taur, Y., Seo, S. K., & Shah, M. K. (2013). International Travel Patterns and Travel Risks of Patients Diagnosed With Cancer. *Journal of Travel Medicine*, *20*(2), 71–77. doi:10.1111/jtm.12013 PMID:23464712

Moorcraft, S. Y., Marriott, C., Peckitt, C., Cunningham, D., Chau, I., Starling, N., ... Rao, S. (2016). Patients' Willingness to Participate in Clinical Trials and Their Views on Aspects of Cancer Research: Results of a Prospective Patient Survey. *Trials*, *17*(17). doi:10.118613063-015-1105-3 PMID:26745891

Patients Beyond Borders. (2011). *Medical Tourism Statistics & Facts*. Retrieved from https://patientsbeyondborders.com/

Perdue, C., & Noble, S. (2007). Foreign Travel for Advanced Cancer Patients: A Guide for Healthcare Professionals. *Postgraduate Medical Journal*, *83*(981), 437–444. doi:10.1136/pgmj.2006.054593 PMID:17621611

Saavedra, K. P. (2015). Millennials as Travelers. *BusinessMirror*. Retrieved from https://businessmirror.com.ph/

Shah, M. K. (2016). The Immunocompromised Traveler. *Oncology*, *30*(2), 142–159. Retrieved from http://www.cancernetwork.com/oncology-journal/immunocompromised-traveler PMID:26888792

Smith, A. K., Shara, N. M., Zeymo, A., Harris, K., Estes, R., Johnson, L. B., & Al-Refaie, W. B. (2015). Travel Patterns of Cancer Surgery Patients in a Regionalized System. *The Journal of Surgical Research*, *199*(1), 97–105. doi:10.1016/j.jss.2015.04.016 PMID:26076685

Snepenger, D., King, J., Marshall, E., & Uysal, M. (2006). Modeling Iso-Ahola's Motivation Theory in the Tourism Context. *Journal of Travel Research*, *45*(2), 140–149. doi:10.1177/0047287506291592

Turner, M., Fielding, S., Ong, Y., Dibben, C., Feng, Z., Brewster, D. H., ... Murchie, P. (2017). A Cancer Geography Paradox? Poorer Cancer Outcomes with Longer Travelling times to Healthcare Facilities despite Prompter Diagnosis and Treatment: A Data-linkage Study. *British Journal of Cancer*, *117*(3), 439–449. doi:10.1038/bjc.2017.180 PMID:28641316

United Nations World Tourism Organization. (2018). *2017 International Tourism Results: The Highest in Seven Years.* Retrieved from http://media.unwto.org/press-release/2018-01-15/2017-international-tourism-results-highest-seven-years

Yousaf, A., Amin, I., & Santos, J. A. C. (2018). Tourists' Motivations To Travel: A Theoretical Perspective On The Existing Literature. *Tourism and Hospitality Management*, *24*(1), 197–211. doi:10.20867/thm.24.1.8

Zain, A. A. (2018). Over 4,500 new cancer cases in UAE this year. *Khaleej Times*. Retrieved from https://www.khaleejtimes.com/

Chapter 6
Medical Tourism in Visakhapatnam by People of South Odisha

Sachin Kumar Behera
North-Eastern Hill University, Shilong, India

ABSTRACT

Vishakhapatnam is a coastal city of Andhra Pradesh, one of the commercial hubs of Andhra Pradesh and very near to the south part of Odisha. The city has many super specialty hospitals and is home to various tourist destinations. People of Southern Odisha do not have good medical facilities always rush to Visakhapatnam for even small treatments. Southern Odisha comprises of the following districts: Gajapati, Rayagada, Koraput, Nabrangpur, Malkangiri, and Ganjam. These districts are still deprived of basic medical facilities, and traveling to Visakhapatnam is more suitable than to the capital of Odisha (Bhubaneswar) due to distance. The methodology of this chapter is based on secondary sources such as a published book, journals, reports, articles, newspapers, and online sources. In this chapter, a descriptive method is employed. Primary data was collected from the people staying in various hospitals in Vishakhapatnam for medical purposes.

INTRODUCTION

India is home to the first plastic surgeon of 600 B.C – Sushruta and he is also considered the father of surgery. India is the land of Yoga which now a tourism product in terms of wellness tourism. Medical tourism has recently grown in India to a large extent. Medical tourism is basically an economic activity based on

DOI: 10.4018/978-1-5225-9787-2.ch006

integration of two sectors i.e. medical and tourism. (Han & Hyun, 2015), patients seeking medical care are willing to travel from developed countries such as Australia, United Kingdom and USA to developing countries such as Costa Rica, India and Thailand for medical treatment and Thailand, Singapore and India have the highest share of medical tourism market in Asia (Yeoh, Othman, & Ahmad, 2013). India has emerged as a major Medical Tourism destination. While Ministry of Tourism does not maintain any data regarding the growth of India's medical tourism vis a vis other countries, Ministry of Commerce informs that as per a The Federation of Indian Chambers of Commerce and Industry - Intercontinental Marketing Services (FICCI-IMS) Knowledge Paper titled, 'Medical Value travel in India: Enhancing value in MVT', published in 2016, India is amongst the top 6 MVT (Medical Value Travel) destinations of the world which include Thailand, Singapore, India, Malaysia, Taiwan and Mexico (India ranked third in the world in 2015). The Niti Aayog has identified medical value travel (MVT) as a major source of foreign exchange earnings. India currently has around 18% of the global medical tourism market. Its medical value travel (MVT) was pegged at $3 billion in 2015, and is estimated to grow at a CAGR of 15%, according to a report by FICCI and IMS Health. It has been estimated that by 2020, India's medical tourism industry could be worth $9 billion, and account for 20% of the global market share. The report also pointed out that in curative care, India was the preferred destination for cardiology, orthopedics, transplants, and ophthalmology. High credibility in wellness, preventive, and alternative medicine was also attributed to India.

The domestic medical tourism market has also seen a boom but a very little research has been done so far. Government of India has realized the potential of medical tourism in India and appropriate polices have been made so far but very few policies are made focusing the domestic medical tourism. People of those states which have poor medical infrastructure are bound to travel to neighbor states for medical and tourism purpose. Although there is no focused policy by central government for domestic medical tourism, most states also do not have any policy.

PROCESS OF MEDICAL TOURISM

Key Initiatives Taken by Ministry of Tourism for Medical Tourism

A National Medical and Wellness Tourism Board has been constituted to provide a dedicated institutional framework to take forward the cause of promotion of Medical Tourism, Wellness Tourism and Yoga, Ayurveda Tourism and any other format of Indian system of medicine covered by Ayurveda, Yoga, Unani, Siddha and

Figure 1.

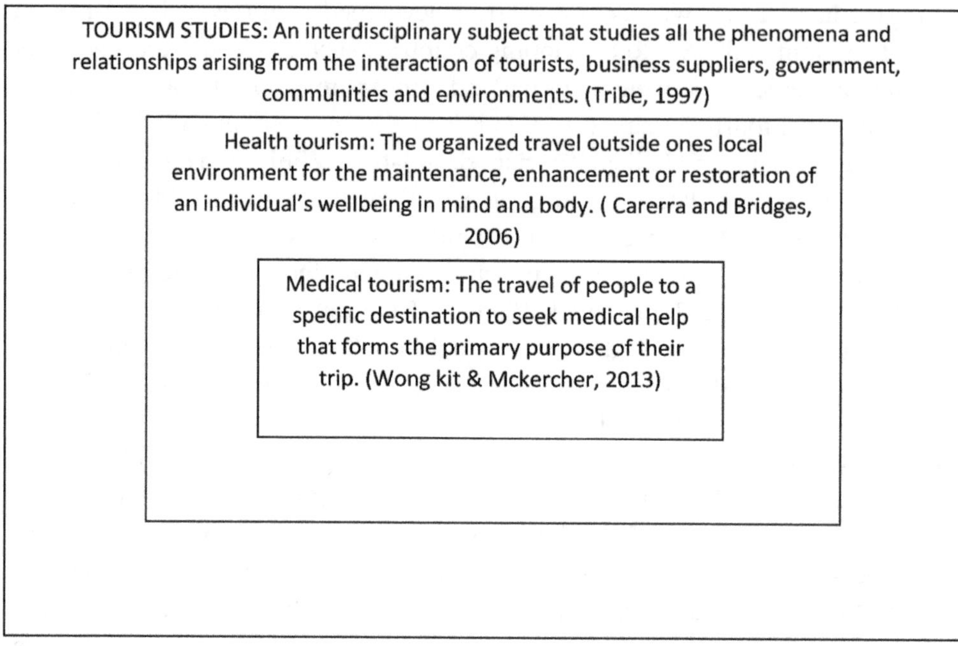

Homeopathy (AYUSH). This Board works as an umbrella organization that governs and promotes this segment of tourism in an organized manner. It has representatives from AYUSH, Quality Council of India, and National Accreditation Board for Hospitals and Healthcare Providers (NABH).

The Department of Commerce and Services Export Promotion Council (SEPC) have launched a Healthcare Portal www.indiahealthcaretourism.com, as a single source platform providing comprehensive information to medical travelers on the top healthcare institutions in the country in English, Arabic, Russian and French.

Facilitation counters has also been set up at the major airports of Delhi, Mumbai, Chennai, Kolkata, Hyderabad and Bengaluru for tourists arriving on Medical Visas.

The total number of foreign medical tourists visiting India was 2.34 lakh in 2015, 4.27 lakh in 2016 and 4.95 lakh in 2017 as per Ministry of Tourism Statistics

Figure 2.
(Adapted from FICCI and IMS Health Report)

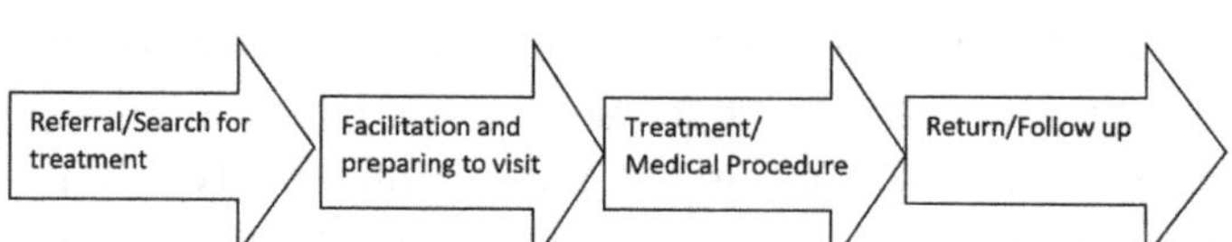

. There is a clear increase seen in the numbers as India has a rare combination of advanced facilities, skilled doctors, and low cost of treatment which made India a popular hub of medical tourism, attracting a large number of foreign patients every year. However, the provisional estimates of the total FEE through medical tourism during 2015, 2016 and 2017 were ₹1,35,193 crore, ₹1,54,146 crore, and ₹1,77,874 crore, respectively.

The aim of the present study was to investigate and describe the aspects of medical tourism in Vishakhapatnam. Factors affecting medical tourism in the region will also be described. This paper intends to respond to the calls for greater theoretical clarification made by numerous researchers, tourism authorities and organizations. It first provides a description of the medical tourism development and medical tourism in Vishakhapatnam.

The methodology employed in this study is discussed in following sections, followed by a presentation of analysis and results of the study.

OBJECTIVES OF THE STUDY

The following are the objectives of the study:

- To know the pattern of Medical Tourism in Vishakhapatnam.
- To explore the different aspects of Medical Tourism in Vishakhapatnam.
- To understand the behavior of medical tourists.

REVIEW OF LITERATURE

In 2002 the economic potential of medical tourism was recognized by Indian Government and initiatives were taken to promote India as a Global Health Destination. Most medical tourists come from Bangladesh, the Middle East, the UK, and the US, Canada and African and other developing countries (Medhekar, 2014).

"Medical tourism as a niche has emerged from the rapid growth of what has become an industry, where people travel often long distances to overseas countries to obtain medical, dental and surgical care while simultaneously being holidaymakers" defines (Connell, 2006). The push and Pull factors of medical tourism was given by (Crompton, 1992) the push factors are mainly related to consumers and includes factors such as socio-demographical (e.g., age, gender, income, education) or health related (e.g., insurance status, health status) hence generating the demand for medical tourism and pull factors include overall country environment (e.g., stable economy, country image), healthcare and tourism industry of the country (e.g., healthcare costs, popular tourist destination) and quality of the medical facility and services (e.g., quality care, accreditation, reputation of doctors). The factors affecting medical tourism in a destination are country environment, medical and tourism industry factors and quality of facilities and services. Country environment includes economic conditions, cultural and religion match, favorable exchange rates, affordability and convenience of travel. The medical and tourism factors include infrastructure, health care costs, policies, tourism potential etc. The quality factors include certification and accreditation of hospitals, expertise and qualification of doctors, service quality of physicians and nurses, reputation of doctors etc (Fetscherin & Stephano, 2016).

People traveling to places in search for quality health services and wellbeing are not a new trend. Medical centers in Europe and the U.S. received wealthy patients from mostly developed countries in the 18th – 20th century. In the 21st century less wealthy people started travelling from developed countries to developing countries for medical treatments due to globalization of communication and transportation technologies (Fetscherin & Stephano, 2016). Only a few of hospitals and countries were promoting themselves as medical tourism destinations a few years ago but today there are hundreds of hospitals and clinics and over thirty different countries promoting it (Saadatnia & Mehregan, 2014).

PLACE OF STUDY

Visakhapatnam is a coastal, port city, often called “The Jewel of the East Coast”, situated in the Indian state of Andhra Pradesh, located on the eastern shore of India, and nestled in the midst of the hills of the Eastern Ghats and facing the Bay of Bengal to the east. Telugu is the language spoken by most of the people of the place. Vishakhapatnam has quite a few historical, natural, religious and cultural attractions; therefore, it would be of interest to tourists. It has temperate summers. The average annual temperature is 27.8 °C in Visakhapatnam and the average rainfall is 1008 mm. There are many places of interest for tourists such as Varaha Lakshmi Narasimha templ in Simhachalam, INS Kursura museum, RK beach, Kailasgiri Hills, Indira Gandhi Zoological park, Rushikonda Beach. It is also a economic hub for most south Odisha districts and northern Andhra Pradesh.

Vishakhapatnam is selected for the study due to its proximity to the districts of South Odisha. This city is quite popular among the residents of south Odisha for Medical purpose, tourism, shopping and other commercial activities.

Vishakhapatnam has mainly 2 government hospitals and many private hospitals such as Apollo, Care, Pinnacle, 7 Hills, Omni- RK, Manipal Hospital, King George Hospital etc.

Figure 3. Most people travelled by public transport due to frequent availability of buses and trains from Odisha. People who travelled by private taxi wanted to have flexibility in their schedule so that they can visit places.

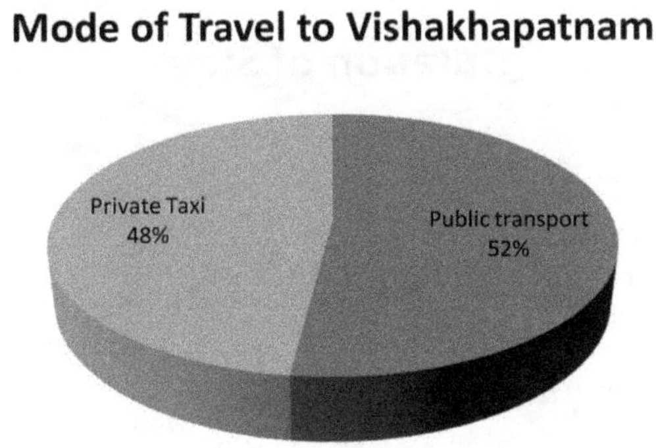

There are many small hotels, lodges and guesthouses near the hospitals to accommodate attendants and relatives of patients. Even many Odia restaurants mushroomed in the area to cater the need of people travelling for medical tourism.

METHODOLOGY

Owing to the exploratory nature of the present study quantitative method was applied. A total of 100 samples were taken from 5 major hospitals in Vishakhapatnam. The sample size was 20 from each hospital. The instrument used to collect data is questionnaire. Data was only collected from attendants/ relatives of patients coming from Odisha for medical purposes. The type of sampling used was random. The five hospitals were namely Apollo, Care, Pinnacle, 7 Hills and King George Hospital.

Figure 4. Most of the patients stayed for more than a week for treatment, while some were same day visitors who returned to their home in the same day after medical and tourism purpose was fulfilled

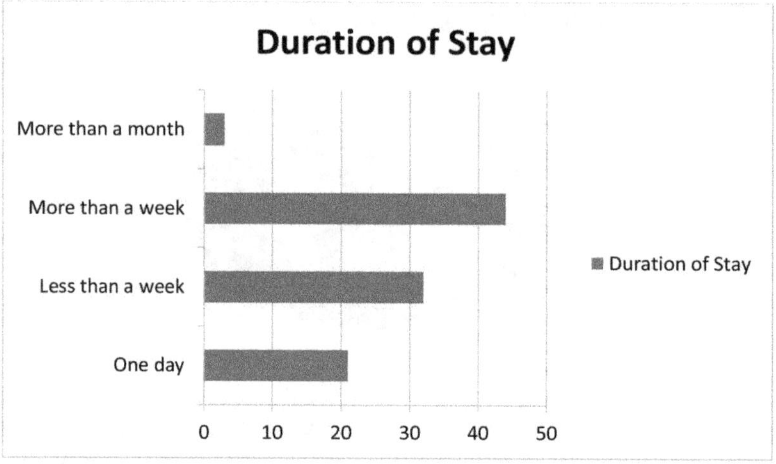

FINDINGS AND DISCUSSIONS

SUGGESTIONS

After analyzing the data and interpretation, my suggestions are as follows:

- As no respondent came through medical tourism operator, medical tourism is not formalized in this area. There is huge market for facilitation and medical tourism in South Odisha. Tour Operators should star offering similar services.
- Most people visited the same place 2-3 times; hospitals should focus on customer retention and after treatment services so that patients visit again. Tour operators of Vizag should also target people coming for medical purpose.
- Medical tourism was the mostly said reason to visit the place; government should bring a comprehensive policy for medical tourism.
- Hospitals need to focus on their marketing policies as very less patients visit hospitals by going through their website or advertisements.
- As many people are accompanied by more than 3 members, tour operators should focus on arranging tours during the treatment of the patient. The accompanying members can go around in the free time.
- Government may consider conducting an extensive study on medical tourism destination and marketing.

Figure 5. The purpose of visit was mostly for medical and tourism but a very few people visited only for medical purpose

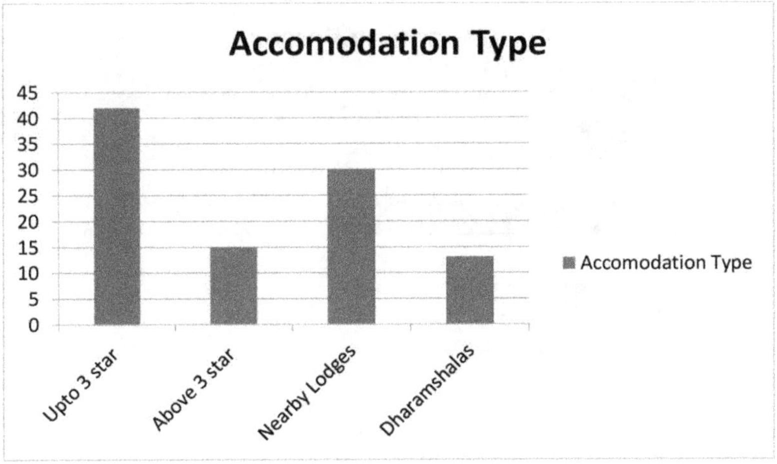

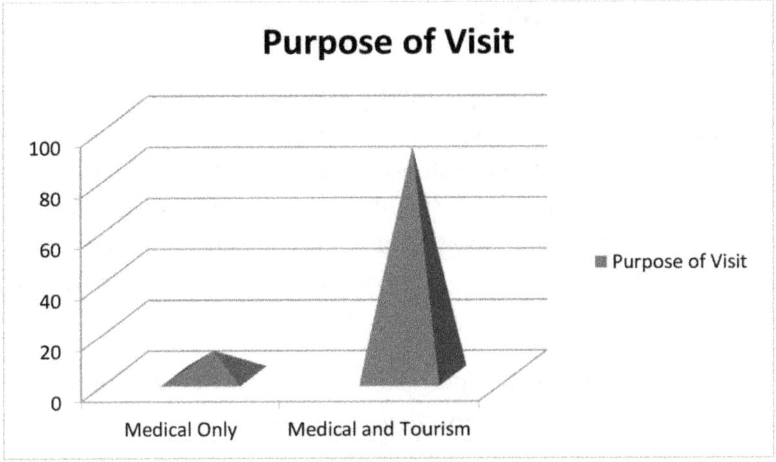

- Surrogacy Tourism, Reproductive Tourism, Fertility Tourism can also be introduced in this destination as it is in high demand these days.
- Positioning of healthcare industry in Vishakhapatnam should be as a high quality complete healthcare solution.
- The countries like Japan, South Korea, etc. have positioned themselves for specific specialties – Similarly India as a whole should also have a focused approach.

Figure 6. Most respondents were accompanied by 4 persons as parents couldn't leave their children back home for treatment

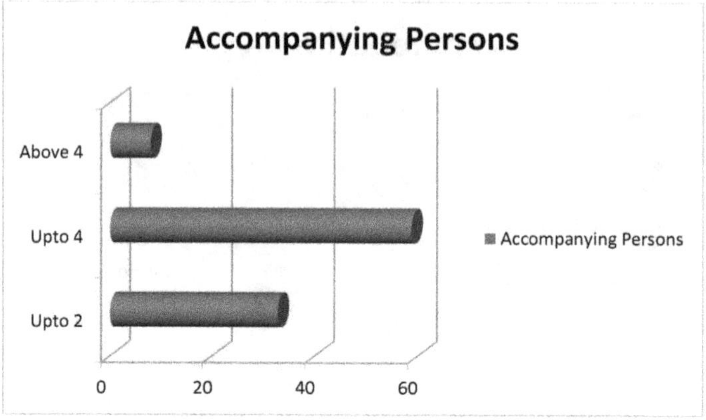

LIMITATIONS OF THE STUDY

One of the limitations of this study is low response rate, which is relatively lower than other studies on medical tourism that have employed questionnaire methods, the reason of low response is due to the stress of illness of their close ones. Therefore, results might not be fully accurate of the whole population because of hard-to-convince respondents and lack of a non response bias check. In addition, the sample profile is consistent with the demographics of residents of several south Odisha districts

Figure 7. Most people spent money between Rs 10000-15000. It includes accommodation, travel, medical fees, medicines, food etc.

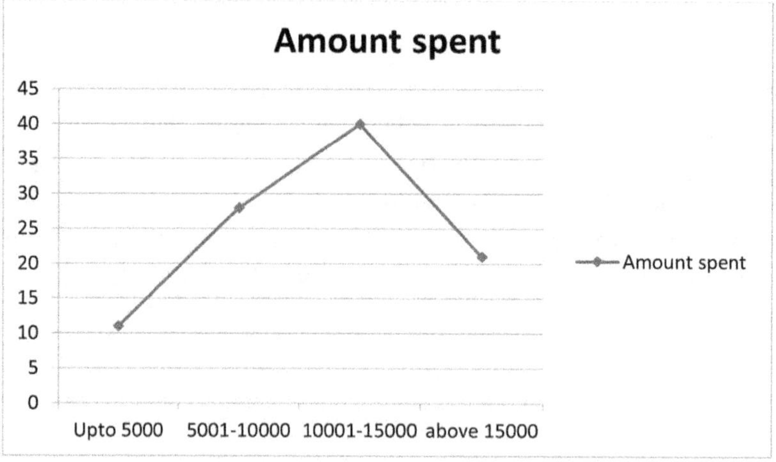

Figure 8. The domicile district of most of the respondents was South Odisha. They cited several reasons for this such as proximity to Vizag, lack of development in southern part, Vizag being the most famous tourist destination near to South Odisha etc. South Odisha includes Gajapati, Rayagada, Koraput, Nabrangpur, Malkangiri and Ganjam district.

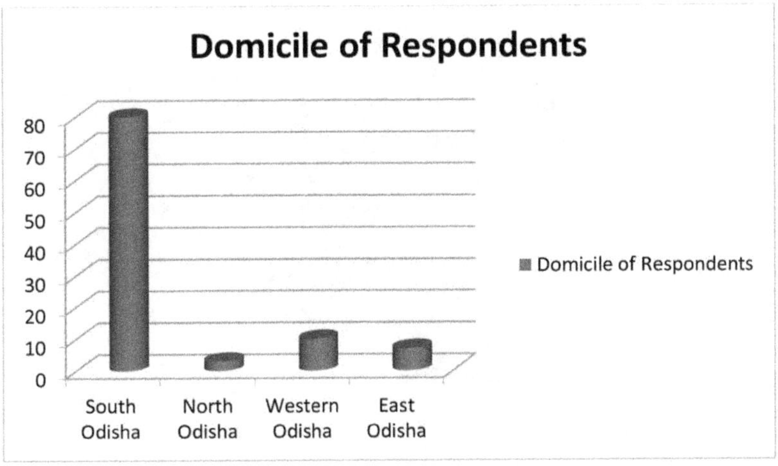

Figure 9. Mostly medical tourism was the reason given by respondents with a significant impact of perception on quality treatment available in comparison to South Odisha

Figure 10. Most respondents belonged to the middle class; many had even borrowed money and took loan for treatment of their family members

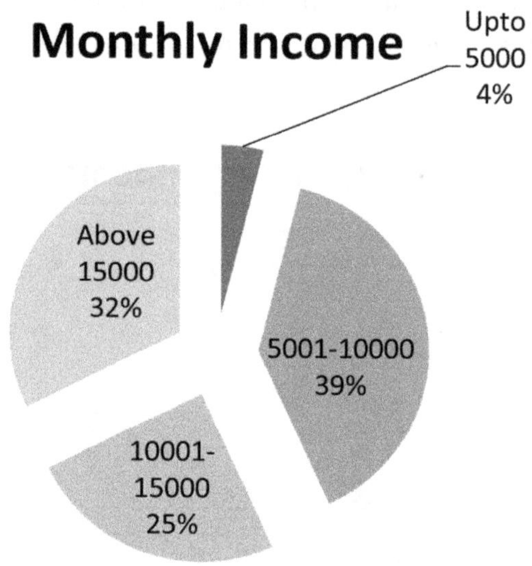

Figure 11. Most people visited Vishakhapatnam 2-3 times on an average for medical and tourism purpose

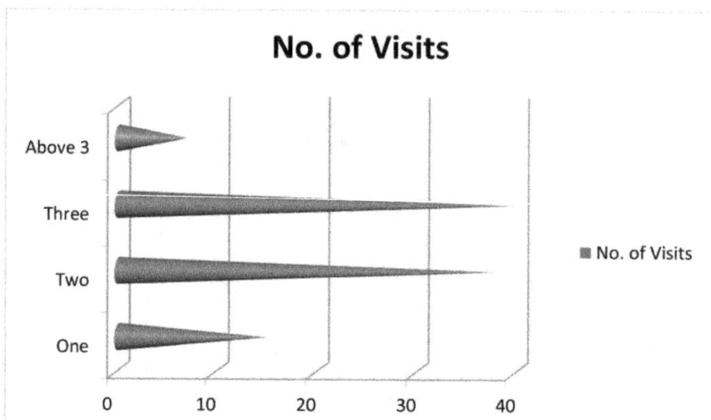

Figure 12. Most respondents came to a specific hospital due to word of mouth publicity, as many people of South Odisha visit the place they propagate the message to others as well. No respondent came through medical tourism operators.

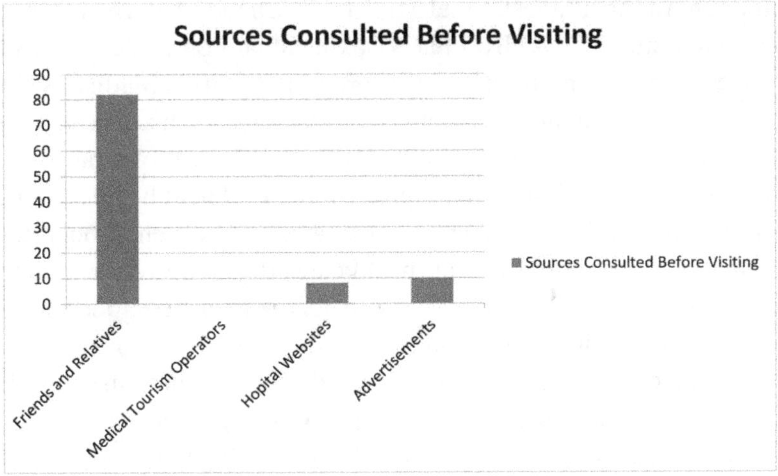

in state of Odisha; the survey instrument was administered in English only, which would have resulted in a lower sample size for this category. The actual behaviors may be different from self-expressed intentions.

CONCLUSION

In this chapter, the definitions and models of medical tourism need to be more encompassing and should include domestic medical tourists—particularly those crossing state boundaries and those traveling abroad for treatments.

With domestic medical tourism likely to expand under Indian healthcare reform, research is needed to identify existing barriers to such tourism and to provide a strong foundation for a domestic medical tourism strategy. Research is needed that can examine, in detail, both the medical and tourism sectors to find destinations most appropriate for medical tourism.

State involvement in development of the medical tourism industry is still awaited. More availability of data on medical tourism will help the city to flourish. Emphasis should be on medical tourism but over emphasis could result in poor health care for the locals. Hospitals and medical clinics need to differentiate themselves as there are many players. Accreditation of hospitals alone is not enough to attract medical tourists, marketing and facilitation plays an important role in maintenance of competitiveness.

In order to cater to international tourists visa on arrival is required and the infrastructure and support services should be of international standards. More direct flights to South East and Middle East nations can help medical tourists to directly arrive. Although Andhra Pradesh Chief Minister N. Chandrababu Naidu inaugurated AP Medical Tourism Hub (AMRIT) at Visakhapatnam on 21 June 2018 but a lot has to be done to implement the scheme. There is no certified Medical Value Travel Facilitator in Vishakhapatnam as per NABH statistics, which acts as a deterrent for medical tourism. The vast healthcare market is fueled by the proliferation of lifestyle diseases, changing population demographics, increased healthcare spending and a demand for better medical services, which has created unprecedented opportunities for Indian companies in medical tourism and healthcare provision. Overcrowded hospitals in India and patient complaints about high costs, poor services, poor facilities and widespread lack of trust in doctors and the healthcare system in general, is leading to India's medical tourism market grow at a rapid pace. Cultural dissimilarities with India such as language and food habits still persists in current scenario and strong competition from nearby countries like Thailand and Singapore because of relaxed visa norms and good flight connectivity is also seen.

REFERENCES

Carrera, P., & Bridges, J. (2006). Globalization and healthcare: Understanding health and medical tourism. *Expert Review of Pharmacoeconomics & Outcomes Research*, *4*(6), 447–454. doi:10.1586/14737167.6.4.447 PMID:20528514

Carrera, P., & Lunt, N. (2010). A European perspective on medical tourism: The need for a knowledge base. *International Journal of Health Services*, *3*(40), 669–684. PMID:20799671

Connell, J. (2006). Medical tourism: Sea, sun, sand and… surgery. *Tourism Management*, *6*(27), 1093–1100. doi:10.1016/j.tourman.2005.11.005

Crompton, J. (1992). Structure of vacation destination choice sets. *Annals of Tourism Research*, *19*(3), 420–434. doi:10.1016/0160-7383(92)90128-C

Crooks, V., Turner, L., Snyder, J., Johnston, R., & Kingsbury, P. (2011). Promoting medical tourism to India: Messages, images, and the marketing of international patient travel. *Social Science & Medicine*, *5*(72), 726–732. doi:10.1016/j.socscimed.2010.12.022 PMID:21310519

Fetscherin, M., & Stephano, R.-M. (2016). The medical tourism index: Scale development and validation. *Tourism Management,* (52), 539-556.

Goodrich, J., & Goodrich, G. (1987). Health-care tourism— An exploratory study. *Tourism Management*, *3*(8), 217–222. doi:10.1016/0261-5177(87)90053-7

Han, H., & Hyun, S. (2015). Customer retention in the medical tourism industry: Impact of quality, satisfaction, trust, and price reasonableness. *Tourism Management*, *46*, 20–29. doi:10.1016/j.tourman.2014.06.003

Hanefeld, J., Smith, R., Horsfall, D., & Lunt, N. (2014). What do we know about medical tourism? A review of the literature with discussion of its implications for the UK national health service as an example of a public health care system. *Journal of Travel Medicine*, *6*(21), 410–417. doi:10.1111/jtm.12147 PMID:25156070

Heung, V., Kucukusta, D., & Song, H. (2010). A conceptual model of medical Tourism: Implications for future research. *Journal of Travel & Tourism Marketing*, *3*(27), 1–30.

Hopkins, L., Labonté, R., Runnels, V., & Packer, C. (2010). Medical tourism today: What is the state of existing knowledge? *Journal of Public Health Policy*, *2*(31), 185–198. doi:10.1057/jphp.2010.10 PMID:20535101

Horowitz, M., & Rosensweig, J. (2007). Medical tourism - health care in the global economy. *Physician Executive*, *6*(33), 24–30. PMID:18092615

Inhorn, M., Shrivastav, P., & Patrizio, P. (2012). Assisted reproductive technologies and fertility 'tourism': Examples from global Dubai and the Ivy League. *Medical Anthropology*, *3*(31), 249–265. doi:10.1080/01459740.2011.596495 PMID:22540317

Lunt, N., & Carrera, P. (2011). Advice for prospective medical tourists: Systematic review of consumer sites. *Tourism Review*, (66): 57–67. doi:10.1108/16605371111127224

Medhekar, A. (2014). Government policy initiatives for developing sustainable medical tourism industry. *Journal on Business Review*, *3*(3), 267–283.

Ormond, M., & Sothern, M. (2012). You, too, can be an international medical traveler:reading medical travel guidebooks. *Health & Place*, *5*(18), 935–941. doi:10.1016/j.healthplace.2012.06.018 PMID:22809711

Saadatnia, F., & Mehregan, M. R. (2014). Determining and prioritizing factors affecting to increase customers attraction of medical tourism from the perspective of Arabic countries. *International Journal of Marketing Studies*, *3*(6), 155.

Singh, J., Cuttler, L., & Silvers, J. (2007). Toward understanding consumers' role in medical decisions for emerging treatments: Issues, framework and hypothesis. *Journal of Business Research*, (57): 1054–1065.

Smith, R., Martínez, Á. M., & Chanda, R. (2011). Medical tourism: A review of the literature and analysis of a role for bi-lateral trade. *Health Policy (Amsterdam)*, *2*(103), 276–282. doi:10.1016/j.healthpol.2011.06.009 PMID:21767892

Tribe, J. (1997). The indiscipline of tourism. *Annals of Tourism Research*, *3*(24), 638–657. doi:10.1016/S0160-7383(97)00020-0

Turner, L. (2007). "First World health care at third World Prices": Globalization, bioethics and medical tourism. *Biosocieties*, *2*(3), 303–325. doi:10.1017/S1745855207005765

Wongkit, M., & McKercher, B. (2013). Toward a typology of medical tourists: A case study of Thailand. *Tourism Management*, *38*, 4–12. doi:10.1016/j.tourman.2013.02.003

Ye, B., Qiu, H., & Yuen, P. (2011). Motivations and experiences of mainland Chinese medical tourists in Hong Kong. *Tourism Management*, *5*(32), 1125–1127. doi:10.1016/j.tourman.2010.09.018

Yeoh, E., Othman, K., & Ahmad, H. (2013). Understanding medical tourists: Word-ofmouth and viral marketing as potent marketing tools. *Tourism Management*, *34*, 19–201. doi:10.1016/j.tourman.2012.04.010

APPENDIX

Questionnaire

1. Name:________________________________
2. Accompanying Persons Up to 2 Up to 4 Above 4
3. Domicile District ________________________
4. Duration of Stay One day Less than a week More than a week More than a month
5. Purpose of Visit Medical Only Medical and Tourism
6. Type of Accommodation

Above 3 star Up to 3 star Nearby Lodges Dharamshalas

7. Amount spent

0-5000 5001-1000 10001-15000 Above 15000

8. Reason of visiting Vishakhapatnam

Low medical Expense Quality treatment Medical and tourism Lack of facilities in Odisha

9. Monthly Income

Upto 5000 5001-10000 10001-15000 Above 15000

10. No of Visits

One Two Three Above 3

11. Sources Consulted before Visiting

Friends and relatives Medical tourism Operators Advertisements
Hospital Websites

Chapter 7
Perspectives for Medical Tourism Development in Portugal's Central Region:
The View of Healthcare Stakeholders

Gonçalo Santinha
https://orcid.org/0000-0002-4732-5959
GOVCOPP, University of Aveiro, Portugal

Zélia Breda
https://orcid.org/0000-0002-5882-063X
GOVCOPP, University of Aveiro, Portugal

Vítor Rodrigues
University of Aveiro, Portugal

ABSTRACT

The European Directive 2011/24/EU establishes the rules for the access to cross-border healthcare to ensure the mobility of patients and promote cooperation between the different Member States. This study aims to understand its impact and the role that medical tourism can play in the healthcare context in Portugal. On the one hand, it makes a reflection on the challenges arising from its adoption, and, on the other hand, it discusses the possible impacts of its implementation, specifically in two sub-regions of the Central Region, and the role of medical tourism in light of the views of health policymakers and other local and regional stakeholders. The attractive conditions of Portugal translate into a potential destination for medical tourism; however, the transposition of the Directive reveals several weaknesses. Only through the design of a strategic plan of action, necessarily collective, participative, and accountable, that lists the supply, the potential demand, and priority options for the country and for each region, it is possible to effectively develop medical tourism.

DOI: 10.4018/978-1-5225-9787-2.ch007

INTRODUCTION

The growth of travel for health purposes had its beginning in the late 1990s, with an increasing number of individuals traveling, within and outside their countries of origin, pursuing specific medical treatments or any other therapies, as well as engaging in complementary and leisure activities (Connell, 2008). In fact, this type of travel can be traced back to the ancient times, namely the Roman period, due to the proliferation of thermal facilities and public baths throughout the entire empire (Jakšić- Stojanović, Janković, & Šerić, 2019). Nevertheless, the product known as health tourism, as well as its subcategories, is still a recent phenomenon.

Dunn (1959) stated, more than fifty years ago, the need for developing a new health paradigm in line with demographic, social, economic and policy changes. More recently, the widening of the "travel motivation basis" (Cunha, 2006, p. 79), as well as higher life standards, which generate new health challenges and, consequently, the need for improved physical, mental and psychological states/conditions, led to the multiplication or branching of tourism forms (Cunha, 2006), namely health tourism. In some way, these needs led to the globalization of healthcare, which, in turn, generated differentiated patterns of consumption and production of healthcare services (OECD, 2014). Due to an extended globalization process, the health industry started to generate visitors (patients) traveling from their origin country to the destination in pursuit of medical and non-medical (or prevention) treatments (Freitas, 2010; Henama, 2014; OEDC, 2014). Although being a secular activity, the increasing interest in healthy lifestyles (Charity, Walter, Forbes, Kumbirai, & Margaret, 2013) recently promoted the development of several concepts linked to health tourism, that "collide or cross with other pre-existing forms, giving rise to scenarios of conflict" (Cunha, 2006, p. 79). Charity et al. (2013) found that the term medical tourism was used to refer to both dimensions of health tourism (Lee & Spisto, 2007, cited in Charity et al., 2013) or, in a different approach, as a specific term meaning medical treatments (Pollock & Williams, 2000, cited in Charity et al., 2013). The health tourism concept is, however, in the great majority of the cases, established in the same theoretical framework and understood as a unifying concept from which two other crucial terms emerge: medical tourism and wellness tourism (Cunha, 2006; Mueller & Kaufmann, 2000; Smith & Puczkó, 2009; Yoong, Sulaiman, & Balday, 2013).

The health tourism sector has been growing due to the rising costs of medical treatments and healthcare in developed countries (Martins, Lunt, Freitas, Ribeiro, & Klein, 2014), long waiting lists, higher incomes, and improved human and technological resources and services in developing countries (Connell, 2008)[1]. This is clearly a great opportunity for developing countries, given that the globalization of healthcare services becomes obligatory (Martins et al., 2014).

Maybe because its poorly defined boundaries, it is difficult to measure the health tourism market. Nonetheless, it is estimated that 3-4% of the world population travels internationally for medical treatment and, in the European context, health motivation accounted for a total of 9.4 million trips in 2011 (IPK International, 2012). In terms of revenue, Martins et al. (2014) estimate a share of 20% for medical tourism and 80% for health tourism. SRI International (2010) has developed a model of the wellness industry that includes nine industry sectors, estimating that this cluster represents a market of nearly US$ 2 trillion dollars globally, revealing that the wellness tourism market has reached US$ 106 billion, more than double the size of the medical tourism market at US$ 50 billion.

The study of Beladi, Chao, Ee and Hollas (2017) confirms that medical tourism, on average, has a positive effect on host economies' output growth, particularly in non-OECD countries. Medical tourism, in fact, entails many opportunities, but European healthcare providers and decision makers have to face many challenges, including the implementation of the Directive 2011/24/EU, on the application of patients' rights with regard to cross-border healthcare. The rules for the access to healthcare are thus established, in order to ensure the mobility of patients and promote cooperation in this field between the different Member States[2]. In fact, the demand for cross-border care is not new, with mobility of patients already existing, to a greater or lesser extent, in different contexts. However, the Directive clarifies some dubious issues, particularly with respect to certain administrative procedures and reimbursement of healthcare costs incurred in another country, also introducing obligations to be met by each Member State in the provision of care and information to patients. The Directive makes it easier to access information on available healthcare in other European countries and alternative healthcare options, and/or specialized treatment abroad. The provisions aim the right balance between maintaining the sustainability of health systems, while protecting patients' right to seek treatment outside their home country. For that, the Directive (i) creates a network of National Contact Points to provide clear, accurate information on cross-border healthcare; (ii) creates rules on a minimum list of elements to be included in a medical prescription taken from one EU country to another (cross-border prescription); and (iii) encourages further development of European Reference Networks of medical expertise, broadening cooperation between EU countries, with added benefits to health technology assessments and e-health (European Commission, 2019).

This study aims to understand the impact of the cross-border healthcare Directive and the role that tourism can play in the healthcare context in Portugal. The increasing growth of tourism and hospitality industry in Portugal is now widely recognized for the country's economic contribution, representing about 18% of the country's global exports (Turismo de Portugal, 2017) and contributing to 13.7% of GDP (INE, 2018) in 2017. On the one hand, this chapter makes a reflection on the challenges arising from the adoption of the Directive, as well as the potential contributions, from a theoretical point of view, that medical tourism can produce in the healthcare context. On the other hand, it discusses the possible impacts of the implementation of the Directive in Portugal (in general) and in two sub-regions of the Central Region (in particular), and the role of medical tourism, in light of the views of health policy makers and other local and regional stakeholders. It is increasingly clear that this debate should occur, and this study seeks to contribute to it. A debate that necessarily mobilizes arguments and different stakeholders, but with a common background: the need to find solutions to the economic development of the country and of the regions, in order to take advantage of the excellent geographical conditions, climate, hospitality, tourist infrastructures and quality of healthcare.

The chapter is organized as follows: first, the literature on health tourism is reviewed, following which health tourism in Portugal as an export of healthcare services is addressed. Subsequently, the methodology used for the empirical study is described in more detail. Finally, research findings are reported and discussed, and their implications for further research and applications are highlighted.

LITERATURE REVIEW

Health Tourism

Considered as a segment of the tourism industry, the concept of health tourism is the result of some inconsistencies found in the literature regarding health, wellness and medical travel. The discussion seems to be related to the motivations or, in other perspective, to the activities or services that the visitor will enjoy in the destination. Connell (2008) considers that medical tourism, although being linked to direct medical treatments or interventions, should be the major concept to the detriment of health tourism. On the other hand, other authors defend health tourism as a unifying concept (Cunha, 2006; Mueller & Kaufmann, 2000; Smith & Puczkó, 2009). For Charity et al. (2010, p. 26), health tourism "is more appealing for branding purpose" and it also congregates all the travel motivated by health reasons that have been taking place since ancient times. In the same line of reasoning, Henama (2014, p. 3) considers that the "health tourism market is not limited to people travelling for medical procedures", but also for those seeking to enhance their beauty. Cunha (2006) summarizes these considerations by grouping, all the activities developed in order to provide a specific medical treatment/healing or to improve health, in a so-called 'umbrella' concept, i.e., health tourism.

Figure 1 illustrates the basis in which domestic and international healthcare travel experience is developed. First, health tourism, as a holistic concept (Smith &

Figure 1. The health tourism system
Source: Based on Charity et al. (2013); Mueller and Kaufmann (2000); Smith and Puczkó (2009); UNWTO and ETC (2018); Voigt et al. (2010)

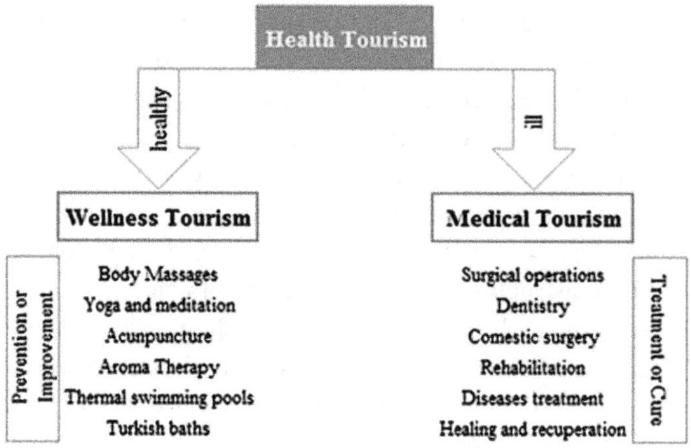

Puczkó, 2009), covers both wellness tourism and medical tourism (Caballero-Danell & Mugomba, 2007; Charity et al., 2013; Mueller & Kaufmann, 2000; Voigt et al., 2010), and comprehends those trips aiming to benefit from treatments, therapies or activities that improve and/or maintain health conditions (Bookman & Bookman, 2007; Caballero-Danell & Mugomba, 2007; Joppe & Choi, 2010; Tooman, 2013). As stated by Bookman and Bookman (2007), the term personifies the link between medicine and tourism.

According to the World Tourism Organization and European Travel Commission, health tourism is a form of tourism which have as a primary motivation the contribution to physical, mental and spiritual health of individuals, through medical and wellness-based activities (UNWTO & ETC, 2018). Although this helps to frame health tourism, there is no agreed definition of this type of tourism (Ridderstaat, Singh & DeMicco, 2019; Ross, 2001), nor its role and position are defined in the educational programs and curricula related to tourism (Savaşan, Yalvaç, Uzunboylu, & Tuncel, 2018). In addition, "participation in tourism either before or after treatments and the degree of participation [...] can be highly diverse and really depends on the types of treatments medical tourists have" (Hongnphadol, 2010, p. 77). Despite these shortcomings, this paper adopts the aforementioned view.

The increasing consciousness regarding health conditions, which stimulates people to adopt healthy lifestyles, but also the great economic growth, can be directly linked to the development of health tourism (Azman & Chan, 2010). In respect to the specific case of medical tourism, Connell (2008) identifies the same 'development' on consumers' mind, adding that the rising costs of medical treatments and healthcare, long waiting lists and better human and technological resources and services in developing countries, had a significant contribute to the emergence of a new globalization of healthcare. So, when a potential traveller buys a healthcare product, he/she is looking to get a typical tourism package that congregates the usual air transport, transfers and accommodation, but with two distinct components: treatment and postoperative vacation (Bookman & Bookman, 2007). As advocated by Novo (2014), the emergence of medical tourism was prompted by the internationalization of medical care, ranging from surgical operations to rehabilitation or dentistry services (Figure 1). Thus, Connell (2008) links the visitor to a direct medical intervention to outline medical tourism, in what seems to be a synthetical way to define it. Smith and Puczkó's (2009) contribution goes a little further, introducing the travel component and detailing the purposes. Therefore, medical tourism is described as the travel to a distinct place to achieve a specific cure for a disease, ailment or condition, taken by patients who are looking for lower costs, higher quality, better access and/or different healthcare. This definition highlights the 'requisite' to travel for medical purposes, i.e., being illness-oriented because the primarily travel motivation is related to cure or treatment of a particular illness or medical condition. According to Hallem, Barth and Triki (2010), this health tourism segment is a profitable activity for both developing and developed countries. In his research, Hongnaphadol (2010) corroborates this, by asserting that Asian countries, during the Asian economic crisis, considered medical tourism as a potential growth engine for the economy. Thailand was used as a case study to demonstrate the importance of medical tourism as a nuclear player to face off the currency collapse and rapid devaluation of the Thai baht. However, a study presenting an extensive and detailed research on medical tourism and its effects on the private health system in Thailand revealed that there is an evident need for the Thai government to consider carefully the overall cost of the "medical hub" policy (Noree, 2015). In the study of Beladi, Chao, Ee and Hollas (2017), it was unveiled that the output contribution of medical tourism is usually overestimated by an average of 26.8% if the unfavourable indirect productivity effect is not taken into account.

On the other hand, wellness tourism can be defined as the type of travel whose tourists who go on vacation aim to reach higher levels of wellness (Miller, 2005). The expression 'wellness' has distinct interpretations depending on the context. Regardless its diversity, in this study it is understood as a holistic concept of health, combining physical, mental, spiritual and social wellbeing (Miller, 2005). According to Joppe and Choi (2010), each individual has the responsibility for making lifestyle choices and self-care decisions in order to improve quality of life, achieving a superior level of wellness. This is also supported by Cunha (2006), setting human concerns with body and mind as influential factors to physical conditions and social inclusion. In parallel, he adds that total equilibrium (comprehending body, spirit and mind) can be achieved through beauty care, healthy nutrition, relaxation and mental activity. This sub-category of health tourism differs from medical tourism in several ways, being the first related to healthier conditions of the travellers. In Ross's (2001) perspective, this statement could be better explained in the way that wellness suggests helping healthy people prevent problems so that they stay well, both physically and mentally. Therefore, wellness tourism is the sum of all the relationships and phenomena resulting from a journey to a different place to proactively pursue activities that preserve or promote personal health and wellbeing (Mueller & Kaufmann, 2000).

Health Tourism in Portugal as an Export of Healthcare Services

Health tourism is one of the ten strategic products for tourism development defined in 2007 in Portugal. Despite this recognition, the number of tourists travelling to Portugal motivated by health reasons does not have a significant position in the global tourism panorama. The latest data highlights a market share of less than 2% or, approximately, 235 thousand health tourists (MEI, 2007). The absence of updated data is a big obstacle by disallowing a better understanding of the health tourism evolution and development in the Portuguese context. Nonetheless, it is possible to say that this product has been growing in Europe at an annual average rate of 7-8% since 2000 (MEE, 2013), providing scope for its development in Portugal[3]. In order to take advantage of this growth, Portuguese authorities should promote the country's competitive factors, namely (MEE, 2013): (i) a quality National Health System (NHS) (according to the World Health Organization, Portugal is the 12th country at the international level with a better health system); (ii) qualified professionals with international experience; (iii) international accredited hospital facilities; and (iv) a great number of spa and thermal facilities along with other natural resources with therapeutic characteristics.

Despite these so-called 'competitive advantages' and the promotion of health tourism as a strategic tourism product, there is no structured plan to stimulate it, nor it is possible to compete with other developed health tourism destinations. Despite being a small country, Portugal offers a great variety of natural characteristics that only satisfy one side of health tourism, thanks to exceptional conditions regarding natural resources (thermal and sea water), as well as wellness-oriented services (MEE, 2013). It is, therefore, essential for the promotion of this tourism product to take into account the determinants for its success. Being aware of the challenges promoted by the European Directive, it is expected a considerable advance on medical tourism practices, regardless the 'commitment' established on the National Strategic Plan for Tourism (Horizon 2013-2015).

To some extent, the investment on the medical tourism segment has already tangible components, due to private companies linked to healthcare services. Novo (2014) identified a set of health-related companies which developed projects oriented to the medical segment. From partnerships between Portuguese and Spanish hospitals, and online platforms that promote 'surgical vacations', to the development of integrated medical tour packages and also the idealization and subsequent implementation of networks involving different actors, such as health tourism operators, medical care services, hospitality, cultural, sport and leisure activities, these stakeholders could play a significant role within the health tourism segment.

A study sponsored by the Portuguese Entrepreneurial Association and by the Health Cluster Portugal, has concluded that health tourism could play a significant role, generating more than 400 million euros to the Portuguese economy in 2020 (Campos, 2014). In accordance with Martins et al. (2014), the conclusions of the study also set wellness tourism as the main source of revenue, while medical tourism should be responsible for, approximately, a fourth of the total. For the medical segment, United Kingdom, Germany and France are the target markets, but it is also argued that to attract them, the costs of medical procedures should be reduced, becoming more competitive. Regarding the wellness segment, the United States, Germany, Japan, France and Austria are positioned as the most important markets. In a global perspective, there is the need of Portuguese authorities to primarily adopt a strategy oriented to medical and therapeutic treatments where the destination is truly competitive, namely esthetical surgeries, arthroplasties and dentistry. It is also recommended to develop an 'all-inclusive' package that includes the clinical procedure, as well as the trip and the accommodation.

The law proposal providing for the transposition of the European Directive 2011/24/EU, on the application of patients' rights regarding cross-border healthcare, has been approved in 2014 by the Portuguese Council of Ministers on January 30. It is still not possible to predict the actual impacts emerging from the implementation of the Directive in the Portuguese context. However, to the best of our knowledge, there is no national strategy aiming to anticipate the risks arising from this 'market opening' in healthcare provision. In essence, it seeks to promote greater freedom of choice for patients and, simultaneously, increased competition among providers. This can endanger not only the quality of services and the timely access to healthcare, but also the decision of the country in becoming a healthcare exporter. That is, the benefits arising from healthcare export to the economic development of the territories (associated with an increased volume of healthcare and the emergence of other service activities) can, thus, be underexploited because the lack of a strategic vision and planning.

METHODOLOGY

In order to understand the impact of the cross-border healthcare Directive and the role that tourism can play in the health context in Portugal, a study was developed between 2012 and 2013[4] and comprehended two phases of data collection. Phase I consisted of face-to-face semi-structured interviews to 23 key actors in the area of healthcare, at the governmental level, as well as in central and regional administrations. The sample of the interviewed decision-makers comprised current and former health ministries and secretaries of state (from both social democrat and socialist governments), directors/presidents of central level institutions (e.g. Directorate-General of Health) and independent administration entities (e.g. Health Regulation Authority), and presidents of Regional Health Administrations. Consistency was addressed by means of interview topic guidelines to make sure that significant issues regarding the concept of governance were covered systematically (Table 1), while allowing participants freedom to describe their own experiences.

Phase II followed the same approach of phase I, with similar guiding questions. However, in this case, the analysis was centred in two NUTS III regions in the central region of Portugal: Baixo Vouga and Beira Interior Sul (Figure 2). From a methodological viewpoint, face-to-face semi-structured interviews were once more conducted as the principal source of primary data collection, in order to assess the challenges related to the phenomenon under study, but also the level of involvement and motivation of the different stakeholders. However, differently from phase I, in this case the type of actors chosen for the interviews varied, in order to receive feedback from regional and local structures that, even if indirectly, are usually referred to

Table 1. Thematic objectives (analytical domains) of the interviews and the analytical dimensions of the territorial cohesion principle

Analytic domain	Dimension	Subdimension	Purpose
Trade-off equity / efficiency and territorial dimension in healthcare	Territorial heterogeneity	disparities	Spatial justice
External factors to healthcare	Territorial organization	Urban system Urban / Rural	Balanced and networked urban development Proximity territorial integration
Healthcare as an export activity	Territorial heterogeneity	Diversity	Appreciation of territorial capital
Governance mechanisms in healthcare	Territorial governance	Vertical coordination Horizontal coordination	Multilevel governance Institutional cooperation and coherence of policies

Figure 2. Location of NUT II Centro Region and NUT III Baixo Vouga and Beira Interior Sul
Source: Adapted from INE (2012)

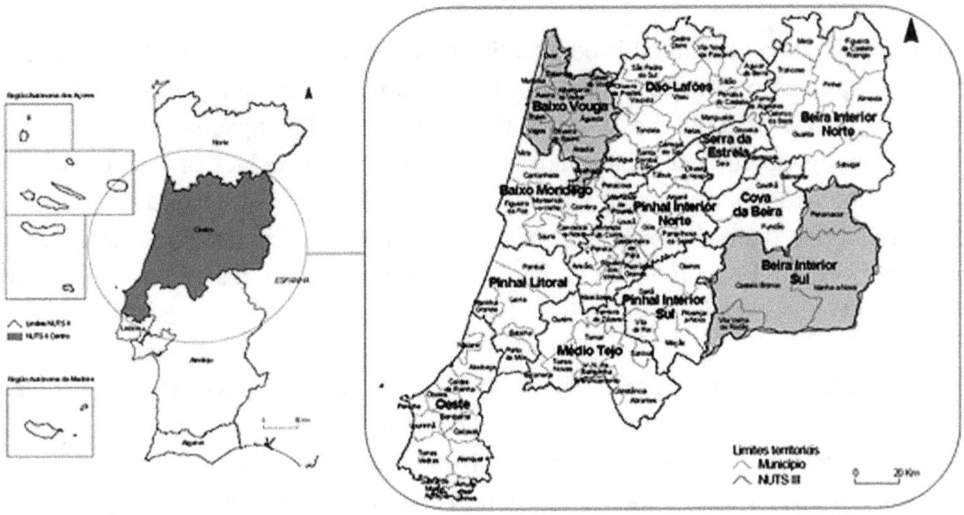

in the literature as also being involved in health policy-making, such as healthcare providers, city councils, universities and non-profit institutions with social purposes (*Misericórdias*). In this sense, a total of 12 interviews were conducted to key actors to understand the impact of the Directive and the role that tourism can play in the health context of Baixo Vouga and Beira Interior Sul regions.

It should be noted that this data collection falls within the context of a broader research, which intends to gain a deeper understanding of the construction process of health policies and on how the territorial component is considered, joining the perspective of combating disparities to the logic of territorial recovery.

This study is exploratory in nature and, therefore, presents a set of constraints that, in the future, should be taken into consideration so that the findings can be generalized. Reference should be made to three limitations in particular. Firstly, the fact that these results are within the scope of a broader scientific research, not specifically focusing on the topic under study, limited the depth of the discussion on this matter during the interviews. For this reason, and secondly, tourism entities linked to the development and promotion of health and wellness products were not auscultated. Their perception and point of view on the phenomenon under study is important for the effective link between healthcare, leisure and wellness, and tourism. Thirdly, the number of local and regional actors was limited, both in nature and in number, to effectively be able to move forward with concrete arguments about the role of health tourism in the region.

RESULTS

Phase I: National Level

From the discussion around this perspective on healthcare, the new reality resulting from the application of the Directive of cross-border healthcare was recurrently discussed. Given that little is known about the possible impacts in the national context, owing the current situation of uncertainty due to the lack of information at this level, sometimes the debate was centred in the history of the adoption process of the Directive itself, in the Portuguese positioning and in the characteristics of the health system. From the data gathered from health policy makers, it is possible to emphasize three main ideas:

- The Directive favours countries whose health system works through a social health insurance: *when operating in a reimbursement system (for example, the patient goes to a French private hospital or a French private doctor and is reimbursed by the social security), things do not change much: the protected market of healthcare providers in each country is thus seen in the perspective of a global market and the patient has a bigger range of choice. Therefore, the Directive will have a huge impact in countries that have a social health insurance (France, Germany, Netherlands ...). These are countries which, moreover, are in the same geographical area. In countries that have a national healthcare system model, many questions arise.*;
- The Directive focuses on healthcare providers and not on the users' needs: *the cross-border Directive looked at the concerns of providers and not of the patients and, as such, is a Directive that certainly has more risks to healthcare systems than benefits. It was designed more in the dominant perspective of the European thought of the Franco-German axis and, therefore, it is a healthcare system that certainly has nothing to do with us. But the biggest problem does not lie there: this approach involves more risks than benefits to users.*;
- Being a fait accompli, Portugal should have adapted to the Directive much quicker and in a timely manner: *at the time, three countries were against the Directive: Portugal, Spain and England. In practice, countries that have a public healthcare system. The problem is that Spain and England started preparing for it... Portugal did not!*

The discourse of the respondents then highlighted that the 'market opening' in healthcare entails both risks and benefits. The greatest risk lies in Portugal becoming more an importer of healthcare than exporter, i.e. the Portuguese population may go to other countries to seek health care services. This question, arising mainly from the fact that the NHS have a response time longer than expected, made six respondents to question the State's role in this process. And if, on the one hand, half of the respondents advocated a strong State intervention in the provision of healthcare in this cross-border perspective, either for the economic externalities or for a 'humanist' reason, on the other hand, other respondents expressed a different position, stressing the need for a strong (and only) involvement of the private sector in this area: *while the access constraints in the public sector are not resolved, it should be the private sector to invest in the Directive issue.*

Furthermore, the possibility to take advantage of the quality of healthcare professionals, the installed technical capacity, the country's geographical position and amenities is an opportunity that can and should be harnessed in the scope of this Directive. After all, as noted by one respondent, *either by threat or by opportunity it requires a very careful analysis of the pros and cons and the definition of a strategic plan of action to make it as advantageous as possible for Portugal and for the Portuguese citizens.* Another issue focused was the uncertainty that exists regarding the assurance of quality (e.g., dealing with malpractice or misleading advertising) and the international projection, which are crucial factors for Portugal place itself in this global matter.

The discussion on the Directive and the aforementioned benefits served as a starting point to bring out the role of health tourism in the interrelationship between healthcare and economic development. In this context, it was pointed out, on several occasions, that medical tourism (more directed to solving clinical problems and in close link with the issues brought by the Directive) should not be confused with health tourism (comprising both relaxation – spas – and some specialization – thermal spas with therapeutic abilities), although health tourism is generally used to encompass both concepts.

Regarding medical tourism, about a dozen of respondents stressed out that Portugal presents a set of key success factors that should be used and valued, in particular climate, geographical location, gastronomy and the quality of medical resources (skills, clinical practices and technologies). On the other hand, the country presents very satisfactory health and wellness indicators, which contributes to a good image of the country internationally. The target population and treatment costs are factors that clearly influence the demand and should also be considered. In relation to the target population, a minority of respondents focused on the importance of the Diaspora, to the extent that its ties with Portugal could encourage medical tourism. With regards to costs, the arguments presented by the minority who addressed this issue were not consensual. If, for some, the treatments made in Portugal are competitive at this level, other respondents think the opposite: *in terms of medical tourism, the key issue has to do with prices. Our healthcare private sector is expensive. And, therefore, the climate can be magnificent, as well as the food and hospitality, but prices must be competitive. There will always be hundreds of people who can think of coming under the current conditions, but there is no single health tourism project that can hold with just that number of potential patients / tourists.*

These questions about the success of medical tourism were also mentioned by other respondents, albeit by a minority. Three main aspects are important to retain:

- The quality of medical resources should be recognized and valued, not only domestically, but also by potential 'users' of medical tourism. It also was stressed the fact that this type of tourism is more directed to 'collective patients' (such as an intermediary entity – insurance company – responsible for health costs) than to patients that pay directly, given the type of clinic interventions and medical procedures that are likely to be more performed;
- The quality must be certified and mapped to better recognition. But this raises other questions: who certifies internationally, what are the deciding factors (price, quality ...), and how to disseminate the information (which should be reliable);
- To make medical tourism a reality, proximity care must operate in full, which is not currently the case. In this context, one of the respondents mentioned that: *medical tourism is very important, but the country is not prepared for it, because there is no proximity care. Tourists do not come here looking for a hospital. They come because of tourism, which means that there must be an approach to healthcare, organized in a way to provide security, trust... that is, to have communities prepared to meet the needs. Because they also have hospital care in their countries; they do not travel to Portugal to be hospitalized for a surgery.*

In the context of medical tourism, another issue was also addressed, albeit by a minority of respondents: can medical tourism be an opportunity to leverage low density territories through the use of natural resources? The (few) responses reveal that more importantly than the existing amenities is the quality of healthcare: *it is true that, in terms of the location of natural resources, the most interesting tourist attractions may be in more remote locations, we should not forget that intensive care units or other higher quality healthcare services are not located in these sites [...]. And a good hospital supply is also a means of attracting tourists.* Therefore, if medical tourism mainly focuses on hospital care, which is located in major urban areas, health tourism can be applied to more remote areas. However, these respondents believe that it is not in health tourism that the bet should be made.

Phase II: Regional and Sub-Regional Level

The Directive aiming to establish the rules for facilitating access to cross-border healthcare in the EU and promote greater mobility of patients was the central point of discussion for three of the respondents, stressing that the establishment of these new rules should be urgently and rapidly considered, not only from regional and local actors, but especially by policy makers, in order to determine a concerted policy response between the various actors associated with this issue, in particular the different healthcare providers. But if for these actors the Directive is something on which they are informed and have already reflected, one of the respondents mentioned that there are others who are not aware or informed about this issue.

Generally speaking, the actors who are informed about the Directive believe that this is an opportunity to be seized, particularly when associated with health tourism (Table 2). Despite everything, several questions were raised, both regarding equal access to healthcare services and in relation to the provision of services by the public sector, leaving a greater opportunity, in their opinion, for the private sector. In this context, the role of government was, albeit superficially, discussed by some of the actors, raising the question of whether the increase of patients from other countries would not overload public healthcare providers.

If for these actors the discussion on the Directive served as a motto to bring out the role of health tourism in the interrelationship between healthcare and economic development, for most respondents tourism was the main topic of conversation. And the opinions were unanimous: in general, the country has excellent conditions to take advantage of climate, hospitality and gastronomy, jointly with healthcare (medical specialization and general medicine) and the existing technology. Indeed, if it is possible to combine excellent medical services to amenities and the geographical location of the country, it is a window of opportunity that should be used to promote economic development.

Some reservations were addressed regarding the role of the State in this process, and the regions' context and conditions to respond effectively to this challenge. Concerning the first issue, the State must encourage and create the necessary conditions for the development of medical tourism, but always being aware of the effects that this may have on the NHS, particularly regarding the waiting time for patients. The idea is that this constitutes an investment opportunity mainly for private entities. Regarding the regions, several questions were raised: in the case of Baixo Vouga, although its attractive capacity was highlighted, essentially for geographical reasons (e.g. proximity to the sea and natural resources linked to the Ria de Aveiro), it was addressed the importance of healthcare quality and the strong positive image that providers must have internationally, which is not the case of the Hospital Centre of Baixo Vouga; in the case of Beira Interior Sul, it was noted that not only the existing

Table 2. Assessment of the cross-border healthcare directive and health tourism

Aspects evaluated as positive		Aspects evaluated as negative	
Evaluation domain	**Consensus level**	**Evaluation domain**	**Consensus level**
Diretive Installed technical and technological capabilities in terms of healthcare, amenities and geographical position of the country Experience demonstrated in the treatment of chronic patients from outside Portugal Government policies point to a bet in this area Private hospitals begin to position themselves well to respond to the challenge **Health tourism** Technical and technological capabilities in terms of healthcare, amenities and geographical position of the country, gastronomy and hospitality Aging population is an opportunity for senior tourism Expansion of thermal spas and spas	+++ + + + +++ + +	**Diretive** It is not morally acceptable to extend the waiting lists on the NHS Possible loss of users in the interior of the country to Spain High and non-competitive costs of medical interventions Lack of communication between different carers Late political reaction to the challenge Possibility to increase inequality of access to healthcare as it favours those who have more access to information and higher incomes **Health tourism** Reduced organization and integration of the various areas and respective actors that should work together It is not morally acceptable to extend waiting lists in the NHS Lack of practice and knowledge to respond efficiently and in an articulate way (tourism / health) Few policy orientations for health tourism	++ + + + + ++ ++ + +

amenities are more conducive to a different type of tourism more associated with thermal spas and hydrotherapy, but also there is not a willingness on the part of healthcarers to look with interest to this issue.

The assessment of healthcare as an export activity was tendentiously negative by the majority of respondents. It is true that, regarding the installed healthcare technical and technological capacities, the amenities and the country's geographical position, the opinions were overwhelmingly positive. In this point of view, Portugal is in a position to, not only be able to meet the challenge launched by the Directive, but also invest in medical tourism to promote economic and territorial development. However, the prospect of the NHS not being able to adequately respond to this opportunity (with consequences, for example, on the waiting lists), the reduced organization and integration of different areas, and the respective actors that should work together, or even the little political guidance for effective investment in this area, are factors that make these issues more difficult to deal with.

When the diagnosis is particularized to the sub-regions under study, it is widely recognized that in both cases there is no favourable conditions for effective commitment to medical tourism development and the response to the challenge posed by the Directive will have to be well thought out, because there is a set of strong barriers to an efficient immediate response. Briefly, the comments were:

- In the Baixo Vouga region, on a positive point of view, the characteristics of natural spaces and the geographical location were highlighted, being identified as barriers the reduced image of the region as healthcare provider (namely the Hospital of the Baixo Vouga) and the lack of organization and leadership to deal effectively with the issue under discussion;
- In the Beira Interior Sul region, respondents mentioned the good conditions for the effective development of senior and wellness tourism (spas and hydrotherapy), and, from a negative point of view, they highlighted the lack of resources (health professionals and infrastructure), medical differentiation and even the lack of medical expertise to make the region competitive at this level.

DISCUSSION AND POLICY IMPLICATIONS

Health tourism provides great opportunities for destination development in Portugal; however, it also entails challenges, namely to healthcare stakeholders, especially concerning the implementation of the Directive 2011/24/EU. The debate on the impacts of its implementation in the Portuguese context is still to deepen regarding its potential and its relevance as a tool for destinations' economic development. From the data gathered from health policy makers and from local and regional stakeholders, it is possible to emphasize three main ideas:

1. The application of the cross-border healthcare Directive entails a number of risks. First, the philosophy of the Directive, favouring countries whose health system works through a social health insurance, makes Portugal less competitive in this sphere. Secondly, the fact that the Portuguese government has not responded quickly to adapt to the challenges arising from the transposition of the Directive into the national context suggests a delay in the ability to overcome existing weaknesses and take advantage of any potential resulting therefrom for the country. Thirdly, given the response time of the NHS, which is lower than expected, Portugal may prove to be mainly an importer of healthcare, with the Portuguese population preferring to seek medical services in other countries.

2. Although it does not derive directly from the Directive, health tourism (in general) and medical tourism (in particular) can be differentiating factors in this interrelationship between healthcare and economic development. There is a common belief that the country has excellent conditions to take advantage of the good climate, hospitality and gastronomy, combined with healthcare (specialties and general medicine) and the existing technology. The combination of these factors with very satisfactory health and well-being indicators provides a good brand image, which is crucial to attract potential health tourists. According to respondents, another factor that clearly influences the demand is the treatments' cost (which must be competitive). Additionally, there is the question regarding the role that the State should play in this process. And the answer is not unanimous: if, for some respondents, there should be a strong intervention in the provision of cross-border healthcare – due the economic externalities or the right to healthcare –, for others, the State must create the necessary conditions for strong investment mainly coming from the private sector, focusing its attention on solving problems (e.g. reduction of waiting lists for treatment of patients). Therefore, the development of a strategy for the implementation of the Directive, which considers the relevant role of health tourism in the process, constitutes a window of opportunity to turn the challenge into a competitive advantage.
3. The depth of knowledge about this matter exhibits different degrees among health policy makers and local and regional stakeholders. Whilst to the former this question, globally, has deserved their attention, either because the positions they hold or their interest in the subject, for a good part of regional and local stakeholders this is a subject on which information is still vague. This suggests, firstly, that the discussion on this topic has been focused mainly at the decision-making level, which corroborates the argument that there is still a long way to go before the country is able to deal with this challenge, and, on the other hand, this information is mainly on the agenda of those who work directly in the health sector, since unawareness was mainly showed by actors who pursue their activity in areas other than healthcare. It is, thus, important to reflect on how the Directive and medical tourism are being discussed and how the processes of decision making, which a fortiori must be articulated, are conducted.

Generally speaking, the empirical analysis allowed to infer that an effective response to this issue implies the design of a national strategy for health (medical) tourism, with the development of studies on the potential demand and the existing supply, opening spaces for discussion, creating niche markets (competing for differentiation), defining new organizational forms by hospitals and enhancing existing infrastructure, also promoting communication between health institutions and the tourism sector. And public intervention should have a decisive role in boosting this effort: either in the design of the strategy, which should be combined with public policies formulated under other sectoral areas, or in creating instruments to promote the implementation of the formulated guidelines.

Another issue relates to the relationship between this type of tourism and low-density areas: can medical tourism constitute an opportunity to leverage low-density areas through the development of natural resources? Although this issue has not deserved special attention from the respondents, the arguments still show that more importantly than the existing amenities is the quality of healthcare. Therefore, the focus should be primarily on areas where specialised healthcare constitutes a reference, which tends to mostly happen in developed and densely populated territorial areas. The issue of quality of provided services received special attention from local and regional actors. In the sub-region of Baixo Vouga, for example, although its attractive capacity has been highlighted essentially for geographical reasons (e.g. proximity to the sea and natural resources linked to the Ria de Aveiro), the poor image of the Baixo Vouga Hospital Center was highlighted, making it difficult for the region to develop medical tourism. Similarly, the reduced number of health professionals and hospitals in Beira Interior Sul also hinders the potential of this region to develop this type of tourism. Therefore, it seems fair the idea that more remote areas that no longer are a reference in providing special healthcare should focus on wellness tourism, more associated with spas.

CONCLUSION

Healthcare services may support other economic activities, being complementary in relation to directly productive capital and even allowing generating an economic multiplier effect. An example lies in its strong links with tourism. First, because health care can play a decisive role for tourists, particularly the elderly, being a differentiating factor for destinations. Second, because health tourism has gained expression over the last decades due to health care high costs and long waiting lists in some countries (or the unavailability or low priority of specific treatments), higher incomes, new technology and skills in destination countries, alongside reduced transport costs and internet marketing. It concerns people travelling beyond national boundaries in search of specific treatments or operations, or the search for an improved physical and psychological well-being, or better health conditions in general. It is an economic activity that entails trade in services and represents the combination of at least two sectors: medicine and tourism. Presently, medical tourism is small in comparison to the overall service trade or the consumption of medical services or even the trade in tourism services. However, it is a growing product with enormous economic implications for destinations.

Regarding this issue, a new reality has emerged from the implementation of the cross-border healthcare Directive, which aims to establish rules to facilitate access to cross-border healthcare in the EU and to promote greater mobility of patients. From the empirical study it is clear that the depth of knowledge on this subject differs between health policy makers and local and regional actors in Portugal. In fact, while for the former this question has deserved their attention, either for their professional responsibilities or for their interest in the subject, for a good part of the local and regional stakeholders this is a subject on which information is still vague. This suggests, on the one hand, that the discussion on this issue has focused mainly on decision-making, which corroborates the argument that there is still a long way to go for Portugal to be able to deal with this challenge, and, on the other hand, that this information is fundamentally on the agenda of those who work directly in the healthcare sector. Although not deriving directly from the Directive, health tourism (in general) and medical tourism (in particular) can be differentiating factors in this interrelation of healthcare / economic development. The combination of excellent geographical, climatic and hospitality conditions with very satisfactory indicators of health and well-being, which also derive from medical care, symbolizes a good brand image abroad, a crucial issue for attracting potential health tourists. These are factors that clearly influence demand and to which two other issues must be added: the population to be attracted and the costs of treatments.

REFERENCES

Azman, I., & Chan, J. (2010, 1-3 September). *Health and spa tourism business: Tourists' profiles and motivational factors*. Paper presented at the conference "Health, wellness and tourism: Healthy tourists, healthy business?", Dalarna.

Beladi, H., Chao, C.-C., Ee, M. S., & Hollas, D. (2017). Does medical tourism promote economic growth? A cross-country analysis. *Journal of Travel Research, 58*(1), 121–135.

Bookman, M. Z., & Bookman, K. R. (2007). *Medical tourism in developing countries*. New York: Palgrave Macmillan.

Caballero-Danell, S., & Mugomba, C. (2007). *Medical tourism and its entrepreneurial opportunities: A conceptual framework for entry into the industry* (Master Dissertation). Goteborg University, Goteborg.

Campos, A. (2014, Abril). *Turismo de saúde e bem-estar pode render 400 milhões/ano*. Público.

Charity, M., Walter, M., Forbes, K., Kumbirai, M., & Margaret, N. (2013). Stakeholders' knowledge, attitudes and practises towards health tourism development in Zimbabwe. *Australian Journal of Business and Management Research*, *3*(2), 24–31.

Connell, J. (2008). Tummy tucks and the Taj Mahal? Medical tourism and the globalization of health care. In A. Woodside & D. Martin (Eds.), *Tourism management analysis, behaviour and strategy* (pp. 232–244). Wallingford: CABI Publishing.

Cunha, L. (2006). Turismo de saúde: Conceitos e mercados. *Revista Lusófona de Humanidades e Tecnologias*, *10*, 79–84.

Dunn, H. (1959). High-level wellness for man and society. *American Journal of Public Health and the Nation's Health*, *49*(6), 786–792. PMID:13661471

European Commission. (2019). *Cross-border healthcare*. Retrieved on July 8, 2019, from https://ec.europa.eu/health/cross_border_care/overview_en

Freitas, H. (2010). *Turismo médico: A globalização da saúde* (Master Dissertation). University of Porto, Porto.

Hallem, Y., Barth, I., & Triki, A. (2010, September 1-3). *Customer perceived value of medical tourism: An exploratory study – The case of cosmetic surgery in Tunisia*. Article presented at the conference "Health, wellness and tourism: Healthy tourists, healthy business?", Dalarna.

Henama, U. (2014). Health tourism in South Africa: Opportunities and possibilities. *African Journal of Hospitality, Tourism and Leisure*, *3*(1), 1–9.

Hongnaphadol, W. (2010, September 1-3). *An exploratory study of consumer choice and motivation of medical tourism in Thailand: A case study of healthcare consumers visiting a private hospital in Pattaya*. Article presented at conference "Health, wellness and tourism: Healthy tourists, healthy business?", Dalarna.

INE. (2012). *Anuário Estatístico da Região Centro 2011*. Lisboa: INE.

INE. (2018). *Conta Satélite do Turismo em Portugal: Destaque à comunicação social*. Retrieved on June 8, 2019, from https://www.ine.pt

International, I. P. K. (2012). *ITB world travel trends report 2012/2013*. Munich: IPK International.

International, S. R. I. (2010). *Spas and the global wellness market: Synergies and opportunities*. Retrieved on July 25, 2019, from https://www.sri.com/sites/default/files/publications/gss_sri_spasandwellnessreport_rev_82010.pdf

Jakšić- Stojanović, A., Janković, M., & Šerić, N. (2019). Montenegro as a high-quality health tourism destination: Trends and Perspectives. *African Journal of Hospitality, Tourism and Leisure*, *8*(3), 1–9.

Joppe, M., & Choi, H. (2010, September 1-3). *The evolution of attitudes towards spa holidays in Canada*. Article presented at conference "Health, Wellness and tourism: Healthy tourists, healthy business?", Dalarna.

Martins, A., Lunt, N., Freitas, R., Ribeiro, S., & Klein, U. (2014). *Atlas de oportunidades para o turismo de saúde e bem-estar*. Leça da Palmeira: AEP – Câmara de Comércio e Indústria.

MEE. (2013). *Plano Estratégico Nacional do Turismo: Horizonte 2013-2015*. Lisboa: Ministério da Economia e do Emprego.

MEI. (2007). *Plano Estratégico Nacional do Turismo*. Lisboa: Ministério da Economia e da Inovação.

Miller, J. (2005). Wellness: The history and development of a concept. *Spektrum Freizeit*, *1*, 84–102.

Mueller, H., & Kaufmann, E. (2001). Wellness tourism: Market analysis of a special health tourism segment and implications for the hotel industry. *Journal of Vacation Marketing*, *7*(1), 5–17.

Noree, T. (2015). *The impact of medical tourism on the domestic economy and private health system: A case study of Thailand* (PhD thesis). London School of Hygiene & Tropical Medicine. doi:10.17037/PUBS.02267963

Novo, A. (2014). *Internacionalização na saúde: O cluster do turismo médico em Portugal* (Master dissertation). University of Minho, Braga.

OECD. (2014). *Health at a glance: Europe 2014*. Paris: Organization for Economic Co-operation and Development.

Ridderstaat, J., Singh, D., & DeMicco, F. (2019). The impact of major tourist markets on health tourism spending in the United States. *Journal of Destination Marketing & Management*, *11*, 270–280. doi:10.1016/j.jdmm.2018.05.003

Ross, K. (2001). *Health tourism: An overview by Kim Ross*. Retrieved on February 25, 2015, from http://www.hospitalitynet.org/news/4010521.html

Savaşan, A., Yalvaç, M., Uzunboylu, H., & Tuncel, E. (2018). Article. *Quality & Quantity*, *52*(Suppl 1), 285–303. doi:10.100711135-017-0612-6

Smith, M., & Puczkó, L. (2009). *Health and wellness tourism*. Oxford, UK: Elsevier.

Tooman, H. (2013, May 24). *A framework for health tourism*. Article presented at conference "The future of health tourism: Creativity, innovation and sustainability", Parnu.

Turismo de Portugal. (2017). *Turismo em Portugal 2017*. Retrieved on August 14, 2019, from http://travelbi.turismodeportugal.pt/pt-pt/Documents/Turismo%20em%20Portugal/turismo-em-portugal-2017.pdf

UNWTO & ETC. (2018). *Exploring health tourism*. Madrid: World Tourism Organization.

Voigt, C., Laing, J., Wray, M., Brown, G., Howat, G., Weiler, B., & Trembath, R. (2010). *Health tourism in Australia: Supply, demand and opportunities*. Queensland: CRC for Sustainable Tourism Pty.

Yoong, W., Sulaiman, N., & Baldry, D. (2013, December). *A framework development for promoting medical tourism (MT to Malaysia using Internet strategy for international patient tourists (IPT)*. Article present at FPTP Postgraduate Seminar, Johor.

ENDNOTES

1 Psychological factors can be added, such as new concerns about illness prevention that prompted the appearance of several activities and products linked to wellness, prevention and physical recovery (Cunha, 2006).

2 Austria, Belgium, Bulgaria, Croatia, Republic of Cyprus, Czech Republic, Denmark, Estonia, Finland, France, Germany, Greece, Hungary, Ireland, Italy, Latvia, Lithuania, Luxembourg, Malta, Netherlands, Poland, Portugal, Romania, Slovakia, Slovenia, Spain, Sweden and the United Kingdom.

3 For example, the number of health tourists in Turkey grew from 74 to 156 thousand in the period of 2008-2011, due to a great promotion and investment in the country's health facilities (Campos, 2014).

4 Despite the study has been conducted between 2012 and 2013, during the last years there was no relevant changes in policies in the tourism and the healthcare sectors that could have significant impact on the study.

Chapter 8
Investigation of Alcohol Consumption Determinants in Turkey With Multinomial Probit Model

Ömer Alkan
https://orcid.org/0000-0002-3814-3539
Atatürk University, Turkey

İkram Yusuf Yarbaşı
https://orcid.org/0000-0003-4689-5121
Erzurum Technical University, Turkey

ABSTRACT

The main objective of this study is to determine key factors that may have a significant effect on alcohol consumption in Turkey. For this purpose, the cross-sectional data obtained from the Turkish Health Survey conducted in 2010 and 2012 by the Turkish Statistical Institute were analyzed through the multinomial probit model. Results revealed that several key variables were found to be a significant determinant of alcohol consumption, such as gender, age, education, marital status, income, general health status, tooth brushing frequency, situation of violence, fruit consumption frequency, tobacco use, exposure to tobacco smoke, and survey year. It is apparent that alcoholics need help to get rid of an addiction. Therefore, it would be inevitable for governments to intervene through national and international public health authorities. In particular, the ability of governments to design and implement comprehensive prevention strategies that combine the strengths of different policy approaches is critical to success.

DOI: 10.4018/978-1-5225-9787-2.ch008

INTRODUCTION

Alcohol is legal psychoactive substance that is widely used in the world and has addictive properties. Particularly, excessive alcohol consumption increases the probability of cancer, cardiovascular diseases and many other chronic disease occurrences, besides this is a reason for preventable premature deaths. The protection of the health of population by preventing and reducing the harmful use of alcohol is one of the main objectives of the governments. More alcohol use than alcohol consumption limits recommended by the National Institute of Health and Care Excellence (NICE) has been defined as the use of bad alcohol. It is stated that alcohol abuse can cause physical, psychological, economic and social negative effects on individuals in this situation.

Since extraction of alcohol from the body is slower than the absorption, it causes a structure that r drunkenness and intoxications that disrupt the normal functioning of the body. Excessive alcohol consumption can lead to undesirable consequences such as intoxication, accidents, violence and reduced productivity. It can also contribute to the development of cancer, brain, liver, heart and bone pathologies and mental disorders.

In 2012, nearly 3.3 million deaths or 5.9% of global deaths were associated with alcohol consumption. There are significant gender differences in the proportion of alcohol-related global deaths. For example, 7.6% of deaths among males in 2012 and 4% of deaths among females were alcohol-dependent. In 2012, there were 139 million lives that resulted in disability due to alcohol consumption. There is also wide geographical variability in the rates of alcohol-related deaths and disabilities.

In order to avoid the negative consequences of excessive alcohol use, governments and public health organizations have approved the rules of "sensitive drinking" globally. For example, NICE recommends that those who choose to consume alcohol on a regular basis should not exceed three to four units per day. The World Health Organization (WHO) states that alcohol use is the third most important risk factor that increases the burden of disease in developed countries. Besides, thanks to the alcohol policies they developed, governments aim to reduce the harmful use of alcohol and the health and social burden that can be linked to alcohol in society. Such policies can be formulated at a global, regional, multinational, national and sub-national level. Most of the countries that are members of the World Health Organization have been working to reduce the use of alcohol in recent years. The majority of reporting countries have implemented enacted national alcohol policies. High-rate tax or price implementation for the solution of the problem of excessive alcohol consumption has attracted great attention among public health experts and policy makers (Nelson, 2014).

Young adulthood, defined between the ages of 18 and 29, refers to a critical period of development in a person's life. It is evident that the health behaviors adopted by young adults in these ages will affect long-term body health, which will continue in the following years. Therefore, the positive habits they will gain during this period will have a positive effect on their overall health status. The health behaviors adopted by young adults not only have profound and long-term consequences for their health in their later lives but will play a crucial role in future generations when they become parents as well.

Average alcohol consumption per capita for adults remained almost constant in the last twenty years between 1992 and 2012, but an increase has been observed in the last five years. In young people, alcohol consumption is increasing, especially in low-income and middle-income countries (WHO, 2014). Some of the reasons for young people consuming more alcohol are low cost of alcoholic beverages, the presence of more extensive alcohol use areas, alcohol promotion especially for young people and in many societies these can be considered as the acceptable form of alcohol consumption.

Alcohol is the most ubiquitous psychoactive substance in the world and excessive alcohol consumption causes many health-related, social and economic problems. Alcohol consumption can result in negative effects on public health, the economy, productivity and society in general. Problems created by alcohol consumption are a major source of concern for developing countries such as Turkey. Alcohol consumption has become a prevalent problem among individuals and unless controlled could have critical or fatal consequences. For that reason, it is essential to investigate the underlying factors behind regular or excessive alcohol consumption. In this study, the aim is to detect socio-demographic, economic and personal factors as well as healthy-life indicators that affect alcohol consumption in Turkey. As a result, it will be possible to determine the effect of such factors on alcohol consumption. The unique aspects of this study are its focus on Turkey as a whole, having a large sample size and the simultaneous analysis of many different variables.

This study, which aims to examine determinants of alcohol consumption of adults in Turkey, consists of five chapters. In the second chapter, the literature review of the studies on determinants of alcohol consumption is shown. In the third chapter, the material-method of the study was examined and also the data, variables and statistical analysis methods used in the study were discussed. In the fourth chapter, the results of the estimation obtained through the multinomial probit model were analyzed, and interpretations were made over marginal effects. In the final chapter, policy recommendations were developed by taking the studies that coincide with the results obtained into account.

BACKGROUND

Alcohol is the third most important risk factor for global disease and disability. Approximately 4% of all deaths worldwide are due to the harmful use of alcohol. Alcohol, which is a causal factor in 60 disease types and injuries, is also associated with more than 200 diseases (Pathak & Kumar, 2016). The abuse of alcohol has caused a number of health problems, traffic accidents, suicides as well as the commission of crime and the deterioration of family integrity and has become a major problem both psychosocially and economically because it has a negative impact on some areas of the economy and business life (Ekuklu, Deveci, Eskiocak, Berberoglu, & Saltik, 2004).

Alcohol use, which affects the mortality rates of societies, also paves the way for economic costs, poverty, disruption of family dynamics and lessening of efforts to raise healthy individuals. In addition, the negative impact of alcohol and tobacco use is an area that needs to be examined in detail because it affects society, the cultural structure in society, and the social structure that extends to the economic process (Varona, Chang, García, & Bonet, 2011).

According to the OECD Health Statistics for 2016, Turkey ranks last among OECD countries with 1.3 liters per person for alcohol consumption among individuals over 15 years of age. In 2012, an average adult in the OECD country consumed 9.1 liters of pure alcohol per year. The highest alcohol consumption was recorded in Austria, Estonia, and France, where 12 liters and above are consumed per person per year. The lowest alcohol consumption was reported in Turkey and Israel. In countries such as Turkey, Israel, Indonesia and India, low alcohol consumption can be said to be associated with religious and cultural structure (OECD, 2015).

Again, in OECD reports, between 2008 and 2010, alcohol consumption for males and females in Turkey and European countries was compared. According to this, the ratio of alcohol consumption per capita for males and females aged 15 years and over in Turkey is 4.4 liters and 0.5 liters, which is lower than the average consumption value of countries in the European continent that is 10.6 liters. If we look at 2010 in Turkey, 15 years and older persons consume drinks in such portions as 63% beer, 9% wine and 23% whiskey, vodka, spirits such as raki that constitute luxury drinks. In Turkey, the ratio of the population of the heavy drinkers aged 15 years and over to the total population was 0.2%, and the ratio between alcohol users was 1.3%. In 2010, in Turkey, 65.9% of males age 15 years and older, 92.4% of females and 79.6% of both sexes did not use alcohol at all. 11.6% of men age 15 years and older, 2% of females and 6.7% of both sexes in total used to be drinkers.

ECONOMIC BURDEN OF ALCOHOL CONSUMPTION

There is an interdependency between alcohol abuse and the economic welfare of a society, country or region and the socio-economic health of its citizens. Damage to human health caused by alcohol consumption leads to an increased economic burden from unemployment, productivity loss, crime, traffic accidents, premature death, and the like. The social costs of alcohol consumption represent 9-24% of health sector costs (WHO, 2014).

Alcohol consumption plays a vital role in increased ratios of morbidity and mortality and creates a burden on the health service. To introduce effective strategies to minimize the losses caused by excessive alcohol consumption, it is essential to know how this behavior affects utilization of the health service (Miquel et al., 2018).

According to research conducted in the United States in 1992, the total cost of alcohol abuse was $148.021 billion. Based on inflation, increased population and miscellaneous factors the total economic cost was estimated to be $184.636 billion in 1998. The estimated total cost through productivity loss caused by alcohol-abuse was $134.206 billion (72.7%) and the total cost for health services was $26,338 billion (14.3%). A vast proportion (71.6%) of total health cost was caused by the medical consequences of alcohol consumption, a huge proportion (65.2%) of productivity loss stemmed from alcohol-relevant disease and the majority of the other effects (65.3%) were from traffic accidents (Harwood, Fountain, & Livermore, 1998).

The estimated economic cost of excessive drinking was $223.5 billion in 2006 (72.2% from lost productivity, 11.0% from healthcare costs, 9.4% from criminal justice costs, and 7.5% from other effects) or approximately $1.90 per alcoholic drink. Binge drinking resulted in costs of $170.7 billion (76.4% of the total); underage drinking $27.0 billion; and drinking during pregnancy $5.2 billion. The cost of alcohol-attributable crime was $73.3 billion. The cost to government was $94.2 billion (42.1% of the total cost), which corresponds to about $0.80 per alcoholic drink consumed in 2006 (categories are not mutually exclusive and may overlap). On a per capita basis, the economic impact of excessive alcohol consumption in the U.S.A is approximately $746 per person, most of which is attributable to binge drinking (Bouchery, Harwood, Sacks, Simon, & Brewer, 2011).

In Canada, the total annual cost of substance use in 2002 was computed as $39.8 billion. $14.6 billion dollars of the total cost was connected to alcohol abuse (death, disease, law enforcement, productivity loss etc.,) and $17 billion to tobacco use. In 2002, the share of alcohol consumption in direct health care costs was estimated to be $3.3 billion (Rehm et al., 2006). In another Canadian study into the direct and indirect costs in healthcare induced by Fetal Alcohol Spectrum Disorder, the estimated annual cost was measured at $344.2 million (Stade, Ungar, Stevens, Beyene, & Koren, 2006).

Alcohol addiction is another additional cost for communities. In a study focusing on Europe in particular, it was detected that alcohol addiction caused a huge economic burden in Europe. On a national level, direct costs in a year constituted 0.04-0.31% of a country's GDP and in 2012 the total cost was reported to range between one billion and 7.8 billion Euros (Laramée et al., 2013).

In Turkey, the amount spent on alcoholic drinks, tobacco products and cigarettes in 2007 was one trillion 22 million 760 thousand 174 ₺ and 2014 this sum jumped to 2 trillion 580 million 277 thousand 760 ₺. According to the Turkish Statistical Institute 2014 report on Turkish Household Budget Spending, households devoted 2.4% of their household budget to education, 2.1% to health, and 4.2% to alcoholic drinks, cigarettes and tobacco products. The total budget devoted to education and health is far lower than the amount spent on alcoholic drinks, cigarettes and tobacco products. Spending on alcoholic drinks, cigarettes and tobacco products increased each year from 2002 to 2014.

In Turkey, the total cost of alcohol consumption is 15.3 billion ₺ in a single year, far exceeding the budget of many ministries. In addition to tangible costs such as material damage, treatment costs, and labor costs, it is estimated that intangible costs bring the amount to around 31 billion ₺ (Varol, 2011).

LITERATURE REVIEW

As a consequence of the negative social effects of alcohol consumption, there is a vast body of research focusing on this issue. In these studies, researchers achieved significant results by analyzing specific determinant factors.

There are numerous studies on the effect of personal income on alcohol consumption (Barrett, 2002; French & Zarkin, 1995; Hamilton & Hamilton, 1997; Heien, 1996). In particular, earlier studies accentuated that the treatment of alcohol consumption as an external factor weakened the importance of the research. Some studies proved that individuals with low incomes are disposed to greater alcohol consumption (Bryden, Roberts, Petticrew, & McKee, 2013; Easwaran, Bazroy, Jayaseelan, & Singh, 2015; Vaeth, Caetano, & Durazo, 2014). However, other studies reported that those with higher incomes are disposed to greater alcohol consumption (Cheah & Rasiah, 2017; Grittner, Kuntsche, Gmel, & Bloomfield, 2012; Touvier et al., 2014). As proven by these conflicting results, there is no conclusive agreement on the effect of income on alcohol consumption. It has been suggested that this disagreement may be related to the socio-cultural differences in the regions in which the studies were executed. The region a person lives in and his culture determine the relationship between his income level and alcohol consumption.

Religion is classified as a significant variable determining perspectives towards alcohol and consumption levels. As a result, Christians were reported to consume higher amounts of alcohol than the followers of other religions (Auld, 2005; Burazeri & Kark, 2010; Clausen et al., 2005; Welcome, Razvodovsky, & Pereverzev, 2011). In Judaism and Islam, there is an emphasis on avoiding self-harm for reasons of health but compared to other faiths Christians tend to act in quite the opposite fashion. It has been reported that alcohol consumption - already low among Muslims - is particularly low during the holy month of Ramadan (Çelen, 2015).). It has also been suggested that observers of religious rules consume alcohol differently from those less faithful (Mangeloja, 2005). These studies confirm that among people whose religion bans alcohol there is a correspondingly lower level of alcohol consumption.

Some studies indicate that there is also a rise in alcohol consumption in parallel with tobacco consumption. Based on these studies, there is a unidirectional and significant relationship between the smoking and alcohol consumption habits of people aged 18 and above (Barrett, 2002; Cheah & Rasiah, 2017; Coulson et al., 2014; Dias, Oliveira, & Lopes, 2011; Easwaran et al., 2015; Moore et al., 2005). In some other research, the link between tobacco use and alcohol consumption was investigated based on gender. It was found that male smokers were more prone to alcohol consumption than females (Soler-Vila et al., 2014; Touvier et al., 2014).

Regarding marital status, it is suggested that because he has more responsibility a married individual would be more conscientious about self-harming behavior. In the same vein, it was determined that compared to single people married individuals were less likely to consume alcohol (Alavi, Mehrdad, & Makarem, 2016; Gius, 2005; Soler-Vila et al., 2014). However, the tendency for alcohol consumption was higher among divorced or widowed people (Vaeth et al., 2014).

Unemployment has always negatively affected human activity. The correlation between unemployment and alcohol consumption has been widely investigated by researchers (Lundborg, 2002; Tomkins et al., 2007). Researchers attest that once the responsibility of unemployment has been removed and the stress levels of the person peak there is a greater likelihood to consume alcohol (Andréasson, Danielsson, & Hallgren, 2013; Bryden et al., 2013; Chonviharnpan & Lewis, 2015; Mossakowski, 2008; O'Hare & Sherrer, 2006).

Education is a salient variable for the personal development of any human. It might be expected that highly educated people would be more responsible regarding alcohol consumption and so there would be a lower likelihood of self-harming acts among them. It has been postulated that with higher education levels there is a heightened awareness of the potential risks of alcohol consumption (Austin & Ressler, 2012). It is likely that individuals who have invested in their future would be less likely to damage that future with self-destructive behavior. Indeed, other studies reveal that the higher the level of education the lower the likelihood of alcohol consumption (Burazeri & Kark, 2010; Dias et al., 2011; Easwaran et al., 2015; Vaeth et al., 2014). However, contrary to common expectations, some studies underline the higher tendency for alcohol consumption among highly educated people (Huerta & Borgonovi, 2010).

There is a divergence between age groups and alcohol consumption in the researched regions. Some studies indicate that among elderly people the tendency for alcohol consumption is greater (Coulson et al., 2014; Dias et al., 2011; Easwaran et al., 2015; Zhou et al., 2006). In other studies based on a comparative analysis of gender, it was found that elderly males had a higher tendency toward alcohol consumption (Bonevski, Regan, Paul, Baker, & Bisquera, 2014), while among elderly females the opposite was observed (Vaeth et al., 2014). On the other hand, there were significant same-directional links between youth and excessive alcohol consumption (Andréasson et al., 2013; Grittner et al., 2012; Soler-Vila et al., 2014; Subady, Assanangkornchai, & Chongsuvivatwong, 2013).

In conjunction with the physical, psychological and financial damage of excessive alcohol consumption to the individual, certain results may jeopardize societal security. In a study examining excessive alcohol consumption among university students between 18 and 24, it was shown that alcohol consumption heightened crime rates. Each year, around 646,000 students faced abuse from alcohol consumers and 97,000 students were exposed to sexual harassment or rape. The data show that in the last twelve months roughly 1.2%-1.5% of university students attempted suicide due to alcohol or drug use (White & Hingson, 2013).

In some other studies in which determinants of alcohol consumption were extended, the aim was to measure whether alcohol consumption varied based on such variables. Andrews-Chavez, Lee, Houser, Falcon, and Tucker (2015) detected a negative relationship between Body Mass Index and alcohol consumption. Sjölund, Hemmingsson, and Allebeck (2015) postulated that people with low IQ scores tended toward excessive alcohol consumption. In contrast, Belasen and Hafer (2013) determined that there is a significant and positive relationship between high levels of alcohol consumption and high IQ scores. Dias et al. (2011) found a negative link between fruit and vegetable consumption and excessive alcohol consumption. Zhou et al. (2006) focused on city-village distinctions and pointed out that urban females had higher alcohol consumption than women in villages whilst men in villages had a higher tendency toward alcohol consumption. Vanassche, Sodermans, Matthijs, and Swicegood (2014) suggested that domestic problems played a role in alcohol consumption among female children. Coulson et al. (2014) concluded in their study that depression elevated the likelihood of alcohol consumption. Touvier et al. (2014) reported that compared to nondrinkers, alcohol drinkers had an increased risk for cancer. Yaogo, Fombonne, Kouanda, Lert, and Melchior (2013) found that those with a psychological disorder and a family member consuming alcohol posed a higher risk for excessive alcohol consumption. Vaeth et al. (2014), Mutalip, Kamarudin, Manickam, Abd Hamid, and Saari (2014) showed that ethnic roots played a role in shaping the alcohol consumption patterns of humans. Bryden et al. (2013) stated that increased alcohol consumption leads to higher crime rates.

MATERIAL AND METHOD

Data

In this study, data were employed from the Turkey Health Survey conducted by the Turkish Statistical Institute between 2010 and 2012. The objective in conducting the Turkey Health Survey was to provide data showing that health indicators play a significant role in the development level of countries and to fill a void in data shown in the existing structure.

All Turkish households were included in the scope of the sample selection. Populations termed as corporate (military personnel, permanent residents of dorms, prisons, hospitals, nursing homes etc.) were excluded from the sample. In addition, settlements where the population was below 1% of the country (small villages, hamlets etc.) thereby failing to provide an adequate number of households for the sample (population <132) were also excluded.

The stratified two-stage sampling method was employed in calculating the sample size for the Turkey Health Survey. The city-village division was used as the external stratification criteria (settlements with populations of 20,000 and below were categorized as villages, populations with 20,001 individuals and above were categorized as cities). The first-stage sampling unit was composed of blocks of approximately 100 households. The second-stage was composed of households systematically selected from each block.

The sampling size of the Turkey Health Survey was created to draw estimations of the entire country as well as the city and village base. For the design, the total sample size was selected as 7,886 households in 2010 and 14,400 in 2012. Among the households constituting the sampling size, 14,447 individuals from 2010 and 28,055 individuals from 2012 - a total of 42,502 individuals - constituted the data set of this study (TurkStat, 2010, 2012)

Variables

Employed variables in this research were selected from the questions in the Turkey Health Survey. A literature analysis was conducted to decide which variables to include in the model. The most widely used variables in the literature were then included in the model.

The dependent variable of the study is the state of alcohol use measured with questions "Have you ever used alcohol?" (Yes; No) and "Do you still drink alcohol?" (Yes, every day; yes, occasionally; I am not currently using). These two questions were combined into a four-choice variable, "yes, every day; yes, occasionally; s/he does not currently using; s/he did not use it at all."

The independent variables in the study were determined by conducting a literature review. Independent variables are, place of residence (urban, rural), age (15-24, 25-34, 35-44, 45-54, 55-64, and 65+), gender (male, female), educational status (literacy/read and write but not finished any school, primary school, elementary/secondary/vocational secondary school, high school, and equivalent schools, college/faculty/graduate/doctorate), marital status (never married, married, and wife died/divorced), monthly average income (less than ₺500, ₺501-1100, ₺1101-1700, ₺1701-₺2300, and ₺2301+), general health status (very good/good, medium, and bad/very bad), primary health care provider psycho-social support health care status (yes, no), tooth brushing frequency (1 time per day/2 or more, 1 time per week/more than 1, and never), body mass index (underweight, normal weight, overweight, and obese), fruit consumption frequency (at least once a day, at least once a week, at least once a month, and not at all), exposure to violence (severely, slightly, and not exposed), exposure to tobacco smoke at home (never, less than 1 hour per day, 1-5 hours per day, and more than 5 hours per day), survey year (2010, 2012), and tobacco use (yes, no).

Research Methodology

In this study, a multinomial probit regression model was employed to designate factors that affected alcohol consumption. In research that examines the links between dependent and independent variables, if the dependent variable is a qualitative variable, discrete choice models are employed. Since the dependent variable in this study is a four-category qualitative variable measurable in a nominal scale, it is viable to employ the multinomial probit regression model. Provided that the dependent variable has more than two categories, it is recommended to employ multinomial logistic regression or multinomial probit regression models. If assumption of independence of irrelevant alternatives is unavailable for the multinomial logistic regression model, the alternative multinomial probit regression model is recommended. In this research, since the key assumption of the multinomial logistic regression model could not be attained, the multinomial probit regression model was selected (Greene, 2012).

Multinomial probit model; zero mean, arbitrary variance-common variable matrix and common multivariate normal distribution are expressed as a coincidental utility function model with error terms. In this case, the variation of the error term in the multinomial probit model may be different and related (Daganzo, 1979). Although the multinomial probit model is one of the intriguing models of alternatives among the hidden benefits of the alternatives, the attractive models and the preference behavior models, it is not widely used in the literature since the problem of calculating the highest likelihood estimator in the application is encountered (Geweke, Keane, & Runkle, 1994).

The structural equations of the multinomial probit model are

$$U_{ij} = x_{ij}^{'}\beta + v,\ j = 1,\ldots,J,\left[\blacklozenge_{i1},\blacklozenge_{i2},\ldots,\blacklozenge_{iJ}\right] \sim \mathrm{N}\left[0,\pounds\right]. \tag{1}$$

The term in the log-likelihood that corresponds to the choice of alternative q is

$$Prob\left[choice_{iq}\right] = Prob[U_{iq} > U_{ij}, j = 1,\ldots,J, j \neq q]. \tag{2}$$

The probability for this occurrence is

$$Prob\left[choice_{iq}\right] = Prob[\blacklozenge_{i1} - \blacklozenge_{iq} < \left(x_{iq} - x_{i1}\right)^{'}\beta,\ldots,\blacklozenge_{iJ} - \blacklozenge_{iq} < \left(x_{iq} - x_{iJ}\right)^{'}\beta]. \tag{3}$$

for the J – 1 other choices, which is a cumulative probability from a (J – 1)-variate normal distribution (Greene, 2012).

RESULTS

Descriptive Statistics

Socio-economic and demographic variables are shown in Table 1. In this study, the total values of some variables are different due to the loss observation values. 73% of the individuals in the study reside in the city. The highest participation is in the 25-54 age group. While the percentage of males is 45%, the percentage of females is 55%. While 36% of individuals are primary school graduates, 12% are university graduates and higher education graduates. The rate of married people is about 70%. Approximately 40% of the individuals in the study have monthly net income of TL 501-1100. It was determined that 54% of the individuals have good health, 62% brush their teeth once or twice a day, and 43% have a normal weight. Also, 57% of individuals consume fruits at least once a day, while 67% consume vegetables at least once a day. It was determined that 23% of individuals are exposed to tobacco smoke for at least one hour or more a day.

Model Estimation

In the present study, the multinomial probit regression model was used to determine the factors that are effective in alcohol use in individuals over 15 years of age. The results of the estimated multinomial probit regression model are shown in Table 2.

In the estimated multinomial probit model, the state of "not used alcohol at all" was determined as the reference group. The coefficient cannot be interpreted from the estimated model, but only the signs of variables can be determined through this model. Table 3 shows the marginal effects estimated from the model.

According to the results of the analysis, gender has a significant effect on alcohol use. It has been determined that males are 0.3% more likely to drink alcohol every day than females and 9.5% more likely to use alcohol occasionally. When the age factor was examined, it was detected that individuals in 25-34, 35-44, 45-54 and 55-64 age groups have a higher probability of occasional alcohol use than individuals in 15-24 age group (4.3%, 5.7%, 5.8%, and 5.5%, respectively). It has been determined that the individuals 65 age years and older are 1.2% more likely to consume alcohol occasionally than individuals 15-24 years of age, and 11.4% are more likely to have used alcohol previously. Primary School, elementary, High School, and university graduates have been detected to be, more likely to consume alcohol occasionally than those who do not know how to read and write (8.6%, 12.2%, 16.4% and 24.3%, respectively).

It has been determined that singles are 2% more likely to use alcohol occasionally than the married ones. It has been determined that people who are widowed or divorced 3.1% more likely to use alcohol occasionally than the married ones. When monthly income was examined, it was discovered that those whose income is between ₺1101-1700 are 2.7% more likely to use alcohol occasionally than those whose income is less than ₺500. It has been obtained that those whose income is between ₺1701-2300 are 1.9% more likely to use alcohol occasionally than the reference group. It has been determined that those with the income of ₺2301 and above are 8.2% more likely to use alcohol occasionally than the reference group.

According to the general health status, it was discovered that those with moderate health status were 2.04% more likely to use alcohol occasionally than those with poor health status and those with good health status are 1.93% more likely to use alcohol occasionally than those with poor health status. It has been determined that the individuals who brush daily are 1.7% more likely to use alcohol occasionally than those who do not brush at all.

Table 1. Frequency of risk factors that are effective in alcohol use

Variables		f(%)	Alcohol Use n(%)				P*	
			Every day	Occasionally	Not currently using	Not used alcohol at allw		
Place of residence	Rural	11570(27.2)	44(22.8)	798(18.1)	1199(25.9)	9529(28.6)	0.001^c	
	Urban	30932(72.8)	149(77.2)	3613(81.9)	3425(74.1)	23745(71.4)		
Gender	Female	23290(54.8)	6(3.1)	1030(23.4)	1109(24.0)	21145(63.5)	0.001^c	
	Male	19212(45.2)	187(96.9)	3381(76.6)	3515(76.0)	12129(36.5)		
Age	15-24	7786(18.3)	15(7.8)	594(13.5)	470(10.2)	6707(20.2)	0.001^c	
	25-34	8507(20.0)	23(11.9)	1178(26.7)	796(17.2)	6510(19.6)		
	35-44	8374(19.7)	22(11.4)	1110(25.2)	919(19.9)	6323(19.0)		
	45-54	7426(17.5)	62(32.1)	899(20.4)	931(20.1)	5534(16.6)		
	55-64	5215(12.3)	54(28.0)	456(10.3)	790(17.1)	3915(11.8)		
	65+	5194(12.2)	17(8.8)	174(3.9)	718(15.5)	4285(12.9)		
Education	Literacy/ read and write but not finished any school	7334(17.3)	4(2.1)	81(1.8)	311(6.7)	6938(20.9)	0.001^c	
	Primary school	15319(36.0)	81(42.0)	1183(26.8)	1935(41.8)	12120(36.4)		
	Elementary/ secondary/ vocational secondary school	7774(18.3)	24(12.4)	746(16.9)	754(16.3)	6250(18.8)		
	High school and equivalent schools	7212(17.0)	45(23.3)	1171(26.5)	939(20.3)	5062(15.2)		
	College/ faculty/ graduate/ doctorate	4858(11.4)	39(20.2)	1230(27.9)	685(14.8)	2904(8.7)		
Marital status	Never married	9566(22.5)	31(16.1)	1118(25.3)	660(14.3)	7757(23.3)	0.001^c	
	Married	29250(68.8)	145(75.1)	3044(69.3)	3672(79.4)	22378(67.3)		
	Wife died/ divorced	3686(8.7)	17(8.8)	238(5.4)	292(6.3)	3139(9.4)		
Monthly average income	Less than ₺500	5026(12.0)	10 (5.3)	275 (6.3)	451 (9.8)	4290 (13.0)	0.001^c	
	₺501-1100	16449(39.1)	60 (31.6)	1154 (26.4)	1728 (37.6)	13507 (41.1)		
	₺1101-1700	9078(21.6)	47 (24.7)	957 (21.9)	1035 (22.5)	7039 (21.4)		
	₺1701-2300	4873(11.6)	21 (11.1)	581 (13.3)	560 (12.2)	3711 (11.3)		
	₺2301 +	6620(15.7)	52 (27.4)	1400 (32.1)	825 (17.9)	4343 (13.2)		

continued on following page

Table 1. Continued

Variables		f(%)	Alcohol Use n(%)				P*
			Every day	Occasionally	Not currently using	Not used alcohol at allw	
General health status	Bad/very bad	3848(9.1)	19(9.8)	144(3.3)	481(10.4)	3204(9.6)	0.001[c]
	Medium	10611(25)	49(25.4)	818(18.6)	1298(28.1)	8446(25.4)	
	Very good/ good	28025(66)	125(64.8)	3446(78.2)	2843(61.5)	21611(65.0)	
Psycho-social support	No	41996(98.8)	188(97.4)	4368(99.0)	4567(98.8)	32873(98.8)	0.165
	Yes	506(1.2)	5(2.6)	43(1.0)	57(1.29)	401(1.2)	
Tooth brushing frequency	1 time per day/2 or more	26538(62.6)	108(56.0)	3118(70.8)	2732(59.3)	20580(62.0)	0.001[c]
	1 time per week/more than 1	9633(22.7)	52(26.9)	906(20.6)	1234(26.8)	7441(22.4)	
	Never	6209(14.7)	33(17.1)	379(8.6)	644(14.0)	5153(15.5)	
Body mass index	Underweight	1519(4.0)	6(3.2)	108(2.5)	119(2.7)	1286(4.4)	0.001[c]
	Normal weight	16386(42.6)	89(47.1)	1911(44.4)	1713(38.7)	12673(42.9)	
	Overweight	13309(34.6)	63(33.3)	1638(38.0)	1760(39.7)	9848(33.4)	
	Obese	7218(18.8)	31(16.4)	649(15.1)	836(18.9)	5702(19.3)	
Fruit consumption frequency	At least once a day	24041(53.6)	114(59.1)	2574(58.4)	2736(59.2)	18617(56.0)	0.001[c]
	At least once a week	15009(35.4)	63(32.6)	1487(33.7)	1529(33.1)	11930(35.9)	
	At least once a month	2830(6.7)	10(5.2)	258(5.9)	283(6.1)	2279(6.9)	
	Not at all	574(1.4)	6(3.1)	88(2.0)	74(1.6)	406(1.2)	
Exposure to violence	Severely	337(0.8)	6(3.1)	51(1.2)	48(1.0)	232(0.7)	0.001[c]
	Slightly	764(1.8)	7(3.6)	105(2.4)	100(2.2)	552(1.7)	
	Not exposed	41312(97.4)	180(93.3)	4250(96.5)	4471(96.8)	32411(97.6)	
Exposure to tobacco smoke at home	Never	32718(77.0)	99(51.3)	3061(69.4)	3466(75.0)	26092(78.4)	0.001[c]
	Less than 1 hour per day	4578(10.8)	32(16.6)	538(12.2)	536(11.6)	3472(10.4)	
	1-5 hours per day	3985(9.4)	35(18.1)	596(13.5)	458(9.9)	2896(8.7)	
	More than 5 hours per day	1221(2.9)	27(14.0)	216(4.9)	164(3.5)	814(2.4)	
Tobacco use	No	31274(73.6)	53(27.5)	1742(39.5)	2676(57.9)	26803(80.6)	0.001[c]
	Yes	11228(26.4)	140(72.5)	2669(60.5)	1948(42.1)	6471(19.4)	
Survey year	2010	14447(34.0)	73(37.8)	1641(37.2)	1802(39.0)	10931(32.9)	0.001[c]
	2012	28055(66.0)	120(62.2)	2770(62.8)	2822(61.0)	22343(67.1)	

* p value is calculated according to two- tail Pearson χ^2 test; [c]p<.01

Table 2. Multinomial probit model analysis results

Variables		Every day		Occasionally		Not currently using		VIF
		β	Std. error	β	Std. error	β	Std. error	
Place of residence (reference: rural)								
	Urban	0.003	0.11	0.002	0.04	-0.025	0.04	1.16
Gender (reference: female)								
	Male	2.123[c]	0.20	1.125[c]	0.03	1.067[c]	0.03	1.27
Age (reference: 15-24)								
	25-34	0.245	0.21	0.390[c]	0.06	0.130[b]	0.07	2.95
	35-44	0.211	0.23	0.508[c]	0.07	0.215[c]	0.07	3.65
	45-54	0.985[c]	0.23	0.543[c]	0.08	0.365[c]	0.08	3.58
	55-64	1.299[c]	0.24	0.570[c]	0.09	0.590[c]	0.08	3.00
	65+	0.846[c]	0.27	0.311[c]	0.10	0.722[c]	0.08	3.16
Education (reference: literacy/read and write but not finished any school)								
	Primary school	1.111[c]	0.25	0.887[c]	0.09	0.779[c]	0.06	2.72
	Elementary/secondary/vocational secondary school	0.958[c]	0.27	1.086[c]	0.10	0.896[c]	0.07	2.69
	High school and equivalent schools	1.432[c]	0.26	1.351[c]	0.10	1.050[c]	0.07	2.60
	College/faculty/graduate/doctorate	1.706[c]	0.28	1.711[c]	0.10	1.226[c]	0.08	2.49
Marital status (reference: never married)								
	Married	0.195	0.16	0.128[b]	0.05	-0.292[c]	0.06	2.45
	Wife died/divorced	0.346[b]	0.16	0.250[c]	0.07	-0.060	0.06	1.20
Monthly average income (reference: less than ₺500)								
	₺501-1100	0.329[a]	0.18	0.078	0.06	0.012	0.05	3.09
	₺1101-1700	0.654[c]	0.19	0.258[c]	0.07	0.090	0.06	2.75
	₺1701-2300	0.196	0.20	0.183[b]	0.07	0.059	0.07	2.21
	₺2301 +	0.880[c]	0.20	0.675[c]	0.07	0.257[c]	0.07	2.21
General health status (reference: bad/very bad)								
	Medium	-0.117	0.17	0.159[a]	0.08	-0.133[b]	0.06	3.23
	Very good/good	-0.311[a]	0.16	0.107	0.08	-0.399[c]	0.06	3.76
Psycho-social support (reference: no)								
	Yes	0.472[a]	0.29	0.005	0.15	0.208	0.13	1.01
Tooth brushing frequency (reference: never)								
	1 time per day/2 or more	0.082	0.13	0.199[c]	0.06	0.159[c]	0.05	2.64
	1 time per week/more than 1	0.103	0.14	0.159[c]	0.06	0.233[c]	0.05	2.27
Body mass index (reference: obese)								
	Underweight	0.227	0.27	-0.083	0.10	0.028	0.09	1.32
	Normal weight	0.020	0.14	-0.058	0.05	-0.026	0.04	2.21
	Overweight	-0.168	0.13	-0.071	0.05	-0.022	0.04	1.94
Fruit consumption frequency (reference: at least once a day)								

continued on following page

Table 2. Continued

Variables		Every day		Occasionally		Not currently using		VIF
		β	Std. error	β	Std. error	β	Std. error	
	At least once a week	-0.032	0.10	-0.011	0.03	-0.023	0.03	1.10
	At least once a month	-0.022	0.18	0.079	0.07	0.050	0.06	1.09
	Not at all	0.601[b]	0.26	0.447[c]	0.12	0.310[b]	0.12	1.02
Exposure to violence (reference: not exposed)								
	Severely	0.622[b]	0.30	0.449[c]	0.16	0.447[c]	0.16	1.00
	Slightly	0.358[a]	0.21	0.218[b]	0.10	0.286[c]	0.10	1.00
Exposure to tobacco smoke at home (reference: never)								
	Less than 1 hour per day	0.467[c]	0.13	0.026	0.05	0.115[b]	0.05	1.08
	1-5 hours per day	0.443[c]	0.12	0.125[b]	0.05	0.048	0.05	1.10
	More than 5 hours per day	0.880[c]	0.15	0.353[c]	0.08	0.171[a]	0.09	1.06
Tobacco use (reference: no)								
	Yes	1.003[c]	0.09	1.043[c]	0.04	0.588[c]	0.04	1.32
Year (reference: 2010)								
	2012	-0.258[c]	0.08	-0.314[c]	0.03	-0.300[c]	0.03	1.04
Constant		-7.415[c]	0.45	-4.486[c]	0.15	-3.124[c]	0.12	

[a]p<.10;[b]p<.05; [c]p<.01

When the situation of violence is examined, it was assigned that individuals who are severely exposed to violence are 4.4% more likely to use alcohol occasionally than those who are not subjected to violence, and those who are exposed to some violence are 1.8% more likely to use alcohol occasionally compared to the reference group. It has been determined that those who are exposed to 5 hours of tobacco at home are 1.3% more likely to use alcohol occasionally than those who are not exposed to it and are 0.1% more likely to use alcohol every day. It was discovered that individuals who are exposed to smoking for more than 5 hours at home are 0.3% more likely to drink alcohol every day than those who do not. It has been determined that tobacco users are 11.9% more likely to use alcohol occasionally and are 0.1% more likely to use alcohol every day than the those do not use tobacco.

CONCLUSION

This study aims to examine the socio-economic determinants of alcohol consumption of adults in Turkey. For this purpose, the cross-sectional data obtained from the Turkish Health Survey conducted in 2010 and 2012 by the Turkish Statistical Institute were analyzed through the multinomial probit model. According to the analysis results, gender differences are one of the primary factors in alcohol use. All the age groups

Table 3. Marginal effects of variables affecting alcohol consumption

Variables	Every day		Occasionally		Not currently using		Not used alcohol at all	
	dy/dx	Std. error	dy/dx	Std. error	dy/dx	Std. error	dy/dx	Std. error
Place of residence (reference: rural)								
Urban	0.000	0.0001	0.0006	0.004	-0.003	0.005	0.0030	0.006
Gender (reference: female)								
Male	0.003[c]	0.0006	0.0949[c]	0.002	0.116[c]	0.004	-0.2150[c]	0.005
Age (reference: 15-24)								
25-34	0.001	0.0003	0.0425[c]	0.008	0.009	0.009	-0.0510[c]	0.011
35-44	0.000	0.0003	0.0570[c]	0.010	0.017[a]	0.010	-0.0740[c]	0.014
45-54	0.002[a]	0.0012	0.0580[c]	0.011	0.039[c]	0.012	-0.0990[c]	0.015
55-64	0.004	0.0025	0.0546[c]	0.012	0.077[c]	0.014	-0.1357[c]	0.017
65+	0.001	0.0012	0.0149	0.011	0.114[c]	0.017	-0.1305[c]	0.019
Education (reference: literacy/read and write but not finished any school)								
Primary school	0.001[a]	0.0007	0.0859[c]	0.012	0.091[c]	0.009	-0.1783[c]	0.013
Elementary/secondary/vocational secondary school	0.001	0.0008	0.1218[c]	0.016	0.108[c]	0.013	-0.2312[c]	0.017
High school and equivalent schools	0.002[a]	0.0015	0.1641[c]	0.018	0.124[c]	0.012	-0.2908[c]	0.017
College/faculty/graduate/doctorate	0.003	0.0025	0.2426[c]	0.023	0.135[c]	0.017	-0.3817[c]	0.020
Marital status (reference: never married)								
Married	0.001	0.0003	0.0199[c]	0.006	-0.039[c]	0.007	0.0188[c]	0.008
Wife died/divorced	0.001	0.0004	0.0309[c]	0.010	-0.013[a]	0.008	-0.0180	0.011
Monthly average income (reference: less than ₺500)								
₺501-1100	0.001	0.0003	0.0079	0.007	-0.0001	0.007	-0.0080	0.009
₺1101-1700	0.001[a]	0.0006	0.0270[c]	0.008	0.006	0.008	-0.0340[c]	0.011
₺1701-2300	0.000	0.0003	0.0193[b]	0.009	0.004	0.009	-0.0230[b]	0.012
₺2301 +	0.002[a]	0.0009	0.0819[c]	0.011	0.018[a]	0.009	-0.1010[c]	0.013
General health status (reference: bad/very bad)								
Medium	-0.001	0.0002	0.0204[b]	0.010	-0.020[c]	0.007	7.73e-06	0.012
Very good/good	-0.001	0.0003	0.0193[b]	0.008	-0.060[c]	0.009	0.0410[c]	0.011
Psycho-social support (reference: no)								
Yes	0.001	0.0010	-0.0042	0.015	0.030	0.020	-0.0270	0.024
Tooth brushing frequency (reference: never)								
1 time per day/2 or more	0.001	0.0001	0.0172[a]	0.005	0.017[c]	0.006	-0.0340[c]	0.008
1 time per week/more than 1	0.001	0.0002	0.0122	0.007	0.029[c]	0.007	-0.0410[c]	0.009
Body mass index (reference: obese)								
Underweight	0.001	0.0006	-0.0089	0.009	0.005	0.012	0.0030	0.015
Normal weight	0.001	0.0002	-0.0056	0.005	-0.002	0.005	0.0080	0.007
Overweight	-0.0002	0.0002	-0.0069	0.005	-0.002	0.005	0.0090	0.007

continued on following page

Table 3. Continued

Variables	Every day		Occasionally		Not currently using		Not used alcohol at all	
	dy/dx	Std. error	dy/dx	Std. error	dy/dx	Std. error	dy/dx	Std. error
Fruit consumption frequency (reference: at least once a day)								
At least once a week	-0.0000	0.0001	-0.0007	0.003	-0.003	0.004	0.0040	0.005
At least once a month	-0.0001	0.0002	0.0075	0.007	0.005	0.008	-0.0130	0.011
Not at all	0.001	0.0009	0.0490	0.018	0.034[a]	0.020	-0.0835[c]	0.025
Exposure to violence (reference: not exposed)								
Severely	0.001	0.0009	0.0440[b]	0.022	0.058[b]	0.028	-0.1025[c]	0.035
Slightly	0.0004	0.0045	0.0179	0.012	0.037[b]	0.017	-.05551[c]	0.020
Exposure to tobacco smoke at home (reference: never)								
Less than 1 hour per day	0.001[a]	0.0004	0.0002	0.005	0.015[b]	0.007	-0.0162[a]	0.008
1-5 hours per day	0.001[a]	0.0004	0.013[b]	0.006	0.004	0.007	-0.0170[a]	0.009
More than 5 hours per day	0.003[b]	0.0012	0.039	0.011	0.015	0.012	-0.0561[c]	0.016
Tobacco use (reference: no)								
Yes	0.001[c]	0.0004	0.119[c]	0.005	0.056[c]	0.005	-0.1765[c]	0.007
Year (reference: 2010)								
2012	-0.0002	0.0001	-0.027[c]	0.003	-0.034[c]	0.004	0.0609[c]	0.005

[a]p<.10;[b]p<.05; [c]p<.01

are effective in alcohol consumption. Income was detected to have a positive effect on alcohol use. One of the indicators for healthy life is fruit consumption frequency. It has been determined that the state of none-fruit consumption is a decisive factor in occasional alcohol use. The same-way relationship was found between alcohol consumption and psycho-social support for individuals who consume excessive alcohol and the inverse relationship was found between alcohol consumption of people who have good health status. Education has been shown to be effective in alcohol use in all groups. It has been determined that individuals with an income of ₺2500 and above tend to drink alcohol. It has been discovered that individuals who use tobacco tend to use alcohol.

In parallel with the results obtained by Burazeri and Kark (2010), Andréasson et al. (2013), Pärna, Rahu, Helakorpi, and Tekkel (2010), Grittner et al. (2012), Zhou et al. (2006), and Andrews-Chavez et al. (2015), the study determined that gender has significant effects on alcohol use. It is determined that males are more prone to alcohol consumption and dependency than females. Easwaran et al. (2015), Dias et al. (2011), Coulson et al. (2014), Vaeth et al. (2014), and Soler-Vila et al. (2014) reported that age has a significant effect on alcohol consumption. However, it is observed that the age group in which alcohol consumption is higher varies according to the regions where the study was conducted. In this study, adult individuals in particular are more likely to use alcohol occasionally compared to young people. While the findings Easwaran et al. (2015) and Dias et al. (2011) are similar, Vaeth et al. (2014) reported that young people tend to use more alcohol than older people. In most of the studies, it was perceived that the education variable was used. According to the study, the increase in educational levels also raises the possibility of an individual using alcohol occasionally. The findings obtained by Huerta and Borgonovi (2010) coincide with the results of the study, in their studies Easwaran et al. (2015), Burazeri and Kark (2010), and Vaeth et al. (2014) reported that people with low education tend to consume more alcohol. The increase in the income of the individual has been detected to have led to an increase in the probability of alcohol consumption. Similar results were obtained from the papers of Bryden et al. (2013), (Bonevski et al., 2014), and Çelen (2015)'s papers. The probability of alcohol consumption of tobacco users was also high. Alavi et al. (2016), Cheah and Rasiah (2017), Yaogo et al. (2013), Huerta and Borgonovi (2010), and Dias et al. (2011) found the same results in their studies and stated that the use of tobacco products in the individual increased alcohol use in the individual.

In the case of marital status, the probability of alcohol consumption of married and divorced or widowed spouses was determined to be higher than singles. Soler-Vila et al. (2014), and Martinez, Røislien, Naidoo, and Clausen (2011) in their study, they stated that married individuals are affected by alcohol consumption. Zhou et al. (2006) reported in their studies that divorced or separated people tend to consume alcohol.

Alcohol use is an individual choice, but it can have many social effects. In particular, excessive alcohol use can damage the individual's health, career, and personal relationships, as well as causing anti-social, violent behavior or traffic accidents, which can damage others.

It is apparent that alcoholics need help to get rid of an addiction. Therefore, it would be inevitable for governments to intervene through national and international public health authorities. In particular, the ability of governments to design and implement comprehensive prevention strategies that combine the strengths of different policy approaches is critical for success. Alcohol advertisements become uncontrollable because of use of the internet and social media. In particular, it is essential to reduce the probability of the young individuals to encounter these advertisements. It is seen that the sanctions used in the Prevention of alcohol use by individuals vary according to countries. This situation needs to be put into a certain standard and to be implemented worldwide.

FUTURE RESEARCH DIRECTIONS

The data in the study are a second hand source. The variables necessary for statistical analysis consist of variables present in data set. However, some variables missing from the data set such as individual's occupation, home ownership status, alcohol consumption status of parents, siblings, and other individuals at home, and exposure to alcohol commercials status were not taken into analysis. Since data are cross-sectional, definite causal relationship between smoking and related socioeconomic factors cannot be inferred. Since test measurements related to individual's alcohol consumption were not conducted in laboratory environment, the obtained data consist of individuals' personal responses. Because of that, data collected using this method can be biased. In future studies, consumption on different types of alcohol such as beer, champagne, raki can be determined. In addition, the study can be expanded by taking into consideration individuals with different stress levels and psychological problems.

ACKNOWLEDGMENT

This research received no specific grant from any funding agency in the public, commercial, or not-for-profit sectors. The authors would like to thank the Turkish Statistical Institute for the data. The views and opinions expressed in this manuscript are those of the authors only and do not necessarily represent the views, official policy, or position of the Turkish Statistical Institute.

REFERENCES

Alavi, S. S., Mehrdad, R., & Makarem, J. (2016). Prevalence of substance abuse/alcohol consumption and their predictors among patients admitted in operating rooms of a General Educational Hospital, Tehran, Iran. *Asian Journal of Pharmaceutical Research and Health Care*, *8*(S1), 63–71. doi:10.18311/ajprhc/2016/7651

Andréasson, S., Danielsson, A.-K., & Hallgren, M. (2013). Severity of alcohol dependence in the Swedish adult population: Association with consumption and social factors. *Alcohol (Fayetteville, N.Y.)*, *47*(1), 21–25. doi:10.1016/j.alcohol.2012.10.001 PMID:23084032

Andrews-Chavez, J. Y., Lee, C. S., Houser, R. F., Falcon, L. M., & Tucker, K. L. (2015). Factors associated with alcohol consumption patterns in a Puerto Rican urban cohort. *Public Health Nutrition*, *18*(3), 464–473. doi:10.1017/S1368980014000433 PMID:24713083

Auld, M. C. (2005). Smoking, drinking, and income. *The Journal of Human Resources*, *40*(2), 505–518. doi:10.3368/jhr.XL.2.505

Austin, W. A., & Ressler, R. W. (2012). Do designated drivers and workplace policies effect alcohol consumption? *Journal of Socio-Economics*, *41*(1), 104–109. doi:10.1016/j.socec.2011.10.013

Barrett, G. F. (2002). The effect of alcohol consumption on earnings. *The Economic Record*, *78*(240), 79–96. doi:10.1111/1475-4932.00041

Belasen, A., & Hafer, R. W. (2013). IQ and alcohol consumption: International data. *Intelligence*, *41*(5), 615–621. doi:10.1016/j.intell.2013.07.019

Bonevski, B., Regan, T., Paul, C., Baker, A. L., & Bisquera, A. (2014). Associations between alcohol, smoking, socioeconomic status and comorbidities: Evidence from the 45 and U p S tudy. *Drug and Alcohol Review*, *33*(2), 169–176. doi:10.1111/dar.12104 PMID:24372899

Bouchery, E. E., Harwood, H. J., Sacks, J. J., Simon, C. J., & Brewer, R. D. (2011). Economic costs of excessive alcohol consumption in the US, 2006. *American Journal of Preventive Medicine*, *41*(5), 516–524. doi:10.1016/j.amepre.2011.06.045 PMID:22011424

Bryden, A., Roberts, B., Petticrew, M., & McKee, M. (2013). A systematic review of the influence of community level social factors on alcohol use. *Health & Place*, *21*, 70–85. doi:10.1016/j.healthplace.2013.01.012 PMID:23454663

Burazeri, G., & Kark, J. D. (2010). Prevalence and determinants of binge drinking in middle age in a transitional post-communist country: A population-based study in Tirana, Albania. *Alcohol and Alcoholism (Oxford, Oxfordshire)*, *45*(2), 180–187. doi:10.1093/alcalc/agp089 PMID:20061509

Çelen, A. (2015). Influence of holy month Ramadan on alcohol consumption in Turkey. *Journal of Religion and Health*, *54*(6), 2122–2133. doi:10.100710943-014-9875-6 PMID:24810139

Cheah, Y. K., & Rasiah, R. (2017). Analysis of the determinants of alcohol consumption among adult males in Malaysia. *Journal of Health Management*, *19*(1), 28–38. doi:10.1177/0972063416682548

Chonviharnpan, B., & Lewis, P. (2015). The demand for alcohol in Thailand. *Economic Papers: A Journal of Applied Economics and Policy, 34*(1-2), 23-35.

Clausen, T., Romøren, T. I., Rossow, I., Ingstad, B., Molebatsi, R. M., & Holmboe-Ottesen, G. (2005). Patterns of alcohol consumption among older persons in Botswana. *Contemporary Drug Problems, 32*(2), 171–193. doi:10.1177/009145090503200202

Coulson, C. E., Williams, L. J., Berk, M., Lubman, D. I., Quirk, S. E., & Pasco, J. A. (2014). Association between alcohol consumption and self-reported depression among elderly Australian men. *Geriatric Mental Health Care, 2*(1-2), 3–8. doi:10.1016/j.gmhc.2014.09.001

Daganzo, C. (1979). *Multinomial Probit: The Theory and Its Application to Demand Forecasting*. New York: Academic Press.

Dias, P., Oliveira, A., & Lopes, C. (2011). Social and behavioural determinants of alcohol consumption. *Annals of Human Biology, 38*(3), 337–344. doi:10.3109/03014460.2010.548831 PMID:21434759

Easwaran, M., Bazroy, J., Jayaseelan, V., & Singh, Z. (2015). Prevalence and determinants of alcohol consumption among adult men in a coastal area of South India. *International Journal of Medical Science and Public Health, 4*(3), 360–364. doi:10.5455/ijmsph.2015.1010201479

Ekuklu, G., Deveci, S., Eskiocak, M., Berberoglu, U., & Saltik, A. (2004). Alcoholism prevalence and some related factors in Edirne, Turkey. *Yonsei Medical Journal, 45*(2), 207–214. doi:10.3349/ymj.2004.45.2.207 PMID:15118990

French, M. T., & Zarkin, G. A. (1995). Is moderate alcohol use related to wages? Evidence from four worksites. *Journal of Health Economics, 14*(3), 319–344. doi:10.1016/0167-6296(95)90921-R PMID:10145138

Geweke, J., Keane, M., & Runkle, D. (1994). Alternative computational approaches to inference in the multinomial probit model. *The Review of Economics and Statistics, 76*(4), 609–632. doi:10.2307/2109766

Gius, M. P. (2005). An estimate of the effects of age, taxes, and other socioeconomic variables on the alcoholic beverage demand of young adults. *The Social Science Journal, 42*(1), 13–24. doi:10.1016/j.soscij.2004.11.002

Greene, W. H. (2012). *Econometric analysis* (7th ed.). Boston: Pearson Education India.

Grittner, U., Kuntsche, S., Gmel, G., & Bloomfield, K. (2012). Alcohol consumption and social inequality at the individual and country levels—Results from an international study. *European Journal of Public Health, 23*(2), 332–339. doi:10.1093/eurpub/cks044 PMID:22562712

Hamilton, V., & Hamilton, B. H. (1997). Alcohol and earnings: Does drinking yield a wage premium? *The Canadian Journal of Economics. Revue Canadienne d'Economique, 30*(1), 135–151. doi:10.2307/136363

Harwood, H. J., Fountain, D., & Livermore, G. (1998). *The economic costs of alcohol and drug abuse in the United States, 1992*. Washington, DC: US Department of Health and Human Services.

Heien, D. M. (1996). Do drinkers earn less? *Southern Economic Journal, 63*(1), 60–68. doi:10.2307/1061303

Huerta, M. C., & Borgonovi, F. (2010). Education, alcohol use and abuse among young adults in Britain. *Social Science & Medicine, 71*(1), 143–151. doi:10.1016/j.socscimed.2010.03.022 PMID:20452109

Laramée, P., Kusel, J., Leonard, S., Aubin, H.-J., François, C., & Daeppen, J.-B. (2013). The economic burden of alcohol dependence in Europe. *Alcohol and Alcoholism (Oxford, Oxfordshire), 48*(3), 259–269. doi:10.1093/alcalc/agt004 PMID:23371284

Lundborg, P. (2002). Young people and alcohol: An econometric analysis. *Addiction (Abingdon, England), 97*(12), 1573–1582. doi:10.1046/j.1360-0443.2002.00231.x PMID:12472641

Mangeloja, E. (2005). Economic growth and religious production efficiency. *Applied Economics, 37*(20), 2349–2359. doi:10.1080/00036840500217531

Martinez, P., Røislien, J., Naidoo, N., & Clausen, T. (2011). Alcohol abstinence and drinking among African women: Data from the World Health Surveys. *BMC Public Health, 11*(1), 160. doi:10.1186/1471-2458-11-160 PMID:21392398

Miquel, L., Manthey, J., Rehm, J., Vela, E., Bustins, M., Segura, L., ... Gual, A. (2018). Risky alcohol use: The impact on health service use. *European Addiction Research, 24*(5), 234–244. doi:10.1159/000493884 PMID:30282079

Moore, A. A., Gould, R., Reuben, D. B., Greendale, G. A., Carter, M. K., Zhou, K., & Karlamangla, A. (2005). Longitudinal patterns and predictors of alcohol consumption in the United States. *American Journal of Public Health, 95*(3), 458–464. doi:10.2105/AJPH.2003.019471 PMID:15727977

Mossakowski, K. N. (2008). Is the duration of poverty and unemployment a risk factor for heavy drinking? *Social Science & Medicine*, *67*(6), 947–955. doi:10.1016/j.socscimed.2008.05.019 PMID:18573582

Mutalip, M. H. B. A., Kamarudin, R. B., Manickam, M., Abd Hamid, H. A. B., & Saari, R. B. (2014). Alcohol consumption and risky drinking patterns in Malaysia: Findings from NHMS 2011. *Alcohol and Alcoholism (Oxford, Oxfordshire)*, *49*(5), 593–599. doi:10.1093/alcalc/agu042 PMID:25015981

Nelson, J. P. (2014). Gender differences in alcohol demand: A systematic review of the role of prices and taxes. *Health Economics*, *23*(10), 1260–1280. doi:10.1002/hec.2974 PMID:23868570

O'Hare, T., & Sherrer, M. V. (2006). Stress, Recent Changes in Alcohol Consumption Level, and Problem Drinking in FreshmanFirst Offenders. *Journal of Human Behavior in the Social Environment*, *13*(3), 33–50. doi:10.1300/J137v13n03_03

OECD. (2015). *Tackling Harmful Alcohol Use: Economics and Public Health Policy*. OECD publishing.

Pärna, K., Rahu, K., Helakorpi, S., & Tekkel, M. (2010). Alcohol consumption in Estonia and Finland: Finbalt survey 1994-2006. *BMC Public Health*, *10*(1), 261. doi:10.1186/1471-2458-10-261 PMID:20482852

Pathak, N. K., & Kumar, P. (2016). Alcohol and tobacco use among male aged 15 year and above in urban area of Ghaziabad city, Uttar Pradesh, India: An epidemiological study. *International Journal Of Community Medicine And Public Health*, *3*(11), 3026–3029. doi:10.18203/2394-6040.ijcmph20163904

Rehm, J., Baliunas, D., Brochu, S., Fischer, B., Gnam, W., Patra, J., & Adlaf, E. (2006). *The costs of substance abuse in Canada 2002*. Ottawa: Canadian Centre on Substance Abuse.

Sjölund, S., Hemmingsson, T., & Allebeck, P. (2015). IQ and level of alcohol consumption—Findings from a national survey of Swedish conscripts. *Alcoholism, Clinical and Experimental Research*, *39*(3), 548–555. doi:10.1111/acer.12656 PMID:25702705

Soler-Vila, H., Galán, I., Donado-Campos, J., Sánchez-Alfonso, F., Valencia-Martín, J. L., Morilla, F., ... Rodríguez-Artalejo, F. (2014). Three-year changes in drinking patterns in Spain: A prospective population-based cohort study. *Drug and Alcohol Dependence*, *140*, 123–129. doi:10.1016/j.drugalcdep.2014.04.006 PMID:24799288

Stade, B., Ungar, W. J., Stevens, B., Beyene, J., & Koren, G. (2006). The burden of prenatal exposure to alcohol: Measurement of cost. *Journal of FAS International, 4*, e5.

Subady, B. N., Assanangkornchai, S., & Chongsuvivatwong, V. (2013). Prevalence, patterns and predictors of alcohol consumption in a mountainous district of B hutan. *Drug and Alcohol Review, 32*(4), 435–442. doi:10.1111/dar.12015 PMID:23231462

Tomkins, S., Saburova, L., Kiryanov, N., Andreev, E., McKee, M., Shkolnikov, V., & Leon, D. A. (2007). Prevalence and socio-economic distribution of hazardous patterns of alcohol drinking: Study of alcohol consumption in men aged 25–54 years in Izhevsk, Russia. *Addiction (Abingdon, England), 102*(4), 544–553. doi:10.1111/j.1360-0443.2006.01693.x PMID:17362291

Touvier, M., Druesne-Pecollo, N., Kesse-Guyot, E., Andreeva, V. A., Galan, P., Hercberg, S., & Latino-Martel, P. (2014). Demographic, socioeconomic, disease history, dietary and lifestyle cancer risk factors associated with alcohol consumption. *International Journal of Cancer, 134*(2), 445–459. doi:10.1002/ijc.28365 PMID:23824873

TurkStat. (2010). Health Survey 2010. Ankara: Turkish Statistical Institute Publication Number: 3654.

TurkStat. (2012). Health Survey 2012. Ankara: Turkish Statistical Institute Publication Number: 4117.

Vaeth, P. A., Caetano, R., & Durazo, E. M. (2014). Ethnicity and alcohol consumption among US adults with diabetes. *Annals of Epidemiology, 24*(10), 720–726. doi:10.1016/j.annepidem.2014.07.007 PMID:25169682

Vanassche, S., Sodermans, A. K., Matthijs, K., & Swicegood, G. (2014). The effects of family type, family relationships and parental role models on delinquency and alcohol use among Flemish adolescents. *Journal of Child and Family Studies, 23*(1), 128–143. doi:10.100710826-012-9699-5

Varol, M. (2011). *Alkol Raporu*. İstanbul: Türkiye Yeşilay Cemiyeti.

Varona, P., Chang, M., García, R. G., & Bonet, M. (2011). Tobacco and alcohol use in Cuban women. *MEDICC Review, 13*(4), 38–44. doi:10.1590/S1555-79602011000400009 PMID:22143606

Welcome, M. O., Razvodovsky, Y. E., & Pereverzev, V. A. (2011). Prevalence of alcohol-related problems among the Slavs and Arabs in Belarus: A University survey. *The American Journal of Drug and Alcohol Abuse*, *37*(3), 189–195. doi:10.3109/00952990.2011.563334 PMID:21453193

White, A., & Hingson, R. (2013). The burden of alcohol use: Excessive alcohol consumption and related consequences among college students. *Alcohol Research: Current Reviews*, *35*(2), 201–218. PMID:24881329

WHO. (2014). *Global status report on alcohol and health, 2014*. Luxembourg: World Health Organization.

Yaogo, A., Fombonne, E., Kouanda, S., Lert, F., & Melchior, M. (2013). Lifecourse socioeconomic position and alcohol use in young adulthood: Results from the French TEMPO cohort study. *Alcohol and Alcoholism (Oxford, Oxfordshire)*, *49*(1), 109–116. doi:10.1093/alcalc/agt128 PMID:23900495

Zhou, X., Su, Z., Deng, H., Xiang, X., Chen, H., & Hao, W. (2006). A comparative survey on alcohol and tobacco use in urban and rural populations in the Huaihua District of Hunan Province, China. *Alcohol (Fayetteville, N.Y.)*, *39*(2), 87–96. doi:10.1016/j.alcohol.2006.07.003 PMID:17134661

ADDITIONAL READING

Costanzo, S., Mukamal, K., Di Castelnuovo, A., Bonaccio, M., Olivieri, M., Persichillo, M., . . . de Gaetano, G. (2018). Impact of Alcohol Consumption upon Healthcare Utilization: Evidence from Moli-sani study. *European Journal of Public Health, 28*(suppl_4), cky213. 406.

Costanzo, S., Mukamal, K. J., Di Castelnuovo, A., Bonaccio, M., Olivieri, M., Persichillo, M., ... de Gaetano, G. (2019). Alcohol consumption and hospitalization burden in an adult Italian population: Prospective results from the Moli-sani study. *Addiction (Abingdon, England)*, *114*(4), 636–650. doi:10.1111/add.14490 PMID:30548347

Dall, T. M., Zhang, Y., Chen, Y. J., Wagner, R. C. A., Hogan, P. F., Fagan, N. K., ... Tornberg, D. N. (2007). Cost Associated with Being Overweight and with Obesity, High Alcohol Consumption, and Tobacco Use within the Military Health System's TRICARE Prime—Enrolled Population. *American Journal of Health Promotion*, *22*(2), 120–139. doi:10.4278/0890-1171-22.2.120 PMID:18019889

Degenhardt, L., Charlson, F., Ferrari, A., Santomauro, D., Erskine, H., Mantilla-Herrara, A., ... Griswold, M. (2018). The global burden of disease attributable to alcohol and drug use in 195 countries and territories, 1990–2016: A systematic analysis for the Global Burden of Disease Study 2016. *The Lancet. Psychiatry*, *5*(12), 987–1012. doi:10.1016/S2215-0366(18)30337-7 PMID:30392731

Delobelle, P., Sanders, D., Puoane, T., & Freudenberg, N. (2016). Reducing the role of the food, tobacco, and alcohol industries in noncommunicable disease risk in South Africa. *Health Education & Behavior, 43*(1_suppl), 70S-81S.

Nelson, E.-U. E. (2018). Alcohol consumption and related problems: Treatment and policy responses in Nigeria. *Journal of Substance Use*, *23*(4), 339–344. doi:10.1080/14659891.2017.1421271

Segura, L., Anderson, P., & Gual, A. (2018). Optimizing the delivery of interventions for harmful alcohol use in primary healthcare: An update. *Current Opinion in Psychiatry*, *31*(4), 324–332. doi:10.1097/YCO.0000000000000435 PMID:29846264

Sturm, R., An, R., Maroba, J., & Patel, D. (2013). The effects of obesity, smoking, and excessive alcohol intake on healthcare expenditure in a comprehensive medical scheme. *South African Medical Journal*, *103*(11), 840–844. doi:10.7196/SAMJ.7260 PMID:24148168

Urbanoski, K. A. (2003). The use of preventive healthcare by Canadian women who drink alcohol. *Preventive Medicine*, *37*(4), 334–341. doi:10.1016/S0091-7435(03)00141-5 PMID:14507490

Yan, T., Xu, H., Ettner, S. L., Barnes, A. J., & Moore, A. A. (2014). At-risk drinking and outpatient healthcare expenditures in older adults. *Journal of the American Geriatrics Society*, *62*(2), 325–328. doi:10.1111/jgs.12636 PMID:24417471

KEY TERMS AND DEFINITIONS

Binge Drinking: Four or more drinks consumed on one occasion for female and five or more drinks consumed on one occasion for male.

Cross-Sectional Data: The data collected from different units at a given moment of time is called cross-sectional data.

Dependent Variable: The dependent variable is the primary variable of the study. It is thought to be influenced by other variables.

Economic Costs of Alcohol: The price paid for alcohol consumption and cost of invisible expenses including expenses that seem such as material damage, treatment costs, and loss of labor.

Excessive Alcohol Consumption: It can be defined in two groups for female and male.

Healthcare Expenditures: Theoretically, health expenditures used in the calculation of health expenditures are expenditures for preventive, rehabilitative health services, medications and out-of-pocket payments.

Heavy Drinking: Eight or more drinks per week for female and 15 or more drinks per week for male.

Independent Variable: The independent variable is variable that affect the dependent variable. So, it is variable investigated and examined the effect.

Multinomial Probit Regression: It is a method employed in the analysis of categorical data. Multinomial probit regression can be utilized when the dependent variable has more than two categories. If assumption of independence of irrelevant alternatives is unavailable for the multinomial logistic regression model, the alternative multinomial probit regression model is recommended.

Statistical Model: The statistical model is a mathematical model for formalizing the relations between variables in the form of mathematical equations.

Chapter 9
Effects of Stress Management and Healthcare Issues

Pinki Paul
https://orcid.org/0000-0003-4964-3042
Sikkim Manupal University, India

ABSTRACT

Modern life is full of hassles, deadlines, frustrations, and demands. Stress is defined as perspective of mind or as mental health disorder. It is of equal importance compared with others in the 21st century. Stress management is a common phenomenon globally. The imbalance of any occasion creates stress. The most significant factors include separated from family, loneliness, fatigue, multi-nationality, limited recreation activity, and dissatisfaction of job opportunity, which tends to cause healthcare issues, especially sleep deprivation and depression. The long-lasting stress causes chronic mental fatigue. It has positive and negative impacts, which depend on situations. Sometimes it plays as a motivating factor for peak performance and great opportunity, or sometimes negative like when a person faces social, physical, organizational, and emotional problems.

INTRODUCTION

Stress

Stress is a rare preventable significance of modern goal-oriented life. Modern life is full of struggle, morbidity, disappointment, and demands etc. It has significantly impacted both ways of life; either positively in our lives or negatively in our lives. Stress is also a psychological factor behind that causing nervousness, anxiety like

DOI: 10.4018/978-1-5225-9787-2.ch009

many other mental health problems. So, one should concern how they control these managerial strategies like planning, organizing, finding. This application is really helpful for achieving goal to minimize the stress. In other words, if we find any misbalance occurs in job challenge, and thenone should need more strength and stamina, must speed their gaining power within timeperiod. Today's work stress is recognized universal as a considerable challenge to workers' health and the wellness of their organizations. People who are in stress they are not able to motivate in their work and less productive. Therefore, if employees are not able to give their best effort in work, organization cannot achieve their desire objectives. The current scenario of work requires faster and excellent quality of work with minimum time. Today, employer`s demands are best performance as both quality and quantity of work to achieve the target. Hence, to prohibit incomplete tasks, the outcome is stress. Always organizational process is long-term process, so during this procedure many employees feel degenerate with their work performance and mostly facing attention deficit disorder followed by depression(Jahanian, Tabatabaei, & Behdad, 2012).

As per psychology factors, decision making is significance as cognitive process. It is a belief of course of action within several possibilities. But in stress, employees are very limited to make any important decision;hence it is a reflection of motor activity process slow down and memory become weakened. As a result, interpersonal relationship isobstructing by conflict in the workplace, psychological panic occur in the workplace(Cropanzano, Howes, Grandey, & Toth, 1997).

Role of Management

Stress arises of many reasons like- demotivation, no-one care about the feelings, no support of colleagues, no time management, feeling nervousness to taking challenges, too much work load making mad etc.Research studies have proved that the *work performance decreases*, if employees are not find appropriate*working conditions* like*Bad lighting, noise, wrong temperature, lackof oxygen* and *insufficient or no air-conditioning*create *negative environment as depicted in figure 1.* Organizational culture is one of the key factorsin determining how successful an organization will be inmanaging work stress. It isalso consider in the attitudes of staffs, beliefsabout the organization, their shared value systems andcommon and approved ways of behaving at work. It is very important that pressure of overloaded work withindeadline conduct with lots of work could result under stress(Nekoranec & Kmosena, 2015).

The main causes of work related stress are as follows:

- Lack of management support
- Work related violence

Figure 1. Negative environment that creates stress

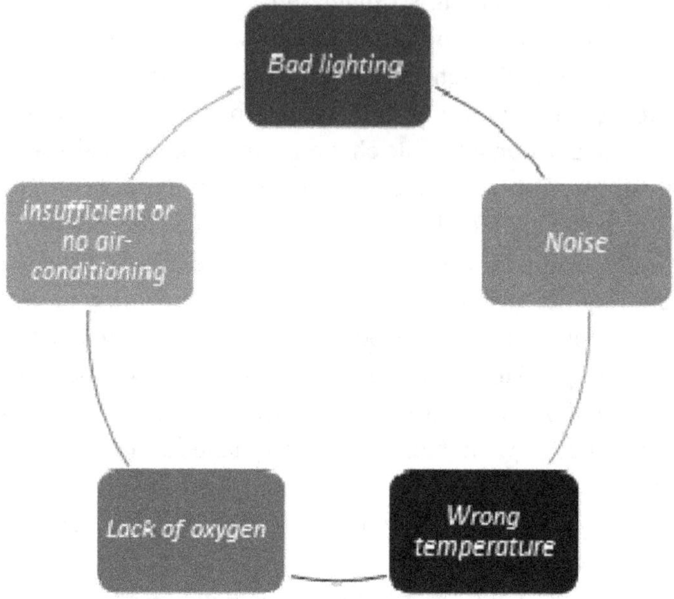

Employers, managers and trade unionrepresentatives must become aware of theculture of an organization, and build it strong relation tothe management of work stress. As per requisition, theseparties must involve in culture change activities if required, as animportant aspect of improving the management ofstress at workplace. Management plays a very crucial part of any organization for their consequential role. Moreover employees are asset of every establishment. Hence, manager should more focus on their satisfaction and motivational factors. When employees undergo in the work related stress and psychological difficulties, they usually tend to overlook the importance of work and failed to complete their assigned work during time period. Many times organizations are faced national economy deficit for employee's work related stress (McGonagle & Kessler, 1990).

Every establishment should appoint stress management team for reducing employee's stress relaxedness program, like planning, implementation, follow up, and evaluation. The management team must incorporate with occupational and environmental medicine (OEM) specialists, professional nurses. In this procedure, human resource department was tried to incorporate the suitable working place, communicate with employees and their intrinsic and extrinsic motivation factors, encourage workers to participate in the stress management program in the starting phase, provide some training program to motivate them, correlate between superior, subordinate and peers etc. Every work has own stress factor and it cannot be avoided.

Preferably, avoid fearing, taking action to manage this. Normally organization plan is a long term plan, during these strategies workers are faced threats are likely- Heavy targets and workloads, Poor communication, Insufficient resources, Lack of involvement, Long working hours, Poor delegation, Rapid change, Lack of trust in management, Conflicting priorities, Management style, Uncertainty/insecurity and Lack of control.

There are a number of organizational changes that managers and employers can make to reduce workplace stress. These include:

Improve Communication

- Share information with subordinates to reduce unpredictability about their jobs and futures.
- Clearly define employees' roles and responsibilities.

Consult Your Employees

- Give workers opportunities to participate in decisions making.
- Before conduct scheduling and work rules must consult with workers.
- Be sure the workload is suitable to employees' abilities and resources; avoid unrealistic deadlines.
- Offer rewards and incentives.
- Praise good work performance, both verbally and officially, through schemes such as Employee of the Month.
- Provide opportunities for career development.
- Promote an "entrepreneurial" work climate that gives employees more control over their work, suggest some orientation program so that they can improve their ability.

Create a Friendly Social Climate

- Social interaction among employees is created enthusiasm.
- Establish a policy for harassment.
- Make harmonious management actions with organizational value.

Physiological Aspects

When one`s perceive a threat, their nervous system responds by releasing a flood of stress hormones, including adrenaline and cortical. These hormones rouse the body for emergency action. Figure 2 describes that the heart beats faster, muscles rigidity,

Figure 2. Stress and it`s physiological effects

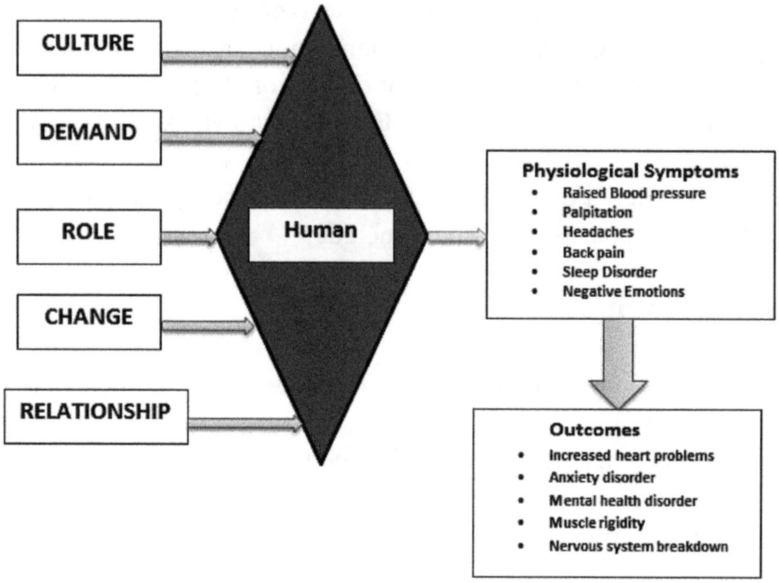

blood pressure rises, breath quickens, mental health disorders and senses become sharper(Nekoranec & Kmosena, 2015; Rekha Sahoo, 2016). These physical changes increase the strength, stamina and also speed up reaction time. There are two basic neurotransmitters involved with stress factor, like Dopamine and Serotonin. These neurotransmitters are rapidly changing with stress and other neuronal behavioral conditions. Dopamine plays an important role for bot movement, facial gesture and balancing of the human body. If the person having stress, so obviously the level will change and their movement will also unusual with normal pattern, gait cycle also changed. When a person used to face tough challenges or loosing desired achievements then the neuronal excitation takes place, neuronal firing occurs, as a result uncontrolled tremors, increased reflexes and body temperature increased. This is because of the level of serotonin changes and it is called serotonin syndrome.

OBJECTIVES AND METHODOLOGY

Many researches have been conducted into stress over the last decades. The main objective of the present research work is as follows-

1. Effect of stress.
2. Stress and anxiety management.

3. Technologies involvement to assess the stress
4. Identification the different methods & techniques for stress relief.

Data Collection and Sampling

The data was collected from primary as well as secondary sources. In this study we obtained data from male, female with age group of 25±10 years. The sample size was 70 in which 35 were male and 35 were female.

The primary data was collected by direct interview through questionnaires and face to face. The secondary data was collected from Journals, magazines and periodicals. The primary and secondary data collected was analyzed with the help of statistical tools.

RESULTS AND DISCSSION

The present study emphasizes on an analysis of data collected by representing it in tabular form.

From the table 1 we can directly getting the results between two groups like- persons having under stress and not under stress. The result showed that 77.2% of population among total of 70 nos. having under stress and 22.8% of total population having not under stress. The above results were mathematically calculated based on the questionnaires factors are Culture, Demand, Role, Change and Relationship.

In figure 3 represents that the male subject who are under stress in (blue colour) and not under stress in (red colour). Similarly in figure 4 represents those female subjects with the same colour combinations. Both the graphs were plotted as per the feedback received after face to face interview and questionnaire methods. It is very significant that the female gender group is under more stress than male. Among the total number of under stressed (54 no) the male subject was 23 and female was 31. Similarly, it was observed that the persons not having under stress is total of 16 (male 12 and female is 4).

Table 1. Represents the percentage of population

Category (Male and female together)	Respondents (Total= 70)	Percentage of respondents
Under Stressed condition	54	77.2%
Not under Stressed (based on their opinion)	16	22.8%

Figure 3. Represents the male subject responding the questionnaires

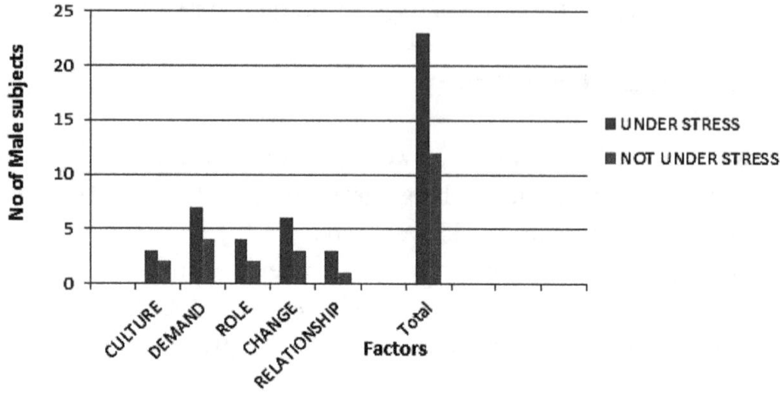

According to the previous gender group studies also proved that female are more talented than male to be involved in stress (Griffin & Moorhead, 2009). 47% of Americans are worry about stress. Females believe stress is more effective in them than male (%53 to %43). Female group who are under stress report feelings such as anger, desire to cry and physical weakness, while male group complain about difficulties in sleep, anger and sensitivity. According to past research also proved that female involve in high blood pressure, anxiety, depression and obesity more than male(Kazemi, 2007).

STRESS AND ANXIETY MANAGEMENT

Stress and anxiety share many of the same physical symptoms. From the outside looking in, it can be difficult to spot the differences between stress and anxiety. Both can lead to sleepless nights, exhaustion, excessive worry, lack of focus, and irritability etc. Even physical symptoms like- rapid heart rate, muscle tension, and headaches can impact both people experiencing stress and those diagnosed with an anxiety disorder. *Anxiety, on the other hand, is a sustained mental health disorder that can be triggered by stress.* It doesn't fade into the distance once the threat is mediated and also hangs around for the long haul, and can cause significant impairment in social, occupational, and other important areas of functioning. It is one of the popular forms of mental illness. If anyone wants to be healthy without anxiety problem, research studies suggest that healthy eating, are aware of smoking and drinking alcohol, exercise, time take out, be mindful, get some restful sleep, take a few minutes every day to appreciate. Sometimes stress can be positive impact for the work, it stimulates better performance; as a result one who get their better

Figure 4. Represents the female subject responding the questionnaires

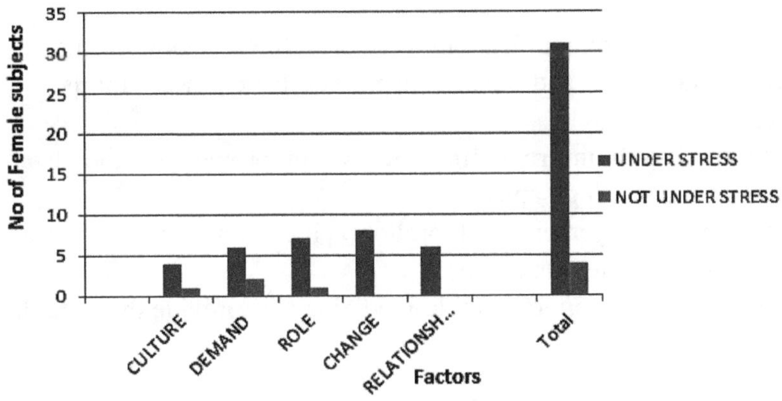

achievement. Hence, employees will be happy with their performance, their mental satisfaction works and stress may overcome.so physical health and mental health is interrelated.Hypnotherapy for anxiety works at a subconscious level to create more calming and empowering patterns of thought and feeling. During a session of hypnosis for anxiety management, one will literally get to experience the relief, desire and be given the ability to recreate that experience whenever they need or want.

TECHNOLOGIES INVOLVEMENT FOR ASSESSMENT OF STRESS

The following technologies are involved for assessment of stress. Researchers suggest that there are a number of emotional and physical disorders linked to stress(Koncul, 2012).

Data Recording

These data can be directly recorded from the subject under stress. The results prove that the person stress level and risk factors. Using different technology we can assess the stress.

- Body measurement
- Electrophysiological measures
- Sleep studies
- Bioenergetics testing

Data Analysis and Knowledge Management

- Information and communications technology plays a vital role in 21st century, where social media and email can provide better assess the person having stress.
- Electronic health information systems can provide us the data through e-governess or through apps.
- Knowledge management and bibliographical databases can lead us the database for the stress in a zone.
- Clinical decision support and tele-medicine also provide the suitable support for assessing the stress.

Direct Questioning

Sometimes researchers ask questions to the persons having stress through formal and informal medical history on current and past illnesses, family, occupational, travel, dietary, lifestyle, and sex details.

Tissue Sampling

This is related with biophysical parameters like- blood and urine analysis; hair, sweat, semen, breast milk, ear wax, finger nails and tissue biopsies etc.

Functional Testing

There are certain functional testing like- lung functions, cognitive performance, auditory and visual function as well as fitness assessment, cardiovascular stress testing, nutritional challenge tests etc. can be done to assess the stress.

IDENTIFICATION OF THE DIFFERENT METHODS AND TECHNIQUES FOR STRESS RELIEF (PANIGRAHI, 2017)

Spa

Spa treatments and massage therapies, which are quick and relatively affordable, create both mental and physical health benefits. In fact, studies have shown that the frequency of visiting a spa directly correlates with better quality sleep, fewer sick days, reduced absenteeism from work and fewer hospitalizations. The popularity

Figure 5. Stress relief factors

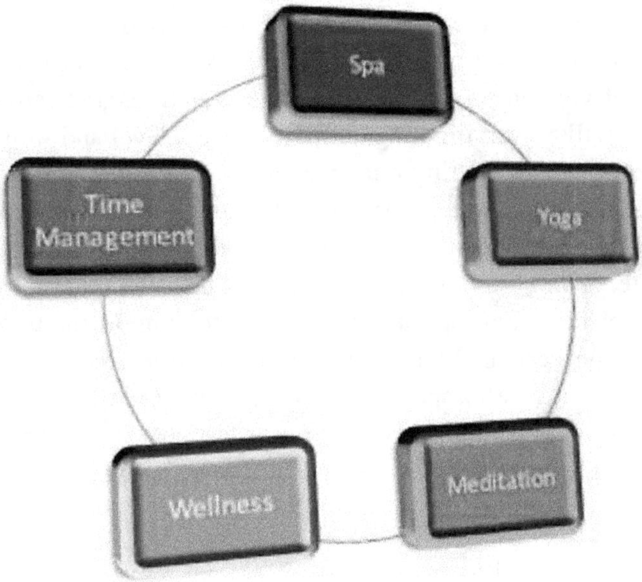

of the spas continued into the 20th century. Since then hydrotherapy, heat therapy and massages both improve blood circulation and manage blood pressure. Some spas even have Pilates and yoga, which improve flexibility and breathing. In the recent past, spas in the U.S. emphasized dietary, exercise, or recreational programs more than traditional bathing activities. Hence one can say that spa is well advanced popular stress relief technology available across the globe especially in Europe and Japan. It will also useful to refresh mind and increase positive thinking ability, so as a result stress reduced. Many researches prove that it is most economic and less side effects after yoga. On the other hand medication can cause the side effects but there is very limited chance in spa.

Yoga

Yoga is an ancient practice to live healthy life. It gives mental and physical energy to become more happy and healthy to minimize stress disorder. It originated in India and now it makes proud to every Indian that is being practiced all over the world to act as global heeler by reaping it's medicinal and therapeutics benefits in health care of the people. Since ancient times, India has always been considered as global Guru for being a spiritual, yoga and meditation. The role of the yoga therapy from its physical factors especially on stem cells trafficking from bone marrow, delays senescence, improves the physiological functions of heart and lung and yoga postures make the body elastic. Yoga breathing exercises increased positive vital energy and consciousness as we know breathing is physical part of thinking and thinking is psychological part of breathing by balancing emotions and bringing peace in the mind. Pranayama part of yoga improves the autonomic functions and cardio respiratory system including will power, thinking, oxidative stress level and weight loss. Over thousands of years, we are getting our own systems of indigenous medicinal and healing practices such as- yoga, ayurveda and naturopathy. Regular yoga practice helps to stay positive attitude offers a lot of possible transformation to live healthy in day to day life. Awareness of different yoga patterns to be in different disease intervention by selection appropriate tool of yoga to support the transformational process. Yoga can be a crucial breakthrough in prevention, treatment and reversion of heart disease if done with appropriate yoga therapeutic tool in regulation with proper dietary control. So, one can say that yoga is fast growing health care's therapy towards which people are getting aware and start learning yoga to live and stay fit and smart life.

Meditation

It is a practice where an individual uses a technique, such as focusing their mind on a particular object, thought or activity, to achieve a mentally clear and emotionally calm state.Meditation has been practiced since antiquity in numerous religious traditions and beliefs. Since the 19th century, it has spread from its origins to other cultures where it is commonly practiced in private and business life. Meditation may be used with the aim of reducing stress, anxiety, depression, and pain, and increasing peace, perception,self-concept, and well-being. Meditation is under research to define its possible health (psychological, neurological, and cardiovascular) and other effects.

Wellness

It is believed that the term 'wellness' has emerged from the World Health Organization (WHO) notion of 'well-being' and the concept of fitness.It is more than being free from illness; also it is a dynamic process of change and growth. According to WHO, it is defined that"*...a state of complete physical, mental, and social well-being, and not merely the absence of disease or infirmity*".Wellness is an useful procedure of creating a healthy and fulfill lifestyle. There are eight dimensions in wellness like – emotional, spiritual, intellectual, physical, environmental, financial, occupational, and social. Above mentioned factors are very influencing in wellness. According to various studies, it is proved that the main concern for the health problem is depression which comes from insomnia, stress, poor nutrition, physical inactivity, obesity, mental

Figure 6. Wellness dimensions

health and heart disease, etc.People are so alert for his quality of life. In this journey they faces lots of challenges, it will be great threats for fulfill their dream. So make a healthier and happier life, one fight with their weaknesses for continued growth and development. Holisms, balance, self-responsibility, positive and proactive are important perspectives for healthy lifestyle. It is important to maintain the work and family life balance to overcome chronic unhappiness.Sometimes, it is found that similar meaning health and wellness but these are not synonyms. Health refers to a healthy physical body, but wellness is an overall balance of physical, social emotional, intellectual and occupational wellbeing.

Time Management

Time management is the intellectual process of planning. It is also referred as the precise control of time spent on specific utilizations; especially to increase effectiveness, efficiency and productivity(Mohsenzade, 2007). Time plays a vital role for achieving all success. So, if one`s neglect the value of time, then it will be difficult to get their desire goal. If someone doesn't complete their assigned work on time, they will be under stress hence; they cannot concentrate in their workplace as well as family environment. To minimize the stress and maximize the healthy condition one should follow Maslow`s Hierarchy of needs theory. The following factors are essential:

- Prioritize: Setting the life by goals.
- Organize: Accomplish timely for success.
- Streamline: Well organized.
- Economize: Cost effectiveness.
- Contribute: Paying attention for remaining things.

CONCLUSION

Stress management is important consideration because it can save life and relationships. Persons having under stress used to break attention on their goals in life. There are plenty of good reasons to learn some stress management techniques. After the effects of yoga, wellness, medication, spa and time management, stress can be reduced and it is helpfuleveryday life to make a man healthy and wealthy, also as it can improve one`s mood, increase immune function, promote longevity and allow one`s to be more productive. The consequences of stress can cause specific disorders in both mind and body. Many peoples do suicide because of under stress. Stress can affectdirectly health, family, relationships, and workplace attitude also leads to marriage breakups, suicides and violence. Therefore, stress management and its implication for more creativity and quicker cursor movement toward the organizational targets is one of the goals which have been recently developed in organizations. The organizations can prevent negative stress and its consequences by training managers and personnel effectively for better recognition and management of stress factors. Hence, stress management is very useful for long happy lives with less trouble.

ACKNOWLEDGMENT

I am highly thankful to the professors and staff members of Sikkim Manipal University for their valuable suggestions and guidance. I am equally thankful to the persons whose who gave their valuable time for sharing knowledge about this field and also share me with the answers of my questions.

REFERENCES

Cropanzano, R., Howes, J. C., Grandey, A. A., & Toth, P. (1997). The relationship of organizational politics and support to work behaviors, attitudes, and stress. *Journal of Organizational Behavior, 18*(2), 159–180. doi:10.1002/(SICI)1099-1379(199703)18:2<159::AID-JOB795>3.0.CO;2-D

Griffin, R. W., & Moorhead, G. (2009). Organizational Behavior: Managing People and Organizations (9th ed.). Mason, OH: South-Western College Pub.

Jahanian, R., Tabatabaei, S. M., & Behdad, B. (2012). Stress management in the workplace. *International Journal of Academic Research in Economics and Management Sciences, 1*(6), 1.

Kazemi, H. (2007). A Study of Unhealthy Behaviors and Stress Managment. *Journal of Psychology and Information*, 40-44.

Koncul, N. (2012). Wellness: A New Mode of tourism. *Economic Research-Ekonomska Istraživanja, 25*(2), 525–534. doi:10.1080/1331677X.2012.11517521

McGonagle, K. A., & Kessler, R. C. (1990). Chronic stress, acute stress, and depressive symptoms. *American Journal of Community Psychology, 18*(5), 681–706. doi:10.1007/BF00931237 PMID:2075897

Mohsenzade, A. (2007). Stress Management. Journal of Management Advice (Industrial Development and Renovation Organization of Iran), 31-44.

Nekoranec, J., & Kmosena, M. (2015). Stress in the workplace-sources, effects and coping strategies. *Review of the Air Force Academy,* (1), 163.

Panigrahi, A. (2017). Managing Stress at Workplace. *Journal of Management Research and Analysis, 3*, 154–160. doi:10.18231/2394-2770.2016.0001

Rekha Sahoo, S. (2016). Management of Stress at Workplace. *Global Journal of Management and Business Research.*

Chapter 10
A Study of Green Marketing Practices in the Selected Ayurvedic Resorts of Kerala

Sheeba Hamid
Aligarh Muslim University, India

Syed Talha Jameel
Aligarh Muslim University, India

ABSTRACT

Ayurveda is a unique system of healthcare with more than 5000 years of history. It is presumed that Ayurveda is one of the oldest scientific ways of keeping, promoting, and conserving a healthy life. The various natural ingredients that are used in Ayurvedic therapy are of great medical value as is described in the Vedic literature on Ayurveda. The Ayurveda's history laid down the instructions of maintaining healthy lifespan as well as fighting against illness by different types of therapies like massages, diet control, herbal medicines, and exercises. Nowadays, green marketing is a rapidly growing concept, and consumers are willing to pay more for green products. Green marketing affects all areas of the economy. It does protect not only the environment but also creates a new market and job opportunities. The study is focused on the concept of Ayurveda especially in the resorts of Kerala. The majority of consumers have felt that their actions had a proportional impact on the environment.

DOI: 10.4018/978-1-5225-9787-2.ch010

INTRODUCTION

The new concept that has arrived in India is Ayurveda tourism. Ayurveda is one of the oldest forms of treatment, which is known as the Vedic system of medicine. It has worldwide recognition. In Sanskrit literature, Ayu means life and Veda means traditional knowledge or science Ayurveda means the science of life. It is a unique system of healthcare with more than 5000 years of history. It is presumed that Ayurveda is the scientific way of promoting, keeping and conserving a healthy life. Ayurveda is not only about the physical health of an individual, but it is a medical therapy that assures overall wellness. The various natural ingredients that are used in the therapy are of great medicinal value as is described in the Vedic literature on Ayurveda. The Ayurveda's history laid down the instructions of maintaining healthy lifespan as well as fighting against illness by different types of therapies like massages, diet control, herbal medicines, and exercises. Removal of toxic and harmful elements from the different parts of the body is the primary function of the ayurvedic treatment. Human body system gets purified when the unwanted items are removed from the body. As a result, the chances of falling with illness has become negligible, which makes one feel good.

The American Marketing Association (AMA) defines "green marketing as the marketing of products that are presumed to be environmentally safe. It incorporates several activities such as product modification, changes to production processes packaging, advertising strategies and also increases awareness on compliance marketing amongst industries". The adverse effect of human activities over the environment is a matter of great concern. Governments of all the countries making efforts to reduce the human influence on the environment. Human beings affect the environment in different ways. These effects include depletion of natural resources, decreased water quality, and increased pollution, greenhouse gas emissions and contribution to global warming.

Here, the term 'green' is the indicator of purity. So Green refers to pure in quality and transparent in dealing. For instance, green advertising means advertising of the product or services without an adverse effect on society. Green marketing is a highly discussed topic right from the layman to highly professionals — the concept of green marketing concerns with the protection and conservation of the ecological environment. Modern marketing has created problems with the environment. Growth in marketing activities increases economic growth, mass production, use of advanced technology, luxurious and comfortable lifestyle, stiff competition, use of unhealthy marketing tactics and techniques to attract customers, enhancement in advertising, creation of MNC's, retailing and distribution by multinational companies etc.

When we talk about green marketing in resorts, especially in resorts of Kerala are provided many health and respectful services. These all activities have threatened welfare ecological balances and welfare of people. Mainly, big resorts are the sources of a different kind of pollution by cutting the forest to build the structure of resorts. Production and consumption of the ingredients affect the environment adversely.

Thus the Green marketing is a marketing philosophy that promotes eco-friendly products production, selling and services with the protection of ecological balance. Green marketing involves different types of activities. Green Marketing increase production of pure products by pure technology, preservation of energy, conservation of the environment, less use of natural resources, and instead of processed foods more use of natural foods. Attempts of people, government and social organisations in this field can be said as green marketing efforts.

Kerala is one of the states in the southwestern Malabar Coast of India. It was formed on 1 November 1956, by combining Malayalam-speaking regions. Kerala is famous for its unique and vibrant culture, moderate weather, incredible art and various colourful festivals. That is why it is one of the best tourist destinations in the country. It has cultural and natural attractions with a healthy and good quality life in respect of other states. That is why the tourism industry in Kerala is flourishing. Kerala is the centre of attraction because of its diverse flora and fauna along with its beaches, backwaters, wildlife sanctuaries and evergreen forests. Kerala is often referred to as the "Green Gateway to India" (Netto, 2004). Another face of the coin is that Kerala is rich in agriculture sector also. Tea, coconut, cashew, coffee and spices are essential crops of the state. Kerala is one of the best tourist destinations of the country, with backwaters, hill stations, beaches, Ayurveda tourism, medical tourism and tropical greenery as its major attractions.

In India, Kerala is one among the few states to have promoted its natural beauty successfully to the tourism sector. Tourist from India and abroad are attracted towards the cultural diversification and unique heritage of the state. According to the BBC Travel Survey, Kerala is at first priority among foreigners travelling to India.

Health Tourism carries high growth opportunities. Yoga, Ayurveda and Rejuvenation therapy are India's ancient system of medication. Kerala is capable of providing medication and Health care facilities at international standards at a low cost. For this Kerala is focusing on tourism along with different types of medication facilities. Hotels and resorts are providing natural therapies at no cost. This is drawing foreign tourist comparatively higher rate with other states.

Statement of Problem

Human beings should use the scarce natural resources of the earth without compromising on the ability of the future generation. Otherwise, humankind will face a considerable environment degradation problem very soon. The remedial action will have to be taken by all the groups of society like the general public, government, individuals, groups, consumer, and producers. The business will have to bear the extra cost in perusing the eco-friendly green processes. So green marketing is the best to approach in a country like India. The Ayurvedic resorts of Kerala will have to go green in the interest of the health of the people and also in the national interest.

It has been observed that the present competitive and technological environment is gradually affecting the psychology and health of the people (Muralidhar & Karthikeyan 2016). The increasing level of stress and pressure, junk food habits and imbalanced diet resulted in a negative impact on the health and the lifespan of people. So increasing awareness of Ayurvedic treatment by using the eco-friendly ingredients is fruitful for both the health of the people and environment of the country.

REVIEW OF LITERATURE

Ramesh and Joseph (2011) This paper focused on the development of advanced marketing strategies in the current scenario for wellness tourism in Kerala. Point out that people from developed countries are turning towards developing countries like India for treatments. Medical and wellness tourism can be a substantial foreign revenue generator for the country. This paper further reveals that the most favourable factor for the growth of tourism in Kerala is ayurvedic heritage and clean environment. Kerala has apex potential to the wellness hub of the world.

According to the World Health Organization (WHO) practicing traditional system of medicine is quite safe and cheaper in a country like India, and it is also culturally acceptable. That is why the alternative method of medicine is prevalent among people seeking cure and wellness.

Nazmal Islam, (2012) 'New Age Orientation: Ayurvedic 'Wellness and Spa Culture' is in the view that Ayurveda and spa have grown to wellness medical therapy in a place of a means to reestablish the health. He claims that now these days Ayurveda is becoming a commercial product that can be bought as a package of 'Ayurveda healthy life'. The paper also discussed commercialization and commoditized kind of Ayurveda. The article also talked about the dangers to the Ayurveda prescription and its confidence as wellbeing treatment rather than Therapeutic Treatment

Jaya and Heera (2002) in their research study on "Role of Ayurveda in primary health care" Explained that health is a full state of physical, mental and social well-being and not only disappearance of diseases. The values of human life and the aims and objective of Ayurveda were discussed to establish the role of Ayurveda in primary health care. They assure that taking into consideration of all these factors, Ayurveda in primary health care is inevitable.

Sharfuddin (2015) is of the view that tourism is one of the growing service sectors in India, and it is economically essential too because it increases the significant share of the National GDP. Ayurveda and Wellness is an integral part of the tourism industry. Traditional medicine system is quite popular in India because of the culture, tradition, faith and beliefs prevalent in the country. Increase in the yearly growth in tourist arrival in India is observed on both national and international levels.

Binokar, Sawant, Bhoyar and Parlikar (2018) this study is based on Ayurveda education & research in India. It also explains challenges & solutions. Paper says Ayurveda is a unique system of health care since ages. It is one of the modern ways of encouraging a healthy lifestyle. An online survey conducted the research through questionnaire taking into account various studies, educational and awareness programs on Ayurveda. Total 1850 participants responded, and the researcher evaluated that 47% of participants did not appreciate the quality of education provided in Ayurvedic institutes. Finally, the authors suggested that Ayurveda education and research could be better with the adoption of various innovative ideas and methods in India.

Jyothis T and v.k. Janardhan (2009) the research is based on Service Quality in Kerala's Health Tourism. An emerging trend is being found out in health tourism providers in Kerala. A good health tourism address picture should be created to attract more health tourists by offering standard and satisfactory health tourism service. Health tourist's satisfaction relies on their outlook and sensitivity of services provided by health tourism service providers. This bailiwick intention to pick out the service tone size of health tourists visiting Kerala.

Sharma (2013) The main aim of the research was to spotlight the capacity of the Indian Medical Tourism industry. Research swot is aimed at challenging the optimistic fiscal remuneration of remedial tourism and focusing on the role of government, tourism ministry and pharmaceutical industries in making India's icon as a high-quality medical tourism destination. The research found that India is in an advantageous situation to exploit the medical tourism sector's worldwide possibilities.

Bindu.V.T and Sivakami (2016), The study directs the focus on the qualities of services at the ayurvedic centres in Palakkad city of Kerala. Findings showed that services and treatment delivered are satisfactory. These services can be improved in future. The author believes that ayurveda has become a wellness therapy in the city and the same is being commercialized and commoditized.This article also addressed threats to ayurvedic medicine and its faith as wellness therapy instead of therapeutic therapy. The paper touched clear areas that make awareness about the threats of ayurveda tourism. The study also says that imperative function of effectual service delivery in customer satisfaction of health tourism practice of ayurvedic centres of Palakkad which needs to be tapped effectively to pave way for sustainable tourism development in the state.

Praful Patel, (2011), globalisation of Ayurveda a global vision for the next decade, International Ayurveda Facilitator. The author believes that there is a need arises for a separate status of ayurveda nationally and internationally. The study focuses on the commercialization of ayurveda and discuses action plan to be implemented in future for growth and development of ayurveda as an entrepreneurship. The study was conducted for relating ayurveda with business.

The paper thoroughly discussed about popularization of ayurveda and provided facts and figures associated with qualifications of ayurvedic doctors and nurses etc.

PURPOSE AND SIGNIFICANCE OF THE STUDY

The aim of the study is to understand the concept of Ayurveda, especially in the resorts of district Thiruvananthapuram of Kerala. This study also focuses on green marketing practices and strategies of the resorts and how they attract tourists and give them a better quality of services. This study provides the idea that tourism in Kerala is mainly in the field of health and wellness doing excellent. Now, these days every individual is conscious about their health and wellness, so when someone plans their vacations, then he/she tries to pick a spot where the environment is relatively better, and he can enjoy the natural environment rather than an artificial tourist spot. Kerala is famous for its natural beauty and cultural assets. Nowadays, people are suffering from many sorts of anxiety and mental pressure, and to overcome all these, and they choose a tourist spot full of the natural environment. By keeping in mind the same concept, tourism in Kerala provides health and wellness tourism. Many of the resorts are entirely working on medical and health tourism. Medical tourism in Kerala grew without many collective efforts. It is an opportunity for the resorts to practice the Ayurvedic system of medicine because the traditional method of medicine like Ayurveda, Siddha and spas are widely accessible and acceptable in Kerala and it is fetching numbers of tourists in the state.

OBJECTIVES OF THE STUDY

- To study the concept of Ayurveda and the relevance of green ideas in Ayurveda.
- To study the green marketing practices in Ayurvedic resorts of Kerala.
- To highlight the importance of Green marketing concepts in resorts of Kerala.
- To increase the awareness about the significance of Going Green in the field of Ayurveda industry.

RESEARCH GAP

The tourism industry is performing excellently in terms of growth, revenue, employment generation and the number of international tourist arrivals among all the service industries in the country. The tourism industry is the highest contributor, i.e. (6.23%) to national GDP as compared to other service industries. In the current scenario, a developing country like India is gradually becoming a tourist hub and witnessing a massive number of foreign tourist arrivals. Among these tourists, a good number of tourists visit India for getting treatments with natural ways as Kerala is the fastest-growing state in India in respect of medical tourism and wellness. So, in the long run, the wellness industry can become the good foreign exchange earning industry in India, especially in Kerala.

The unique specification of Kerala's resorts is Ayurvedic consultant and therapist, treatment care attention, indoor and outdoor recreation, availability of ayurvedic pharmacy and a healthy and hygienic environment. Ayurveda is all about the greenness and purification of the body from the unwanted elements, so this industry should be promoted as a green industry in terms of its services as well as their marketing strategies and promotions.

GREEN MARKETING PRACTICES IN AYURVEDIC RESORTS OF KERALA

The study focuses on three ayurvedic centres in Kerala. These three resorts are identified with the following objectives

The highest number of foreign tourists arrives at Thiruvananthapuram as compared to other places. Moreover, Kovalam in Thiruvananthapuram having maximum ayurvedic health resorts compared to other districts. So, three Ayurvedic health resorts namely Somatheeram, and Coconut Bay and Ayurbay has identified for this study.

AyurBay resorts is a renowned name for wellness resorts-Ayurveda. The resort is located by the ocean, combining the enjoyment of a beach vacation with genuine Ayurvedic therapy and wellness therapy. Dr. K. R. Chandra Babu, the renowned Ayurvedic doctor, founded Ayurbay Beach Resort on Nellikunnu Beach, 4 km from Kovalam and 22 km from Trivandrum (Kerala) Currently, his spouse Dr. Lalitha Babu, a dedicated Ayurvedic physician, administers this accredited "Ayurvedic center of the medical doctor." A lovely rebuilt center has 16 rooms and two flats that attract visitors from Germany in particular.

The resort's lovely place and esthetic interiors embedded in contemporary amenities, yet not losing the ethnic traditions in decoration is an entirely different experience. And the craft masters guide you through refreshing yoga while the chefs are cooking for you delicious vegetarian dishes. In the colors of the waving coconut palms, relax the meal in the open-air dining region.

The personal life guard is always alert to enjoy swimming in the ocean. Or just enjoy the sea breeze from the resort's balcony lounge chairs. And, you can take a break from the therapy to visit exotic Kerala. The Ayurbay resort offers recreational facilities and services such as Doctor on call, laundry services, restaurant, Ayurveda, warm and cold water running, direct dial telephone and satellite television in the room.

In the Ayurbay resorts, which is based on Ayurveda rules, there are eight types of unique massage

Abhyangam

This massage has been performed to relax the mind and the body's adequate blood circulation. Trained masseurs apply lukewarm herbal oil according to the old rules on the head and body. This is a purely natural and healthy massage

Elakkizhi

A individual can enjoy one of the most refreshing and relaxing massages, using fresh cooked herbs in Ayurvedic oils and packed in small bags. Then these bags applied to the body by experts. It helps to lubricate the joints and alleviate the joint pain. It cleans the channels of circulation and expels toxins through humidity.

Navarakkizhi

Through internal application of certain medicinal puddings made from distinctive rice called navara rice cooked in herbal decoctions and milk and packed in muslin bags, the entire body or specific part is generated to transpire. This massage purifies the skin's pores, softens the complexion, strengthens the body's muscles, and heals the joints 'rigidity and increase circulation of blood. It is also prescribed for all kinds of diseases of nervous system and for rheumatism.

Dhara

This is a method created in Kerala where in a unique pattern a constant stream of medicated oil or buttermilk is poured on the forehead. It is performed primarily for mental relaxation and is very efficient for sleep disturbances, insomnia, mental issues and skin diseases.

Sirovasthy

A unique cap is fitted on the head and roughly 30 minutes of hot oil is permitted to remain on the head. This is performed for issues with vision, memory problems, sleep disturbances, he adaches, etc.

Udavarthanam

This massage is provided with the unique herbal powder that is useful for fat depletion and muscle strengthening and is very efficient for obesity. This is solely medical therapy provided by the natural manner.

Nasya

Sprinkles into the nose are medicated and natural herbal oils or powders. This is prescribed for nasal cavity, ear, sinus, headaches, facial paralysis distortion, spondilosis, etc. disorders and is generally component of long-term medicines.

Chavitti Thirummu

This is the oldest type of massage in which the masseur hangs on a cord and provides the massage with his hands, namely Kalari (Martial Arts of Kerala). As an osteopath or chiropractor does, the masseur will correct the alignments of the body.

Another important health resort is Somatheeram Ayurvedic Beach Resort which declared itself as the first resort of its kind, having a combination of both Ayurveda and yoga. It is established on a hillock covering a territory of 15 acres rich in greenery. It has conventional wooden home buildings, stone cottage and mansion with 50 rooms' suite bath. The centre is managed by 18 ayurvedic physicians and instructed by 65 therapists who are actively engaged in supervising Spa activities in the health resort at Kovalam. It has 24 sanitized rooms, out of those six rooms are open that has an extensive oceanic view. The lush greenery of the garden has 600 different kinds of herbs to cure people. The resort provides not only health care facilities to the patients but also several games to fit the body like indoor games, boating and fishing. These herbal products are useful for the body as they do not have any side effects. The health resort is also famous for keeping perfect balance and harmony among mind, body and soul. The Spa centre recommends a balanced diet which is regarded as an essential part of ayurvedic therapy. The centre has 259 several kinds of varieties as recommended by the dieticians and health experts. The ayurvedic centre can also be referred to as an educational institution as it also gives knowledge of Ayurveda. The resort arranged all important herb ingredients from its own Herbal Garden which contained 600 kinds of herbs.

Ayurveda is the core and soul of Somatheeram resort, which has been providing Ayurvedic therapy with the traditional and natural manner for more than 30 years and has rightly gained the goodwill ' The Ayurvedic People.' Ayurveda, meaning life science (Ayur means life and Veda means science), is an ancient medical science created in India thousands of years ago.

Authentic and traditional Kerala Ayurveda resort. This is the award winning Ayurveda Hospital set on South India's tropical garden and prime beachfront place. Here in a blissfully peaceful setting, you can enjoy both traditional Ayurvedic treatment and yoga. Somatheeram, the world's first Ayurveda hospital set in a resort atmosphere to provide people / patients from all over the world with Ayurveda treatments / programs. It is situated on a hill 9 km south of the renowned Kovalam Beach at Chowara Beach with more than 15 acres of greenery all around.

The authorized Coconut Bay Ayurveda Centre is situated in 4 acres of land, with the Arabian Sea facing 25 independent villas, at Vizhinjum place in Kerala. Like the other Ayurvedic resorts, it also has yoga facilities with indoor and outdoor entertainment activities for tourists. Coconut bay resorts offer a special treatment "House by the Sea", this eight-room oasis gives the sounds of the ocean to calm down the senses while relaxing the mind and body. Guests can select from a variety of treatments containing signature organic therapies in ocean view treatment rooms featuring outdoor showers. Whether you desire to calm down the mind, the staff is also pleased to provide their services.

Through the Ayurveda therapy, the coconut bay resorts provide you with relaxation from the quick and hectic life. The resort provides you the perfect getaway, nestled in a lush green coconut grove and surrounded by a quiet and serene beach. Located next to the beach of Kovalam, Coconut Bay has twenty-two cozy deluxe villas and five beach rooms, each with a wonderful ocean perspective., Coconut Bay becomes the perfect place for a memorable vacation because the body and mind need not only relaxation but also a peaceful environment experience.

GOING GREEN: IDEAS FOR THE AYURVEDIC RESORTS

1. A green team can be appointed in a resort which focuses on continuous improvement, scheduled re-evaluation and reporting about green practices.
2. Stimulate and encourage staff to contribute to environmentally friendly practices.
3. Organize regular staff training lectures and program on green practices to motivate workers and staff in the resort.

4. Staff must be educated enough to turn off lights, heating/air conditioning equipment's in unoccupied rooms.
5. Staff must be guided to continuous check for turning off unused kitchen appliances
6. Start Excessive use of reusable handkerchiefs, towels, bedding, sheets, pillowcases, comforters, bedspreads, blankets, quilts, dishtowels, tablecloths, napkins etc.
7. To reduce the usage of water and energy install an ozone laundry system may be installed.
8. Use recycling bins both in public areas and in the back office.
9. Eco-friendly papers can be bought such as toilet paper, copier paper, facial tissue, paper towels, etc.
10. Reduce the usage of paper for maintaining the records in the office and generating invoices to the guests.
11. Resort must buy biodegradable, nontoxic laundry, cleaning and dishwashing products with seals.
12. Guests should be introduced with green practices at the very initial stage to make them understand various green practices done by the resort.
13. It is advisable to follow a Private-Pubic-Partnership Model (PPP) in promoting ayurvedic Tourism in Kerala. The Central Government should also help to popularize the ayurvedic and medical Tourism through different Health Ministries and Embassies in various foreign countries. More financial and fiscal rebates and concessions should also be offered to this sector which has good employment and foreign exchange earning potential for the nation.

CONCLUSION

Most customers thought that their actions had a proportionate environmental impact. Consumers therefore shift non-green products to green products to have a beneficial effect on the environment and the environment. This study article concludes that Kerala's Ayurvedic resorts need to alter their marketing policies by investing in technology. To survive in the green competitive market, research and development are needed to develop the green product, green promotion, green innovation eco-packaging, eco-labeling and green logo to have a beneficial environmental and ecological effect. In Kerala resorts, green marketing is in the early stages, so service providers, consumers, and mediators and to have a strong effect on society and the environment, the government needs to encourage the green marketing and service industries.

REFERENCES

Binorkar, S., Sawant, R., & Bhoyar, M. (2018). Ayurveda education & research in India–present scenario, challenges & solutions. *Int J Complement Alt Med.*, *11*(2), 130–137. doi:10.15406/ijcam.2018.11.00362

Chandra, S. (2016). Ayurvedic research, wellness and consumer rights. *Journal of Ayurveda and Integrative Medicine*, *7*(1), 6–10. doi:10.1016/j.jaim.2016.05.002 PMID:27297503

Islam, N. (2012). New Age Orientation: Ayurvedic 'Wellness and Spa Culture'. Health Sociology Review, 21(2), 270-231.

Kajonborrirak, S. (n.d.). *The Importance of Professional Health Care and Spa Therapist Training in The Tourism Industry*. Retrieved from http://www.sarahorg.com/thaispa/Pata_Pattaya.pdf

Patel. (2011). Globalization of Ayurveda a global vision for the next decade. *International Ayurveda Facilitator*.

Ramesh, U., & Joseph, K. (2012). The holistic approach of ayurveda based wellness tourism in Kerala. *International Journal of Research in Management, 3*(2).

Ramesh, U., & Joseph, K. (2012). The holistic approach of Ayurveda based wellness tourism in Kerala. International Journal of Advanced Research in Management, 29-39.

Sharafuddin, M. A. (2015). Siddha and Wellness tourism: Opportunities and challenges for "Brand Tamilnadu". *Int. J. Res. Ayurveda Pharm.*, *6*(3), 387–394. doi:10.7897/2277-4343.06376

Sungpo Yi, S., & Li, X. (2018). Hotel guests' perception of best green practices: A content analysis of online reviews. *Tourism and Hospitality Research*, *18*(2), 191–202. doi:10.1177/1467358416637251

T, S., & Mariswamy, H. (2016). The Role of Health Tourism on Tourism Development in Kerala State: An Evaluation. *IRA-International Journal of Management & Social Sciences, 4*(2), 494-501.

Vijayraghvan, G. (2013). Green Marketing – Issues Concerning Indian Organisations. *International Journal in Multidisciplinary and Academic Research, 2*(5).

WHO. (2002). *Traditional Medical Strategy 2002-2005*. World Health Organisation. Retrieved from http://whqlibdoc.who.int/hq/2002/who_edm_trm_2002.1.pdf

Chapter 11
A Collaborative Framework for Medical Tourism Service Supply Chain Operations

Saliha Karadayi-Usta
Istanbul Teknik Üniversitesi, Turkey

Seyda Serdarasan
https://orcid.org/0000-0001-9933-0998
Istanbul Teknik Üniversitesi, Turkey

ABSTRACT

Medical tourism is a combination of medical and tourism services that attracts medical travelers to destination countries. Collaboration between the members of the medical tourism service supply chain (MTSSC) is important to maintain a sustainable business. Thus, in this chapter, the authors use Collaborative Planning Forecasting Replenishment (CPFR) model as a reference and adapt it for medical tourism services. The focus of this chapter is on the collaboration between an assistance company and a medical institution. This chapter suggests a collaborative MTSSC operations framework including steps, tools, and techniques for collaboration arrangement and joint business plans, demand planning and forecasting, balancing the demand and capacity, the execution phase, and the final performance measurement. It describes how multiple supply chain partners intelligence could be combined to fulfill demand of medical tourists by aligning the planned actions and available resources with the real execution process by a set of tools and techniques.

DOI: 10.4018/978-1-5225-9787-2.ch011

INTRODUCTION

Medical tourism service is the type of healthcare tourism where patients receive treatment and/or rehabilitation in healthcare institutions outside their country of residence. Medical tourists intend to take the advantage of shorter waiting times in the destination country, relatively low medical intervention costs, availability of well-recognized medical professionals, and the opportunity to discover new countries and touristic locations simultaneously (Connell 2006, Hopkins et al. 2010).

Recent treatment trends in medical tourism include birth tourism (Jaramillo et al., 2019), cancer treatment (Kim et al., 2019), transplant tourism (Nino-Murcia et al., 2018), stem cell tourism (Touré et al., 2018), cosmetic surgery tourism (Pereira et al., 2018), renal replacement therapy (Amahazion, 2018), and bariatric tourism (Peters and Gangemi, 2018). In addition, business reports address that the dental, cardiovascular, orthopedics and ophthalmic treatment trends, and the fertility treatments segment are expected to obtain the highest compound annual growth rate (Mordor Intelligence, 2019).

The most popular medical tourism destination countries are located in Asia and the Pacific region with lower costs as well as better and faster healthcare services. Figure 1 provides the number of medical travelers estimated by country in 2018 (Patients Beyond Borders, 2019).

According to Patients Beyond Borders (2019), the size of the medical tourism market is $65-87.5 billion with an average spending of $3410 per visit per patient, and the worldwide medical tourism market is expected to grow at a rate of 15-25%.

Figure 1. Estimated number of inbound medical travelers by destination country in the year 2018 (Patients Beyond Borders, 2019)

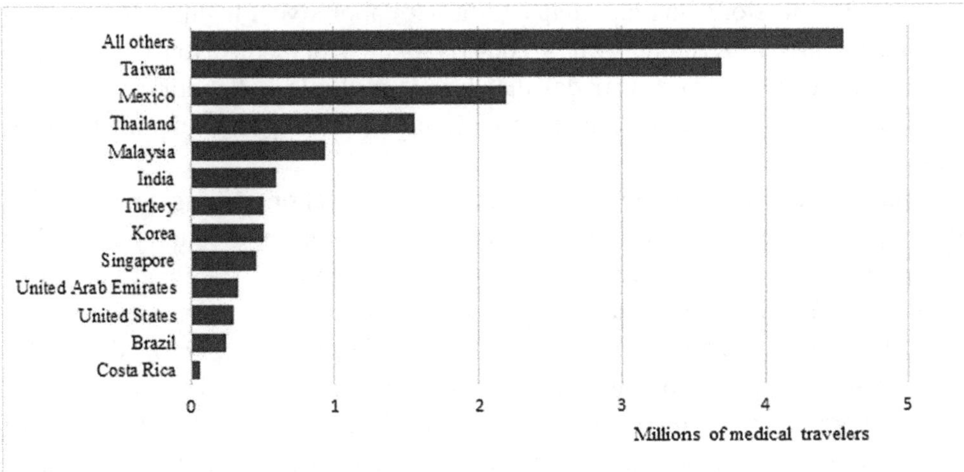

Additionally, more than one thousand medical centers and hospitals around the world have so far been awarded the Joint Commission International (JCI) accreditation and this number is increasing by around 20% per year (JCI, 2019).

Jagyasi (2019) describes the year 2018 as quite exciting with market disruptors emerging and new destination countries breaking into the medical tourism sector, while 2019 is anticipated to exhibit an unprecedented growth with the globalization of healthcare focusing on patient-centric and patient-friendly ambiance. Artificial Intelligence in decision making, patients' preferences towards personalized medicine, web/mobile applications supporting the medical tourism venture, post-operative follow up treatment with telemedicine and advanced software programs, adoption of blockchain technology, cross-border payments through cryptocurrency, government supported information platform to provide authenticity, new popular destination countries, more regional associations, medical cities projects, quality knowledge, and skill building workshops are all trending topics in medical tourism (Jagyasi, 2019).

The medical tourism services, which are a combination of tourism and healthcare services, require the participation of multiple parties such as service providers of medical treatment, transportation, accommodation, touristic activities, translation, insurance, and visa as well as medical tourists. Thus, the medical tourism service supply chain (MTSSC) is a network of multiple businesses and people that plan for medical services, supply necessary resources, deliver medical tourism services and manage information and financial flows between the service providers and the patients (Ferrer and Medhekar, 2012). Typical agents in the MTSSC include patients, healthcare institutions, assistance companies, accommodation service providers, transfer or ambulance service facilitators, flight ticket suppliers, translation service providers, visa service providers, and insurance service providers.

Since the collaboration between these supply chain members is critical to maintaining a sustainable way of business, a framework for a collaborative MTSSC is required. Therefore, in this chapter, the Collaborative Planning Forecasting Replenishment (CPFR) model (VICS, 2004) is adapted for medical tourism services. CPFR is a business process model that brings multiple collaborative partners' intelligence into the same place in order to plan and fulfill customer demand (VICS, 2004).

Collaboration in the MTSSC has a significant impact on gaining a competitive advantage in terms of medical tourism services provided in a country as well as in improving the performance of the supply chain members (Lee and Fernando, 2015). The MTSSC collaboration requires business partners to trust, commit to, cooperate with and share information with each other (Lee and Fernando, 2015). Recent research on medical tourism regarding collaborative approaches emphasize the collaboration of different medicine styles (Eom et al., 2019), the effective collaboration and information sharing to navigate patients' journey (Sandal, 2019), the social integration and cooperative medical scheme (Peng and Ling, 2019), the use of collaborative platforms (Dileep et al., 2019), the cooperative involvements and advancements for medical service/tourism complexes (Jing and Lim, 2018), the effective and efficient trans-border cooperation between health authorities and health facilities (Mathon et al., 2018), and the cross-border cooperation and sustainable economic development (Dunets and Zhogova, 2018).

This chapter introduces a collaborative MTSSC operations framework including the steps, tools, and techniques for collaboration arrangement and strategic planning, demand and supply management, execution and analysis through a literature review. The framework combines multiple supply chain partners' operations to fulfill the expectations of medical tourists by linking the planned actions and resources with real execution processes. The focus of this chapter is on the collaborative MTSSC operations between an assistance company (AC) and a healthcare institution (HI) in aiming to improve patient experience and performance of the supply chain. This chapter stresses the growth and development of healthcare services as an emerging market and the healthcare and assistance company services in improving patient experience within the scope of this book.

The following sections describe, through the review of the related literature, the collaborative MTSSC operations based on the CPFR model and the tools and techniques to support the smooth flow of the supply chain operations between an AC and an HI.

BACKGROUND

Collaborative Planning Forecasting and Replenishment (CPFR) is defined by Voluntary Interindustry Commerce Standards (VICS) as a business process bringing multiple collaborative partners' intelligence into the same place in order to plan and fulfill the customer demand (VICS, 2004). CPFR is a collaborative initiative to develop supply chain partners' relations in a joint planning and management effort to share the information, risks, benefits and costs (Hollmann et al., 2015; Seifert, 2003).

The first CPFR reference model was presented in 1998 by VICS with nine steps categorized into three processes, namely planning, forecasting, and replenishment. Fliedner (2003) suggests a brief version of the VICS 1998 model that contains only five steps. In 2004, VICS updated the CPFR model to its current version accompanied with detailed explanations that offer four activities: strategy and planning, demand and supply planning, execution, and analysis (VICS, 2004). CPFR has been used in sectors beyond retail, such as manufacturing goods (Chung & Leung, 2005), spare parts (Panahifar et al. 2013), apparel and consumer packaged goods (VICS, 2004);

however, its application in the service industry is scarce. Lin & Ho (2014) discussed the benefits of applying CPFR in the healthcare sector.

Although a new version of the CPFR model, named CPFR 2.0, was introduced in 2014, the 2004 model preserves its currency. There is no accessible documentation supporting the CPFR 2.0 model and when the VICS representatives were consulted via e-mail, they confirmed the current version as the 2004 CPFR model. Hence, this study uses the 2004 CPFR model and adapts it for medical tourism services (see Figure 2):

1. Strategy and planning: Arranging collaborative business partnerships, developing joint business plans.
2. Demand and supply planning: Forecasting demand, integrating demand and capacity.
3. Execution: Generating service order, delivering the healthcare service.
4. Analysis: Managing the exceptions, assessing the performance.

The CPFR model has three layers with customer at the center, buyer (e.g. retailer) in the second layer, and seller (e.g. producer) in the third layer. In an MTSSC, patients are end customers located at the center of the model, AC represents the buyer as the mediator located in the second layer, and HI represents the seller as the provider of desired healthcare services as presented in Figure 2.

Although there are other services and associated service providers in medical tourism services such as accommodation, transfer, flight ticket, translation, visa, and insurance, the CPFR model presented focuses on the medical service and related operations between an AC and an HI. The other optional services are out of the scope of this study, yet the CPFR model can be adapted to represent any dyadic relationship (or triadic, including the patient) within the MTSSC. The collaborative business processes in the MTSSC are described in detail in the following section.

Collaborative Tools and Techniques in Medical Tourism Service Supply Chain Operations framework

Following the CPFR steps introduced in Seifert (2003) and Bozarth (2011), the CPFR tasks and keywords were adapted for MTSSC operations, and then the literature is reviewed using these keywords. The CPFR model focuses on the customer (patient), and two collaborating service providers: AC and HI. The service providers have both specific individual tasks and collaborative tasks, a list of which is given in Table 1.

Figure 2. CPFR model for an assistance company and a healthcare institution for medical tourism service supply chain operations (adapted from VICS, 2004)

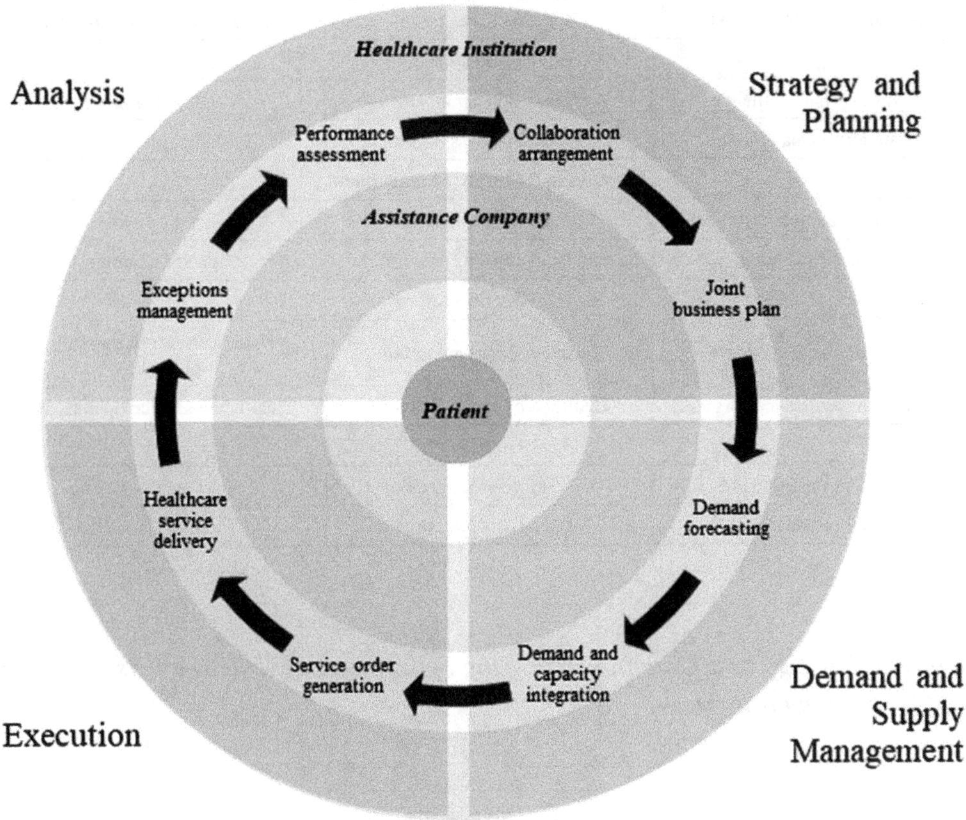

Strategy and Planning

The MTSSC operations start with strategy and planning step covering collaboration arrangement and joint business plan tasks (see Figure 3). Vendor management and category management activities on the AC side and account planning and market planning activities on the HI side support collaborative tasks in this step.

Collaboration Arrangement

The collaboration arrangement is where business goals for the relationship are set, the scope of collaboration is defined and roles, responsibilities, checkpoints and escalation procedures are assigned. This task has 11 activities (Seifert, 2003; Bozarth, 2011):

Table 1. CPFR tasks for medical tourism service supply chain operations framework (adapted from Seifert, 2003; Bozarth, 2011)

Assistance company tasks	Collaboration tasks	Healthcare institution tasks
	Strategy and Planning	
Vendor management	Collaboration arrangement	Account planning
Category management	Joint business plan	Market planning
	Demand and Supply Management	
Point of sale forecasting	Demand forecasting	Market data analysis
Demand planning	Demand and capacity integration	Capacity planning
	Execution	
Service order placement	Service order generation	Healthcare service supply planning
Maintaining assistance services	Healthcare service delivery	Healthcare service operations
	Analysis	
Execution monitoring	Exceptions management	Execution monitoring
Supplier scorecard	Performance assessment	Customer scorecard

Figure 3. Strategy and planning step of the collaborative medical tourism service supply chain operations

1. Defining CPFR mission, clarifying the explanations, signing nondisclosure agreements.
2. Determining CPFR purpose, goals, performance criteria, and exceptions.
3. Discussing the competency of sources, capacity, outsourcing options, and systems.
4. Defining the collaborative points and responsible units.
5. Determining information exchange requirement and frequency, deciding which data to share, limiting the response times, and specifying the forecasting methodology.
6. Adding previous business experiences.
7. Determining service and order commitment.
8. Resource involvement and commitment, deciding on which resource to involve, how much time and how many employees needed.
9. Defining exception resolution, determining rules and standards.
10. Determining revision cycles for collaboration agreements.
11. Top management support, continuous communication, finalizing the arrangement, and updating if necessary.

In addition, parties make decisions related to categorizing their business partners based on their properties and workload (Nylén, 2007; Reniers, 2011), utilizing online tools enabling simultaneous access (Andersson et al., 2015; Bekkers, 2009), updating the arrangement according to business memory (Seifert, 2003; Bozarth, 2011), and terminating the inactive business collaborations (Madzingamiri et al., 2015).

Vendor Management

The AC is required to perform vendor (i.e. service provider) management activities for all services delivered in medical tourism such as services provided by HIs, infrastructure and technologies, finance, transportation, and other facilitators (Chee et al., 2017). If it is the first time to conduct a business partnership, the AC prepares, delivers and collects request for proposals, and then evaluates and categorizes healthcare institutions accordingly (Costello, 2013; Urbach et al., 2014; Levin and Berry, 2010). Next, gap analysis and RACI (responsible, accountable, consulted, informed) matrix are implemented, and credibility of service providers (Nakayama et al., 2018) are assessed to prepare guidelines (Costello, 2013).

In case of a continuous partnership with an HI, AC collects patient satisfaction and experience data by checklists, direct phone calls or surveys and evaluates the performance of the HI using predetermined criteria (Friedman et al., 1995; Costello, 2013). This way, AC decides whether to maintain the partnership or not. In general ACs monitor the capacities and occupancy rates of HIs in order to canalize patients towards another HI when necessary. Besides, they can mobilize patients towards transnational healthcare markets (Hartmann, 2019) by evaluating the performances and capacities of HIs.

Additionally, the contract and commission-based payment system (Chee et al., 2017), and immediate synchronous communication ability to service providers by the use of mutual data formats (Levin and Berry, 2010) regulate the vendor management activities of ACs.

As the intermediary/moderator/broker, an AC offers all-inclusive or tailor-made bundled service packages to patients including air travel, accommodation, transfers, cost of treatment, and local sightseeing trips and excursions. In order to form a creative bundling of medical tourism services, collaboration of HIs and ACs play a critical role (Haarhoff and Mokoena, 2017).

Account Planning

HIs manage their direct sales channels in account planning phase by managing the medical tourist applications of ACs. ACs are important channels in bridging the gap between prospective patients and HIs (Haarhoff and Mokoena, 2017).

HIs, on the other hand, should implement risk management activities by sharing business protocols with ACs (Gan and Frederick, 2018), by credibility assessments of ACs (Nakayama et al., 2018), and by a contract / commission-based payment system (Chee et al., 2017). HIs and ACs define the scope of collaboration and elaborate on this context in order to control contingent cases. Next, commission-based payment details are identified to manage the sales channel. HI managements attempt to regulate the activities of ACs by providing an incentive mechanism to bring patients (Chee et al., 2017).

HIs evaluate the number of patients provided by ACs, overall integration and service delivery ability of ACs, synergy of AC service professionals, follow-up AC services availability and efficiency of supporting activities (Hsu et al., 2013) in account planning.

Synchronous and simultaneous communication is important in managing these sales channels. Moreover, HIs ask medical tourists' opinions to measure the satisfaction level of AC-provided services to make decisions on preserving the collaboration with a particular AC or not.

Joint Business Plan

The joint business plan focuses on internal business operations and outsourcing other services (Accenture, 2012). The joint business plan phase steps are (Accenture, 2012; Smith, 2015):

1. Strategic customer and enterprise planning (market segmentation analysis), attractiveness and performance analysis, preparing 12–18 months joint strategic plans.
2. Trust analysis: Trust = ((credibility + reliability + intimacy) / (self-orientation)).
3. Adopting the KISS (Keep It Simple Stupid) principle, defining business scope with the Pareto principle, reviewing content within 3 months, creating a plan for at most 18 months.
4. Scenario modelling and reconciliation activities.
5. Defining the outcomes to assess, agreeing on the most applicable simple criteria.
6. Execution, alignment, analysis (utilizing cutting-edge technology, inspecting key performance indicators by scenario modeling and dashboards)
7. Evaluating the dashboards and tracking the joint business plan continuously.

Category Management

Category management in medical tourism services corresponds to service type management, which depends on patient preferences. ACs gather patient requests for a treatment type and manage collaborative procedures. The steps and tools of category management include defining and classifying the service (treatment) type (Lindblom and Olkkonen, 2006), primary market research, and CRM tools (e.g. customer scorecards, questionnaires, direct marketing), determining the responsible units and employees (Barrenstein and Tweraser, 2004), identifying specific performance criteria (income per service type, market share of each service type, customer satisfaction level, throughput time etc.), preparing an implementation plan for each service type by pricing, promotion and seasonality (Lindblom and Olkkonen, 2006; Barrenstein and Tweraser, 2004)

Market Planning

For market planning, an HI should adhere to the following steps and tools: Marketing audit (analyzing the current situation: analyzing the market, effectiveness of the marketing unit, strengths and weaknesses against the competitors) (Alderson, 2006; Zallocco and Joseph, 1991), developing strategy (preparing, evaluating, weighing different strategies), portfolio analysis (Alderson, 2006; McCain, 1987), making programs, scheduling (matching the plans and programs with the service calendar), budgeting and control, installation procedure, review and demonstration (Alderson, 2006; Zallocco and Joseph, 1991).

Demand and Supply Management

The MTSSC operations proceed with demand and supply management step that involves demand forecasting and demand - capacity integration tasks (see Figure 4). Point of sale forecasting and demand planning activities on the AC side and market data analysis and capacity planning activities on the HI side support the collaborative tasks in this step.

Demand Forecasting

Future reservations/appointments are required to forecast by taking past demand data of a specific AC bringing patients to a specific HI. Demand forecasting step includes (Bozarth, 2011):

1. Analyzing the current joint business plan, evaluating the effect of the plan for possible demand.
2. Analyzing the causal information.
3. Collecting past demand data.
4. Identifying the planned events (opening/closing offices, holidays, promotions, new service package entries, changes, etc.)

Figure 4. Demand and supply management step of the collaborative medical tourism service supply chain operations

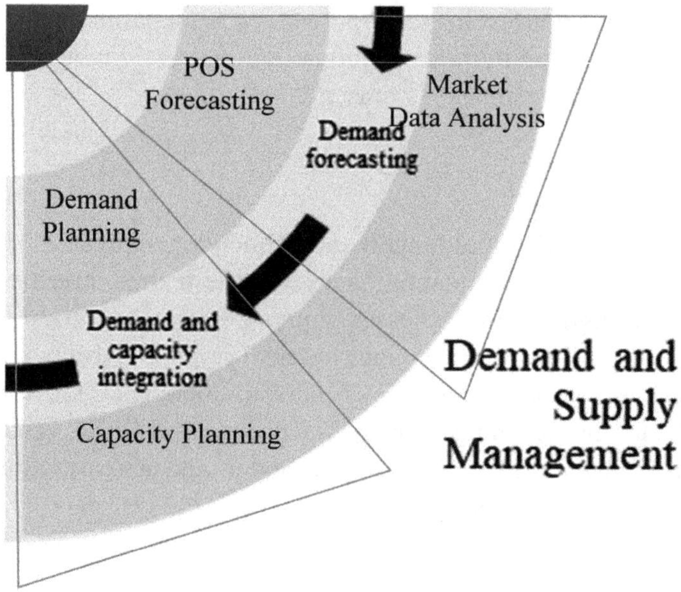

5. Updating the mutual calendar, sharing between business partners, and compromising.
6. Forecasting future reservations/appointments/service demand.

Point of Sale Forecasting

In the medical tourism service (as defined in this chapter), ACs act as points of sale, i.e. a sales channel, for HIs. Since an AC is an intermediary between multiple service providers (hotels, transfer and flight ticket providers, translators, visa and insurance vendors, etc.), demand created by an AC and these suppliers is forecasted in order to predict the future volume of demand. Demand data can be recorded by both the AC and the service providers, and forecasting can be performed by considering all lines of business. The literature review highlights the use of techniques such as time series analysis (Tang and Lau, 2017), multiple regression analysis (Ridderstaat et al., 2019; Johnson and Garman, 2015), econometric models (Tang and Lau, 2017; Cheng, 2016), and machine learning forecasting methods (Dang et al., 2016).

Market Data Analysis

Literature on market data analysis focuses on the factors affecting medical tourism demand such as exchange rates, cost of tourist services, gross domestic product (Tang and Lau, 2017; Vetitnev et al., 2016, Dong and Hu, 2017, Cheng, 2016), undesired situations like epidemic illnesses, security, workforce and medical facility factors (Tang ve Lau, 2017), life expectancy, household spending, gross regional product, sanatorium branch income, regional income per capita (Vetitnev et al., 2016), quality of service (Tang and Lau, 2017, Dong and Hu, 2017), location, environment, resources and society (Dong and Hu, 2017), short-distance flights, low cost treatment and visa requirements (Johnson ve Garman, 2015).

Market data can be forecasted by time series analysis (Tang and Lau, 2017), regression (Ridderstaat et al., 2019; Johnson and Garman, 2015), econometric models (Tang and Lau, 2017; Cheng, 2016), system dynamics models (Vetitnev et al., 2016; Dong and Hu, 2017), and Grey models (Dang et al., 2016). There are papers in the related literature forecasting the number of medical tourists (Dang et al., 2016), modeling medical tourist behavior (Tang and Lau, 2017), forecasting the HI income (Vetitnev et al., 2016). The HI is expected to perform this forecasting task, considering the market pertaining to its specific service business line.

Demand and Capacity Integration

Demand and capacity integration task is carried out by the mutual effort of business partners. The HI plans its own capacity, and the AC plans demand for the integration. The related literature includes applications of industrial engineering approaches such as queuing theory in healthcare systems (Murray and Berwick, 2003; Bittencourt et al., 2018), scheduling (Wang et al., 1995; Xu, 2018) and system dynamics models (Sanden et al., 2005) to integrate demand and capacity into healthcare systems.

There are also training programs such as Care Capacity Demand Management (CCDM) provided by a private company including five steps: patient acuity, core data set, staffing methodology, variance response management, governance, and program monitoring (CCDM, 2019).

Tasks in demand and capacity integration are (Bozarth, 2011):

1. Planning the date and place by taking the forecasting output of the previous step.
2. Implementing the strategies for resources, capacity, inventory, and employees, considering the seasonality factors, analyzing the capacity constraints.
3. Gathering information about whether additional capacity and resource management are needed, and revising the plans.
4. Collecting data on approved and completed operations.
5. Collecting data on whether there is an exception, and how it has been solved.
6. Using this information for balancing and integrating demand and capacity.

Demand Planning

The AC monitors the forecasted and planned demand in this step by observing whether the forecast values match the actual demand and/or whether there is a seasonal or cyclical pattern (Wirtz, 2016). The number, demographics, and requirements of the patients and the expected changes in the patient demand volume should be tracked (Farmer et al., 2016).

In case of inadequate capacity, demand can be planned by reducing the number of patients by canalizing some patients to another HI that is in collaboration with the AC (Farmer et al., 2016), through marketing efforts to redirect the patients, and/or by queueing or through a reservation system (Wirtz, 2016, Bittencourt et al., 2018). In case of excess capacity, the number of patients can be increased through marketing efforts to attract more patients, and/or by shifting the excess capacity to different organizational positions (Wirtz, 2016). Hence, the most important points in demand planning are observing the changing patient demand, controlling the capacity level of business partners, and applying different strategy options.

Capacity Planning

HIs prepare the required materials, employees and rooms in the facility according to planned patient appointments. In relation to medical tourism, patients should not wait for medical intervention, HIs should arrange the visits as far in advance as possible, and after the patient arrives at the institution, delays should be avoided (Murray and Berwick, 2003). The main principle of capacity planning is scheduling patient requests with respect to the healthcare professional's convenience (An & Kritchanchai, 2019; Dubas-Jakóbczyk et al., 2018).

Six components of capacity planning to perform are:

1. Balancing demand and supply by controlling the rooms and inventory to match the planned patient visit requirements (Murray and Berwick, 2003).
2. Working down the backlog, i.e. doing the today' work today, by additional appointment slots and stretching the capacity (Wirtz, 2016), and by investments to expand the capacity in the long run (Murray and Berwick, 2003).
3. Reducing the number of appointment types by controlling for the patient's category (Murray and Berwick, 2003; Farmer et al., 2016).
4. Developing contingency plans for epidemics, influenza season, days following holiday seasons, etc. As a temporary solution, the planned appointments can be shifted to a different date by getting in touch with related patients for their approval (Murray and Berwick, 2003).
5. Reducing and shaping demand for visits by directing patients to a different HI (Tripathi et al., 2018), by obtaining additional facility, equipment and healthcare professional (Wirtz, 2016), by outsourcing specific healthcare services (Sanden et al., 2005), by improving the competency of medical assistants, and by virtual access to care with video telehealth (Farmer et al., 2016).
6. Increasing the effective supply, especially of bottleneck resources (Murray and Berwick, 2003). In the case of ambulatory care, the bottleneck is often the healthcare professionals. Therefore, in order to prevent bottlenecks, medical assistants should be well-trained and part-time healthcare professionals should be hired (Wirtz, 2016).

Execution

Execution phase of the MTSSC operations framework addresses service order generation and healthcare service delivery tasks (see Figure 5). The collaborative service operations execution is directly related to information sharing (Field et al, 2017), not only between business partners but also with the patient (Takahashi and

Figure 5. Execution step of the collaborative medical tourism service supply chain operations

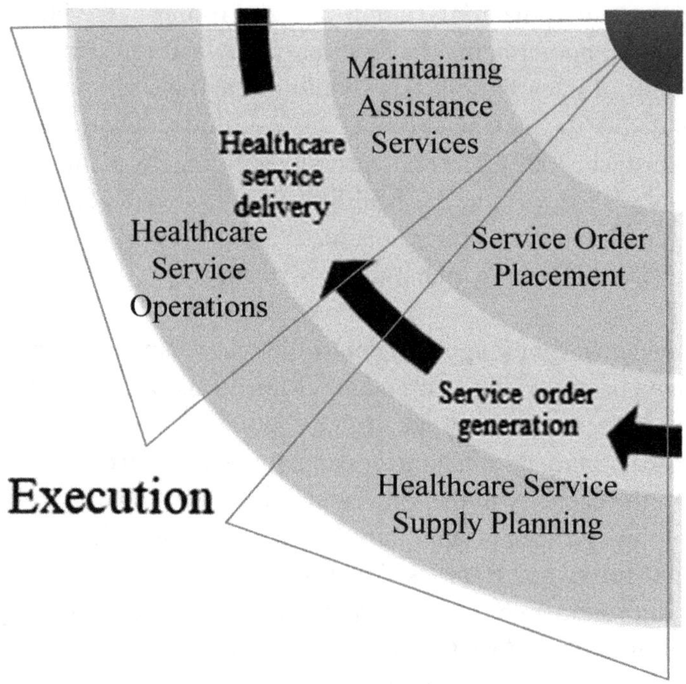

Hayashi, 2017). The collaborative execution perspective shapes the adaptability and flexibility of supply chains (Romero and Molina, 2011).

Service Order Generation

Service order generation, as a mutual collaborative business operation, details the planned medical tourist visit with an exact date and place. There are proactive and reactive approaches in service order generation (Kahiya et al., 2014). The latter takes the patient demand and generates a response, while the former predicts the patient demand for an appointment. Previous research asserts that the mixed use of these proactive and reactive approaches makes it easier in defining strategies by taking the current position of the market into consideration (Kahiya et al., 2014). In the related literature, there exist studies that employ agent-based simulation (Ponta et al., 2012) and linear programming (Deng et al., 2013) for service order generation.

Service Order Placement

Medical tourism service order placement process starts with the request of a patient from an AC for receiving medical treatment outside his/her country of residence. Patients can access an AC through their websites followed by an internet search, acting on referrals on social networking platforms, referrals from individuals who have received a similar treatment before, or via the guidance of an HI or healthcare agency. After the initial contact, medical tourism experience proceeds with the communication between the medical consultants at the AC and the patient(s). The patients are informed about the medical tests that they need to have in their own country before making a decision on the treatment. The test results provided are translated along with the medical reports and they are edited by the AC. Patients are informed about the choice of HI and the costs to guide them through the HI selection process. Once the patient makes a choice, an appointment with the HI is arranged by the AC. The patient's trip is planned. After the service order is placed, a contract between the patient and the service providers is signed to protect their rights. Additionally, optional services such as accommodation, flight ticket, translation, touristic activities can be arranged by the AC if the patient demands.

Service order placement literature emphasizes the importance of delays and the bullwhip effect (Li and Liu, 2013), process flow by using web services (Hon and Chiu, 2006), strategy development in case of high order placement frequency (Elbert and Knigge, 2018). Agent-based simulation (Elbert and Knigge, 2018) and fuzzy momentum analysis (Kablan and Ng, 2010), on the other hand, have been featured in the related literature.

Healthcare Service Supply Planning

HIs procure all the required materials and equipment in healthcare service supply planning task and keep themselves ready for additional tests depending on when and where the treatment service is to be executed. This phase requires the patient information (i.e. his/her category and preferences) and the exact appointment date (Hovav and Tsadikovich, 2015), the schedule of the healthcare professionals, the accessibility of medical and service suppliers, operation room planning, inventory and decision making tools (Xu et al., 2011). Inventory can be continuously or periodically reviewed (Rossetti et al., 2012) and the necessary materials/services are ordered (Al-Qatawneh and Hafeez, 2015).

Methods adopted in healthcare service supply and inventory planning include mathematical modeling (Hovav and Tsadikovich, 2015; Rosales et al., 2015), discrete event simulation (Essoussi, 2015; Rossetti et al., 2012; Zhou and Olsen, 2018), system dynamics model (Al-Qatawneh and Hafeez, 2015), ABC analysis, economic order quantity model, safety stock concept (Xu et al., 2011), simulation with particle swarm optimization (Kim and Lee, 2017), and two-bin method (Xu et al., 2011, Rosales et al., 2015).

Healthcare Service Delivery

In this collaborative operation of the MTSSC partners, the patient arrives at the HI, and all the activities planned beforehand are expected to go as planned. The face-to-face interaction between the healthcare professional and the patient is the most important part of this phase with regards to understanding patient needs and requests. Hence, communication and knowledge transfer skills of healthcare professionals are essential (Mirzaei et al., 2013). Furthermore, the effective use of healthcare information technology makes the treatment process more efficient (Bauer et al., 2014). In order to guarantee expected service quality, service contracts are recommended (Loevinsohn and Harding, 2005). In this way, uncertainty can be eliminated or at least reduced in order to make patients feel secure (Tan et al., 2005). The principles of healthcare service delivery are:

1. Incremental progress in the healthcare service process, for instance, shaping the communication and relation between the healthcare professional and the patient gradually.
2. Feedback systems for improving performance. Receiving direct, rapid, specific, and constructive feedback from the patient.
3. Adopting standard diagnosis and treatment procedures with flexibility.
4. Shortening response and service time with backup redundancy, disallowing backlogs.
5. Intelligent and effective leadership, tolerating minor mistakes, keeping people away from stress (Tan et al., 2005).

In order to assess service quality, Nordin et al. (2018) suggest a patient satisfaction measurement index based on the Kano model.

Healthcare Service Operations

The background operations of HIs is covered in the healthcare service operations task with the preparations of the medical intervention rooms and healthcare professionals. The patient's final decision on receiving the planned treatment is shaped during or right after the first medical examination. In case the patient decides not to receive the treatment, s/he returns to their home country. Otherwise, the treatment is performed immediately. After the medical intervention, communication between the patient and a medical consultant of the AC proceeds. The patient's return to their home country is planned with the medical consultant, and necessary fit to fly documentation or other needs are provided by again the AC.

Healthcare service operations literature highlights applications of the lean principle in healthcare systems in order to reduce variability, to avoid human-based errors by poka-yoke tools, to simplify or to remove unnecessary processes, to minimize the movements and transportation, to optimize the inventory, to prevent delays and waits (Diaz et al., 2012; Salam and Khan, 2016), lean appointment scheduling to increase service capacity (LaGanga, 2011), total productive maintenance, Kaizen and continuous improvement, to shorten the set up times, to standardize the processes, to obtain quality certifications, 5S, to reduce waste, and to produce service just in time (Adebanjo et al., 2016).

There are also studies in the literature employing simulation for the internal healthcare service operations by performing experiments/changes on the processes so that one can plan and schedule service capacity in a proper way (Samaranayake and Kiridena, 2011).

Maintaining Assistance Services

The background operations of ACs are addressed in the maintaining assistance services task. While the patient is in the examination room, additional needs of the patient or his/her relatives are provided by a representative/medical consultant of the AC that is also known as the medical tourism agent or the medical tourism facilitator. ACs keep in touch directly with the patients throughout the process to support them in each phase (Johnston et al., 2011). They guide the patients in deciding on the country and the HI to choose (Gan and Frederick, 2011). Therefore, it is important for an AC representative to be familiar with the culture and customs of the patients in order to make them feel secure in the provision of the related services at the destination country (Frederick ve Gan, 2015).

Depending on the follow-up care arrangements between the AC and the patient, the AC can provide tour/site-seeing, spa, air travel and ground transportation to the HI facility, accommodation, translation, concierge or ancillary services, can offer different insurance packages, can facilitate all kinds of communication with service providers such as arranging appointments or reservations, can pursue the required medical tests of the patient, can supply a medical escort, can purchase an international cell phones and can receive payments (Gan and Frederick, 2011; Cormany and Baloglu, 2011), can also make a follow-up care available (Johnston et al., 2011). In brief, all needs and requests of the patient can be fulfilled for a pre-defined charge (Gan and Frederick, 2011).

Analysis

In the final step of the collaborative MTSSC operations, all planned and implemented phases are evaluated with exception and performance analysis (Kwon et al., 2016) as presented in Figure 6. Execution monitoring and performance assessment activities on both sides support the collaborative tasks in this step.

Exceptions Management

An exception is an event happening out of expectation/ideal flow, and it can occur in both AC and HI business relations, and in the service provision process of the patients with the AC or the HI (Han et al., 2006; Panzarasa et al., 2002). The collaborative exception management activities of ACs and HIs requires rapid responsiveness due to frequent and various patient cases as a barrier to the workflow (Han et al., 2006; Panzarasa et al., 2002). Hence a quick solution for an exception is a necessity.

Exception management includes three main steps: representing the exception, generating a solution, and analyzing (Han et al., 2006). Exception management phases adapted for medical tourism services are (Bozarth, 2011, Han et al., 2006):

Figure 6. Analysis step of the collaborative medical tourism service supply chain operations

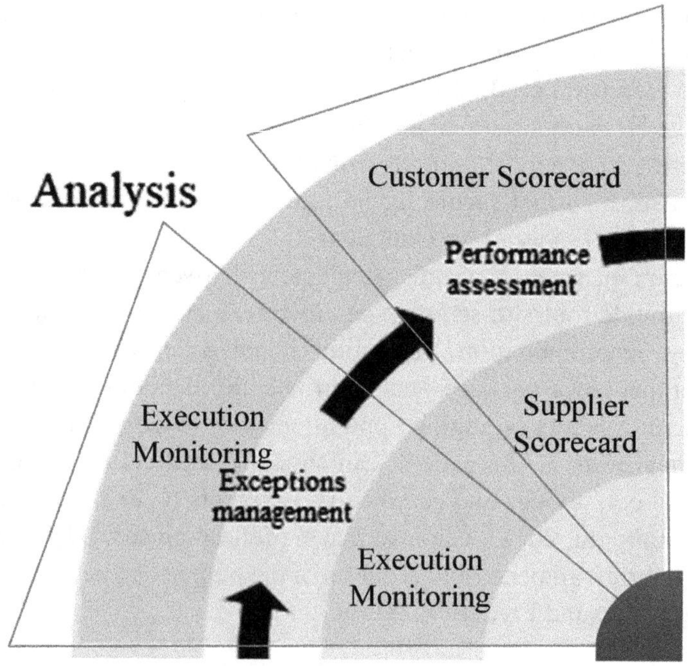

1. Reviewing the pre-defined exception criteria, defining the category of the exception.
2. Identifying the unexpected situation by both AC and HI side, defining the exception environment.
3. Determining the reason for the exception.
4. Comparison in exception criteria and value of the happening by considering the degree of importance (Bozarth, 2011).

The exception definition part can be non-objective because of the personal judgments of the responsible unit (Han et al., 2006). The factors that can trigger the exceptions are incompetence of the healthcare professionals, unusual symptoms (Han et al., 2006), inadequate resources, operating regardless of any prioritization rule (Panzarasa et al., 2002).

The solution generation phase consists of propagation of the patient to the respective healthcare professionals, reviewing the pre-defined decision making procedure, investigating the exceptions, and generating a solution (Bozarth, 2011; Han et al., 2006).

In order to analyze the exceptions, the solution implementation level is controlled (Han et al., 2006), if required, the decision making procedure is updated to standardize the solution generation phase (Panzarasa et al., 2002).

Execution Monitoring

ACs and HIs monitor and control the execution in the exception management phase. In this phase, execution monitoring procedure is defined, data on delivered services are collected (Majumdar et al., 2018), evidence-based data analysis is conducted, and decision making tools are used to support the monitoring process (Prasinos et al., 2017). The monitoring can be online, periodic or on-demand, and can be compared with the pre-specified rules (Piccoli et al., 2010). The responsible units should be known, barriers against the service provision should be detected, context change at run-time should be determined, the problem should be compensated during the service provision process (Marrella and Mecella, 2017). Retrospective compensation approaches are not suggested in medical services.

Performance Assessment

The AC and the HI evaluate their business partnership quality (Lin, 2014) as an input for the next (actually the first) step of the collaborative MTSSC operations framework so that they can form a decision on whether to strengthen or to terminate the collaboration. The factors affecting this partnership quality are external environment uncertainty (i.e. factors affecting medical tourism demand), trust, resource dependence, and inter-organizational partnership. These factors shape the supply chain operational performance directly by adding cooperation experiences, firm size, and the number of partners (Lin, 2014).

Most frequently used performance assessment tools are questionnaires, observations, scorecards, multiple-choice questions, knowledge tests, standard patient simulations, and case audits (Finucane et al., 2003)

Customer and Supplier Scorecards

The HI and the AC are both customers and suppliers of each other in a supply chain structure. They evaluate themselves and each other by scorecards in order to obtain a quantitative measurement. Additionally, patient satisfaction surveys are delivered to the patients by both the HI and the AC. Frequently, patient satisfaction questionnaires are used as a means to receive feedback. These questionnaires should include service quality, service delivery, accessibility level, efficiency aspects of the healthcare service provision.

The HI quality factors are pre-treatment screening, successful diagnosis, patient-centered service, secure environment, competency of the medical assistants, competency of the new medical techniques, hospitality, delays, need for re-treatment, hygiene, accuracy in laboratory tests, undesired situations, satisfactory explanations of healthcare professionals, patient involvement in medical decisions (Gauld et al., 2011), service structure, process and outputs (Sibthorpe and Gardner, 2007).

As a result of the scorecards, business partnership or service provision decisions are made anew in the next cycle of the collaborative MTSSC operations framework.

CONCLUSION

A supply chain management perspective is not so prominent in medical tourism services, but encouraging the authorities to think in terms of a service supply chain would certainly improve the success rate and sustainability of the business. Collaboration in medical tourism services, as in any other supply chain, is essential for the enhanced competitive ability and long-term business success.

This chapter presents the CPFR model adapted for supply chain operations in medical tourism services. Defining the collaborative tasks of ACs and HIs and describing different tools and techniques that would support the collaboration in medical supply chain planning and the execution between ACs and HIs, the related literature has been reviewed to discover the tools and techniques that support each collaborative task.

This chapter emphasizes the growth and development of medical tourism as an emerging market and the collaboration between HIs and ACs ensures an improved patient experience, which is in support of the main theme of the book.

The study lists many approaches to support collaborative operations; however, since there is no one size fits all approach, the relevant parties need to decide on which tools to use considering their own needs and requirements and become skilled in how to use them.

As the next step in this direction, a case study implementing the relevant tools for collaborative planning and execution of supply chain operations in a medical service supply chain can be examined and reported.

REFERENCES

Accenture. (2012). *Joint business planning*. Retrieved from: www.accenture.com

Adebanjo, D., Laosirihongthong, T., & Samaranayake, P. (2016). Prioritizing lean supply chain management initiatives in healthcare service operations: A fuzzy AHP approach. *Production Planning and Control*, *27*(12), 953–966. doi:10.1080/0953 7287.2016.1164909

Al-Qatawneh, L., & Hafeez, K. (2015). Critical-to-life classification for managing inventory in a healthcare supply chain. *International Journal of Intelligent Enterprise*, *3*(1), 54–78. doi:10.1504/IJIE.2015.073491

Alderson, W. (2006). A basic guide to market planning. *A Twenty-First Century Guide to Aldersonian Marketing Thought,* 283-290.

Amahazion, F. (2018). Renal Replacement Therapy in Eritrea. *Transplantation*, *102*(5), 707–710. doi:10.1097/TP.0000000000002152 PMID:29702535

An, T. S., & Kritchanchai, D. (2019). Hospital Capacity Planning for Special Economic Zone in Thailand: A Case Study in Kanchanaburi Province. *IEEE International Conference on Industrial Engineering and Engineering Management*, 1593-1597.

Andersson, A., Wiklund, M., & Hatakka, M. (2015). Emerging collaborative and cooperative practices in 1:1 schools. *Technology, Pedagogy and Education*, *25*(4), 413–430. doi:10.1080/1475939X.2015.1060896

Barrenstein, P., & Tweraser, S. (2004). Category Management: Why Now? In *Collaborative Customer Relationship Management*. Springer-Verlag Berlin Heidelberg. doi:10.1007/978-3-540-24710-4_11

Bauer, A. M., Thielke, S. M., Katon, W., Unützer, J., & Areán, P. (2014). Aligning health information technologies with effective service delivery models to improve chronic disease care. *Preventive Medicine*, *66*, 167–172. doi:10.1016/j.ypmed.2014.06.017 PMID:24963895

Bekkers, V. (2009). Flexible information infrastructures in Dutch E-Government collaboration arrangements: Experiences and policy implications. *Government Information Quarterly*, *26*(1), 60–68. doi:10.1016/j.giq.2007.09.010

Bittencourt, O., Verter, V., & Yalovsky, M. (2018). Hospital capacity management based on the queueing theory. *International Journal of Productivity and Performance Management*, *67*(2), 224–238. doi:10.1108/IJPPM-12-2015-0193

Bozarth, C. (2011). *Lecture notes: Collaborative planning forecasting and replenishment*. Academic Press.

CCDM. (2019). *Care Capacity Demand Management.* Retrieved from: https://www.ccdm.health.nz/

Chee, H. L., Whittaker, A., & Por, H. H. (2017). Medical travel facilitators, private hospitals and international medical travel in assemblage. *Asia Pacific Viewpoint*, *58*(2), 242–254. doi:10.1111/apv.12161

Cheng, K. M. (2016). Medical tourism: Chinese maternity tourism to Hong Kong. *Current Issues in Tourism*, *19*(14), 1479–1486. doi:10.1080/13683500.2015.1042359

Chung, W. W. C., & Leung, S. W. F. (2005). Collaborative planning, forecasting and replenishment: A case study in copper clad laminate industry. *Production Planning and Control*, *16*(6), 563–574. doi:10.1080/09537280500112488

Connell, J. (2006). Medical tourism: Sea, sun, sand and surgery. *Tourism Management*, *27*(6), 1093–1100. doi:10.1016/j.tourman.2005.11.005

Cormany, D., & Baloglu, S. (2011). Medical travel facilitator websites: An exploratory study of web page contents and services offered to the prospective medical tourist. *Tourism Management*, *32*(4), 709–716. doi:10.1016/j.tourman.2010.02.008

Costello, T. (2013). Vendor Management. *IT Professional – IEEE Computer Society*, 1520-9202/13, 70-72.

Dang, H. S., Huang, Y. F., Wang, C. N., & Nguyen, T. M. T. (2016) Estimation of the market size of medical tourism industry using grey models-case study in South Korea. *International Conference on Computational Intelligence and Applications*, *7600313*, 46-50. 10.1109/ICCIA.2016.14

Deng, L., Jin, H., & Wu, S. (2013). Vmerger: Server consolidation in virtualized environment. *Proceedings of IEEE 11th International Conference on Dependable, Autonomic and Secure Computing, 6844434*, 606-612.

Díaz, A., Pons, J., & Solís, L. (2012). Improving healthcare services: Lean lessons from Aravind. *Int. J. Business Excellence*, *5*(4), 413–428. doi:10.1504/IJBEX.2012.047907

Dileep, M. R., Prathyash, V., & Jithin, J. (2019). Ayurtourism:A web based recommendation system for medical tourism. *ACM International Conference Proceeding Series*, 492-495.

Dong, D., & Hu, Y. (2017). Study of System Dynamics for Health Care Housing Development in Panzhihua. *Proceedings of the International Conference on Construction and Real Estate Management*, 175-186. 10.1061/9780784481073.020

Dubas-Jakóbczyk, K., Sowada, C., Domagała, A., & Więckowska, B. (2018). Building hospital capacity planning mechanisms in Poland: The impact of 2016/2017 regulatory changes. *The International Journal of Health Planning and Management*, *33*(2), e403–e415. doi:10.1002/hpm.2493 PMID:29417634

Dunets, A. N., & Zhogova, I. G. (2018). Significant changes of tourism industry in the altai-sayan mountainous region. *Journal of Environmental Management and Tourism*, *9*(4), 869–879. doi:10.14505//jemt.9.4(28).21

Elbert, R., & Knigge, J.-K. (2018). How order placement influences resource allocation and order processing times inside a multi-user warehouse. *Proceedings – Winter Simulation Conference*, *8632468*, 2921-2932. 10.1109/WSC.2018.8632468

Eom, T., Yu, J., & Han, H. (2019). Medical tourism in Korea – recent phenomena, emerging markets, potential threats, and challenge factors: A review. *Asia Pacific Journal of Tourism Research*, *24*(6), 563–573. doi:10.1080/10941665.2019.1610005

Essoussi, I. E. (2016) A performance evaluation of some collaborative inventory management practices in the healthcare supply chain. *Proceedings of International Conference on Industrial Engineering and Systems Management*, *7380171*, 277-284.

Farmer, C. M., Hosek, S. D., & Adamson D. M. (2016). Balancing Demand and Supply for Veterans' Health Care. *RAND Health*.

Ferrer, M., & Medhekar, A. (2012). The factors impacting on the management of global medical tourism service supply chain. *Journal of GSTF Business Review*, *2*(2), 206–211.

Field, J. M., Victorino, L., Buell, R. W., Dixon, M. J., Meyer Goldstein, S., Menor, L. J., ... Zhang, J. J. (2017). Service operations: What's next? *Journal of Service Management*, *29*(1), 55–97. doi:10.1108/JOSM-08-2017-0191

Finucane, P. M., Bourgeois-Law, G. A., Ineson, S. L., & Kaigas, T. M. (2003). A comparison of performance assessment programs for medical practitioners in Canada, Australia, New Zealand, and the United Kingdom. *Academic Medicine*, *78*(8), 837–884. doi:10.1097/00001888-200308000-00020 PMID:12915380

Fliedner, G. (2003). CPFR : An emerging supply chain tool. *Industrial Management & Data Systems*, *103*(1), 14–21. doi:10.1108/02635570310456850

Frederick, J. R., & Gan, L. L. (2015). East-West differences among medical tourism facilitators' websites. *Journal of Destination Marketing & Management*, *4*(2), 98–109. doi:10.1016/j.jdmm.2015.03.002

Friedman, M. D., Bailit, M. H., & Michel, J. O. (1995). Vendor management: A model for collaboration and quality improvement. *The Joint Commission Journal on Quality Improvement*, *21*(11), 635–645. doi:10.1016/S1070-3241(16)30192-4 PMID:8608335

Gan, L. L., & Frederick, J. R. (2011). Medical tourism facilitators: Patterns of service differentiation. *Journal of Vacation Marketing*, *17*(3), 165–183. doi:10.1177/1356766711409181

Gan, L. L., & Frederick, J. R. (2018). The choice of facilitators in medical tourism. *Health Marketing Quarterly*, *35*(1), 65–83. doi:10.1080/07359683.2018.1434891 PMID:29474154

Gauld, R., Al-wahaibi, S., Chisholm, J., Crabbe, R., Kwon, B., Oh, T., ... Sohn, S. (2011). Scorecards for health system performance assessment: The New Zealand example. *Health Policy (Amsterdam)*, *103*(2-3), 200–208. doi:10.1016/j.healthpol.2011.05.016 PMID:21723641

Haarhoff, R., & Mokoena, L. G. (2017). The market place of medical tourism facilitators in South Africa. *African Journal of Hospitality, Tourism and Leisure*, *6*(3).

Han, M., Thiery, T., & Song, X. (2006). Managing Exceptions in the Medical Workflow Systems. ICSE'06, Shanghai, China.

Hartmann, S. (2019). Mobilising patients towards transnational healthcare markets–insights into the mobilising work of medical travel facilitators in Delhi. *Mobilities*, *14*(1), 71–86. doi:10.1080/17450101.2018.1533694

Hollmann, R. L., Scavarda, L. F., & Thomé, A. M. T. (2015). Collaborative planning, forecasting and replenishment: A literature review. *International Journal of Productivity and Performance Management*, *64*(7), 971–993. doi:10.1108/IJPPM-03-2014-0039

Hopkins, L., Labonté, R., Runnels, V., & Packer, C. (2010). Medical tourism today: What is the state of existing knowledge? *Journal of Public Health Policy*, *31*(2), 185–198. doi:10.1057/jphp.2010.10 PMID:20535101

Hovav, S., & Tsadikovich, D. (2015). A network flow model for inventory management and distribution of influenza vaccines through a healthcare supply chain. *Operations Research for Health Care*, *5*, 49–62. doi:10.1016/j.orhc.2015.05.003

Hsu, H.-Y., Chang, M.-H., Ni, Y.-H., Jeng, Y.-M., Chiang, C.-L., Chen, H.-L., ... Chen, P.-J. (2013). Long-term follow-up of children with postnatal immunoprophylaxis failure who were infected with hepatitis B virus surface antigen gene mutant. *The Journal of Infectious Diseases*, *207*(7), 1047–1057. doi:10.1093/infdis/jis943 PMID:23300165

Mordor Intelligence. (2019). *Global Medical Tourism Market Report*. Author.

Jagyasi, P. (2019). *Medical tourism trends to watch*. Retrieved from: https://www.linkedin.com/pulse/medical-tourism-trends-watch-2019-dr-prem-jagyasi/

Jaramillo, J., Goyal, D., & Lung, C. (2019). Birth tourism among Chinese women. *MCN. The American Journal of Maternal Child Nursing*, *44*(2), 94–99. doi:10.1097/NMC.0000000000000500 PMID:30640727

JCI. (2019). *Joint Commission International Accredited Organizations List*. Retrieved from www.jointcommissioninternational.org/about-jci/jci-accredited-organizations/

Jing, F., & Lim, C.-K. (2018). Advancement strategies toward the Chinese market in Korean medical tourism industry. *Asia Life Sciences Supplement*, *15*(3), 2073–2081.

Johnson, T. J., & Garman, A. N. (2015). Demand for international medical travel to the USA. *Tourism Economics*, *21*(5), 1061–1077. doi:10.5367/te.2014.0393

Johnston, R., Crooks, V. A., Adams, K., Snyder, J., & Kingsbury, P. (2011). An industry perspective on Canadian patients' involvement in Medical Tourism: Implications for public health. *BMC Public Health*, *11*(1), 416. doi:10.1186/1471-2458-11-416 PMID:21627830

Kablan, A., & Ng, W. L. (2010). Enhancing High-Frequency Order Placement Strategies with Fuzzy Logic and Fuzzy Inference, *IAENG. International Journal of Computational Science*, *37*(4).

Kahiya, E. T., & Dean, D. L. (2014). Export performance: Multiple predictors and multiple measures approach. *Asia Pacific Journal of Marketing and Logistics*, *26*(3), 378–407. doi:10.1108/APJML-11-2012-0119

Kim, J., & Lee, J. (2017). Particle swarm optimization based inventory policy for wholesale business in Devs-based medicine supply chain. *International Journal of Industrial Engineering: Theory Applications and Practice*, *24*(2), 146–161.

Kim, J. H., Kim, S. Y., Yun, S.-J., Chung, J. I., Choi, H., Yu, H. S., ... Lee, J. Y. (2019). Medical travel among non-Seoul residents to seek prostate cancer treatment in medical facilities of Seoul. *Cancer Research and Treatment*, *51*(1), 53–64. doi:10.4143/crt.2017.468 PMID:29458236

Kwon, I. G., Kim, S. H., & Martin, D. G. (2016). Healthcare supply chain management; strategic areas for quality and financial improvement. *Technological Forecasting and Social Change*, *113*, 422–428. doi:10.1016/j.techfore.2016.07.014

LaGanga, L. R. (2011). Lean service operations: Reflections and new directions for capacity expansion in outpatient clinics. *Journal of Operations Management*, *29*(5), 422–433. doi:10.1016/j.jom.2010.12.005

Lee, H. K., & Fernando, Y. (2015). The antecedents and outcomes of the medical tourism supply chain. *Tourism Management*, *46*, 148–157. doi:10.1016/j.tourman.2014.06.014

Levin, S., & Berry, T. B. (2010). Next-generation vendor management: The experience of Centura Health. Healthcare Financial Management. *Journal of the Healthcare Financial Management Association.*, *64*(6), 106–116. PMID:20533685

Li, C., & Liu, S. (2013). A robust optimization approach to reduce the bullwhip Effect of supply chains with vendor order placement lead time delays in an uncertain environment. *Applied Mathematical Modelling*, *37*(3), 707–718. doi:10.1016/j.apm.2012.02.033

Lin, H. C. (2014). Assessment of the Partnership Quality between Travel Agencies and Health Care Organizations on the International Medical Tourism Market in Taiwan. *Journal of Quality Assurance in Hospitality & Tourism*, *15*(4), 356–381. doi:10.1080/1528008X.2014.921777

Lin, R.-H., & Pei-Yun, H. (2014). The study of CPFR implementation model in medical SCM of Taiwan. *Production Planning and Control*, *25*(3), 260–271. doi: 10.1080/09537287.2012.673646

Lindblom, A., & Olkkonen, R. (2006). Category management tactics: An analysis of manufacturers' control. *International Journal of Retail & Distribution Management, 34*(6), 482–496. doi:10.1108/09590550610667065

Loevinsohn, B., & Harding, A. (2005). Buying results? Contracting for health service delivery in developing countries. *Lancet, 366*(9486), 676–681. doi:10.1016/S0140-6736(05)67140-1 PMID:16112305

Madzingamiri, D., Schouten, M. A. C., & Blokland, M. (2015). Water, sanitation and hygiene partners collaborating to combat severe cholera outbreaks during the State of Emergency in Zimbabwe. *Water Policy, 17*(2), 370–388. doi:10.2166/wp.2014.100

Majumdar, R., Yang, Y. Y., Li, H., Akçapinar, G., Flanagan, B., & Ogata, H. (2018). GOAL: Supporting learner's development of self-direction skills using health and learning data. *Proceedings 26th International Conference on Computers in Education, Main Conference*, 406-415.

Marrella, A., & Mecella, M. (2017). Adaptive process management in cyber-physical domains. *Intelligent Systems Reference Library, 123*, 15–48. doi:10.1007/978-3-319-52181-7_2

Mathon, D., Apparicio, P., & Lachapelle, U. (2018). Cross-border spatial accessibility of health care in the North-East Department of Haiti. *International Journal of Health Geographics, 17*(1), 36. doi:10.118612942-018-0156-6 PMID:30359261

McCain, G. (1987). Black holes, cash pigs, and other hospital portfolio analysis problems. *Journal of Health Care Marketing, 7*(2), 56–64. PMID:10301718

Mirzaei, M., Aspin, C., Essue, B., Jeon, Y. H., Dugdale, P., Usherwood, T., & Leeder, S. (2013). A patient-centered approach to health service delivery: Improving health outcomes for people with chronic illness. *BMC Health Services Research, 13*(1), 251. doi:10.1186/1472-6963-13-251 PMID:23819721

Murray, M., & Berwick, D. M. (2003). Advanced Access Reducing Waiting and Delays in Primary Care. *Innovations in Primary Care., 289*(8), 1035–1040. PMID:12597760

Nakayama, M., Chen, C., & Ractham, P. (2018). Medical tourism for cosmetic procedures: Credibility assessment of service providers via online health forums. Handbook of Research on Emerging Perspectives on Healthcare Information Systems and Informatics, 498-514.

Nino-Murcia, A., Pinto Ramirez, J. L., & Nino-Torres, L. (2018). Organ transplantation in Colombia. *Transplantation, 102*(11), 1779–1783. doi:10.1097/TP.0000000000002409 PMID:30346371

Nordin, N., Norsyafawati, W., Radzi, W. M., Razak, R. C., Abdullah, S., Hamzah, M. R., ... Idrus, S. (2018). Complaints and compliments assessment in developing service delivery measurement. *Management Science Letters*, *8*, 293–304. doi:10.5267/j.msl.2018.4.018

Nylén, U. (2007). Interagency collaboration in human services: Impact of formalization and intensity on effectiveness. *Public Administration*, *85*(1), 143–166. doi:10.1111/j.1467-9299.2007.00638.x

Panahifar, F., Ghadimi, P., Azadnia, A. H., Heavey, C., & Byrne, P. J. (2013). A Study on CPFR Implementation Critical Factors for the Automotive Spare Part Industry. *8th EUROSIM Congress on Modelling and Simulation*, 1-6. 10.1109/EUROSIM.2013.11

Panzarasa, S., Maddé, S., Quaglini, S., Pistarini, C., & Stefanelli, M. (2002). Evidence-based careflow management systems: The case of post-stroke rehabilitation. *Journal of Biomedical Informatics*, *35*(2), 123–139. doi:10.1016/S1532-0464(02)00505-1 PMID:12474426

Patients Beyond Borders. (2019). *Medical Tourism Statistics & Facts*. Retrieved from: https://patientsbeyondborders.com/medical-tourism-statistics-facts

Peng, B.-L., & Ling, L. (2019). Association between rural-to-urban migrants' social medical insurance, social integration and their medical return in China: A nationally representative cross-sectional data analysis. *BMC Public Health*, *19*(1), 86. doi:10.118612889-019-6416-y PMID:30658619

Pereira, R. T., Malone, C. M., & Flaherty, G. T. (2018). Aesthetic journeys: A review of cosmetic surgery tourism. *Journal of Travel Medicine*, *25*(1).

Peters, X., & Gangemi, A. (2018). An update on bariatric tourism: Time for a national registry? *Surgery for Obesity and Related Diseases*, *14*(4), 528–532. doi:10.1016/j.soard.2017.12.018 PMID:29426706

Piccoli, L., Dubey, A., Simone, J. N., & Kowalkowlski, J. B. (2010). LQCD workflow execution framework: Models, provenance and fault-tolerance. *Journal of Physics: Conference Series*, *219*(1 part 7), 072047. doi:10.1088/1742-6596/219/7/072047

Ponta, L., Scalas, E., Raberto, M., & Cincotti, S. (2012) Statistical analysis and agent-based microstructure modeling of high-frequency financial trading. *IEEE Journal on Selected Topics in Signal Processing, 6*(4), 381-387.

Prasinos, M., Spanoudakis, G., & Koutsouris, D. (2017). Towards a model-driven platform for evidence-based public health policymaking. *Proceedings of the International Conference on Software Engineering and Knowledge Engineering*, 566-571. 10.18293/SEKE2017-180

Reniers, G. (2011). Investigating the factors facilitating (a.o. safety and security) collaboration in the chemicals sector. *International Journal of Safety and Security Engineering*, *1*(1), 18–32. doi:10.2495/SAFE-V1-N1-18-32

Ridderstaat, J., Singh, D., & DeMicco, F. (2019). The impact of major tourist markets on health tourism spending in the United States. *Journal of Destination Marketing & Management*, *11*, 270–280. doi:10.1016/j.jdmm.2018.05.003

Romero, D., & Molina, A. (2011). Collaborative networked organizations and customer communities: Value co-creation and co-innovation in the networking era. *Production Planning and Control*, *22*(5-6), 447–472. doi:10.1080/09537287.2010.536619

Rosales, C. R., Magazine, M., & Rao, U. (2015). The 2Bin system for controlling medical supplies at point-of-use. *European Journal of Operational Research*, *243*(1), 271–280. doi:10.1016/j.ejor.2014.10.041

Rossetti, M. D., Buyurgan, N., & Pohl, E. (2012). Medical Supply Logistics, *International Series in Operations Research &. Management Science*, *168*, 245–280.

Salam, M. A., & Khan, S. A. (2016). Value creation through lean management: A case study of healthcare service operations. *International Journal of Services and Operations Management*, *25*(3), 275–293. doi:10.1504/IJSOM.2016.079513

Samaranayake, P., & Kiridena, S. (2011). *Patient Journey Modeling Using Integrated Data Structures in Healthcare Service Operations*. Penang: IEEE CHUSER. doi:10.1109/CHUSER.2011.6163802

Sandal, C. (2019). By the Way. the Last-Minute International Traveler. *Workplace Health & Safety*, *67*(2), 53–55. doi:10.1177/2165079918806535 PMID:30428770

Sanden, R., Everwijn, H., Rouwette, E., & Gubbels, J. (2005). Balancing supply and demand for dementia care in the Netherlands. *The Town Planning Review*, 1–23.

Seifert, D. (2003). Collaborative planning, forecasting, and replenishment: How to create a supply chain advantage. American Management Association.

Sibthorpe, B., & Gardner, K. (2007). A conceptual framework for performance assessment in primary health care. *Australian Journal of Primary Health*, *13*(2), 96–103. doi:10.1071/PY07027

Smith. (2015). *The brave approach to writing a joint business plan with a UK supermarket*. Retrieved from: www.makingbusinessmatter.co.uk

Takahashi, A., & Hayashi, T. (2017). Collaborative quality framework: QoE-centric service operation in collaboration with users, service providers, and network operators. *EICE Transactions on Communications,* (9), 1554-1563.

Tan, J., Wen, H. J., & Awad, N. (2005). Health care and services delivery systems as complex adaptive systems. *Communications of the ACM*, *48*(5), 36–44. doi:10.1145/1060710.1060737

Tang, C. F., & Lau, E. (2017). Modelling the demand for inbound medical tourism: The case of Malaysia. *International Journal of Tourism Research*, *19*(5), 584–593. doi:10.1002/jtr.2131

Touré, S. B., Kleiderman, E., & Knoppers, B. M. (2018). Bridging stem cell research and medicine: A learning health system. *Regenerative Medicine*, *13*(6), 741–752. doi:10.2217/rme-2017-0129 PMID:30043682

Tripathi, V., Elneil, S., & Romanzi, L. (2018). Demand and capacity to integrate pelvic organ prolapse and genital fistula services in low-resource settings. *International Urogynecology Journal and Pelvic Floor Dysfunction*, *29*(10), 1509–1515. doi:10.100700192-018-3561-2 PMID:29411073

Urbach, N., Ahlemann, F., & El Arbi, F. (2014). Towards a design theory for customer satisfaction-oriented it vendor management. *20th Americas Conference on Information Systems*, 1-14.

Vetitnev, A., Kopyirin, A., & Kiseleva, A. (2016). System dynamics modelling and forecasting health tourism demand: The case of Russian resorts. *Current Issues in Tourism*, *19*(7), 618–623. doi:10.1080/13683500.2015.1076382

VICS. (1998). *Collaborative Planning Forecasting and Replenishment (CPFR)*. Voluntary Interindustry Commerce Standards.

VICS. (2004). *Collaborative Planning Forecasting and Replenishment (CPFR): An overview*. Voluntary Interindustry Commerce Standards.

Wang, S. J., Shahidehpour, S. M., Mokhtari, S., Irisarri, G. D., & Kirschen, D. S. (1995). Short-term generation scheduling with transmission and environmental constraints using an augmented Lagrangian relaxation. *IEEE Transactions on Power Systems*, *10*(3), 1294–1301. doi:10.1109/59.466524

Wirtz, J. (2016). Balancing Capacity and Demand in Service Operations. *Winning in Service Markets,* 308 – 343.

Xu, E., Wermus, M., & Bauman, D. B. (2011). Development of an integrated medical supply information system. *Enterprise Information Systems*, *5*(3), 385–399. doi:10.1080/17517575.2011.566630

Xu, Y., Prats, X., & Delahaye, D. (2018) Synchronization of traffic flow and sector opening for collaborative demand and capacity balancing. *Proceedings AIAA/IEEE Digital Avionics Systems Conference*. 10.1109/DASC.2018.8569789

Zallocco, R. L., & Joseph, W. B. (1991). Strategic Market Planning in Hospitals: Is It Done? Does It Work? *Journal of Health Care Marketing*, *11*(1), 5–11. PMID:10110082

Zhou, Q. S., & Olsen, T. L. (2018). Rotating the medical supplies for emergency response: A simulation-based approach. *International Journal of Production Economics*, *196*, 1–11. doi:10.1016/j.ijpe.2017.11.010

Chapter 12
Heal and Revive:
Emerging Trends in Wellness Tourism in Kerala

Bipithalal Balakrishnan Nair
https://orcid.org/0000-0001-5381-4073
University of Bedfordshire, UK

ABSTRACT

During the past decade, health and wellness tourism has become one of the top categories of tourism across the globe. On the other hand, academic deliberations are forged about the classifications and elucidations to differentiate the key terms concomitant with the wellness tourism sector. Arguably, due to the high market competition, the majority of the wellness/wellbeing/health tourism products are closely related and used interchangeably. Therefore, this study attempts to discourse the contemporary trends and developments in Kerala. As the forerunner for Ayurveda tourism and as one of the popular wellness tourist destinations, Kerala persists in the top list. Though, compared to other destinations, there are minimal tourism-oriented researcher studies were conducted. To attend this gap, this chapter explores the wellness sector of Kerala in terms of recent trends and developments. Interestingly, the tourism sector of Kerala observed to be dynamic and innovative by combining various tourism attributes offer a unique experience to the visitors.

DOI: 10.4018/978-1-5225-9787-2.ch012

INTRODUCTION

Tourism is perceived as a course of self-generation as well as recreation, edification or leniency. Smith and Puczkó (2009, p.9) suggest the process of tourism as "enhanced by regular breaks from routine, periods of rest and relaxation, fantasy and escapism, even the mere pleasure of planning and anticipating a trip". To them, the benefits of tourism appears to be more linked to mental health and physical relaxations. Historically, many regions, countries and communities followed their own ethnic wellness treatments; for instance, Indian, Chinese, Egyptian, Persian and Japanese style treatments existed and many are still widely practised through tourism.

Scholars who have worked on the topic of wellness tourism seem to agree that there is not a universally approved definition for the term or often confusion is caused owing to the myriad of associated terms (Grénman and Räikkönen, 2015). Due to interdisciplinary (or *transdisciplinary*) conceptualisation, it has been demarcated in many ways. This plurality of definitions has often contributed to the richness and depth of the area with dialogues bridging the disciplinary boundaries from medical science to sociology. All of these conceptualisations differ in their scope and disciplinary characteristics. In tourism studies, health, well-being and medical tourism are well researched and the *Nordic* scholars have been epitomised at the leading edge of the research.

Following the views of Agner (2010), the term 'well-being' can be classified into three main categories: psychological or mental; satisfaction or fulfilment and purpose. Instead, wellness or well-being is complex to define since it is a personal experience based on the requirements of the individual in need. One of the prime reasons for the growing interest in this field can be hectic lifestyle, stress and changes in the sociological values as well as customs. Tourism has always been seen as a process of relaxation, indulgence or revitalisation. At present it is seen as an escape from daily stress and tension. More people prefer to find ways to revitalise themselves during their holidays, than just through leisure. This trend catalysed the boom in the wellness tourism sector. Instead of health or medicinal tourism, well-being aims to revive mind, body and soul to create a holistic ambience; the psychological and physical benefits of tourism. In this context, it is worth exploring the views of Hallab (2006, p.71) regarding well-being tourism, to demonstrate how "in the fields of travel and tourism, health has been approached from the angle of tourism experiences' effects on an individual's well-being".

Reflecting the intensifying tourism discourse about wellness, Hartwell et al., (2018, p.56), mentioned that there has been "an evolution in thinking about health, wellness, well-being and quality of life in tourism from concerns about product, tourist motivations and attitudes towards tourism, towards [sic!] a more consolidated and deeper appreciation of the range of benefits provided by tourism, both for tourists and residents." Aware of the wealth of studies on health and wellness tourism, Table 1 illustrates various viewpoints and descriptions. In tourism studies, the literature around wellness is witnessing a tremendous expansion, principally focusing on the areas of product development; customer satisfaction; marketing; management and practice; service opportunities; moreover, it has also been conceptualised in association with indigenous and cultural contexts, as noted by Foley (2010). It is perhaps a more industrially converged topic aim to deliver customer satisfaction as well as experience built upon the foundation of 'alternative health' tourism.

From a sociological point of view, by recognising the contemporary trend in tourism it would instead be a philosophical confrontation of the self; the flow from the West to the East. At this juncture, the transdisciplinary understanding about well-being is worth noting: *West Vs East and Materialism Vs Spiritualism,* specifically taking into account the amplified fame of Indian Ayurveda and Yoga, Meditation, Chinese treatments and Thai massage. For these reasons, the scope of wellness tourism must weigh more than the traditional way of relaxation, to include the 'spiritual' borders. Therefore, the following conceptual framework can be used to explain the functions or scope of wellness tourism in a broad spectrum to include the 'self' factor. Ayurveda and Yoga have become the most prevalent one among this. One of the main reasons for this amplified popularity can be the contemporary hectic lifestyle, stress and sociocultural vicissitudes. These trends are also evident in the wellness tourism industry across the globe, especially for Indian destinations. Beyond the boundaries of traditional medical treatments, an increasing number of tourists prefer wellbeing experiences through the rejuvenation of mind, body and soul (Edward and George, 2008). Therefore, the contemporary wellness tourism industry develops innovative products and ideas to facilitate growing customer expectations.

Kerala, India is renowned for its geographical charm, cultural attractions and also as a flourishing wellness tourism destination. One of the pioneers of the wellness tourism sector, the state is also known as *'Land of Ayurveda'*. Thanuskodi (2016, p.34), notes that "Kerala has become one of the leading Medical Tourism destinations of India and gained international attention for health tourism and is becoming a popular health tourism hub." Kerala Ayurveda has been labelled as a 'unique attraction' from three decades ago when the Government of Kerala started to invest in a three-phase project. Through this endeavour Kerala became one of the global destinations in healthcare, which could be further accomplished by collaborating with other businesses, especially within tourism (Pordié, 2013).

LITERATURE REVIEW

An Overview of Kerala Tourism

Edward and George (2008) described Kerala as a prime, top of the line, travel industry goal in the Indian subcontinent. The moderate atmosphere, rich craftsmanship, bright celebrations, unique characteristics and cultural attractions with a personal, physical satisfaction similar to created countries are making the travel industry thrive in Kerala. Contrasted with different states in India, Kerala is distinct due to its fascinating geological variety contained within the smallest conceivable zone. This variety offers vacationers a wide range of attractions and experiences, such as coastlines, backwaters, wildlife, evergreen timberlands and assorted vegetation. It is regularly referred to as the "Green Gateway" to India (Netto, 2004).

It is located at the Southern point of India and is relatively small in size compared to other states in the country. The state is famous for coconut trees, long sandy beaches and spices. Western Ghats, the beautiful mountain range is safeguarding Kerala on the Eastern border and has one of the richest sites for biodiversity with rare species of medicinal plants. This is one of the reasons for the success of Kerala's medicinal tourism. The central region of Kerala is well-known for Backwater tourism. Kerala tourism ministry (2017, p.20) promoted the destination, describing it as "an equable climate, a lengthy shoreline with serene beaches, tranquil stretches of emerald backwaters, lush hill stations and exotic wildlife, waterfalls, sprawling plantations and paddy fields, Ayurvedic health holidays, enchanting art forms, magical festivals, historical and cultural monuments, exotic cuisine - make Kerala a unique experience for all" (ICCCON, 2019).

Due to its stunning natural beauty, foliage and uniqueness, the state has achieved several prestigious tourism awards, such as the Conde Nast Travel Award (2015) and also an award from Travel and Leisure Magazine (2006). *National Geographic Traveler* Magazine chose Kerala as "one of the Ten Paradises of the world" and *The National Geographic Magazine* listed it as "*50 of the world*'s top destinations: places that every curious traveller should visit in a lifetime" (Edward and George, 2008, pp.16-35).

A sliver of a state in India's deep south, Kerala is shaped by its landscape – almost 600 km of glorious Arabian Sea coast and beaches, a languid network of backwaters and the spice and tea-covered hills of the Western Ghats. As relaxing as an Ayurvedic massage, just setting foot on this swathe of soul-quenching green will slow your stride to a blissed-out amble. Kerala is a world away from the frenzy of elsewhere as if India had passed through the Looking Glass and become an altogether more laid-back place" Lonely Planet (2015, p.941).

It is easy to lose yourself in this land of backwaters, 'black gold' and bewitching sunsets. Whether you glide along with the gentle pulse of Kerala's waterways or opt to cleanse your body and soul at an Ayurvedic spa, this peaceful Indian state beckons spirituality and wonder" National Geographic Traveler (2012).

As a renowned destination in the global tourism market with its strategical approach for development and precipitous promotional initiatives, the state has attracted tourists from all over the world. According to Kerala tourism ministry statistics 2017, "foreign Tourist arrival to Kerala during the year 2017 is 1091870 showing an increase of 5.15% over the previous year." Similarly, Foreign exchange earnings for 2017 are 8392.11 Crores, which has increased by 8.29% from 2016. The total tourism revenue during 2017 is 33383.68 Crores, which shows a rise of 12.56% over previous years (Kerala Tourism Ministry, statistics, 2017). Table 1 presents the international and domestic tourist arrivals in Kerala.

Table 1. International and domestic tourist arrivals in Kerala

Year	No.of Domestic Tourist Visits	% of Increase	No.of Foreign Tourist Visits	% of increase	Total no. of tourists	% of increase
2006	6271724	5.47	428534	23.68	6700258	6.47
2007	6642941	5.92	515808	20.37	7158749	6.84
2008	7591250	14.28	598929	16.11	8190179	14.41
2009	7913537	4.25	557258	-6.96	8470795	3.43
2010	8595075	8.61	659265	18.31	9254340	9.25
2011	9381455	9.15	732985	11.18	10114440	9.29
2012	10076854	7.41	793696	8.28	10870550	7.48
2013	10857811	7.75	858143	8.12	11715954	7.78
2014	11695411	7.71	923366	7.60	12618777	7.71
2015	12465571	6.59	977479	5.86	13443050	6.53
2016	13172535	5.67	1038419	6.23	14210954	5.71
2017	14673520	11.39	1091870	5.15	15765390	10.94

(Source: Department of Tourism, Government of Kerala, Tourist Statistics, 2017)

Wellness Through Ayurveda

Ayurveda is an ancient medical system from India and is believed to be the oldest form of medical treatment, dating back from 5000 BC. The term Ayurveda is a unification of two Sanskrit words: Ayus(r), which means life and Veda, which means Knowledge or science; therefore, it is the 'knowledge [science] of life'. It focuses on the healing power of nature by using natural methods of treatment based on medicinal plants and herbs. As derived from Hinduism, Ayurveda follows the sacred principles of spirituality. Osbourne (2000, p. xiii) purports: "at its very heart, Ayurveda can be described as spiritual in its absolute conviction of linking the wholeness of the universe, to the ones within the human body. This connection between nature, as we know it and the universe is the basis for all Ayurveda principles of healing and medical knowledge." Distinct from other therapeutic systems, Ayurveda emphasises healthy living more than treatment of illnesses.

Varier (1986), a famous Ayurvedic practitioner in Kerala notes that life in Ayurveda is perceived as the amalgamation of body, mind and soul. The growth and decay of the body matrix (see figure 1) and its elements revolve around diet, which it receives and processes into humour, muscles and human excreta. According to the principles of Ayurveda, all human beings possess three Doshas (humour or elements) which determine the healthiness of body and mind. Any kind of imbalance might affect the body system and leads to illness.

Furthermore, in Ayurveda, diet is an essential factor since it deems a person's psychological and spiritual growth, as well as his/her character, influenced by the quality and type of foods consumed. Considering the consumed diet is converted initially to chyle, then transformed into muscles, fat, blood and bone-marrow, Ayurveda conceptualises the diet as a fundamental of health. Therefore, the medications must

Figure 1. Philosophy of Ayurveda Bio-matrix of the human body (Source: Osbourne, 2000)

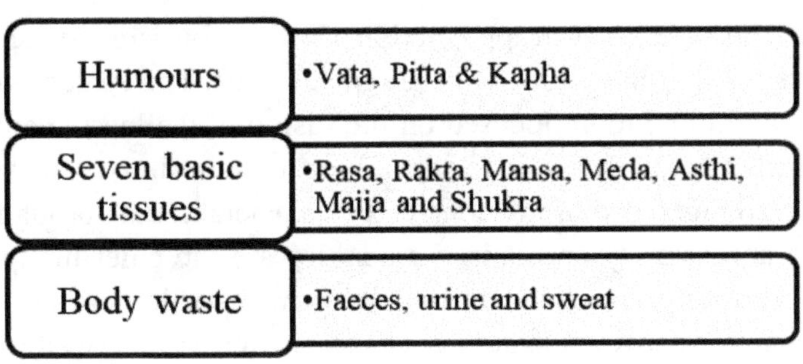

have a diet chart to follow in order to obtain the desired outcome from the therapy. (Varier, 1986)

Food in the human body is transformed first into chyle or Rasa and then continuous processes involve its conversion into blood, muscle, fat, bone, bone marrow, reproductive elements and Ojas. Thus, food is fundamental to all metabolic transformations and life activities. Lack of nutrients in food or improper transformation of food leads to a variety of diseases and conditions. (Varier, 1986)

Consequently, Ayurvedic treatments are based on the balancing of those three senses of humour and five elements through internal purification via the exhalation of toxic substances from the body and revitalisation. This is known as Panchakarma (5 extended treatment) and includes Nasya (medical application through the nose); Vaman (stimulated vomiting); Raktamoksha (induced bloodletting); Viechana (purgation) and Vasti (Enema). Massages, spa treatments and Yoga are contemporary methods of Ayurvedic therapy, of which massages are particularly popular among western tourists, (Mohanlal, 2008).

Ramesh and Joseph (2012, p.31) note that "Ayurveda also has a comprehensive system of massages and body treatments that give relief from a wide range of illnesses, from migraine and sinus to arthritis and paralysis; that detoxifies and cleanse the body through controlled emesis, purgation, making the individual sweat; and that makes the body receptive to further treatment." They also highlight the amazing wellness effect through Ayurveda, as it broadens astounding medications for sicknesses, like Osteo-Arthritis, Rheumatic joint inflammation, tennis elbow and Carpal Tunnel Syndrome, Spondylosis, interventricular plate prolapse, frozen shoulder, insomnia, migraine and skin diseases. Over the past two decades, the need for an all-encompassing methodology in the treatment of illnesses has been a moot point among the researchers of current restorative sciences, toward an arrangement of drugs that kills the infection from the body without bringing about any symptoms, (Ramesh and Jospeh, 2012, pp.31-32)

RECENT TRENDS IN KERALA WELLNESS TOURISM MARKETS

Due to the enduring international appreciation of Kerala tourism, the medical/health/wellness tourism sector has witnessed a pragmatic shift. The contemporary market changes are found to be more focused on the fusion of wellness-medical-cultural tourism elements to provide a unique experience to the visitors. The wide range of products, tailored ambience of the contact zones, social media brought marketing platforms and accessibility specialised amenities are the chief highpoints of the industry. Concentrating on the fundamentals of *'escapism'*, the current treatments are offering rejuvenation and revitalization packages, in line with the wellbeing of mind-body-soul. The combination of wellness, hospitality and tourism have intermingled in unprecedented ways in Kerala to become a wellness tourism destination.

According to Edward and George (2012, p.22) the "increasing the appeal for Ayurvedic rejuvenation holidays and heritage attractions in the international and domestic markets and expanding variety in the accommodation provision of boutique resorts and heritage hotels were some of the landmarks in the successful product development efforts in the tourism industry of Kerala." Various government initiatives have achieved this by converting the old traditional buildings (Nalukettu) into wellness centres, which often creates an ambience of traditionality. See Figure. 2 as an example of a wellness centre in Kerala, which was converted from a traditional Kerala house.

According to Connell (2006, p. 1093) "in the past decade the attempt to achieve better health while on holiday, through relaxation, exercise or visits to spas, has been taken to a new level with the emergence of a new and distinct niche in the tourism industry". Identifying these trends are crucial for tourism destinations to enhance its global competency. This section discusses the recent trends observed in the wellness/medical tourism sector in Kerala to understand contemporary products in demand and how they merge the boundaries of spirituality, culture, health, cuisine and ecotourism into a single platform of wellness tourism to offer innovative products to satisfy the market demands. To understand the current drifts, websites and flyers of the five most popular wellbeing centres were analysed.

Figure 2. Traditional Kerala homes
(Source: Sarovaram wellness centre)

To determine the current trends and practices in any form of tourism, it is necessary to understand the tourist motivations and expectations. In wellbeing tourism, Ayurveda has grown in trustworthiness across the globe, which is primarily due to its holistic nature and by its use of natural, minimal side effect ingredients. Moving away from the traditional leisure concept, a considerable number of tourists are in search for the authentic, innovative experience to revive or rejuvenate their mind or body on short break holidays (Nash, 1996). However, for medical tourism, while crossing very faded boundaries of wellness tourism, the motivation of tourists makes the difference. As Tribe (2009) mentioned, Western travellers whose primary intention is for medical treatments will not take part in other forms of well-being activities. Considering these observations, the wellness tourists in Kerala can be categorised under leisure (or escapist) categories. Therefore, according to contemporary market demand, the wellbeing tourism sector of Kerala *flourishes (or makes use of)* under three segments, namely rejuvenation, spirituality or culture and cuisine.

Kannan and Fernz (2017, p.6) opined that "Kerala mostly offers 'wellness,' which is seen in connection with a pleasant holiday under palm trees, the marketing of Ayurveda as a massage – and wellness package – a 'fashionable', 'flower power' or 'new age' Ayurveda that has been reimported to India." At the same time, they warned of the ethical issues associated with recent marketing trends to project the state as the heart of wellness tourism. Important to all, Gobalakrishnan (2019) suggests that the most important trend is the globalization of Kerala's Ayurveda across the world, either through international fairs, travel trades and so on. Kannan and Fern (2017), also in line with the views of Gobalakrishnan (2019), argue that strategical marketing trends are vital for Kerala's wellness tourism sector.

CHALLENGES AND OPPORTUNISMS

Based on recent studies (Kulkarni, 2008; Ilyas, 2008; Kannan and Fernz, 2017) conducted in leading wellness homes in Kerala, it was identified that there is a mounting demand for the 'wellness packages'. Each type of package is specifically designed for the needs of the tourists, which is rejuvenation, body purification, slimming, stress management, immunisation and beauty care packages. All of these bundles are instituted on the Ayurveda treatments. Notably, the 'so-called' packages are designed in such a manner to maximise the visitor's experience by merging various spiritual, cultural, culinary and entertainment attributes. Following Tribe (2009), the traditional methods of medicinal and wellness tourism has come to an end. Nowadays, the industry offers a unique experience for their clients through the fusion of destination explicit charms.

What is *old is novel yet again*, this was undeniably valid for the present wellbeing tourism choices. In the rejuvenation section, day spas have expanded acceptance and become more flexible with many Ayurvedic rejuvenation selections offering packages that fit tourist's individual needs. Shalini (2017) notes spa tourism as one of the combinations found to be offering massages, along with traditional Ayurvedic treatments, like Panchakarma. Visitors are pampered, de-stressed and made to feel revitalized by fleeing from stifling traumatic city life to detoxification by the natural elements of Ayurveda. The main appeal for the Ayurvedic spa treatments are the natural ingredients used by the spa and derived from nature. It is commonly found to be offered as part of various packages.

Prominently, in Kerala, the current wellness tourism centres are more or less manoeuvred into an ambience of conventional Keralean structural design (see Fig. 2), with pleasant greenery embedded in a serene spiritual tone. This ambience can catalyse the thought-lines of Graburn (1989, p. 22) that tourism is "functionally and symbolically equivalent to other institutions that humans use to embellish and add meaning to their lives". Being a sacred journey, tourism offers a chance to self-discovery by recognising one's spiritual needs. India has always been an accessible terminus of spiritual tourism from ancient times. Spiritual attractions are found to be served as an integral part of many packages. In which medication is practised through Yoga.

Yoga has been perceived to be a central feature of present-day wellness tourism practises in Kerala; marketed as the destressing exercise, the wellness centre claim

Yoga alleviates mental stress and encourages relaxation and inner peace. Furthermore, yoga can also be therapeutic – both as a remedy and as a prophylactic. In the Ayurvedic teachings, yoga and meditation are an essential part of any programme of treatment to establish a balance between the Doshas. In all, but a few cases, yoga and meditation practice are integral parts of the daily schedule. (Naik, 2018)

Spirituality is often mixed with the divine attributes to offer the customers a proper ambience of 'self-revitalisation'. Hindu deities and Buddha idols become the inevitable attractions for the wellness sector. Prayers, Vedic mantra chants, lamps and smells of herbs and medicinal oils together with photographs or idols of deities create a sense of peace and calm in the tourists. All of the Ayurvedic centres are now offering Yoga and meditation packages with both pacification and purification to revitalise mind, body and soul. Yoga and other cultural exports of India are also opening up a great opportunity for the wellness tourism sector of Kerala. However, "the interpretation of yoga tourism is crucial in the choice of marketing approach adopted by destinations offering yoga retreats because, as the study has shown, various perceptions of yoga constitute the basis for particular promotional strategies," (Telej and Gamble, 2019, p.1).

It is interesting to note how wellness centres are trying to combine various niche areas of tourism under the banner of the wellness industry. For example, many tourism centres are now offering cultural events (traditional music and dance), festivals and other activities, like houseboat trips (backwater tourism) to their customers. Diets are also a part of the Ayurvedic treatment, according to the nature of treatments the food offered also differs; thus many of the packages had a combination of the traditional diet to follow. Figure 3 shows a proposed wellness tourism model for Kerala by addressing the recent trends and future implications.

Kerala's wellness tourism sector also faces a myriad of challenges, of which ethical and authenticity issues are predominant one to address. This can be related to popular demand for Ayurvedic products among international and domestic travelers. Innovative products, market competitions and so on are affecting the consumers' experience. Similarly, "many practitioners are concerned about this trend of offering Ayurveda procedures as a massage-spa wellness, as a commercialized product, in

Figure 3. Proposed model of wellness tourism in Kerala

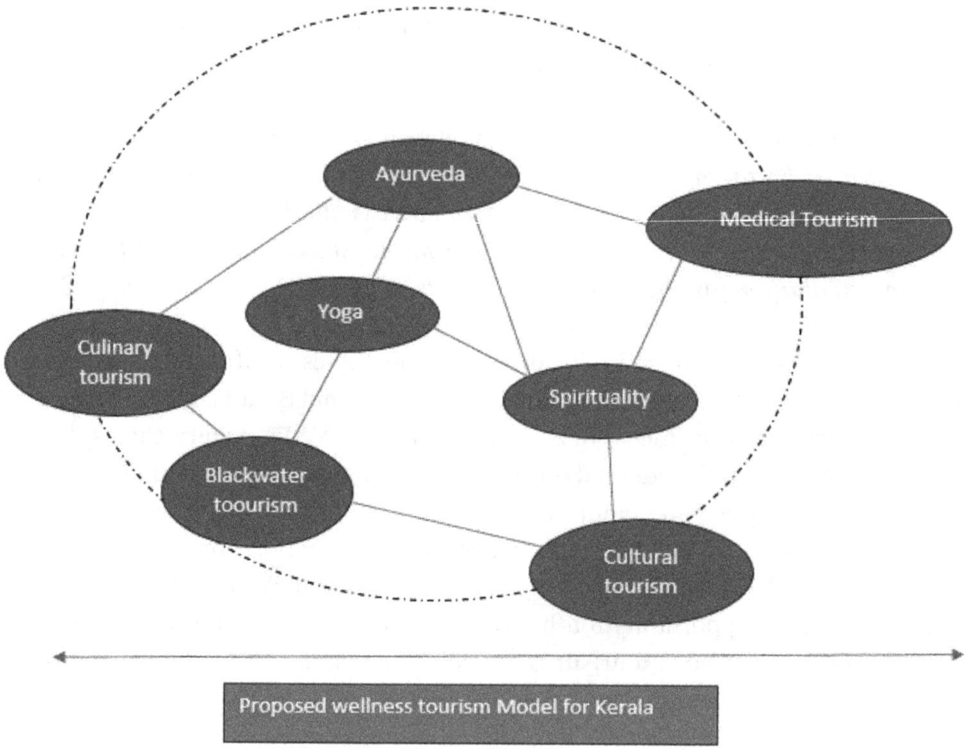

Table 2. Managerial implications and recommendations

Issues identified	*Recommendations*
Ethical and authenticity issues	The authentic tourist experience is crucial for a developing destination like Kerala. Therefore, it is vital to control unethical practices in the Wellness tourism sector by controlling poorly performing practitioners and centres. Collaborative approaches can reduce these issues by providing accreditation to all centres, after a quality control inspection and then allocate license.
Collective Promotion	Collective promotional activities are beneficial for the destination's promotion. This can be done by conducting roadshows and trade fairs by incorporating all the sectors of Medical tourism as a collective approach to create the feeling of a 'unique destination'.
Stakeholders partnerships	This is fundamental for a balanced and steady growth of any tourism destination, a collaboration of public and private bodies, such as government, hospitals and wellness centres.
Community partnerships	Community involvement is one of the essential criteria for sustainable development. As in the case of Kerala, it is beneficial to seek the involvement of local people to collaborate, deliver and practise wellness tourism.

Source: Author's own work

the global market" (Kannan & Fernz, 2017, p. 6). Similar to the practitioners, the mushrooming number of wellness centres are also alarming. The tourism authorities make efforts to deliver a licensed practice, such as green leaf to olive leaf categories (see Ramesh and Joseph, 2012); however, sometimes it is not particularly successful (Kannan and Fernz, 2017).

Bowers and Cheer (2017) discoursed that competitions from other destinations can become one of the challenges. Many Asian and African countries have now entered into Wellness tourism by offering Ayurveda and Yoga practices. Sri Lanka is one of the main competitors for Kerala, since they share numerous similarities, such as climate, low cost of treatment and a wide range of tourist attractions.

In addition, Kerala still lacks the physical and social environment when compared to its tourism potential. Social security and women's safety in the state has been in question for the last two years; Cherukara and Manalel (2008, p.369) emphasis the lack of proper infrastructure as one of the main challenges.

The physical environment includes the improvement in necessary infrastructure, the standard of cleanliness etc. Basic amenities should be excellent—toilets should be user-friendly and well maintained. Excellent standards at lesser cost will make the state a more attractive, value for money destination. For this, we have to improve the physical infrastructure and connectivity.

CONCLUSION

This chapter described the wellness tourism sector of Kerala; God's own country. As a popular tourist destination in India, the state attracts millions of both domestic and international visitors. Its enchanting geographical attractions, backwaters, long-line of beaches and rich cultural heritage are famous in world tourism. As a pioneer of medical tourism in South-East Asia, the place is also known as the land of Ayurveda. Ayurveda is the ancient medical system of India. Due to the side-effect free, natural and renaissance characteristics of Ayurveda, it has becomes one of the fashionable wellness and health tourism attributes across the world. The main intention of this chapter was to acknowledge the recent trends and developments in the wellness tourism sector of Kerala, as one of the famous tourist destinations.

The findings of this case study point out the narrow, fragile and somewhat faded links between health, medical and wellness tourism in its characteristics and definition. In the context of Ayurveda, the current arguments about these forms of tourism could be challenged by demonstrating the heal and revive criteria adopted in the Ayurveda treatments.

Moreover, this study explored the present context of wellness tourism in the state and identified the symbiotic applications of cultural, religious, spiritual, culinary, backwater and art tourism attractions together to create a fantastic ambience for future tourists. The current wellness tourism packages consist of both pacification and purification packages, combined with spiritual (yoga), religious (Hindus ideologies and prayers), cultural (traditional atmosphere), arts (ethnic dances and martial arts), food (regional cuisine of Kerala) and backwater tourism attractions to enhance the visitor experience. Due to the significance this amalgamation of spiritual, wellness, health, cultural and food tourism, it recommended that a further study be undertaken on every single attraction to understand the role and significance in terms of new product development and visitor's satisfaction.

REFERENCES

Agner, E. (2010). Subjective well-being. *Journal of Socio-Economics*, *39*(1), 361–368. doi:10.1016/j.socec.2009.12.001

Bowers, H., & Cheer, J. (2017). Yoga tourism: Commodification and western embracement of eastern spiritual practice. *Tourism Management Perspectives*, *24*(1), 208–216. doi:10.1016/j.tmp.2017.07.013

Cherukara, J., & Manalel, J. (2019). Medical Tourism in Kerala—Challenges and Scope. In *Conference on Tourism in India – Challenges Ahead*, (pp. 369-379). Kochi: IIMK.

Connell, J. (2006). Medical tourism: Sea, sun, sand and … surgery. *Tourism Management*, *27*(6), 1093–1100. doi:10.1016/j.tourman.2005.11.005

Edwards, M., & George, K. (2017). Tourism development in the State of Kerala, India: A study of destination attractiveness. *European Journal of Tourism Research*, *1*(1).

Foley, R. (2010). *Healing Waters Therapeutic Landscapes in Historic and Contemporary Ireland* (1st ed.). London: Routledge.

Gobalakrishnan, C. (2015). *Sociology of Medical tourism* (1st ed.). Chennai: MJP Publishers.

Graburn, N. (1989). Tourism: The Sacred Journey. In V. Smith (Ed.), *Hosts and Guests: The Anthropology of Tourism* (2nd ed.; pp. 21–36). Philadelphia, PA: University of Pennsylvania Press.

Grénman, M., & Räikkönen, J. (2015). Well-being and wellness tourism – Same, same but different? Conceptual discussions and empirical evidence. *Matkailututkimus*, *11*(1), 7–25.

Hallab, Z. (2006). Catering to the healthy-living vacationer. *Journal of Vacation Marketing*, *12*(1), 71–91. doi:10.1177/1356766706059043

Hartwell, H., Fyall, A., Willis, C., Page, S., Ladkin, A., & Hemingway, A. (2016). Progress in tourism and destination wellbeing research. *Current Issues in Tourism*, *21*(16), 1830–1892. doi:10.1080/13683500.2016.1223609

Haseena, V. (2015). The Routes of Wellness in Tourism in Kerala and its Impacts. *Journal Of Tourism. Hospitality And Sports*, *5*(1), 21–26.

ICCCON. (2019). *ICCCON 2019 - 26th Annual Conference, Kochi*. Retrieved 27 July 2019, from http://www.icccon2019kochi.com/experience-kerala

Ilyas, M. (2008). Medical Tourism: India the Right Destination. *Southern Economist*, (1), 37-39.

Kannan, S., & Frenz, M. (2017). Seeking health under palm trees: Ayurveda in Kerala. *Global Public Health: An International Journal for Research, Policy and Practice*, *14*(3), 351–361. doi:10.1080/17441692.2017.1417458 PMID:29272989

Kerala Tourism Ministry. (2017). *Kerala tourism statistics 2017*. Retrieved 27 July 2019, from https://www.keralatourism.org/tourismstatistics/tourist_statistics_2017_book20181221073646.pdf

Kulkarni, A. (2008). Become healthy happy and balanced with Ayurveda. *Medical Tourism*, *2*(1), 38–39.

Lenka, S. (2017). *Health tourism in Kerala: Relative perception study on the determinants of wellness tourism. In Millennial Workforce–A Contemplation* (1st ed.; pp. 180–187). Hyderabad, India: Zenon Academic Publishing.

Lonely Planet. (2015). *Kerala*. Retrieved 20 July 2019, from http://media.lonelyplanet.com/shop/pdfs/india-15-kerala-preview.pdf

Mohanlal, P. (2008). The Holistic Approach of Ayurveda. *Ayurveda &Health Tourism*, *3*(1), 22–26.

Naik, M. (2018). *Best Yoga Retreat in India*. Retrieved 27 July 2019, from https://medium.com/@medhan811/best-yoga-retreat-in-india-aafb1126d1df

Nash, D. (2013). *Anthropology of tourism* (1st ed.). Oxford, UK: Pergamon.

National Geographical Traveller. (2012). *In search of serenity*. Retrieved 18 July 2019, from http://carolineeden.com/CarolineEden/Travel_features_files/NGT1012_104_kerala.pdf

Netto, N. (2004). *Tourism development in Kerala* (1st ed.). New Delhi: Sage.

Osborne, B. (2000). Ayurveda: The Food Balancing Act (1st ed.). London: Janus Publishing Company Limited.

Pordié, L. (2013). Spaces of Connectivity, Shifting Temporality. Enquiries in Transnational Health. European Journal of Transnational Studies. *European Journal Of Transnational Studies*, *5*(1), 6–26.

Ramesh, U., & Joseph, K. (2012). The holistic approach of Ayurveda based wellness tourism in Kerala. *The Holistic Approach of Ayurveda Based Wellness Tourism in Kerala, 3*(2), 29-39.

Shalini, P. (2017). Bridging Healthcare with Wellness Tourism in India. *Indian Journal Of Public Health Research & Development*, *8*(4), 345. doi:10.5958/0976-5506.2017.00367.9

Smith, M., & Puczkó, L. (2013). *Health and wellness tourism*. London: Routledge.

Telej, E., & Gamble, J. (2019). Yoga wellness tourism: a study of marketing strategies in India. *Journal of Consumer Marketing,* 1-12. doi:10.1108/jcm-07-2018-2788

Thanuskodi, A. (2016). A Webometric Analysis of Medical Tourism Websites in Kerala. *Library Philosophy And Practice*, *1*(1), 11–14.

Tribe, J. (2009). *Philosophical issues in tourism*. Bristol, UK: Channel View Publications.

Varier, P. (1986). The management of the problem of ageing, according to the Ayurvedic system of medicine. *Centenary Souvenir, Vasudeva Vilasam Ayurveda Pharmacy*, (1), 1-50.

Chapter 13
HRV:
A Powerful Tool in Medical Diagnosis

Kirti Rawal
Lovely Professional University, Phagwara, India

Gaurav Sethi
Lovely Professional University, Phagwara, India

Barjinder Singh Saini
Dr. B. R. Ambedkar National Institute of Technology, Jalandhar, India

Indu Saini
Dr. B. R. Ambedkar National Institute of Technology, Jalandhar, India

ABSTRACT

The most important factor involved in heart rate variability (HRV) analysis is cardiac input signal, which is achieved in the form of electrocardiogram (ECG). The ECG signal is used for identifying many electrical defects associated with the heart. In this chapter, many issues involved while ECG recording such as type of the recording instrument, various sources of noise, artifacts, and electrical interference from surroundings is presented. Most importantly, this chapter comprises the details about the experimental protocols followed while ECG recording. Also, the brief overview of medical tourism as well as various interpolation methods used for pre-processing of RR intervals are presented in this chapter.

DOI: 10.4018/978-1-5225-9787-2.ch013

INTRODUCTION

The basic function of the human heart is to pump blood around the body via the arterial system in order to transport the vital nutrients and oxygen (Clifford, 2002). The ECG is a signal obtained from the human body which characterizes the electrical activity of the human heart. Heart beats are not evenly spaced in time but they exhibit variations about a mean interval and these variations are commonly termed as heart rate variability. These HRV variations were further analyzed by various doctors for detecting and diagnosing the cardiovascular diseases. Nowadays, Medical tourism plays an important role in providing the medical services in different countries by using Internet of Things (IOT). This chapter comprises the detailed description of human heart, ECG intervals, heart rate variability, various issues of recording an ECG signal, length of recording, sampling frequency, noise and artifacts in the ECG recordings, extraction of RR interval series from the ECG signals.

BACKGROUND

Human Heart

Heart has two chambers in each side: atria and ventricle. Inter-atrial septum separates the two thin-walled atria and two thicker-walled ventricles possessing common wall in the inter-ventricular septum. Fibrous A-V ring is used to connect these atria and ventricles (Saini, 2009). Four valves are used to regulate the blood flow in the heart. The right auricle (RA) collects the impure blood and then the blood passes from the right auricle (RA) to right ventricle (RV) via Tricuspid valve. Thus, it regulates the impure blood flow between the right atria and right ventricles. The impure blood is pumped out through the pulmonary valve to the lungs for its purification by the right ventricle (RV). Afterwards, the blood from the left atrium (LA) is passed to the left ventricle (LV) via mitral valve (Renu Madhavi, 2012). Lastly, the aortic valve is situated at the aortic orifice. The AV ring is penetrated on left side and right side by mitral and tricuspid valve as shown in Figure 1.

The conduction system of the heart consists of Sinoatrial (SA) node, Atrioventricular (AV) node, bundle of His, bundle branches and purkinje fibres as shown in Figure 2. SA node placed at the top of the right atrium, initiates an electrical signal to the AV node which is further transmitted to the left and right bundle branches. The impulse then reaches to the myocardium through the purkinje fibres and contracts it. The two physiological events such as heart mechanical activity (pumping of the blood) and heart electrical activity (the transmission of electrical impulses) gives rise to an orderly heartbeat.

The SA node transmits electrical impulses depending upon the physical demands, stress and hormonal factors (Saini, 2009; Renu Madhavi, 2012). The presence of various cell types such as the atrial cells, ventricular cells, and the cells that constitute the conduction system (Purkinje fibers) and the pacemaker cells in the heart are recognized by the cardiac electrophysiology. The pacemaker cells undergo repetitive cyclic activation which further initiates a contraction. This contraction results in cyclic electrical activity *i.e.,* the periodic heartbeat. This cyclic activation propagates to adjoining atrial tissues by means of local circuit (action) currents. The presence of low resistance intercellular structure facilitates the flow of this current from active to inactive neighboring cells.

The current flow from one cell to another cell until the entire left and right atria are activated. The direct propagation from the atria to ventricles cannot occur because both are separated by fibrous tissue. Initially the conduction in the AV junction is slow and cardiac muscles instigate the successive mechanical contraction which results in the completion of atrial contraction and delay in the ventricular activation and contraction. The ventricular activation occurs over a wide region when electrical impulse reaches the bundles of His where the conduction becomes very fast. The impulse then reaches to the myocardium through the purkinje fibers and contracts it which results in QRS complex. Ventricular repolarisation is the last activity of cycle. The outcome of all these activities of the heart generates the Electrocardiogram (ECG) signal (Saini, 2009; Renu Madhavi, 2012).

Electrocardiogram

There are number of ways by which ECG can be recorded. The idea is to choose the simplest one which gives all the desired information. Moreover, the ECG signal can be acquired from any part of the body, but the foremost requirement is to record the stronger signal with less noise closer to heart (Saini, 2009). ECG can be acquired by putting electrodes on the skin surface with the help of the ECG machine. Due to the depolarization of heart muscle, there are small rises and falls in voltage because of electrodes placed on the skin surface displayed in the form of ECG waveform as shown in Figure 3. The abnormal heart rhythms are also diagnosed by ECG recording (Seaborn, 2010).

The different electrophysiological events occurs in the heart are represented by the salient features of ECG as shown in Figure 3. The P wave represents the atrial depolarization having duration of 80ms approximately. The QRS complex corresponds to the depolarization of the left and right ventricles and repolarization of the atria having approximate duration of 80 to 120ms in length. In the QRS complex, Q-wave and R-wave are the initial downward and upward deflection respectively, and S-wave is the first downward deflection after an upward deflection. The T-wave which has

Figure 1. Cross-section of the human heart (Lovoy Siem, 2007)

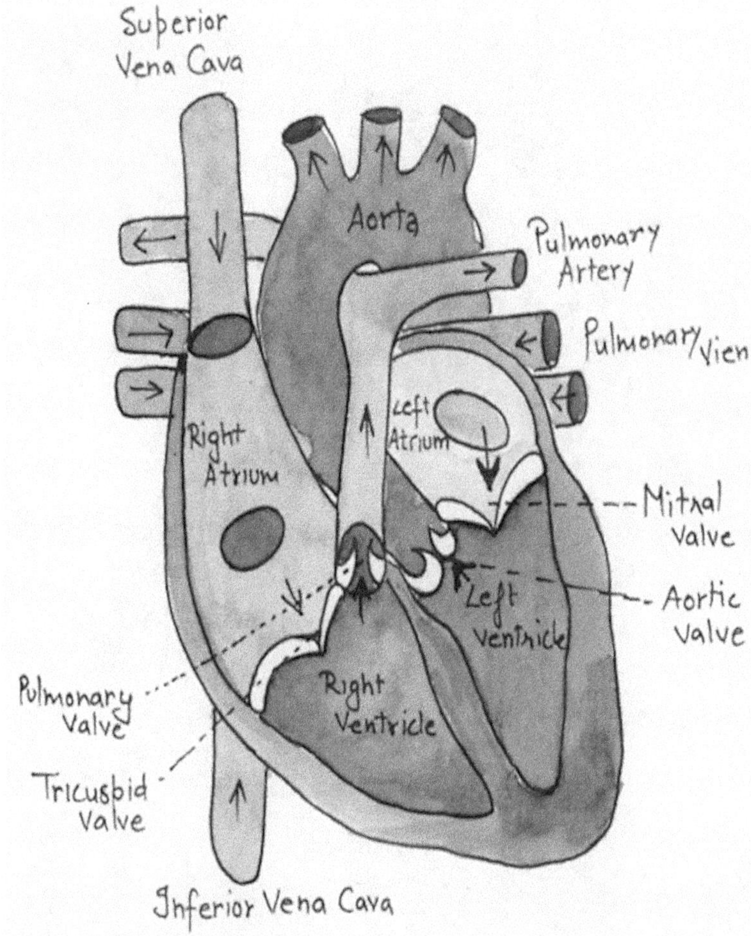

duration of approximately 160ms corresponds to the ventricular repolarization (Saini, 2009; Seaborn, 2010).

The last feature is the U-wave followed by T-wave which is invisible in most of the ECG's represents the repolarization of Purkinje fibers. In ECG based diagnosis, the time intervals are very essential and are indicated in Figure 3.

ECG plays an important role not only for detecting the variety of heart diseases but also diagnosing the various heart patients by providing early diagnosis. Several machine learning algorithms are also used for classifying the ECG signal which is useful for diagnosing the heart diseases.

Figure 2. Electrical conduction system of the human heart (Tze Yeng Chang, 2013)

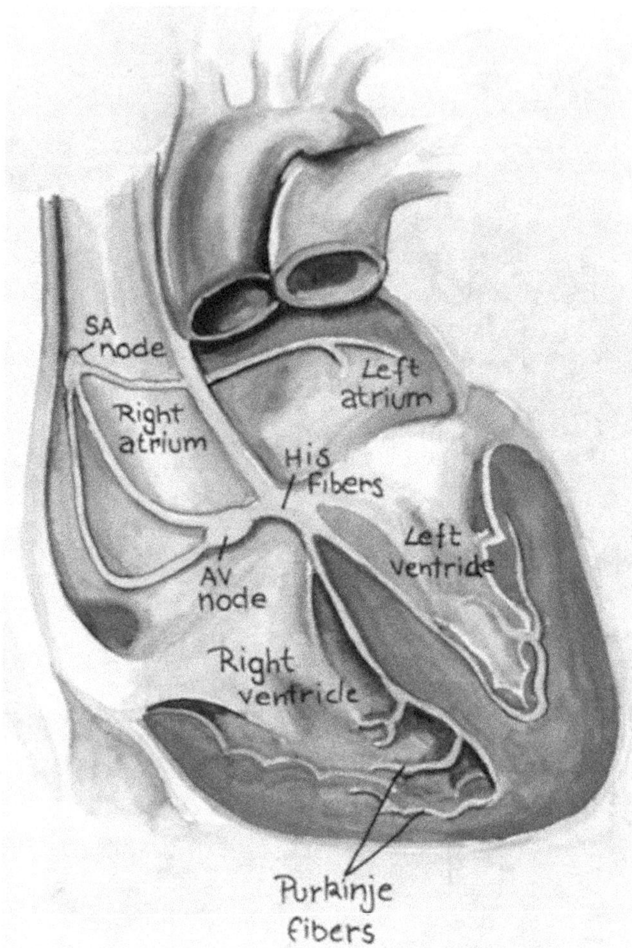

ECG Wave Intervals and Segments

RR-Interval

The distance between two successive R peaks is the RR-interval. If the ventricular rhythm is regular, then heart rate per minute is calculated by dividing the interval (in seconds) between two successive R peaks with 60 seconds. In case of irregular ventricular rhythm, the number of R waves is counted for specific time period (*e.g.*, 10 seconds) and afterwards it is converted into number per minute.

Figure 3. ECG waveform (Seaborn, 2010)

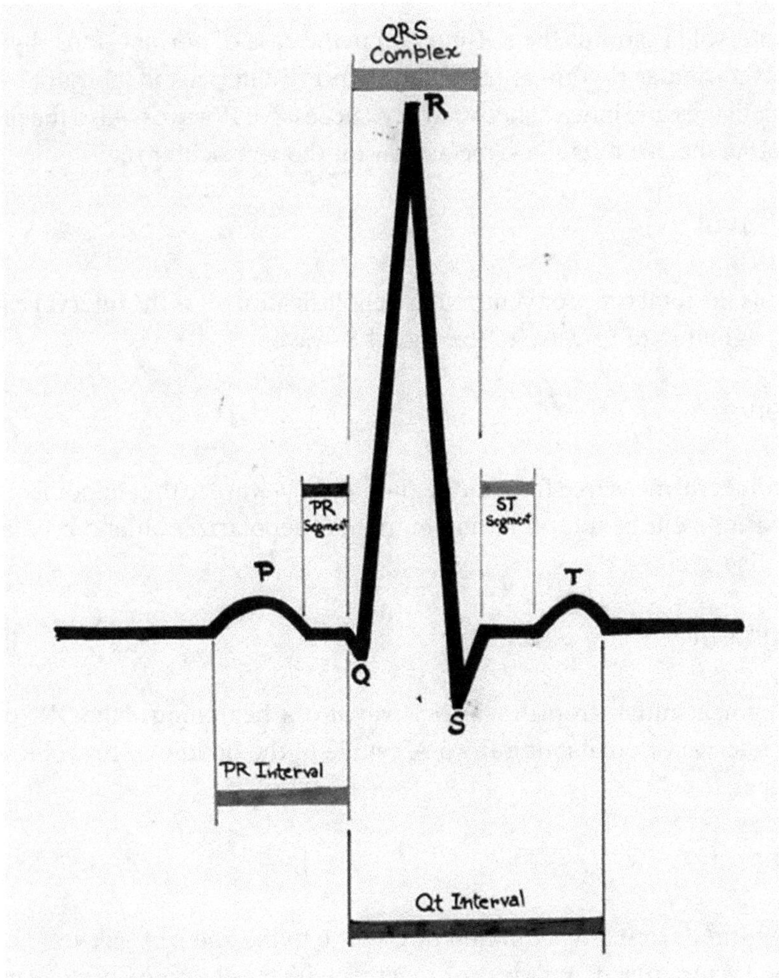

P-R-Interval

It represents the AV conduction time. It includes the time interval from the onset of atrial depolarization to the onset of ventricular depolarization. The normal range of P-R interval is from 0.12 to 0.20sec. The duration of 0.2 sec is well significant only when the heart rate is of 100 beats per minute but it has no clinical significance when the heart rate is of 60 beats per minute.

P-P-Interval

The P-P interval is same as the RR-interval in the case of normal sinus rhythm. But when the ventricular rhythm is irregular, then P-P intervals is measured from the same point in the time interval between two successive P-waves. Also the procedure of calculating the atrial rate is same as that for the ventricular rate.

QRS-Interval

It represents the total time for ventricular depolarization. It is the interval calculated from the beginning of Q-wave to the end of S-wave.

Q-T Interval

This is the interval measured from the beginning of Q-wave to the endpoint of T-wave. It is a measurement of total time in ventricular depolarization and repolarization of the cardiac cycle.

P-R Segment

The P-R segment initiate from the end of P wave to the beginning of the QRS complex. The time interval of conduction from AV node to the bundle of his represents the P-R segment.

Q-U Interval

This is measured from the beginning of Q-wave to the end of U-wave.

The total ventricular depolarization together with the purkinje fibers are measured by Q-U interval.

S-T Interval

This measure the time interval from the QRS offset to the onset of RST segment.

S-T Segment

The time preceding the repolarization of ventricles comprises S-T segment. It is measured from the endpoint of QRS complex to the onset of T-wave.

RST-Junction

It is a portion of ECG at which there is an ending of the QRS complex and beginning of the RST segment (Saini, 2009; Gao, 2003; Singh, 2007; Fatemian, 2009).

Heart Rate Variability

HRV is a physiological phenomenon in which the time interval between heart beats varies as shown in Figure 4. Mathematically it is calculated by using (1)

$$RR = RR_{i+1} - RR_i \tag{1}$$

where RR_i is the ith RR interval and RR_{i+1} is the $i^{th}+1$ RR interval. The overall cardiac health and the state of the ANS can be analyzed by using HRV analysis. One of the biggest advantage of HRV analysis is its non invasive nature to take

Figure 4. Heart rate variability

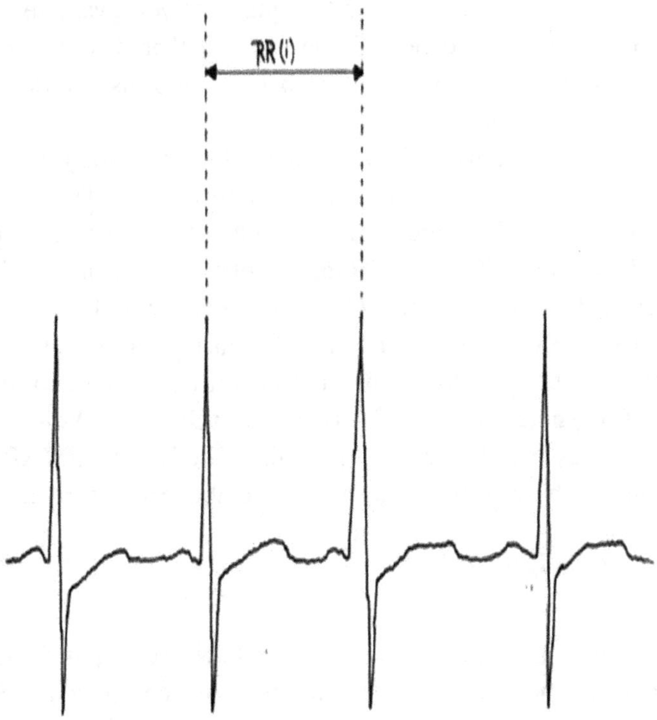

various kinds of measurements, relatively easier to use, and having good reproducibility.

Thus, the analysis of HRV is a vital tool in cardiology because its measurements are noninvasive, simple to perform, and provide prognostic information.

Evolution of HRV

Autonomic Nervous System

The ANS is the main stress regulatory system in human and animals organism. It is influenced by several number of life situations like exercise, rest or illness (Kana, 2010). ANS comprises two systems: (i) SNS and (ii) PNS. Various physiological processes such as BP, heart rate, respiration rate and glucose metabolism are controlled by sympathetic and parasympathetic nervous systems with the help of hormones. The sympathetic nervous system uses epinephrine and norepinephrine hormones in response to "fight-or-flight" response to stress, *i.e.,* fear, pain, or cold exposure. In the parasympathetic nervous system, there is a resting state in which food is digested and BP, heart rate and respiration are decreased. But in sympathetic nervous system, BP, respiration and heart rate increases where as digestion decreases (Simmons, 2013). Therefore, it is necessary to quantitatively evaluate the functioning of ANS in research to understand the pathophysiological processes and physiological regulation, and also in clinical practice to examine the disease development and guide therapy (Kana, 2010).

Both SNS and PNS systems are involved to control the responses to stressors and also in resting states of the body throughout the daily activity. Therefore, ANS plays an important role in controlling the cardiac output, arterial and blood pressure. The product of Cardiac Output (CO) and Total Peripheral Resistance (TPR) estimates the Mean Arterial Pressure (MAP). CO is calculated by multiplying the HR with stroke volume (SV). SV depends on Venous Return (VR) which in turn used to measure the flow of blood into the heart between each contraction and Cardiac Contractility (CC). There are some fluctuations in the Lung Volume (LV) which causes high frequency oscillations in VR (Saini, 2009). Thus, MAP is a function of these components these components expressed above and is given by using (1.2)

$$MAP = f(HR,\ LV, TPR, CC, VR) \tag{1.2}$$

The fluctuations in blood pressure and heart rate with different frequencies occur due to the autonomic modulation of each of the above components (Saini, 2009).

History of HRV

The first person who measured the heart rate was the ancient and Greek scientist named Herophilos (335–280 BC) in ca.300 BC. Herophilos used water clock to time the pulse. The pulse was described by Galen of Pergamon (131-200AD), the ancient scientist and physician in ca.170 AD. He used the pulse for diagnosing and predicting several types of diseases. In 1707, John Floyer was invented the Physician Pulse Watch, *i.e.,* a portable clock which is used to tabulate both the pulse and respiration under a variety of conditions. In this way, the quantitative evaluations of heart rate were increased day by day with the increasing availability of accurate time pieces. Afterwards, the variations in the arterial pressure and beat to beat interval during the respiratory cycle were first reported by Stephen Hales in 1733. In 1847, his invention was used by Carl Ludwig, a first person who invented a device named smoked drum Kymograph to record the variations in the amplitude and timing of atrial pressure with respiration. To further prove his findings, he used dog to demonstrate that pulse is rapidly increasing during inspiration and slowed down during expiration. Several researchers investigated in later half of the 19th century that the variations in the arterial pressure interval occur due to the changes in the neural activity. In 1865, Ludwig Traube investigated that the irradiation from respiratory neurons was responsible for arterial waves but Karl Ewald Hering in 1871, proposed that afferent fibers located in the lungs were responsible for these periodic changes. Franciscus C. Donders demonstated that there is a strong association between the changes in the heart rate and respiration. In 1882, Frredericq examined that the stoppage of lung motion results in continuing the variability of arterial pressure and RSA was eliminated by the inhibition of respiratory motor activity following hyperventilation.

But, Bainbridge (1930) investigated that RSA arises from the mechanical distortion of the atria which occurs because of the changes in thoracic pressure during the respiratory cycle. Later, Anrep et al. (1936) and its associates demonstrated that the beat to beat changes in the heart rate occur due to both the central and peripheral mechanisms. Also the arterial baroreceptor, thermoregulatory control, and the rennin-angiotenism system were responsible for changes in the heart rate (Sayers, 1973). Hering (1910) reported that heart rate is lowered with breathing. Hamlin et al. (1966) observed that the activation of vagal nerves were responsible for RSA in the dogs.

Heart rate variations are also investigated by Hyndman et al. (1971) using power spectral analysis. Thakor & Webster (1980) used two electrodes for ground free ECG recording. DeBoer et al. (1985) established that HRV data can be transformed into signal for analysis. Myers et al. (1986) used power spectral density for categorizing cardiac patients via HRV analysis. Impedance plethysmography is used in 1986 by Jindal (1986) for vascular disorders. Further, Malik et al. (1989) found the automated filtering method for HRV analysis. In order to overcome the nonuniform samples in HRV signal, the resampling is proposed by Schreibman et al. (1989). Merri et al. (1990) recommended a minimum sampling rate of 250 Hz for RR interval measurement. Nollo et al. (1990) examined that low and high frequency oscillations are present in human atrioventricular variability. Malik & camm (1995) performed an extensive survey on use of HRV and its clinical implications. Afterwards, wavelets were used for HRV analysis by Lvanov et al. (1996). Jasson et al. (1997) used time frequency analysis methods for HRV analysis. Laguna et al. (1998) designed a new method for for estimating non-equispaced HRV time series. Hilton et al. (1999) found HRV applications in diagnosing sleep apnea syndrome. In the same year, Huikuri et al. (1999), and Lombardi et al. (1999) provided a detailed review of various HRV analysis methods and future directions in HRV research. Malpas et al. (2001) examined that the blood pressure variability is regulated by sympathetic nervous system. In 2002, Malpas (2002) also reviewed that the variability is associated with respiration. Chan et al. (2003) quantified that HRV changes with different physical activities. Yamamoto et al. (2004) and Osowski et al. (2004) used fractal properties and support vector machine respectively for quantifying the heart rate dynamics. In the same year, Acharya et al. (2005) classified cardiac abnormalities using HRV signals by implementing neural networks. Portet et al. (2005) proposed adaptive QRS detector by quantifying various QRS detection algorithms. Kheder et al. (2006) performed HRV analysis by using a nonlinear method. Hansson-Sandsten & Jonssson (2007) used multiple window approach for finding the correlation between the respiratory frequency and high frequency band. Zhang et al. (2008) used the fractional Fourier transform for detecting the biomedical signals. Yeh et al. (2009) used DFA using empirical mode decomposition for quantifying human heart beat. Rafiee et al. (2011) used various wavelet basis functions in the field of biomedical signal processing. Madhavi ànd Ananth (2012) reviewed HRV analysis methods and its association with diseases. Karthikeyan et al. (2013) used various nonlinear methods for identifying stress using multiple physiological signals. Bolea et al. (2014) used a nonlinear method named correlation dimension for analyzing HRV signals. Various investigators used these physiological signals for developments of healthcare and medical tourism. Venkatesan et al. (2018) used the mobile cloud computing approach for assessing the complexities associated with ECG telehealth care technologies and Coronary Heart Disease (CHD) risk. Various classifiers are compared for classifying the ECG and CHD risk assessment. Mathews et al. (2018) proposed an algorithm based on deep learning methodology for classifying the ECG signals. The proposed algorithm can further be used for classifying other signals like blood pressure, PPG etc. Khowaja et al. (2018) used wearable sensors for providing healthcare monitoring along with the services provided by the doctors. Marcus et al. (2020) presented a brief survey of recent healthcare technologies using Internet of Things (IOT) for diagnosing various cardiovascular diseases. This paper also presents the current developments, open issues as well as future trends in IOT based healthcare monitoring services. Elias et al. (2018) proposed the feature selection method for identifying the unexpected sudden cardiac death due to the loss of the heart function.

Recording Instrument and Data Description

The ECG signal can be recorded using limb leads or chest leads by means of ECG machine such as BIOPAC®MP 150 system All the signals can be recorded at a sampling frequency of 500Hz or 250Hz. The sampling frequency of 250 – 500 Hz or even higher is the optimal range of ECG data recording [1]. The data must be recorded in quiet laboratory settings having maintained temperature levels. For each ECG recording, three Ag-AgCl electrodes were placed as follows: one electrode on the right arm, one on the left leg, and last is ground which is placed on the right leg in lead II arrangement. In order to achieve the most suitable recording conditions and better signal quality, the subject was rested in the lying position for 10 minutes prior to each ECG recording, so that subject may stabilize to the laboratory environment. After 10 minutes rest, ECG signal can be recorded. The RR- intervals were then obtained using software Acknowledge 4.2. To remove the artifacts in the data, all subjects must be instructed to avoid movement of hands, legs and body, talking, coughing and sleeping during recording. Also, subjects should be instructed not to take food, tea or coffee in last two hours prior to the recording. The informed written consent must be taken from all the subjects.

DURATION OF ECG RECORDINGS

Short Term Recordings

In short term recordings of 2 to 5min, the three main frequency components such as Very Low Frequency (VLF), Low Frequency (LF) and High Frequency (HF) are calculated. Out of VLF, LF, and HF, there is much less physiological elucidation of the VLF component. Therefore, the VLF measure can be avoided when interpreting the PSD of short term ECG's. The variations in the LF and HF components are associated with variations in the autonomic modulations of heart. The VLF, LF, and HF components can be measured either in the absolute values of power (ms^2) or in normalized units. The balanced behavior of two branches of ANS is represented by the values of LF and HF in normalized units (Task Force, 1996).

Long Term Recordings

Long term recording comprises the sequence of RR intervals of the entire 24 hour period. Inaddition to VLF, LF and HF components, the Ultra High Frequency (ULF) component is also included in the result due to sufficient length, *i.e.,* 24 hour of the record. Long term recordings are commonly associated with the problem of stationarity. Particularly these heart period modulations for LF and HF components cannot be considered stationary for the entire 24 hour period. Further, the interpretation of results of frequency analysis is less well defined when these modulations are not stable.

Sources of Interference in ECG Recording

The electrodes used for recording the electrical activity of the heart are applied externally on the human body. These ECG signals are recorded in the order of 1 mV in amplitude and are often susceptible to noise, interference and different artifacts. The various sources of interference are power line interference, baseline wander, muscle noise, motion artifacts, and radio frequency interference, *etc* (Levnov et al. 1984; Wachowiak et al. 2000) as shown in Figure 5.

Baseline Wander

The interference in the ECG signal is caused by respiration or movement of subject is called baseline wander as shown in Figure 5(a). In order to produce stable signal for subsequent signal processing and ECG signal analysis and further visualize the ECG signal for meaningful interpretation, baseline wander should be removed.

Electrode Contact Noise and Motion Artifacts

Electrode contact noise occurs due to the variations in the propagation medium between the heart and the electrodes which results in rapid changes in the amplitude of ECG signal. The amplitude of ECG signal is reduced by the poor conductivity between the electrodes and the heart. On the other hand, motion artifacts are caused by deformation of the skin or the disturbance of the skin-electrode interface as shown in Figure 5(b). The subject vibration, movement and respiration are the major causes of motion artifacts. It is also difficult to eliminate them from the ECG recordings. Motion artifacts make the ECG interpretation more difficult when it resembles the QRS complexes of the ECG recordings. Motion artifacts can be limited by designing good quality electrodes, and by reducing the relative movement between the skin and the electrode.

Figure 5. Different sources of interference in ECG (a) Baseline wander (b) Motion artifacts (c) EMG noise (d) Respiration induced noise (Sornmo & Laguna, 2005)

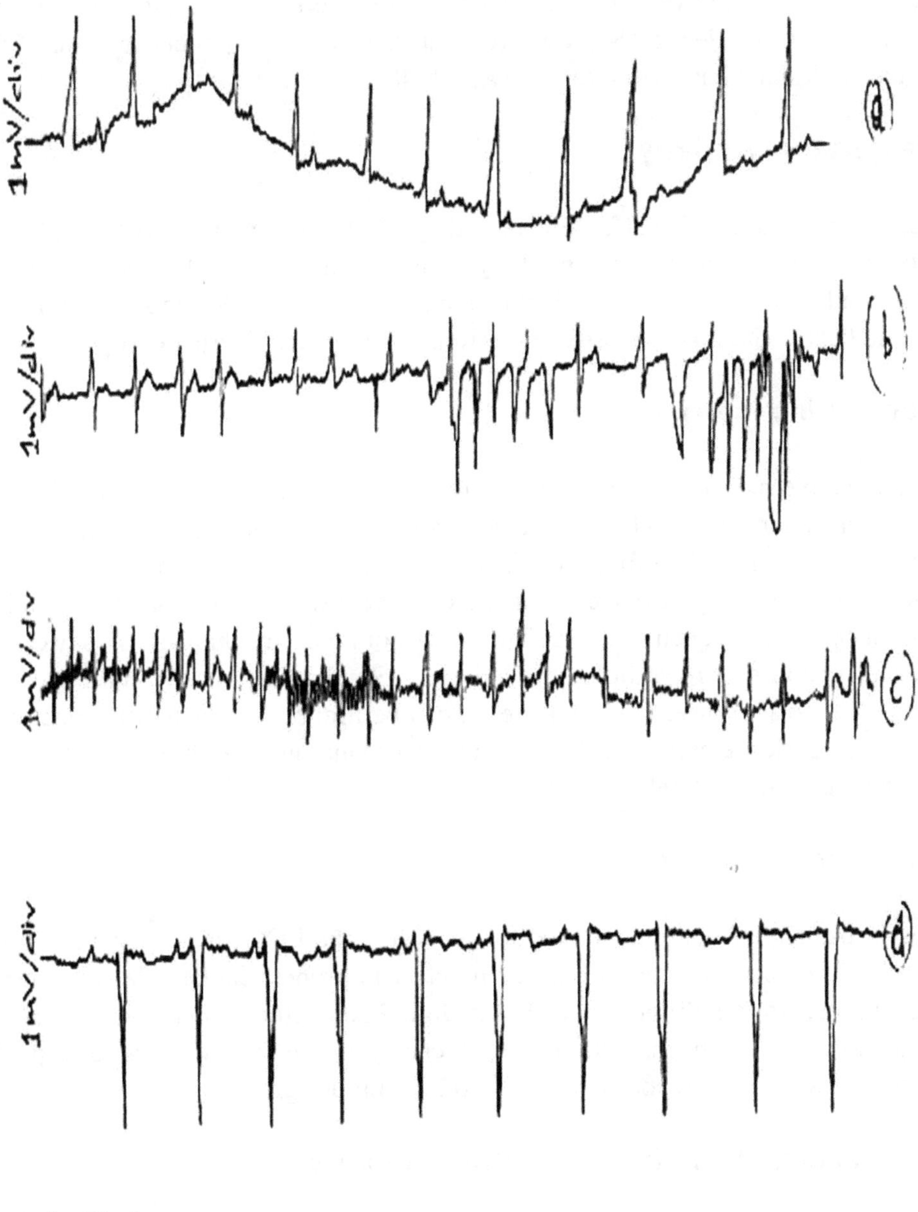

Muscle Noise

Electromyogram (EMG) noise is generated by the contraction of muscles of the human body. The EMG noise is shown in Figure 5(c). The amplitude of EMG noise is proportional to the muscular contraction, *i.e.,* activity undertaken by several muscle groups (subject movement) and the quality of the probes. The amplitude of EMG noise is same as the ECG signals but it occurs at higher frequencies. EMG nose can be limited by: lower muscular contraction while ECG recording, by carefully placing the ECG electrodes (away from large muscle groups) and by amplifying signals in limited bandwidth range, *i.e.,* 0.5-40Hz.

Respiratory Activity

Respiratory activity also effects on recording of ECG signal not only through heart rate but also through beat morphology as shown in Figure 5(d). The variation in lung conductivity, the variations in position of the heart and chest movements causes beat to beat variations in morphology (Reikkinen & Rautaharju, 1976).

Power Line Interference

The inductive and capacitive couplings are the two main mechanisms which induces power line interference. The mutual inductance between the two conductors causes inductive coupling. The magnetic flux is produced when current flows through wires which further generate current in the adjacent wires. The capacitive coupling introduces high frequency noise. The main dominant mechanism of power line interference in electrocardiology is inductive coupling because it introduces low frequency noise. Power line interference can be limited by placing the electrodes properly, no loose wires, and by adequate grounding and shielding of all the components (Saini, 2009)

Instrumentation Noise

The instrument or equipment used for recording the ECG signal generates noise is termed as instrumentation noise. The electric probes, cables, electrode leads, signal processor/amplifier and analog to digital converter (A/D converter) are the major sources of instrumentation noise. It can be eliminated by using good quality instruments for ECG recording and careful circuit design.

Technical and Clinical Recommendations

- There are certain conditions required to be fulfilled for faithful recording of ECG signal which are following:
- The sampling frequency must be properly selected. A sampling frequency of 250 to 500 Hz or even higher is the optimal range of ECG data recording (Task Force, 1996). Low sampling frequency produces jitter in the estimation

of R-wave fiducial point, which changes the spectrum considerably. But if the interpolation algorithm is used, then low sampling frequency (>=100Hz) may behave satisfactorily in the estimation of R-wave fiducial point (Task Force, 1996).

- The QRS fiducial point must be properly chosen. In order to locate a stable and independent R- wave fiducial point, a well-tested QRS fiducial point detection algorithm should be used.
- There are many physiological and technical disturbances occur while ECG recording. During ECG recording, these technical artifacts results due to motion artifacts or use of poorly fastened electrodes. These artifacts in the ECG recording deteriorate the quality of HRV signal. Further, the HRV time series are also non-equispaced in time, so there is a need to transform it into evenly spaced signals. In order to enhance the physiological and clinical information and to remove these artifacts, it is necessary to pre-process these biomedical signals by some suitable pre-processing methods before applying any HRV analysis method. One of the methods to reduce these artifacts is the interpolation of signal. Interpolation is the method by which one can construct new data points by inserting values within known sets of original data points (signal) to make original signal equidistant.

MAIN FOCUS OF THE CHAPTER

Medical Tourism and Healthcare

Medical tourism is a challenging task that addresses the various issues of national healthcare as well as global health care. The main objective of medical tourism is to provide healthcare services all over the world so as to utilize the expertise of various doctors and practitioners (Ridderstaat et al., 2019) The various types of medical treatments are available in indian systems of medicine such as yoga, chakra centres, Ayurveda, panchakarma etc. These medical treatments like Ayurveda are available in india at low cost along with the international standards. Most of the foreign tourists are now visited to india for getting medical Ayurveda treatments. Therefore, india is not only providing these healthcare services at low cost but it also provides world class healthcare by experienced doctors (Daniel & Amy, 2018).

In order to promote the medical tourism, there are various steps which are taken by the ministry of tourism to promote the medical tourism are follows:

1. The medical tourism website is prepared by the ministry of federation on which various hospitals are selected to provide the world class healthcare services.

2. Ministry of tourism also published the material by using pamphlets, CD's in order to provide the exposure to various people all over the world.
3. Some international platforms such as World Travel Mart, London, ITP Berlin are also used to encourage the people to use the medical tourism and healthcare facilities.
4. The foreign tourists can also use the healthcare facilities in India by applying the medical visa.
5. Various Ayurveda and Panchkarma centres are now opened along with the hospitals to provide better healthcare. For providing more publicity about these Ayurveda and Panchkarma centres, the same information is also updated on the medical tourism website.

Various patients need to visit abroad for seeking medical treatments by health care authorities because of the following reasons:

1. High quality healthcare with new developments in the information technology.
2. Better availability of doctors.
3. Affordable healthcare medical treatments.
4. Various medical treatments are not available in their own country.
5. Meet relatives, enjoy their holidays by visiting new places along with the treatment.

Most of the population seeking medical services suffering from cardiovascular diseases along with the cancers, organ transplantation, neurological disorders etc (Courtney et al, 2018). The most preferred countries which provides affordable and quality healthcare are Thailand, Malaysia and Singapore (Soheon & Won, 2019).

Preprocessing of the HRV Signal

There are many physiological and technical disturbances occurs while each ECG recording. During ECG recording, these technical artifacts results due to motion artifacts or use of poorly fastened electrodes. These artifacts in the ECG recording deteriorate the quality of HRV signal and yields incomplete or missing RR interval. Arterial fibrillation, ventricular tachycardia, and ectopic beats, are examples of physiological artifacts in the ECG recording. Further, the HRV time series are also non-equispaced in time, so there is a need to transform it into evenly spaced signals. In order to enhance the physiological and clinical information and to remove these artifacts, it is necessary to preprocess these biomedical signals by some suitable pre processing methods before applying HRV analysis method. There are two basic approaches which are used to preprocess the RR interval time series: (i) Deletion of ectopic beats and (ii) Substitution of a better matching value. The deletion approach is widely suited for time domain analysis, and can also be used with frequency domain analysis if only a few beats are to be deleted. The length of RR intervals is decreased by using deletion preprocessing methods due to the loss of deleted RR intervals. In the second approach, substitution can take the form of simply replacing the ectopic beats with a local mean or median value, but more sophisticated procedures include interpolating of the R-waves from the surrounding beats. Also the initial numbers of samples in HRV time series are preserved by using interpolation methods as compared to deletion methods used for preprocessing (Peltola, 2012).

Interpolation

Interpolation is the method by which one can construct new data points by inserting values within known sets of original data points (signal) to make the original signal equidistant. It is a commonly used method to reduce artifacts of the signal. Despite there are numerous methods of interpolation are available in the literature, but the commonly used methods are: linear interpolation (Singh et al. 2004); Clifford, 2002), spline interpolation (Clifford, 2002; Keseslbrener & Alselrod, 1996), berger interpolation (Berger et al. 1986), and cubic interpolation (Vilal et al. 1992). The different interpolation methods are following:

Linear Interpolation

The simplest method used for interpolation is linear interpolation. Linear interpolation is a method of curve fitting in which linear polynomials are used. If the coordinates (x_0, y_0) and (x_1, y_1) of two known points are given, the linear interpolant is the straight line between these points "Retrieved from http://en.wikipedia.org/wiki/Linear_interpolation"

The formula for the calculation of linear interpolation for the interval (x_0, x_1) is defined using (2)

$$y = y_0 + (x - x_0)\frac{y_1 - y_0}{x_1 - x_0} \tag{2}$$

For a set of data points, linear interpolation can be calculated by concatenating the linear interpolants between each pair of data points. By using the linear interpolation method, a new sequence of RR values is created at each time instant t_i with resampling frequency of 4 Hz. The sequence of new RR values at each time instant t_i using various values is derived using (2.2)

$$r_i = r_a + (t_i - t_a) * ((r_b - r_a) / (t_b - t_a)) \quad (3)$$

where r_i's are the new evenly spaced RR-values and t_a and t_b are the times allied with the before and after t_i. r_a and r_b are their associated RR-values. The main limitation of linear interpolation is that it lacks accuracy. Therefore it can be replaced by other interpolation methods.

Cubic Spline Interpolation

In cubic spline interpolation, the smooth and continuous curve is obtained by fitting a series of unique cubic polynomials between each of the data points. The idea here is to draw smooth curves through several numbers of points. The spline comprises weights connected to a flat surface at the points to be interpolated. Across each weight, a flexible string is subsequently ready to bend which gives smooth curve "Retrieved from http://en.wikipedia.org/wiki/Spline_interpolation". From a mathematical point of view, spline is a special function which can be described piecewise by polynomials. Here, the points used are numerical data. For interpolating the data, the weights are used as coefficients of cubic polynomials. For maintaining the continuity in the line, the line is bended by the coefficients so that it passes through each of the data points. The piecewise function of the form is mathematically using (4) "Retrieved fromhttp://en.wikipedia.org/wiki/Spline_%28mathematics%29"

$$S(x) = \begin{cases} s_1(x) & if \quad x_1 \le x < x_2 \\ s_2(x) & if \quad x_2 \le x < x_3 \\ s_{n-1}(x) & if \quad x_{n-1} \le x < x_n \end{cases} \quad (4)$$

where the third degree polynomial is defined using (2.4)

$$s_i(x) = a_i(x - x_i)^3 + b_i(x - x_i)^2 + c_i(x - x_i) + d_i \ for \ i = 1, 2, ..., n - 1 \quad (5)$$

Where a_i, b_i, c_i, and d_i are the weights which represents the coefficients of cubic polynomial.

Berger's Interpolation

In berger's interpolation, as the time interval increasing from previous sample to the next, a local window is defined over each point t_i (Berger et al. 1986) outcome of assigning each t_i generates a new RR-value corresponding to the RR-values which are associated with the local window. If the location of time interval t_i is situated between two consecutive beats then the new RR-value is calculated using (6)

$$r_i = (t_{i+1} - t_{i-1}) * f_m / (2 * r_b) \tag{6}$$

where f_m is the resampling frequency and r_b is the value RR intervals between two consecutive beats.

Cubic Interpolation

Cubic interpolation is used to transform the entire HRV time series into equidistantly sampled series. Cubic interpolation is used because interpolation using cubic polynomial does not change the nature of the HRV time series. In cubic interpolation, the interpolation of function $f(x)$ in the interval [0, 1] can be performed by using the third degree polynomial. The function $f(x)$ using third degree polynomial and its derivative is defined using (7) and (8) “Retrieved from http://www.paulinternet.nl/?page=bicubic

$$f(x) = ax^3 + bx^2 + cx + d \tag{7}$$

$$f'(x) = 3ax^2 + 2bx + c \tag{8}$$

The values of polynomial at $x = 0$ and $x = 1$ is defined using (9) and (10)

$$f(0) = d \tag{9}$$

$$f(1) = a + b + c + d \tag{10}$$

And its derivatives are given using (11) and (12)

$$f'(0) = c \tag{11}$$

$$f'(1) = 3a + 2b + c \tag{12}$$

The (9) – (12) can be rewritten using (13) – (16)

$$a = 2f(0) - 2f(1) + f'(0) + f'(1) \tag{13}$$

$$b = -3f(0) + 3f(1) - 2f'(0) - f'(1) \tag{14}$$

$$c = f'(0) \tag{15}$$

$$d = f(0) \tag{16}$$

After solving the (13) – (16), the new RR-values which are evenly spaced in time are obtained.

FUTURE RESEARCH DIRECTIONS

There are various applications in which HRV measures are increasingly being employed. The measures of HRV not only provide the fundamental link between the psychological processes and physiological functions as well as basic investigations of cardiac autonomic state. Although the widespread applications of these measures serves as an indication of potential merit, but still there are some issues that are necessary to be resolved, as this would involve the standardization of preprocessing of HRV analysis methods. Some of the issues addressed are following:

1. It was found that in frequency domain analysis two main spectral components, *i.e.,* LF, and HF components are mostly used in the literature. But in the long term HRV, *i.e.,* in ULF and VLF range several physiological mechanisms are responsible. So, in this chapter these ULF and VLF ranges are not studied. Further work in this regard is needed.
2. Further, development and standardization of the conventional preprocessing HRV analysis methods used in this chapter is required for future work.
3. In order to describe the physiological and clinical behavior using HRV, new models of preprocessing the HRV needs to be thoroughly investigated. Moreover,

the bridge between HRV signal processing and physiologic modeling for providing meaningful interpretations and explorations needs to be emphasized.

As this area continues to evolve, it is hoped that the present chapter provides a valuable contribution to the area of preprocessing methods of HRV. The work presented in this chapter would also a contribution for recording and analysing the faithful HRV signals for providing the effective healthcare services.

CONCLUSION

In the present time, it is necessary to provide effective health care services as well as to diagnose the computer based cardiac diseases by using computer aided feature extraction and ECG signal analysis. With increase in population, the pressure at the hospitals also increases. Therefore, day by day the task of cardiac specialists and clinicians are becoming harder. So, in order to provide effective cardiac care, there is a vital need to use computer based expert systems and medical tourism facilities. Medical tourism plays an important role for detecting and diagnosing various types of cardiovascular diseases. Medical Tourism is the new tourism practice for providing medical services to various individuals in different countries. But still, there are no such scientific contributions developed till now which defines the methods, various strategies and the future trends of medical tourism. The other major problem occurs in providing the effective healthcare facilities as well as medical tourism is non availability of data. Therefore, future studies must emphasize on requirement of the medical facilities including the type of treatment in different countries. In computer aided diagnostics, the first step is the recording, identification, and extraction of the features of the ECG signal. Further, this chapter gives a detailed description of ECG signal acquisition, recording requirements, experimental protocols while ECG recording, duration of ECG recordings, various sources of interference in ECG recording, and RR interval pre-processing methods such as interpolation used to remove the artifacts.

The pre-processing methods have a significant role in HRV signal analysis. This chapter gives a brief overview of various interpolation methods used for pre-processing of RR intervals.

REFERENCES

Acharya, R., Kannathal, N., Mei Hua, L., & Mei Yi, L. (2005). Study of heart rate variability signals in at sitting and lying postures. *Journal of Bodywork and Movement Therapies*, *9*(2), 134–141. doi:10.1016/j.jbmt.2004.04.001

Anrep, G. V., Pascua, W., & Rossler, R. (1936a). Respiratory variations in the heart rate I. The reflex mechanism of respiratory arrhythmia. *Proceedings of the Royal Society of London. Series B, Biological Sciences*, *119*(813), 191–217. doi:10.1098/rspb.1936.0005

Bainbridge, F. A. (1930). The relation between respiration and the pulse-rate. *The Journal of Physiology*, *54*(3), 192–202. doi:10.1113/jphysiol.1920.sp001918 PMID:16993458

Berger, R. D., Akselrod, S., Gordon, D., & Cohen, R. J. (1986). An efficient algorithm for spectral analysis of heart rate variability. *IEEE Transactions on Biomedical Engineering*, *33*(9), 900–904. doi:10.1109/TBME.1986.325789 PMID:3759126

Bolea, J., Laguna, P., Remartinez, J. M., Rovira, E., Navarro, A., & Bailon, R. (2014). Methodological Framework for Estimating the Correlation Dimension in HRV Signals. C*omputational and Mathematical Methods in Medicine*. *Article ID*, *129248*, 11.

Chan, H. L., Lin, C. H., & Ko, Y. L. (2003). Segmentation of HRV in different physical activities. *Proceedings of IEEE Conference on Computers in Cardiology*, 30, 97-100.

Clifford, G. D. (2002). *Signal Processing Methods for Heart Rate Variability Analysis* (Ph.D. Thesis). St. Cross College, Oxford, UK.

Courtney, S., Seyhmus, B., & James, A. B. (2018). Perceived impacts of medical tourism development on community wellbeing. *Tourism Management*, *69*, 232–245. doi:10.1016/j.tourman.2018.06.006

Cubic Interpolation. (n.d.). Retrieved from the Cubic Interpolation http://www.paulinternet.nl/?page=bicubic

Daniel, B., & Amy, Z. (2018). Medical tourism and national health care systems: An institutionalist research agenda. *Globalization and Health*, *68*(14), 1–7. PMID:30012218

DeBoer, R. W., Karemaker, J. M., & Strackee, J. (1985). Description of heart rate variability data in accordance with a physiological model for the genesis of heart beats. *Psychophysiology, 22*(2), 147–155. doi:10.1111/j.1469-8986.1985.tb01577.x PMID:3991842

Elias Ebrahimzadeh, E., Manuchehri, M. S., Amoozegar, S., Araabi, B. N., & Zadeh, H. S. (2018). A time local subset feature selection for prediction of sudden cardiac death from ECG signal. *Medical & Biological Engineering & Computing, 56*(7), 1253–1270. doi:10.100711517-017-1764-1 PMID:29238903

Fatemian, S. Z. (2009). *A Wavelet based Approach to Electrocardiogram (ECG) and Phonocardiogram (PCG) Subject Recognition* (Master of Applied Science Thesis). University of Toronto, Toronto, Canada.

Gao, G. Q. (2003). *Computerised Detection and Classification of five Cardiac Conditions* (M. E. Thesis). Auckland University of Technology, Auckland, New Zealand.

Hamlin, R. L., Smith, R. C., & Smetzer, D. L. (1966). Sinus arrhythmia in the dog. *The American Journal of Physiology, 210*(2), 321–328. doi:10.1152/ajplegacy.1966.210.2.321 PMID:5901470

Hansson-Sandsten, M., & Jonsson, P. (2007). Multiple window correlation analysis of HRV power and respiratory frequency. *IEEE Transactions on Biomedical Engineering, 54*(10), 1770–1779. doi:10.1109/TBME.2007.904527 PMID:17926675

Hering, H. E. (1910). A functional test of heart vagi in man. *Men-schen München Medizinische Wochenschrift, 57*, 1931–1933.

Hilton, M. F., Bates, R. A., Godfrey, K. R., Chappell, M. J., & Cayton, R. M. (1999). Evaluation of frequency and time frequency spectral analysis of heart rate variability as a diagnostic marker of the sleep apnea syndrome. *Medical & Biological Engineering & Computing, 37*(6), 760–769. doi:10.1007/BF02513379 PMID:10723884

Huikuri, H. V., Makikallio, T., Airaksinen, K. E., Mitrani, R., Castellanos, A., & Myerburg, R. J. (1999). Measurement of heart rate variability. A clinical tool or research toy? *Journal of the American College of Cardiology, 34*(7), 1878–1883. doi:10.1016/S0735-1097(99)00468-4 PMID:10588197

Hyndman, B. W., Kitney, R. I., & Sayers, B. M. (1971). Spontaneous rhythms in physiological control systems. *Nature, 233*(5318), 339–341. doi:10.1038/233339a0 PMID:4940430

Jasson, S., Medigue, C., Maison-Blanche, P., Montano, N., Meyer, L., Vermeiren, C., ... Swynghedauw, B. (1997). Instant power spectrum analysis of HRV during orthostatic tilt using a time/frequency domain method. *Circulation*, *96*, 3521–3526. doi:10.1161/01.CIR.96.10.3521 PMID:9396450

Jindal, G. D. (1986). Impedance plethysmography for screening vascular diseases. *Journal of Postgraduate Medicine*, *32*, 1–3. PMID:3746705

Kana, M. (2010). *Mathematical Models of Cardiovascular Control by the Autonomic Nervous System* (Ph. D. Thesis). Czech Technical University in Prague, Prague, Czech Republic.

Karthikeyan, P., Murugappan, M., & Yaacob, S. (2013). Multiple Physiological Signal-Based Human Stress identification Using Non-Linear Classifiers. *Electronics and Electrical Engineering, 19*(7).

Keseslbrener, L., & Alselrod, S. (1996). Selective discrete Fourier transform algorithm for time frequency analysis: Method and application on simulated and cardiovascular signals. *IEEE Transactions on Biomedical Engineering*, *43*(8), 789–802. doi:10.1109/10.508542 PMID:9216151

Khedder, G., Kachouri, A., Messouad, M. B., & Samet, M. (2004). Application of nonlinear dynamic method in the analysis of HRV towards clinical application: Tiresome diagnosis. In *Proceedings of the International conference on Information and Communication Technologies: From Theory to applications*, (*vol. 1*, pp. 177-182). Academic Press.

Khowaja, S. A., Prabono, A. B., Setiawan, F., Yahya, B. N., & Lee, S. L. (2018). Contextual activity based Healthcare Internet of Things, Services, and People (HIoTSP): An architectural framework for healthcare monitoring using wearable sensors. *Computer Networks*, *145*(9), 190–206. doi:10.1016/j.comnet.2018.09.003

Laguna, P., Moody, G. B., & Mark, R. G. (1998). Power spectral density of unevenly sampled data by least square analysis: Performance and application to heart rate signals. *IEEE Transactions on Biomedical Engineering*, *45*(6), 698–715. doi:10.1109/10.678605 PMID:9609935

Levkov, C., Micchov, G., Lyanov, R., & Daskalov, I. K. (1984). Subtraction of 50 Hz interference from the electrocardiogram. *Medical & Biological Engineering & Computing*, *22*(4), 371–373. doi:10.1007/BF02442109 PMID:6748774

Linear Interpolation. (n.d.). Retrieved from the Linear Interpolation Wiki: http://en.wikipedia.org/wiki/Linear_interpolation

Lombardi, F. (1999). Heart rate variability: A contribution to better understanding of the clinical role of heart rate. *European Heart Journal Supplements*, *1*, H44–H51.

Lovoy Siem, K. V. (2007). *Modelling fibre orientation of the left ventricular human heart wall* (M. S. Thesis). Norwegian University of Science and Technology.

Lvanov, P. C., Rosenblum, M. G., Peng, C. K., Mietus, J., Havlin, S., Stanley, H. E., & Goldberger, A. L. (1996). Scaling behavior of heart beat intervals obtained by wavelet based time series analysis. *Nature*, *383*(6598), 323–327. doi:10.1038/383323a0 PMID:8848043

Malik, M., & Camm Eds, A. J. (1995). *Heart Rate Variability*. Armonk, NY: Futura.

Malik, M., Cripps, T., Farrel, T., & Camm, A. J. (1989). Prognostic value of heart rate variability after myocardial infarction. A comparison of different data processing methods. *Medical & Biological Engineering & Computing*, *27*(6), 603–611. doi:10.1007/BF02441642

Malpas, S. C. (2002). Neural influences on cardiovascular variability: Posiibilities and pitfalls. *American Journal of Physiology. Heart and Circulatory Physiology*, *282*(1), H6–H20. doi:10.1152/ajpheart.2002.282.1.H6 PMID:11748042

Malpas, S. C., Leonard, B. L., Guild, S., Ringwood, J. V., Navakatikyan, M., Austin, P. C., ... Burgess, D. E. (2001). The sympathetic nervous system's role in regulating blood pressure variability: Understanding how SNA controls vascular tone is an important step in determining the pathogenesis of hypertension. *IEEE Engineering in Medicine and Biology*, *20*(2), 17–24. doi:10.1109/51.917720

Marcus, A. G., Munoz, M., Olivares, R., Reboucas Filho, P. P., Ser, J. D., & Victor Hugo, C. (2020). Online heart monitoring systems on the internet of health things environments: A survey, a reference model and an outlook. *Information Fusion*, *53*, 222–239. doi:10.1016/j.inffus.2019.06.004

Mathews, S. M., Kambhamettu, C., & Barner, K. (2018). A novel application of deep learning for single-lead ECG classification. *Computers in Biology and Medicine*, *99*(1), 53–62. doi:10.1016/j.compbiomed.2018.05.013 PMID:29886261

Merri, M., Areden, D. C., & Motley, J. G. (1990). Sampling frequency of the electrocardiogram for spectral analysis of heart rate variability. *IEEE Transactions on Biomedical Engineering*, *37*(1), 99–106. doi:10.1109/10.43621 PMID:2303276

Myers, G., Martin, G., Magid, N., Barnett, P., Wiess, J., Lesch, M., & Singer, D. H. (1986). Power spectral analysis of heart rate variability in sudden cardiac death: Comparison to other methods. *IEEE Transactions on Biomedical Engineering*, *BME-33*(12), 1149–1156. doi:10.1109/TBME.1986.325694 PMID:3817848

Nollo, G., Del Greco, M., Ravelli, F., & Disertori, M. (1994). Evidence of low and high frequency oscillations in human AV interval variability: Evaluation with spectral analysis. *American Journal of Physiology. Heart and Circulatory Physiology*, *267*(4), H1410–h-1418. doi:10.1152/ajpheart.1994.267.4.H1410 PMID:7943386

Osowski, S., Hoai, L. T., & Markiewicz, T. (2004). Support vector machine-based expert system for reliable heart beat recognition. *IEEE Transactions on Biomedical Engineering*, *51*(4), 582–589. doi:10.1109/TBME.2004.824138 PMID:15072212

Peltola, M. A. (2012). Role of Editing of R–R Intervals in the Analysis of Heart Rate Variability. *Frontiers in Physiology*, *3*(148), 1–10. PMID:22654764

Portet, F., Hernanadez, A. I., & Carrault, G. (2005). Evaluation of real time QRS detection algorithm in variable contexts. *Medical & Biological Engineering & Computing*, *43*(3), 379–385. doi:10.1007/BF02345816 PMID:16035227

Rafiee, J., Rafiee, M. A., Prause, N., & Schoen, M. P. (2011). Wavelet basis functions in biomedical signal processing Expert Systems with Applications. *Expert Systems with Applications*, *38*(5), 6190–6201. doi:10.1016/j.eswa.2010.11.050

Reikkinen, H., & Rautaharju, P. (1976). Body position, electrode level and respiration effects on the Frank lead electrocardiogram. *Circulation*, *53*(1), 40–45. doi:10.1161/01.CIR.53.1.40 PMID:127674

Renu Madhavi, C. H. (2012). *Characterisation of Heart Rate Variability of Healthy, Cardiac and Non-cardiac Diseased Subjects using Nonlinear Techniques* (Ph. D. Thesis). Avinashilingam University for Women, Coimbatore, India.

Renu Madhavi, C. H., & Ananth, A. G. (2012). A Review of Heart Rate Variability and It's Association with Diseases. *International Journal of Soft Computing and Engineering*, *2*(3), 2231–2307.

Ridderstaat, J., Singh, D., & DeMicco, F. (2019). The impact of major tourist markets on health tourism spending in the United States. *Journal of Destination Marketing & Management*, *11*, 270–280. doi:10.1016/j.jdmm.2018.05.003

Saini, B. S. (2009). *Signal Processing of Heart Rate Variability* (Ph. D. Thesis). Dr. B. R. Ambedkar National Institute of Technology, Jalandhar, India.

Sayers, B. M. (1973). Analysis of heart rate variability. *Ergonomics*, *16*(1), 17–32. doi:10.1080/00140137308924479 PMID:4702060

Schreibman, K. L., Thomas, C. W., & Levy, M. N. (1989). Spectral analysis of cardiac cycle length variations: Resampling overcomes effects of nonuniform spacing. In *Proceedings of the 11th Annual International Conference of the IEEE EMBS* (vol. 1, pp. 40-41). IEEE. 10.1109/IEMBS.1989.95561

Seaborn, G. (2010). *Changes in Autonomic Tone Resulting from Circumferential Pulmonary Vein Isolation* (M. S. Thesis). Queen's University, Kingston, Ontario, Canada.

Simmons, J. (2013). *Autonomic Nervous System Response to Repeated Cold Exposure* (M. S. Thesis). Louisiana State University.

Singh, D., Vinod, K., Saxena, S. C., & Deepak, K. K. (2004). Effects of RR segment duration on HRV spectrum estimation. *Physiological Measurement*, *25*(3), 721–735. doi:10.1088/0967-3334/25/3/012 PMID:15253123

Singh, Y. N. (2007). *ECG Delineation and its Application in Individual Identification* (M. Tech Thesis). Indian Institute of Technology, Kanpur, India.

Sohyeon, K., & Won, S. L. (2019). Network text analysis of medical tourism in newspapers using text mining: The South Korea case. *Tourism Management Perspectives*, *31*, 332–339. doi:10.1016/j.tmp.2019.05.010

Sornmo, L., & Laguna, P. (2005). *Bioelectrical Signal processing in cardiac and neurological applications*. Elsevier Academic Press.

Spline Interpolation. (n.d.). Retrieved from the Spline Interpolation Wiki: http://en.wikipedia.org/wiki/Spline_interpolation

Spline Mathematics. (n.d.). Retrieved from the Sline Mathematics. Wiki: http://en.wikipedia.org/wiki/Spline_%28mathematics%29

Task force of the European society of cardiology and the North American society of pacing and electrophysiology Heart rate variability - standards of measurement. Physiological interpretation and clinical use (1996). *Circulation*, *93*(5), 1043–1065.

Thakor, N. V., & Webster, J. G. (1980). Ground free ECG recording using two electrodes. *IEEE Transactions on Biomedical Engineering*, *27*(12), 699–704. doi:10.1109/TBME.1980.326595 PMID:7461645

Tze-Yeng Chang, E. (2013). *Towards understanding the Electrogram: Theoretical & experimental multiscale modelling of factors affecting action potential propagation in cardiac tissue* (Ph. D. Thesis). Imperial College, London, UK.

Venkatesan, C., Karthigaikumar, P., & Satheeskumaran, S. (2018). Mobile cloud computing for ECG telemonitoring and real-time coronary heart disease risk detection. *Biomedical Signal Processing and Control*, *44*, 138–145. doi:10.1016/j.bspc.2018.04.013

Vilal, J., Barro, S., Presedo, J., Ruiz, R., & Palacios, F. (1992). Analysis of heart rate variability with evenly spaced time values. *IEEE Transactions on Engineering in Medicine and Biology*, *2*, 575–576. doi:10.1109/IEMBS.1992.595719

Wachowiak, M. P., & Shah, G. S. (2000). Wavelet-based noise removal for biomedical signals: A comparative study. *IEEE Transactions on Biomedical Engineering*, *47*(3), 360–368. doi:10.1109/10.827298 PMID:10743778

Yamamoto, Y., Kiyono, K., & Struzik, Z. R. (2004). Measurement analysis, interpretation of long term heart rate variability. In *Proceedings of SICE Annual Conference*, (pp. 2598-2605). Academic Press.

Yeh, J., Fa, S., & Shieh, J. (2009). Human heart beat analysis using a modified algorithm of detrended fluctuation analysis based on empirical mode decomposition. *Medical Engineering & Physics*, *31*(1), 92–100. doi:10.1016/j.medengphy.2008.04.011 PMID:18547859

Zhang, Y., Zhang, Q., & Wu, S. (2008). Biomedical signal detection based on fractional Fourier transform. In *Proceedings of 5th International Conference on Information Technology and Application in Biomedicine*, (pp. 349-352) Shenzhen, China: Academic Press.

Chapter 14
Prospects and Challenges of Medical Tourism:
Evidences From Manipur

Sunildro LS Akoijam
North-Eastern Hill University, India

Tabassum Khan
Unity College, India

ABSTRACT

Medical tourism has seen rapid growth in the past few years in Manipur from neighboring states as well as countries, particularly Myanmar. Manipur is also trying to be on the medical tourism map of India with eminent medical practitioners across the state trying to take advantage of the Act East Policy of the Indian Government. Manipur witnessed a significant investment in healthcare over the last decade. With the emergence of some of the eminent hospitals and research institutes with advanced technology in the state, the diagnosis of many of the complicated medical problems are done effectively with minimal cost. The prospect looks bright, but challenges such as tag of being a 'disturbed area' and complex visa procedures for foreign nationals could constraints to the exponential growth of medical tourism in Manipur, especially from neighboring countries. The chapter is an attempt to study the prospects and challenges of medical tourism in Manipur. The study is exploratory in nature with insights from available literature and data from various sources.

DOI: 10.4018/978-1-5225-9787-2.ch014

INTRODUCTION

Medical Tourism is the convergence of foreign tourist arrivals with medical assistance. When distinguished from mere medical tourism, wellness pertains to preventive while medical invariably refers to curative care. Even within medical tourism, the therapeutic drivers range from cosmetic or dental treatments to highly complex transplants, cardiac and replacement procedures. The global medical tourism market size is expected to reach USD 179.6 billion by 2026, according to a new report by Grand View Research, Inc., registering a 21.9% CAGR during the forecast period. Medical tourism generates direct foreign exchange income and contributes to the overall development of any economy. It also provides employment and business opportunities for residents. Moreover, it aids the growth of associated businesses such as pharmaceuticals, medical devices, and tourism. Government support to maintain the general reputation and political stability of the host country is a key factor driving the medical tourism market. The global medical tourism market will reach the market value of US$ 40 billion by next year, 2020 at a CAGR of 17%. India along with countries like Thailand, Malaysia, Singapore, Mexico etc. plays a key role in shaping this market opportunity. Availability of cheaper medical treatment options along with better quality care is the primary factor that drives preference for offshore medical tourism. Patients can save in between 30% to 80% of the total treatment costs in these destinations. Moreover, benefits such as better healthcare, latest technologies, innovative medicines, advanced devices, better hospitality and personalized healthcare services are some of the major forces driving the market.

Government authorities are willing to invest in local enterprises to capitalize on the growth of medical tourism. Such government bodies have been authorizing projects that help in the overall development of infrastructure in a country, such as public transport system and water supply facilities, to attract high-end medical travelers.

Medical tourism has led to a rise in state-of-the-art medical facilities in developing countries to attract foreign nationals, resulting in fast growth of healthcare infrastructure in such countries. Moreover, healthcare providers now offer comprehensive medical tourism packages that include services ranging from ticket booking to hotel stay and medical insurance.

Thailand dominated the market in terms of revenue in 2018 owing to low cost and good quality medical services offered in the country. In 2016, Thailand ranked 18th in the International Healthcare Research Center's Medical Tourism Index. Moreover, the country ranked 13th on the same index in terms of quality of facilities and services provided owing to well-developed healthcare infrastructure and increasing number of medical professionals. Thailand is also home to Asia's first largest private hospital, Bumrungrad International Hospital, which is also the

Figure 1. Global medical tourism market

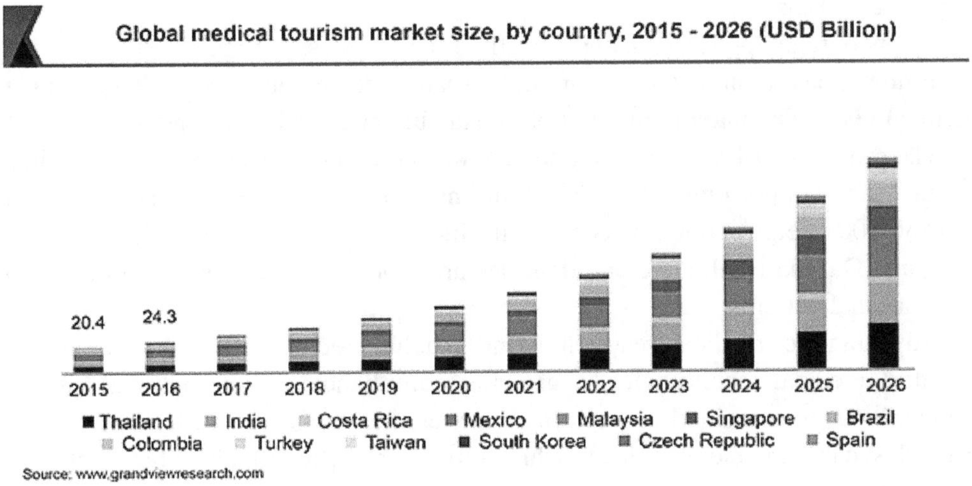

first hospital to receive a JCI accreditation and ISO 9001 certification. Till date, over 53 private hospitals have received JCI accreditation.

Medical Tourism in India

Medical tourism is a growing sector in India. This is mainly due to the cost, facilities, technologies as well as expertise of medical practitioners. India is among the fastest growing medical tourism destinations in Asia. In the BBIN sub-region, Bangladesh, Bhutan and Nepal depend on India for speciality health services. A large number of patients from Nepal, Bhutan and Bangladesh come to India for health treatment. In 2013, a total of 56,129 people came to India on medical visas, of which 9,482 were from Afghanistan, 17,814 from Bangladesh, 1,090 from Pakistan. Most of these patients have been treated in hospitals located in Kolkata, Chennai, Mumbai and Delhi.

India's medical tourism sector is expected to grow at an annual rate of 30 percent in the next few years. In October 2015, India's medical tourism sector was estimated to be worth US$3 billion. It is projected to grow at a CAGR of 200% by 2020, hitting $9 billion by 2020. In the BBIN sub-region, Bangladesh, Bhutan and Nepal depend on India for specialty health services. In 2013, a total of 56,129 people came to India on medical visas, of which 9,482 were from Afghanistan, 17,814 from Bangladesh, 1,090 from Pakistan. Most of these patients have been treated in hospitals located in Kolkata, Chennai, Mumbai and Delhi. In contrast to 2013, in the year 2017, 495,056 patients visited India to seek medical care. The top 10 source countries for patients were Bangladesh, Afghanistan, Iraq, Maldives, Oman, Yemen, Uzbekistan, Kenya, Nigeria and Tanzania.

To encourage applications and ease the travel process for medical tourists, the government has expanded its e-tourism VISA regime on February 2019, to include medical visas. The maximum duration of stay under this visa is 6 months.

The promotion of Medical Tourism in India has helped private players capitalize on this market opportunity. Private institutions such as Max Healthcare have treated up to 50,000 foreign patients in its hospitals. Industrialist Sanjay Dalmia's healthcare company Dalmia Healthcare on 2018, declared medical treatment consultation to international patients.

Advantages of medical treatment in India include reduced costs, the availability of latest medical technologies, a growing compliance on international quality standards, doctors trained in western countries including US and UK, as well as English speaking personnel, due to which foreigners are less likely to face language barrier in India.

Reddy (2000), from the recent studies, analyzes that the prospective of the healthcare industry has same challenges and development that the software and pharmaceuticals business which have shown in the previous years. Health care industry is emerging and largest service sector in developing countries.

Baxi (2004) and Pankaj Mochi (2013) analyzed that the position of India in health care industry in increasing day by day. According to research that has been already conducted, global healthcare industry is increasing to the extent of about $3-trillion due to the amenities and facilities it proposes and also by providing the brand equity of Indian healthcare specialized from corner to corner of the world. As compared to other countries in the world the medical expertise by India is finest in the globe and the job done by doctors in India is accepted all over. The main cause for India's coming out as significant destination for healthcare is because of good reputation of Indian health care givers who are recognized world-wide. In US itself there are about 35,000 expert doctors of Indian origin. International tourists mostly prefer Indian nurses for their caring approach as they feel it is just like a motherly treatment.

Rao (2005) examined the cost of medical treatment all over the world and found that the quality of medical treatment in India is at its best and cost is very low as compared to other countries, due to which large number of foreign tourists are approaching India to benefit from health care services, mainly in the field of cardiology, joint replacement, cardiac surgery, pathology, and ophthalmology.

Mohanty and Madhav (2006) has found that the Indian health care businesses began to come out as a major destination for tourists coming for medical treatment as compared to other countries in the world because Indian Industry is upgrading its knowledge, skill, fasting better familiarity with many advanced medical practices and humanizing its picture in terms of eminence and price.

Simon Hudson and Xiang Li (2012), in their study focused on the literature on medical tourism which studies about the International medical tourism and where people travel to acquire best health care services. They emphasized that not only foreign patients but there is increasing number of domestic patients who travel for health care services inside their own country.

Muralidar Trivedi (2013), studied about yoga and meditation in his research work. He found that it has been more than 5,000 years ago that yoga has come into existence. Many group of students from health care and medical background travel to India to be trained more on Yoga and other forms of natural and ayurvedic medicines. He also mentioned that it was 2,500 years ago when Buddhism came to India, then it achieved a status as the center of Eastern artistic, divine, and therapeuticprogress.

OBJECTIVES

1. To identify various prospects of Medical Tourism in Manipur in line with the India's Act East Policy
2. To explore various challenges in the growth and development of Manipur as a medical tourist destination.

METHODOLOGY

The paper is exploratory and descriptive in nature. Only secondary data are used for the study. The data are collected from various sources including officials of tourism department of state and central government, tourist guides, medical practitioner, travel agents etc. The data collected are then analyzed and presented to fulfill the objectives.

PROSPECTS OF TOURISM IN MANIPUR

Manipur is a unique and beautiful state of India located in the eastern most corner of North East India. The state has numerous attractive tourist destinations which attract large number of tourists not only from within the country but also from abroad. It has variety of attractions for tourists including lake, parks, historical places, gardens, waterfalls, mountains etc.

Manipur, with her comfortable climate, mystique cultural heritage and sublime natural beauty, located strategically in a hitherto considered disadvantageous geographical area, promises to be a huge potential for the growth of tourism. The majesty of the Loktak Lake, the strategic location of Moreh, the uniqueness of the Keibul Lamjao floating National Park & the Sangai Deer, the beauty of the Siroy & Dzukou Lilies, along with the naturally formed limestone caves, pristine green hills and valleys, meandering rivers, cascading rapids, exotic flora & fauna compounded by a rich arts and culture, folklore, myths and legends, indigenous games and artistic handloom & handicrafts, makes Manipur a little paradise on earth and a fertile ground for a tourist to explore. The Asian Development Bank has identified the region as a Key Area due to its unrealized potential as an ecotourism product. The mystery of the Indian Classical Dance form Ras Leela with their intricate costume design, the wonder of the Pung Cholom (Drum Dance), the vibrant tribal dances are some of the precious treasures any tourist will find appealing. The exotic cuisines, the unique tribal cultures and the soothing native music can be an enchanting discovery for various tourists visiting the State. The birthplace of modern Polo, the indigenous games of Yubi Lakpi, Kang Sanaba, Arambai, Thang-Ta and Mukna could prove to be a thrilling experience for any enthusiastic tourist. Weaving is a time-honoured occupation in the land and has been fine-tuned to an art form with its intricate designs most popularly the Wangkhei Phee and Haophee.

With regard to tourism prospects, the abolishment of the Inner Line Permit System from the State can be exploited to accelerate the growth of domestic tourism. Similarly, the relaxation and exclusion of Manipur from the Protected Area Regime since January 2011 can be a major boost to inflow of foreign high-end tourists to the State. However, further steps are required to modify the relaxation so that citizens of Myanmar, who are our primary foreign target, can visit the State beyond the mandatory 16 Kms to enable them to fully explore freely the land and also to avail medical facilities. This will also boost the Indo-Myanmar Border Trade to a great extent. Furthermore, Manipur, which was the great and last battlefield in World War II, can receive a big impetus in the tourism sector from many foreign tourists especially from Japan and the Commonwealth countries whose relatives, ancestors and countrymen lost their lives in the battlefield here.

Manipur and its tourism policies become all the more important in view of India's Act East Policy and the Trans-Asian Highways and Railways. The Government is keen to take advantage of these developments and therefore seeks to create a unique brand to market Manipur Tourism as the "Gateway to South-East Asia" in conformity with its modernity, relevance, competitiveness, strategic location and commercial aspects. It is the belief of the Government that once the appropriate infrastructure and services are suitably placed, Manipur is destined to become a rich commercial hub and a tourist hotspot in South-East Asia akin to Bangkok. In terms of connectivity, Manipur is well connected with major cities of the country including capital city like Delhi, Kolkata, Bengaluru, Mumbai, Guwahati, Hyderabad etc by Air through the Imphal International Airport. Recently an MOU has been signed to operate a direct

Figure 2. India, Myanmar, and Thailand Trilateral Highway via Moreh (Manipur)

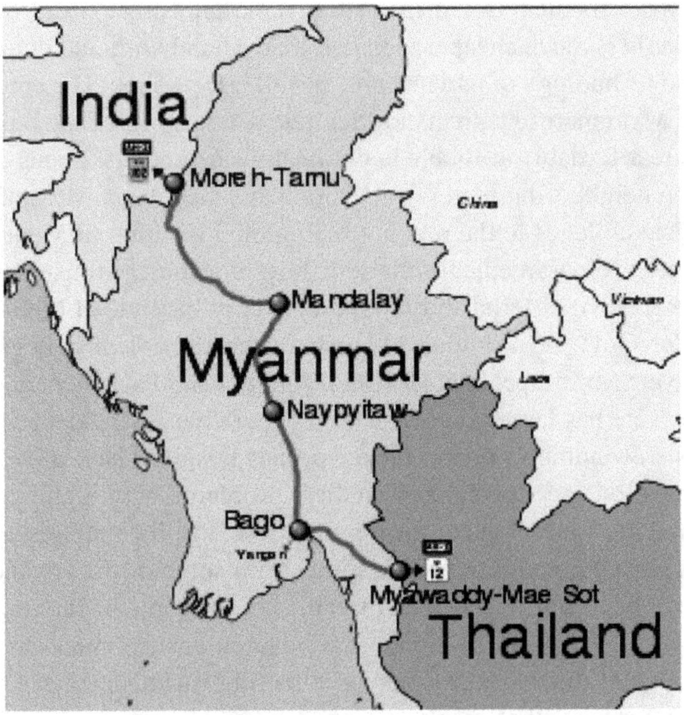

flight between Imphal and Mandalay which will further fly to Bangkok. The MOU was signed by the Myammar Private Airline KBZ and KB enterprise with Imphal set to begin the flight from October 2019. With this development, Manipur will have good connectivity with various countries from South East Asian countries. The Moreh Integrated Check post was inaugurated by Prime Minister of India, Shri Narendra Modi. It will facilitate custom clearance, foreign currency exchange, immigration clearance etc. With the opening of this facility, more tourists from South East Asia particularly Myanmar can come to India via Moreh (Manipur).

Healthcare is one aspect where Manipur is already well ahead in the region and if properly nurtured, can become a principal patient-tourist attraction from the neighbouring States and Nations. The State has a high percentage of qualified health specialists who can cater to different ailments both in terms of allopathic and ayurvedic medicines. Healthcare is expected to create 70 million to 80 million jobs in the next 10 yrs, adding 2 to 3% p.a. to the Nation's GDP. There is a huge requirement for health care workforce in India as every new bed creates employment for 5 personnel directly and about 25 personnel indirectly. In 2006, more than 2 million medical tourists availed medical services in South-east Asia from all corners of the world.

Due to of lack of adequate medical facilities in their own country, most Myanmarese patients also avail medical treatment in Bangkok and Singapore. Comparatively, treatment in India is much cheaper than that in Thailand without compromising on the quality and technology of patient care, and all efforts should be concentrated on attracting the Myanmarese patients to Manipur where some of the best treatments in the world are affordably available in our health care centers. Focus also needs to be given to the neighboring States of Mizoram and Nagaland. Manipur has two of the best medical colleges in the region viz Regional Institute of Medical Sciences (RIMS); one of the oldest medical college in the region under Ministry of Health and Family Welfare, Govt. of India and Jawaharlal Nehru Institute of Medical Sciences (JNIMS) under Govt. of Manipur. Other than these medical colleges, there are numerous Private Multi Specialty Hospital, Nursing and Para Medical Institutes in the state. The state has large number of well experienced Medical Practitioners in various fields. Few numbers of specialized private hospitals have also come up that cater to the need of very specialized medical problems with highly sophisticated equipments and machines. One of the region's best Hospital and Research Institute namely Shija Hospital and Research Institute with some of the advanced medical equipments has been offering medical treatments for some of the major ailments like kidney transplant, cornea transplant, cardiovascular surgery etc at very minimal costs. This is one of the major reasons for attracting various medical tourists from neigbouring states as well as neighbouring country, Myanmar.

CHALLENGES

The development of state of Manipur as a medical tourism destination has been initiated but the pace at which the development is going on is not upto the mark. The state still lacks in terms of development in infrastructure and most importantly, the state still lacks in terms of investments in health infrastructure particularly FDI. Even though the support from both state and central government have been visible since last few years, still the support in terms of promoting and developing the state as medical tourism destination is lacking. The financial support in health infrastructure development in the state is negligible that may hinder the pace of development of the state as a medical tourist destination in the country. The government has initiated the improvement of connectivity of the state with other states and neighbouring countries under the aegis of "Act East Policy". Even though the construction of National highway as well as Asian Highway connecting Manipur to Bangkok Via Mandalay has finally begun, yet the progress of the work is very slow and it will hamper the growth of tourist flows from other states as well as neighbouring countries. The absence of railway connectivity of the state with other regions and counties is also a major hurdle in the heavy flow of medical tourists in Manipur. Another major issue is the poor accessibility of medical Visa to patient from the bordering Myanmarese states- Sagaing, Chin and others. Lack of Consular services in the state that would facilitate medical tourism is a major blow to the growth of the sector. The positioning of image of Manipur as a Medical Tourist Hub for overall physical, mental and spiritual well being through various promotional tools is lacking. Rather the image of the state is perceived as the most disturbed state in the North East with insurgent groups and also linked with various unlawful activities like frequent blockades, bomb blasts and attacks. Moreover, the level of awareness among the people about the excellent medical facilities at much affordable prices in Manipur is very low due to the lack of promotional strategies by any of the hospitals as well as the government authority. There is also a major challenge in the form of lack of MOUs or agreements with neighbouring countries for hassle free cross border movement of medical professionals for efficient medical treatment in both countries. Lessons are yet to be learnt from countries such as Maldives which has entered into agreements with Sri Lanka and very recently with India to expand the coverage of Maldivians under the national health insurance scheme. Shortage of skilled force to promote medical tourism in Manipur and lack of an integrated agency to streamline medical tourism and handle all aspects of a foreign patient's availing of health services in Manipur in order to make a medical tourist's visit smooth and hassle free are also important issues. There is also lack of coordination between various players in the industry-airline operators, hotels and hospitals. Last but not the least, competition from neighbouring countries like Thailand, Malaysia and Singapore in terms of Myanmar's geographical and cultural proximity with them is a big challenge in the growth of medical tourism from Myanmar.

CONCLUSION AND SUGGESTIONS

Manipur with all the prospects and strengths can become a global medical tourism destination in the years to come. It offers various complicated medical treatment at very affordable prices to nearby states as well as neighbouring countries mainly from South East Asian countries. In line with India's Act East policy, the government; both state and central have initiated the process of development of Manipur as a hub for various purposes including trade and tourism. Healthcare is a major service that Manipur can sell to neighboring states and countries. Medical Tourism is a big economic potential for Manipur. But barriers to health services trade are innumerable and very complicated. Removing some of the barriers would lead to generate economic welfare, strengthen the medical networks, and deepen the regional integration centering Manipur. Following suggestions could go a long way in strengthening medical tourism in Manipur:

1. Financial transaction particularly payment of fees from origin countries to India is a major barrier, which not only generate informal payment but also reduces the revenue for government. Steps can be taken to facilitate region-wise e-transaction for medical payment purpose. At the same time, strengthening banking networks between neighboring countries and Manipur would ease the burdens on patients aiming to get treated in Manipur.
2. Connectivity is the backbone of health tourism. To allow health tourism to grow fast, Imphal should be linked with Dhaka, Kathmandu, Thimpu (Paro) and Yangon by direct air. Bus services especially for medical tourists should also be considered.
3. The prospects of opening branches of Indian hospital in neighboring countries like Bangladesh, Bhutan and Nepal should be taken up on priority basis. Signing of Mutual Recognition Agreement (MRAs) for health services would allow doctors and nurses to move without much hassle across the border and carry their services.
4. Skill shortage is another factor which is a big barrier to the promotion of medical tourism in Manipur. Although, Manipur has medical colleges and has been producing medical professionals, still the demand far surpasses the supply. To sustain the medical tourism in Manipur, the state should give more focus on medical education.
5. Consular services would help facilitate the health tourism. Opening of consulates of neighbouring countries at Imphal will be quite apt for the health sector reforms in Manipur.
6. Medical care can be combined with related tourism activities such as spiritual and eco-tourism. Medical tourism could be teamed up with the natural beauty of Manipur to project Manipur as a destination for overall physical, mental and spiritual wellbeing. In other words, it could be offered as a tourism package.
7. Manipur should take policy measures to train the youth and conduct skill development programmes that will groom the young population in the medical tourism sector in the state.
8. Air, rail and road access to Manipur should be expanded and enhanced if medical tourism development is to take off.
9. Imphal should host frequent conferences and seminars of health services as more and more hospital chains are coming up.
10. An integrated agency to streamline medical tourism and handle all aspects of a foreign patient's availing of health services in Manipur is needed.

11. The private players would need to dapper up their expertise, technology and services. The State government also needs to ensure minimum necessary infrastructure such as assured Power supply and hygienic potable water.
12. Lawlessness too must be taken care of. The image of Manipur as a troubled state with incidences of frequent blockades, bomb blasts and attacks needs to be tackled.

REFERENCES

Badwe, A. N., Giri, P. A., & Lati, R. G. (2012). Medical Tourism in India: A New Avenue. *International Journal of Biomedical and Advance Research*, *3*(3), 144–148. doi:10.7439/ijbar.v3i3.337

Baxi, A. (2004, April 1). Prescribe core support- Special Report. *The Economic Times*, 5.

Bose, P. R. (2017). *Visa hurdles choke Manipur's medical tourism*. Retrieved from www.thehindubusinessline.com%2Fnews%2Fvisa-hurdles-choke-manipurs-medical-tourism%2Farticle9929765.ece

Chravarthy, K., Ravi Kumar, C., & Deepthi, K. (2008). *SWOT analysis on: Medical Tourism*. Paper presented in Conference on Medical Tourism in India Challenges Ahead, IIMK.

Eva Ruka Pascal Garel. (2015). *HOPE*. European Hospital and Healthcare Federation.

Glinos, I., & Baeten, R. (2006). *A literature Review of Cross-Border Patient Mobility in the European Union*. Europe For Patients Project.

Hudson, S., & Li, X. (2012). Domestic medical tourism: A neglected dimension of medical tourism research. *Journal of Hospitality Marketing & Management*, *21*(3), 227–246. doi:10.1080/19368623.2011.615018

Kumar, A. (2017). Medical Tourism emerging as a next growth driver. *Travel Trends Today- T3 Magazine*. Retrieved from https://www.traveltrendstoday.in/news/india-tourism/item/5439-medical-tourism-emerging-as-a-next-growth-driver

Kumar, G.S., & Raj, R.K. (2015). Status, growth and impact of medical tourism in India. *International Journal of Pharmaceutical Sciences Review and Research*, *34*, 284-91.

Mochi, P., Shetty, N., & Vahoniya, D. (2013). Medical tourism-destination India. *Commerce and Management*, *2*(3), 29–39.

Mohanty, D., & Madhav, T. P. (2006). Medical Tourism: India's Competitive Advantage. In *Health tourism an Introduction*. ICFAI University Press.

Naik, N., & Lal, S. (2013). Economic Analysis of Indian Medical Tourism (International Healthcare Destination). *International Journal of Business Management, Economics and Information Technology*, *5*, 269–277.

Pachanee, C-. (2009) Implications on Public Health from Mode 2 Trade in Health Services: Empirical Evidence [A Case of Thailand]. *Workshop on the Movement of Patients Across International Borders- Emerging Challenges and Opportunities for Health Care Systems.*

Rao, K. S., Nundy, M., & Dua, A. S. (2005). *Delivery of health services in the private sector." Financing and delivery of health care services in India. National Commission on Macroeconomics and Health–Background papers. Ministry of Health and Family Welfare*. Government of India.

Rath, S. P., Das, B., Mishra, S., & Puthan, P. (2012). New Avenue of Tourism & Revenue Generation in India-Medical Tourism. *International Journal of Business and Management Tomorrow*, *2*(1), 11–14.

Reddy, P. C. (2000). Healthcare Services in the New Millennium. *Management and Labour Studies*, 115.

Trivedi, M. (2013). *Medical Tourism in India*. Academic Press.

Wellness and Medical Tourism & the Ministry of Tourism. (2015). Retrieved from http://tourism.gov.in/wellness-medical-tourism

WHO. (2011). *Medical visas mark growth of Indian medical tourism*. WHO.

Chapter 15
United Arab Emirates as a Global Medical Tourism Destination:
An Explorative Study

Prof. Umendra Narayan Shukla
Dr. Bhimrao Ambedkar University, India

Sharad Kumar Kulshreshtha
North-Eastern Hill University, India

ABSTRACT

UAE is also known as the fastest-growing medical tourism hub due to its most advanced medical technology, affordable treatments cost, and highly specialized doctors with world-class healthcare services. In this context, the Dubai Health Experience (DXH) is developed by Dubai Health Authority as a brand name for global healthcare and medical tourism, which aims to build up Dubai as a medical tourism hub. Dubai Health Experience (DXH) the United Arab Emirates is also widening its opportunity for the medical tourism market in the Gulf Cooperation Council is a political and economic alliance of six countries in the Arabian Peninsula where UAE is itself member country. In this continuation, Dubai Tourism Strategy 2020 is also a strategic roadmap with the target of attracting 20 million visitors per year by 2020. This chapter will reveal the emerging medical tourism and healthcare trends, healthcare policy of UAE, investment in healthcare and medical tourism, government initiatives, public-private partnership, and key initiatives to achieving sustainable development goals.

DOI: 10.4018/978-1-5225-9787-2.ch015

INTRODUCTION

Healthy people make healthy nation. Public healthcare is an inclusive social welfare concerned to everyone for essential primary and endemic diseases. In this context, every country always tries its best to provide accessible quality healthcare to the people with all sort of facilities. Only an effective health policy can create an efficient mechanism deliver inclusive healthcare which covers all stakeholders to achieve sustainable development goals. The rapid developments world class infrastructure is the most significant move to revival of health and medical sector in UAE. The health sector has opened a new opportunities to multi-stakeholders for state-of-the-art infrastructure of hospitals, affordable treatment to deliver patients, application of new edge technology for healthcare and medical services throughout the world. United Arab Emirates (UAE)has transformed health care system into cutting-edge global medical care destination in Middle East. The UAE continues to associate its reputation as a popular destination for medical tourism. In medical tourism, the UAE expects to see a significant rise in the number of visitors seeking treatments ranging from simple surgeries to sophisticated specialized treatments in areas of dentistry, physical therapy, rehabilitation, major surgeries and cosmetic procedures. Now medical tourists are experiencing healthcare services with world-class hospital and multi specialized team of doctors. UAE is an emerging, attractive, most appealing place to seek quality healthcare and treatments at affordable price, compared to similar healthcare access in the West. In 2019, the UAE healthcare industry is expected to focus more on artificial intelligence, machine learning, robotics and other cutting edge technologies, patient-centric services, and precision medicine.

The *United Arab Emirates (UAE)* is a constitutional federation of seven emirates i.e., *Abu Dhabi Ajman, Dubai, Fujairah, Ras Al Khaimah, Sharjah and Umm Al Quwain.* Abu Dhabi is the capital of the UAE. These seven emirates have diverse mosaic, each with its own character and allure. According to the *Medical Tourism Index*, UAE is the 31st largest economy by nominal GDP with more than 9.4 million populations. UAE is now considered to be the world's most vibrant tourism destination with marvelous luxurious tourism& hospitality services and contributing major share in the economy. UAE is also known as fastest growing medical tourism hub due to its most advance medical technology, affordable treatments cost, and highly specialized doctors with the following specializations: orthopedic, oncology, ophthalmology, urology, dental, dermatology, preventive medicine care, plastic surgery, vascular surgery, normal surgery, sports medicine and world-class healthcare services in the recent years. The government is infusing more funds to develop this sector. In this regard Dubai government launched its medical tourism vision in 2014, to attract half a million medical tourists by 2020.According to the *Medical Tourism Index (MTI) which* is a new type of country-based performance measure to assess the attractiveness of a country as a medical tourist destination in 2016 indicated that Dubai and Abu Dhabi were respectively ranked as the 16th and 25th best global destinations for medical tourism. UAE is very proactive in developing its healthcare infrastructure and launched Dubai Health Strategy 2021 with the aim to provide the highest quality of medical and health care. In this context, the Dubai Health Experience (DXH) is developed by Dubai Health Authority as a brand name for global healthcare & medical tourism which aims to build up Dubai as a medical tourism hub. Dubai Health Experience (DXH) manages complete health solution, travel and hospitality, visa services through the website of Dubai Health Authority. United Arab Emirates is also widening its opportunity for medical tourism market in the Gulf Cooperation Council (GCC) that is a political and economic alliance of six countries in the Arabian Peninsula, namely; Bahrain, Kuwait, Oman, Qatar, Saudi Arabia and the United Arab Emirates where UAE is itself a member country. In this continuation, Dubai Tourism Strategy 2020 is also a strategic roadmap with the target of attracting 20 million visitors per year by 2020.

About United Arab Emirates

The United Arab Emirates covers diverse landforms including desert, coastal areas, plains, wetlands, and mountains. Its area is approximately 71,023.6sq km of land, in addition to 27,624.9sq km of territorial water. The capital of the UAE Federation is Abu Dhabi which is 84 per cent of the country's total landmass. The UAE maintains a desert climate. The Emirati Dirham is the official currency of the UAE, Islam is the official religion in the UAE; practice of other religions is allowed. The UAE is a constitutional federation of seven emirates *(Abu Dhabi Ajman, Dubai, Fujairah, Ras Al Khaimah, Sharjah, UAE and Umm Al Quwain*). According to Federal Competitiveness and Statistics Authority, the total population of UAE was 9,304,277 including 6,415,942 males and 2,888,335 females in 2017 (UAE, 2019).

Drivers for the Growth of Medical Tourism in UAE

The development of the healthcare sector in UAE is growing very faster pace of manner with effective planning and policy implementation. These initiatives have transformed scenario of healthcare and medical services in the country. It is supportive to develop the country as an emerging medical tourism destination in the Middle East. There are numbers of growth drivers responsible to develop UAE as a global medical tourism destination, some of them are such as:

- Research and Development in the field of Medical Sciences.
- Development of new medicines and advanced medical equipment, devices

- Globalization and International connectivity advantages
- Advent of Information Technology and its applications in smart medical care
- Frequent mobility and connectivity of UAE with Arab and Middle East Countries as well as European countries
- Ease of medical services
- Medical visa assistance
- Growing emerging middle class with higher disposable income with health conscious
- Specialization – Availability of medical specialists
- Focus and firmness of UAE Government for quality and inclusive healthcare services
- Government spending on healthcare and investment in health sector
- Affordable medical treatment packages
- Medical Insurance program
- Destination Attractions in terms of natural and manmade tourism attractions

REVIEW OF LITERATURE

Health tourism, such as wellbeing, wellness, holistic, medical and spiritual, are analysed and explored, as is the role that health and health tourism play in quality-of-life enhancement, wellbeing, life satisfaction and happiness (Smith, M.K. and Puczkó, L. 2016).The supply side of Wellness tourism from a destination perspective in terms of the generation and delivery of products and services for tourists who seek to maintain and improve their health (Voigt, Cornelia and Pforr, Christof 2013). The study introduces the evolution of health-related tourism products and services from all around the world and provides insights into the current situation of the industry, as well as the future potential (UN-WTO & ETC, 2018)

The global healthcare market had a turnover of $7 trillion in 2015 (Deloitte, 2017). Medical tourism is a recent example of niche tourism, with the rapid rise of international travel in search of cosmetic surgery and solution to various medical conditions, benefiting, healthcare providers, local economies and tourism industry (Connell, J. 2011). Medical tourism is the practice of patient outsourcing healthcare service to an area outside of his/her home country (Claster et al. 2015). Medical tourism is driven by numbers of factors, including healthcare quality, social factors and political issues. People want best medical at lowest cost (Stolley, K. and Watson, S. 2012). According to the reports, is expected to reach US$ 144 billion by 2020. Western patients are increasingly traveling to developing countries for health care and developing countries are increasingly offering their skills and facilities to paying foreign customers (Bookman, M.Z. & Bookman, K.R. 2007). Medical tourism is emerging economic driver in Middle East and North Africa (MENA) Region, especially in the Arabian Gulf region, where hyper-development is closely associated with the increasingly prominent role of luxury real estate and shopping, retail, medical tourism, cruises and transit tourism (Connell, J. 2019). This increase in international association gives citizens more availability to take advantage of opportunities in other nations, such as medical assistance and accompanying services (Cooper, Malcolm J. M. and Vafadari, Kazem and Hieda, Mayumi 2015)

A classification system for medical tourism travel may include three important broad areas and six categories:

1. Intrusive medical procedure includes *cosmetic surgery, medical surgery life threatening, medical surgery nonlife threatening,*
2. Diagnostic procedure including *stress test,*
3. Lifestyle procedure includes *spa treatment, consultation and neurological alternative therapies* (Khan, M.A. 2017).

The Joint Commission International has various programmes of accreditation, for laboratories, hospitals, ambulatory care, home and long-term care, medical transport, primary care centres, or for specific area or clinical care certification. For hospital accreditation, the Joint Commission International standards are designed to improve the quality of care and the patient safety in hospitals *(Joint Commission International, n.d.)*. In medical tourism the ethical issues involved, such as traveling to have a black-market organ transplanted; and the significant impact of medical tourism on health care systems--that of the United States, and those of the destination countries (S. Stolley, Kathy, and Watson, Stephanie, 2012)

JUSTIFICATION OF THE STUDY

This study has tried to justify about how is UAE generating revenues from tourism sector slight shift from oil sector after economic crisis. Tourism is now one of the main sources of revenue in the UAE, with not only some of the world's most luxurious hotels being based there, but also huge hub airports with state of the art facilities. The recent development of medical tourism is in United Arab Emirates as an emerging medical tourism destination. The Government of UAE has taken various initiatives to transform healthcare sector as well as promoting medical tourism. In this regards government has introduced Dubai Health Experience (DHX) and Dubai Health Investment Programme towards a healthier & happier community.

Gaps of the Study

There are very few studies have been conducted related to healthcare and medical tourism of UAE. There is an urgent need to highlights and tap the potential of this emerging sector. This study will support to better insights to understand the policies and implementations for the prospective growth and development of medical tourism in UAE as a global destination.

OBJECTIVES:

The objectives of the study focus on how is UAE as an emerging global medical tourism destination, these are as such:

- To study the recent development of healthcare system in United Arab Emirates.
- To review healthcare policy and Government initiatives for the promotion of medical tourism.
- To introduce the UAE as medical hub centre for the aspirants in healthcare field.

METHODOLOGY

This paper is based on exploratory research method through the review of recent policies and reports of medical tourism practices adopted in UAE. This study explores the medical tourism prospects in UAE as global medical tourism destination.In this regard extensive and in-depth review of literature and published data have been analysed. The published data have been referred from the reports, guides, official brochures and official websites of Health Ministry of UAE.

EMERGING MEDICAL TOURISM AND HEALTHCARE TRENDS IN UAE

According to the Dubai Health Authority, medical tourism generated more than $381 million for the Emirate in 2016. As per the Medical Tourism Index, a tool that ranks countries and cities based on attractiveness as medical tourism destination, “UAE’s rises to the top 20 list of popular medical tourism destinations worldwide”. Most recent initiative of Dubai Government has launched *‘Dubai Health Experience*

Table 1. Medical Tourists in UAE for Treatment

Countries Generating Medical Tourists	Medical Treatments	Percentages
Asian Countries	*Orthopedics, Dermatology*	37%
Arab and GCC	*cancer cosmetic surgery*	31%
Europe	*cardiovascular, dental surgery*	15%
Others	*Neurology treatments, fertility/IVF*	17%

Sources: The Khaleej Times one of the leading English Dailies in the UAE dated August 19, 2018.

(DXH)' and invite global investors to invest in health sector by providing investor friendly environment to develop medical hubs like Dubai Healthcare City.

Medical Tourism VISA

Dubai offers a 90 days medical tourism visa in cooperation with General Directorate of Residency and Foreigners Affairs – Dubai that is renewable and can be applied for through the healthcare facility in which the patient is receiving treatment (Dubai Health, 2019)

Table 2. Available treatment specialty in UAE

Pediatrics	Allied Health
Respiratory Medicine	General Medicine
Neurology	Endocrinology
Oncology & Hematology	Gastroenterology
Immunology & Infections	Orthopedics & Rheumatology
Trauma and Injury	Urology
Dentistry	Renal Medicine
Neonatology	Vascular Surgery
Neurosurgery	Psychiatry
Obstetrics	ENT
Cardiology & Cardiothoracic	General Surgery
Plastic Surgery	Ophthalmology
Dermatology	Gynecology

Source: Dubai Health Investment Guide 2019, Dubai Health care Authority

Table 3. Top visiting nations in UAE

1.	UK
2.	USA
3.	Germany
4.	Russia
5.	China
6.	India
7.	Saudi Arabia

Source: (Visit Dubai, 2019)

Healthcare Cities

To provide better healthcare services and to ease access to health facilities, the UAE has opened healthcare cities. These are complexes having clinics of various specialties. Presently, there are three healthcare cities in the UAE. They are: *Sheikh Khalifa Medical City, Dubai Healthcare City, Sharjah Healthcare City.*

Medical Tourism Portals

The UAE launched medical tourism portals which allow international medical tourists to book procedures and access a wide range of tourism services such as direct contact with healthcare providers, visa issuance, booking appointments, hotels, transportation and other recreational activities.

Dubai Health Experience (DXH)

Dubai Health Experience (DXH) is the repute brand developed by the Dubai Health Authority (DHA) to provide global recognition of Dubai as a world-class medical tourism destination under the directive of HH Sheikh Hamdan Bin Mohammed Bin Rashid Al Maktoum, Crown Prince of Dubai and Chairman of the Dubai Executive Council.

Table 4. Key metrics of health tourism in Dubai

Year 2012 (Health tourists in Thousands)	Year 2016 (Health tourists in Thousands)	Year 2020 (Health tourists in Thousands)
107	326	500

Source: (Visit Dubai, 2019)

Table 5. List of hospitals under DXH groups

Al Garhoud Private Hospital	Burjeel Hospital	Emirates Hospital Dubai
Al Zahra Hospital Dubai	Canadian Specialist Hospital Dubai	Iranian Hospital Dubai
American Hospital Dubai	Dubai London Clinic and Specialty Hospital	Medcare Hospital Dubai
Neuro Spinal Hospital Dubai	Prime Hospital Dubai	Zulekha Hospital Dubai
Nmc Specialty Hospital Dubai	Saudi German Hospital Dubai	

Source: Brochure of Dubai Health Experience, Dubai Health Authority (2018)

There are some unique features of Dubai Health Experience which deliver through cutting edge quality healthcare services as follows:

- *Online Consultation Second Medical Opinion*
- *Patient Protection Plan*
- *Smart care*
- *Packages and Comprehensive Packages*
- *Visa Facilitation-Medical Tourism Visa*
- *Deals and Offers: UAE*
- *Transfer cases*
- *Medical Insurance*
- *Inbound medical tourism*

HEALTHCARE POLICY OF UAE

The UAE National Agenda includes a set of national indicators in the sectors of education, healthcare, economy, police and security, justice, society, housing, infrastructure and government services. World class healthcare, Competitive Knowledge Economy, safe public and fair judiciary, cohesive society and preserved

Table 6. List of clinic under DHX group members

Aesthetics International Plastic Surgery Clinic	City Centre Clinic
Al Shunnar Plastic Surgery	Cocoona Aesthetic And Day Surgical Hospital
Armada Medical Centre	Drs. Nicolas & Asp
Bourn Hall Clinic	Infinity Family Medicine Clinic
Mediclinic Dubai Mall	Silkor Laser Medical Center

Source: Brochure of Dubai Health Experience, Dubai Health Authority (2018)

Table 7. Medical tourism facilitators in UAE

Doctors	*The official website of the Ministry of Health and Prevention offers online facility for searching professional doctor in the Northern Emirates of the UAE. Over 33,000 healthcare and medical professionals*
International Patient care Agencies	*Medical tourists have look after by international patientcare agencies with 24x7 care support including visa assistance, book appointment with doctors, other follow-up and recuperation*
Travel Agents	*DNATA Travel provide full assistance for medical tourism*
Hotels	*Hotels are also offerings wellness rejuvenations packages with luxury.*
Airlines	*UAE national airlines Emirates Airlines, Etihad Airways also promoting and supporting medical tourists worldwide by offering special packages and*
Medical Visa	*Visas can be arranged through travel agents, UAE Airlines, hotels and through close family members who are UAE Nationals or Residents*

Source: Authors

identity, first rate education system, sustainable environment and infrastructure (UAE Vision, 2018).

In December 2014, the Department of health - Abu Dhabi announced Abu Dhabi Healthcare Strategic Plan. The priority areas include:

- *Reducing capacity gaps*
- *Improving the quality of healthcare services, patient safety and experience*
- *Attracting, training and retaining qualified healthcare professionals*
- *Improving preparedness during emergencies*
- *Ensuring value for money and sustainability of healthcare spending, including encouragement of Private investment in healthcare*
- *Introducing an E-Health programme as a facilitator for the other priorities.*

INVESTMENT IN HEALTHCARE AND MEDICAL TOURISM

Medical tourism in UAE is lucrative healthcare projects. Government and private sector is willing to infuse funds in this sector. The recent investment policies have created a favorable eco-system for investors and thus following fields have been emerged for investment in medical areas:

Drivers for Investment in Medical Tourism

- Rapid growing population looking better health services

- Infrastructure development of the healthcare sector
- Chances of occurrence of chronic and non-communicable diseases
- Health coverage for all of Dubai's population
- Public private participation in medical tourism
- Digital transformation in the healthcare sector
- Investor friendly investment climate and support system

GOVERNMENT INITIATIVES PROMOTION OF MEDICAL TOURISM

Dubai's Healthcare Authority reports that more than 300,000 medical tourists traveled to the Emirate in 2016, up nearly 10 percent from the previous year. Dubai's Tourism Vision for 2020 aims to welcome 20 million tourists per year by 2020. There were 13.2 million international overnight visitors in 2014 alone, and 2015 numbers reached approx.14 million. For the year 2016, the UAE Government had allocated 7.9 per cent of the budget amounting to approximately AED 3.83 billion for the health sector alone.

PUBLIC-PRIVATE PARTNERSHIP IN HEALTHCARE

The Investments & Public Private Partnership's Department at Dubai Health Authority has been set-up the healthcare and medical tourism centric goals to support Dubai as a sustainable and economical center for investment in healthcare medical sector for providing the best service for investors and to enable sustainable public-private models in Dubai. Its role is, therefore, to support DHA's objective of providing healthcare in line with global best practices, fostering innovation in all health-related sectors and of becoming a medical hub for the region by attracting investors and encouraging these to contribute to the development of targeted areas.

DHA's Investment Strategy 2017-2020 focused on the following initiatives:

- Investment promotion and facilitation
- Healthcare certificate of need
- Inward investment need
- Health investment guidelines
- Commercial investment and policies
- Enabling healthcare regulations

Source: Dubai Health Investment Guide-2019

KEY INITIATIVES FOR ACHIEVING SUSTAINABLE DEVELOPMENT GOALS

The 17 Sustainable Development Goals build on the success of the Millennium Development Goals (MDGs) (2000-2015), and it includes four main themes, environmental, social, economic, and partnerships. The goals include 169 targets and 233 indicators. The SDG 3 is very much concern with health and wellbeing. The goal aims to ensure healthy life and promote wellbeing for all ages. In this regards, the UAE's medical tourism policy is effectively driving the policy vehicle to meet the Sustainable Development Goal 2030, especially, through sustainable good health and well-being (Al-Talabani et al. 2019). Providing world-class healthcare is one of the six pillars of the UAE National Agenda in line with Vision 2021. UAE Government has made special provision to provide for quality healthcare facilities. Mandatory insurance is one of the pillars of the Insurance System for Advancing Healthcare in Dubai (ISAHD) which aims tocreate an integrated and innovative insurance system for all Dubai citizens and residents, and to provide sustainable high-quality healthcare in Dubai for nationals, residents and visitors in order to position Dubai as the best healthcare system globally.

There are some key initiatives, taken by UAE's Ministry of Health and Prevention:

1. Ministry of Health and Prevention has launched*Smart Patient Portal* through which patients can directly see and their health status as well as day to day doctor's appointment schedule.
2. There is a special provision for *Air Ambulance*in any medical emergencyjust calling on tollfree 998 from anywhere in the UAE.
3. '*Thiqa Programme*' for health insurance for UAE Nationals which is run by Abu Dhabi Health Authority and *Saada* is another health insurance programme for the citizens in the emirate of Dubai.
4. There is special provision for alternative medicine in which *Ayurveda, Homeopathy, Unanai medicine* and *therapeutic massage are some prominent cures in UAE.*
5. All most clinics and hospitals displayed information on the websites of Health Authority – Abu Dhabi and Dubai Health Authority so the patient can access their rights and responsibilities for senior citizen and other residents.
6. Support of health innovation projects through national innovation strategy. (Federal Competitiveness and Statistics Authority, 2018).

CONCLUSION

Earlier medical tourism is only growing and developed in Central America and Southeast Asia due to quality medical healthcare and advanced medical technology with better marketing strategies. But cost of expenditure of medical care is very high which can only affordable by elite class of society. After socio-economic devotement of Middle East countries, especially UAE has started to develop as a global healthcare destination with cutting edge medical facilities, world-class state of art medical infrastructure, team of specialists' doctors and nursing staffs dedicated to deliver best medical services to medical tourists. Apart of these, worldwide air connectivity and international airports have make UAE most significant and economic tourism destination. UAE has foster innovative technological applications for develop tech enabled healthcare system. The UAE government has emphasis on healthcare software applications in which artificial intelligence, block chain technology, smart medical devices are able to deliver quality and prompt healthcare services. Finally, the future of United Arab Emirates as a global medical tourism destination is very prospective and progressive.

REFERENCES

Al-Talabani, H., Kilic, H., Ozturen, A., & Qasim, S. O. (2019). Advancing Medical Tourism in the United Arab Emirates: Toward a Sustainable Health Care System. *Sustainability*, *11*(1), 230. doi:10.3390u11010230

Bookman, M. Z., & Bookman, K. R. (2007). *Medical Tourism in Developing Countries*. Palgrave Macmillan. doi:10.1057/9780230605657

Stolley, K., & Watson, S. (2012). Contemporary World Issue: Medical Tourism. *ABC-CLIO*, 3.

Claster. (2015). *Gathering Medical Tourism Information through Algorithmic Text Analysis of Tweets*. Academic Press.

Connell, J. (2011). *Medical Tourism. CABI* Publication.

Dubai Health Investment Guide. (2019). A comprehensive guide on health investment in Dubai with a listing of investment needs and opportunities for health services-Towards a healthier & happier community. Dubai Health Authority, Government of Dubai.

Connell, J. (2019). Medical tourism: In search of an economic niche. In Routledge Hand Book on Tourism in the Middle East and North Africa, (pp. 352-353). Routledge Publication.

Cooper, M. J. M., Vafadari, K., & Hieda, M. (2015). Current Issues and Emerging Trends in Medical Tourism. IGI Global.

Smith, M. K., & Puczkó, L. (2016). The Routledge Handbook of Health Tourism. Routledge Publication.

Voigt, C., & Pforr, C. (2013). *Wellness Tourism: A Destination Perspective.* Routledge Publication.

Stolley, K., & Watson, S. (2012). *Medical Tourism: A Reference Handbook -Contemporary world issues.* Retrieved from https://www.visitdubai.com

Health, D. (2019). *DXH Wellness*. Retrieved from https://dxh.ae/en-US/wellness-dubai

UAE Vision. (2018). *Vision 2021: National Agenda*. Retrieved from https://www.vision2021.ae/en/national-agenda-2021

Federal Competitiveness and Statics Authority. (2018). *Sustainable Development Goals*. Retrieved from http://fcsa.gov.ae/en-us/Pages/SDGs/The-Global-Goals.aspx

UAE. (2019). *Fact Shee*t. Retrieved from https://www.government.ae/en/about-the-uae/fact-sheet

Joint Commission International. (n.d.). *Joint Commission International*. Retrieved from http://www.jointcommissioninternational.org/

Compilation of References

Accenture. (2012). *Joint business planning*. Retrieved from: www.accenture.com

Acharya, R., Kannathal, N., Mei Hua, L., & Mei Yi, L. (2005). Study of heart rate variability signals in at sitting and lying postures. *Journal of Bodywork and Movement Therapies*, *9*(2), 134–141. doi:10.1016/j.jbmt.2004.04.001

Adam, K., Snyder, J., Crooks, V. A., & Johnston, R. (2015). Tourism discourse and medical tourists' motivations to travel. *Tourism Review*, *70*(2), 85–96. doi:10.1108/TR-04-2014-0015

Adebanjo, D., Laosirihongthong, T., & Samaranayake, P. (2016). Prioritizing lean supply chain management initiatives in healthcare service operations: A fuzzy AHP approach. *Production Planning and Control*, *27*(12), 953–966. doi:10.1080/09537287.2016.1164909

Agner, E. (2010). Subjective well-being. *Journal of Socio-Economics*, *39*(1), 361–368. doi:10.1016/j.socec.2009.12.001

Al-Amin, M., Makarem, S. C., & Pradhan, R. (2011). Hospital ability to attract international patients: A conceptual framework. *International Journal of Pharmaceutical and Healthcare Marketing*, *5*(3), 205–221. doi:10.1108/17506121111172211

Alavi, S. S., Mehrdad, R., & Makarem, J. (2016). Prevalence of substance abuse/alcohol consumption and their predictors among patients admitted in operating rooms of a General Educational Hospital, Tehran, Iran. *Asian Journal of Pharmaceutical Research and Health Care*, *8*(S1), 63–71. doi:10.18311/ajprhc/2016/7651

Alderson, W. (2006). A basic guide to market planning. *A Twenty-First Century Guide to Aldersonian Marketing Thought,* 283-290.

Al-Harbi, M. H. (2018). *How UAE became a medical tourism hub*. Retrieved from https://gulfnews.com/opinion/op-eds/how-uae-became-a-medical-tourism-hub-1.2239792

Alhosani, N., & Zaidan, E. (2014). Shopping Tourism and Destination Development: Dubai as a Case Study. *Arab World Geographer*, *17*(1), 66–81.

Al-Qatawneh, L., & Hafeez, K. (2015). Critical-to-life classification for managing inventory in a healthcare supply chain. *International Journal of Intelligent Enterprise*, *3*(1), 54–78. doi:10.1504/IJIE.2015.073491

Al-Talabani, H., Kilic, H., Ozturen, A., & Qasim, S. O. (2019). Advancing Medical Tourism in the United Arab Emirates: Toward a Sustainable Health Care System. *Sustainability, 11*(1), 230. doi:10.3390u11010230

Amahazion, F. (2018). Renal Replacement Therapy in Eritrea. *Transplantation, 102*(5), 707–710. doi:10.1097/TP.0000000000002152 PMID:29702535

An, T. S., & Kritchanchai, D. (2019). Hospital Capacity Planning for Special Economic Zone in Thailand: A Case Study in Kanchanaburi Province. *IEEE International Conference on Industrial Engineering and Engineering Management*, 1593-1597.

Andersson, A., Wiklund, M., & Hatakka, M. (2015). Emerging collaborative and cooperative practices in 1:1 schools. *Technology, Pedagogy and Education, 25*(4), 413–430. doi:10.1080/1475939X.2015.1060896

Andréasson, S., Danielsson, A.-K., & Hallgren, M. (2013). Severity of alcohol dependence in the Swedish adult population: Association with consumption and social factors. *Alcohol (Fayetteville, N.Y.), 47*(1), 21–25. doi:10.1016/j.alcohol.2012.10.001 PMID:23084032

Andrews-Chavez, J. Y., Lee, C. S., Houser, R. F., Falcon, L. M., & Tucker, K. L. (2015). Factors associated with alcohol consumption patterns in a Puerto Rican urban cohort. *Public Health Nutrition, 18*(3), 464–473. doi:10.1017/S1368980014000433 PMID:24713083

Anrep, G. V., Pascua, W., & Rossler, R. (1936a). Respiratory variations in the heart rate I. The reflex mechanism of respiratory arrhythmia. *Proceedings of the Royal Society of London. Series B, Biological Sciences, 119*(813), 191–217. doi:10.1098/rspb.1936.0005

Asia's Medical Tourism. (2012). *Truly A Leading Medical Tourism Hub.* Retrieved from asiasmedicaltourism.com/medical-tourism/medical-tourism-singapore

Auld, M. C. (2005). Smoking, drinking, and income. *The Journal of Human Resources, 40*(2), 505–518. doi:10.3368/jhr.XL.2.505

Austin, W. A., & Ressler, R. W. (2012). Do designated drivers and workplace policies effect alcohol consumption? *Journal of Socio-Economics, 41*(1), 104–109. doi:10.1016/j.socec.2011.10.013

Awadzi, W., & Panda, D. (2006). Medical tourism: Globalization and the marketing of medical services. *Journal of Hospitality and Tourism, 11*(1), 75–81.

Azman, I., & Chan, J. (2010, 1-3 September). *Health and spa tourism business: Tourists' profiles and motivational factors*. Paper presented at the conference "Health, wellness and tourism: Healthy tourists, healthy business?", Dalarna.

Badwe, A. N., Giri, P. A., & Lati, R. G. (2012). Medical Tourism in India: A New Avenue. *International Journal of Biomedical and Advance Research, 3*(3), 144–148. doi:10.7439/ijbar.v3i3.337

Bagaeen, S. (2007). Brand Dubai: The Instant city; or the instantly recognizable city. *International Planning Studies, 1*(2), 173–197. doi:10.1080/13563470701486372

Bainbridge, F. A. (1930). The relation between respiration and the pulse-rate. *The Journal of Physiology*, *54*(3), 192–202. doi:10.1113/jphysiol.1920.sp001918 PMID:16993458

Balakrishnan, M. S. (2008). Dubai- A star in the East. *Journal of Place Management and Development*, *1*(1), 62–91.

Baliga, H. (2006). Medical Tourism is the new wave of outsourcing from India. *India Daily*, *21*(4), 16–19.

Ballentyne, B. (2015). Huge opportunity for health tourism. *Middle East Economic Digest*, *59*(6), 1–3.

Bandyopadhyay, A., Bhuyan, L., Panda, A., & Kailash, C. (2017, June). Assessment of Oral Hygiene Knowledge, Practices, and Concepts of Tobacco Usage among Engineering Students in Bhubaneswar, Odisha, India. *The Journal of Contemporary Dental Practice*, *18*(6), 1–6. PMID:28621268

Barrenstein, P., & Tweraser, S. (2004). Category Management: Why Now? In *Collaborative Customer Relationship Management*. Springer-Verlag Berlin Heidelberg. doi:10.1007/978-3-540-24710-4_11

Barrett, G. F. (2002). The effect of alcohol consumption on earnings. *The Economic Record*, *78*(240), 79–96. doi:10.1111/1475-4932.00041

Bauer, A. M., Thielke, S. M., Katon, W., Unützer, J., & Areán, P. (2014). Aligning health information technologies with effective service delivery models to improve chronic disease care. *Preventive Medicine*, *66*, 167–172. doi:10.1016/j.ypmed.2014.06.017 PMID:24963895

Baxi, A. (2004, April 1). Prescribe core support- Special Report. *The Economic Times*, 5.

Bekkers, V. (2009). Flexible information infrastructures in Dutch E-Government collaboration arrangements: Experiences and policy implications. *Government Information Quarterly*, *26*(1), 60–68. doi:10.1016/j.giq.2007.09.010

Beladi, H., Chao, C.-C., Ee, M. S., & Hollas, D. (2017). Does medical tourism promote economic growth? A cross-country analysis. *Journal of Travel Research*, *58*(1), 121–135.

Belasen, A., & Hafer, R. W. (2013). IQ and alcohol consumption: International data. *Intelligence*, *41*(5), 615–621. doi:10.1016/j.intell.2013.07.019

Berger, R. D., Akselrod, S., Gordon, D., & Cohen, R. J. (1986). An efficient algorithm for spectral analysis of heart rate variability. *IEEE Transactions on Biomedical Engineering*, *33*(9), 900–904. doi:10.1109/TBME.1986.325789 PMID:3759126

Bialy, C., Horne, K., Dendle, C., Kanellis, J., Littlejohn, G., Ratnam, I., & Woolley, I. (2015). International travel in the immunocompromised patient: A cross-sectional survey of travel advice in 254 consecutive patients. *Internal Medicine Journal*, *45*(6), 618–623. doi:10.1111/imj.12753 PMID:25827660

Bicudo, P., Reis, J., Deus, A. M., Reis, L., & Vaz, M. F. (2016). Mechanical behaviour of dental implants. *Procedia Structural Integrity*, *1*, 26–33. doi:10.1016/j.prostr.2016.02.005

Binorkar, S., Sawant, R., & Bhoyar, M. (2018). Ayurveda education & research in India–present scenario, challenges & solutions. *Int J Complement Alt Med.*, *11*(2), 130–137. doi:10.15406/ijcam.2018.11.00362

Birkic, D., Pilija, I. C., & Sebrek, J. K. (2014). T*he role of local government in planning of sustainable tourism of coastal destination.* Faculty of Tourism and Hospitality Management in Opatija. Biennial International Congress. Retrieved from https://search.proquest.com/docview/1658462265?accountid=33975

Biswas, M. (2008). *Confirmatory factor analysis of Iso-Ahola's motivational theory. An Application of structural equation modelling*. Paper presented at the Conference on Tourism in India - Challenge Ahead, Kozhikode, India.

Bittencourt, O., Verter, V., & Yalovsky, M. (2018). Hospital capacity management based on the queueing theory. *International Journal of Productivity and Performance Management*, *67*(2), 224–238. doi:10.1108/IJPPM-12-2015-0193

Bolea, J., Laguna, P., Remartinez, J. M., Rovira, E., Navarro, A., & Bailon, R. (2014). Methodological Framework for Estimating the Correlation Dimension in HRV Signals. C*omputational and Mathematical Methods in Medicine. Article ID*, *129248*, 11.

Bonevski, B., Regan, T., Paul, C., Baker, A. L., & Bisquera, A. (2014). Associations between alcohol, smoking, socioeconomic status and comorbidities: Evidence from the 45 and U p S tudy. *Drug and Alcohol Review*, *33*(2), 169–176. doi:10.1111/dar.12104 PMID:24372899

Bookman, M. Z., & Bookman, K. R. (2007). *Medical tourism in developing countries.* New York: Palgrave MacMillan. doi:10.1057/9780230605657

Bose, P. R. (2017). *Visa hurdles choke Manipur's medical tourism.* Retrieved from www.thehindubusinessline.com%2Fnews%2Fvisa-hurdles-choke-manipurs-medical-tourism%2Farticle9929765.ece

Bostan, S., & Yalcin, B. (2016). Factors, affecting the medical destination selection of health tourists. *The Journal of International Social Research*, *9*(43), 1729–1735. doi:10.17719/jisr.20164317741

Bouchery, E. E., Harwood, H. J., Sacks, J. J., Simon, C. J., & Brewer, R. D. (2011). Economic costs of excessive alcohol consumption in the US, 2006. *American Journal of Preventive Medicine*, *41*(5), 516–524. doi:10.1016/j.amepre.2011.06.045 PMID:22011424

Bowers, H., & Cheer, J. (2017). Yoga tourism: Commodification and western embracement of eastern spiritual practice. *Tourism Management Perspectives*, *24*(1), 208–216. doi:10.1016/j.tmp.2017.07.013

Bozarth, C. (2011). *Lecture notes: Collaborative planning forecasting and replenishment.* Academic Press.

Brotman, B. A. (2010). Medical tourism private hospitals: Focus India. *Journal of Health Care Finance*, *37*(1), 45–50. PMID:20973373

Brotman, B. A. (2010). Medical Tourism Private Hospitals: Focus India. *Journal of Health Care Finance*, *37*(1), 45–50. PMID:20973373

Bryden, A., Roberts, B., Petticrew, M., & McKee, M. (2013). A systematic review of the influence of community level social factors on alcohol use. *Health & Place*, *21*, 70–85. doi:10.1016/j.healthplace.2013.01.012 PMID:23454663

Burazeri, G., & Kark, J. D. (2010). Prevalence and determinants of binge drinking in middle age in a transitional post-communist country: A population-based study in Tirana, Albania. *Alcohol and Alcoholism (Oxford, Oxfordshire)*, *45*(2), 180–187. doi:10.1093/alcalc/agp089 PMID:20061509

Burkett, L. (2007). Medical Tourism: Concerns, benefits and the American perspective. *The Journal of Legal Medicine*, *28*, 223-245.

Burns, R. L. (2015). Medical tourism opportunities and challenges: Illustration from US-India trade. *International Journal of Healthcare Management*, *8*(1), 15–26. doi:10.1179/2047971914Y.0000000091

Business Standard. (2016). *The foreign tourists who visited India for medical purpose during 2012, 2013, and 2014*. Retrieved from http://www.business-standard.com/article/news-cm/the-116042500714_1.html

Caballero-Danell, S., & Mugomba, C. (2007). *Medical tourism and its entrepreneurial opportunities: A conceptual framework for entry into the industry* (Master Dissertation). Goteborg University, Goteborg.

Caballero-Danell, S., & Mugomba, C. (2007). *Medical tourism and its entrepreneurial opportunities: A conceptual framework for entry into the industry (Unpublished master's thesis)*. University of Gothenburg. Retrieved from http://gupea.ub.gu.se/dspace/handle/ 2077/4671

Campos, A. (2014, Abril). *Turismo de saúde e bem-estar pode render 400 milhões/ano*. Público.

Carrera, P. M., & Bridges, J. P. (2006). Globalisation and healthcare: Understanding health and medical tourism, Expert Review of Pharmacoeconomics & Outcomes Research. *Future Drugs*, *7*(1), 447–445.

Carrera, P., & Bridges, J. (2006). Globalization and healthcare: Understanding health and medical tourism. *Expert Review of Pharmacoeconomics & Outcomes Research*, *4*(6), 447–454. doi:10.1586/14737167.6.4.447 PMID:20528514

Carrera, P., & Lunt, N. (2010). A European perspective on medical tourism: The need for a knowledge base. *International Journal of Health Services*, *3*(40), 669–684. PMID:20799671

Carruth, P. J., & Carruth, A. K. (2010). The financial and cost accounting implications of medical tourism. *International Business and Economics Research Journal*, *9*(8), 135–140.

CCDM. (2019). *Care Capacity Demand Management.* Retrieved from: https://www.ccdm.health.nz/

Çelen, A. (2015). Influence of holy month Ramadan on alcohol consumption in Turkey. *Journal of Religion and Health, 54*(6), 2122–2133. doi:10.100710943-014-9875-6 PMID:24810139

Chandra, S. (2016). Ayurvedic research, wellness and consumer rights. *Journal of Ayurveda and Integrative Medicine, 7*(1), 6–10. doi:10.1016/j.jaim.2016.05.002 PMID:27297503

Chan, H. L., Lin, C. H., & Ko, Y. L. (2003). Segmentation of HRV in different physical activities. *Proceedings of IEEE Conference on Computers in Cardiology*, 30, 97-100.

Charity, M., Walter, M., Forbes, K., Kumbirai, M., & Margaret, N. (2013). Stakeholders' knowledge, attitudes and practises towards health tourism development in Zimbabwe. *Australian Journal of Business and Management Research, 3*(2), 24–31.

Cheah, Y. K., & Rasiah, R. (2017). Analysis of the determinants of alcohol consumption among adult males in Malaysia. *Journal of Health Management, 19*(1), 28–38. doi:10.1177/0972063416682548

Chee, H. L., Whittaker, A., & Por, H. H. (2017). Medical travel facilitators, private hospitals and international medical travel in assemblage. *Asia Pacific Viewpoint, 58*(2), 242–254. doi:10.1111/apv.12161

Cheng, K. M. (2016). Medical tourism: Chinese maternity tourism to Hong Kong. *Current Issues in Tourism, 19*(14), 1479–1486. doi:10.1080/13683500.2015.1042359

Chen, K.-H., Chang, F.-H., & Wu, C. (2013). Investigating the wellness tourism factors in hot springs hotel customer service. *International Journal of Contemporary Hospitality Management, 25*(7), 1092–1114. doi:10.1108/IJCHM-06-2012-0086

Cherukara, J., & Manalel, J. (2019). Medical Tourism in Kerala—Challenges and Scope. In *Conference on Tourism in India – Challenges Ahead*, (pp. 369-379). Kochi: IIMK.

Chinai, R., & Goswami, R. (2007). Medical visas mark growth of Indian medical tourism. *Bulletin of the World Health Organization, 85*(3), 164–165. doi:10.2471/BLT.07.010307 PMID:17486202

Chonviharnpan, B., & Lewis, P. (2015). The demand for alcohol in Thailand. *Economic Papers: A Journal of Applied Economics and Policy, 34*(1-2), 23-35.

Chravarthy, K., Ravi Kumar, C., & Deepthi, K. (2008). *SWOT analysis on: Medical Tourism.* Paper presented in Conference on Medical Tourism in India Challenges Ahead, IIMK.

Chuang, T. C., Liu, J. S., Lu, L. Y., & Lee, Y. (2014). The main paths of medical tourism, from transplantation to beautification. *Tourism Management, 45*(1), 49–58. doi:10.1016/j.tourman.2014.03.016

Chung, W. W. C., & Leung, S. W. F. (2005). Collaborative planning, forecasting and replenishment: A case study in copper clad laminate industry. *Production Planning and Control, 16*(6), 563–574. doi:10.1080/09537280500112488

CII & McKinsey. (2002). *Healthcare in India: The road ahead*. New Delhi: Confederation of Indian Industries & McKinsey & Company.

Claster. (2015). *Gathering Medical Tourism Information through Algorithmic Text Analysis of Tweets*. Academic Press.

Clausen, T., Romøren, T. I., Rossow, I., Ingstad, B., Molebatsi, R. M., & Holmboe-Ottesen, G. (2005). Patterns of alcohol consumption among older persons in Botswana. *Contemporary Drug Problems*, *32*(2), 171–193. doi:10.1177/009145090503200202

Clifford, G. D. (2002). *Signal Processing Methods for Heart Rate Variability Analysis* (Ph.D. Thesis). St. Cross College, Oxford, UK.

Collins, A., Medhekar, A., Wong, H. Y., & Cobanoglu, C. (2019). Factors influencing outbound medical travel from the USA. *Tourism Review*, *74*(3), 463–479. doi:10.1108/TR-06-2018-0083

Connell, J. (2019). Medical tourism: In search of an economic niche. In Routledge Hand Book on Tourism in the Middle East and North Africa, (pp. 352-353). Routledge Publication.

Connell, J. (2006). Medical tourism: Sea, sun, sand and … surgery. *Tourism Management*, *26*(6), 1093–1100. doi:10.1016/j.tourman.2005.11.005

Connell, J. (2008). Tummy tucks and the Taj Mahal? Medical tourism and the globalization of health care. In A. Woodside & D. Martin (Eds.), *Tourism management analysis, behaviour and strategy* (pp. 232–244). Wallingford: CABI Publishing.

Connell, J. (2011). *Medical Tourism. CABI* Publication.

Connell, J. (2013). Contemporary medical tourism: Conceptualisation, culture and commodification. *Tourism Management*, *34*, 1–13. doi:10.1016/j.tourman.2012.05.009

Connell, J. (2015). From medical tourism to transnational health care? An epilogue for the future. *Social Science & Medicine*, *124*, 398–401. doi:10.1016/j.socscimed.2014.11.015 PMID:25467883

Cooper, M. J. M., Vafadari, K., & Hieda, M. (2015). Current Issues and Emerging Trends in Medical Tourism. IGI Global.

Cormany, D., & Baloglu, S. (2011). Medical travel facilitator websites: An exploratory study of web page contents and services offered to the prospective medical tourist. *Tourism Management*, *32*(4), 709–716. doi:10.1016/j.tourman.2010.02.008

Correa, D. R. N., Vicente, F. B., Donato, T. A. G., Arana-Chavez, V. E., Buzalaf, M. A. R., & Grandini, C. R. (2014). The effect of the solute on the structure, selected mechanical properties, and biocompatibility of Ti–Zr system alloys for dental applications. *Materials Science and Engineering C*, *34*, 354–359. doi:10.1016/j.msec.2013.09.032 PMID:24268269

Costa, C., Quintela, J., & Mendes, J. (2015). Health and Wellness Tourism: A Strategic Plan for Tourism and Thermalism Valorization of São Pedro do Sul. In M. Peris - Ortiz & J. Á. García (Eds.), Health and wellness tourism. Emergence of a new market segment (pp. 77-99). Heidelberg, Germany: Springer. doi:10.1007/978-3-319-11490-3_2

Costello, T. (2013). Vendor Management. *IT Professional – IEEE Computer Society*, 1520-9202/13, 70-72.

Cotton, M., Henry, A., & Hasek, L. (2014). Value innovation: An important aspect of global surgical care. *Globalization and Health*, *10*(1), 1–5. doi:10.1186/1744-8603-10-1 PMID:24393237

Coulson, C. E., Williams, L. J., Berk, M., Lubman, D. I., Quirk, S. E., & Pasco, J. A. (2014). Association between alcohol consumption and self-reported depression among elderly Australian men. *Geriatric Mental Health Care*, *2*(1-2), 3–8. doi:10.1016/j.gmhc.2014.09.001

Courtney, S., Seyhmus, B., & James, A. B. (2018). Perceived impacts of medical tourism development on community wellbeing. *Tourism Management*, *69*, 232–245. doi:10.1016/j.tourman.2018.06.006

Crompton, J. (1992). Structure of vacation destination choice sets. *Annals of Tourism Research*, *19*(3), 420–434. doi:10.1016/0160-7383(92)90128-C

Crooks, V. A., Turner, L., Snyder, J., Johnston, R., & Kingsbury, P. (2011). Promoting medical tourism in India: Messages, images, and the marketing of international patient travel. *Social Science & Medicine*, *72*(5), 726–732. doi:10.1016/j.socscimed.2010.12.022 PMID:21310519

Cropanzano, R., Howes, J. C., Grandey, A. A., & Toth, P. (1997). The relationship of organizational politics and support to work behaviors, attitudes, and stress. *Journal of Organizational Behavior*, *18*(2), 159–180. doi:10.1002/(SICI)1099-1379(199703)18:2<159::AID-JOB795>3.0.CO;2-D

Cubic Interpolation. (n.d.). Retrieved from the Cubic Interpolation http://www.paulinternet.nl/?page=bicubic

Cunha, L. (2006). Turismo de saúde: Conceitos e mercados. *Revista Lusófona de Humanidades e Tecnologias*, *10*, 79–84.

Daganzo, C. (1979). *Multinomial Probit: The Theory and Its Application to Demand Forecasting*. New York: Academic Press.

Dang, H. S., Huang, Y. F., Wang, C. N., & Nguyen, T. M. T. (2016) Estimation of the market size of medical tourism industry using grey models-case study in South Korea. *International Conference on Computational Intelligence and Applications*, *7600313*, 46-50. 10.1109/ICCIA.2016.14

Daniel, B., & Amy, Z. (2018). Medical tourism and national health care systems: An institutionalist research agenda. *Globalization and Health*, *68*(14), 1–7. PMID:30012218

Dann, G. M. (1977). Anomie, ego-enhancement and tourism. *Annals of Tourism Research*, *4*(4), 184–194. doi:10.1016/0160-7383(77)90037-8

Dasgupta, S., & Dasgupta, D. (2014). *Globalisation and transnational surrogacy in India: Outsourcing life*. Plymouth, UK: Lexington Books.

De Guzman, L. E. P. (2016). Filipinos among World's Biggest Spenders on Travel. *Business World*. Retrieved from http://www.bworldonline.com/

DeBoer, R. W., Karemaker, J. M., & Strackee, J. (1985). Description of heart rate variability data in accordance with a physiological model for the genesis of heart beats. *Psychophysiology*, *22*(2), 147–155. doi:10.1111/j.1469-8986.1985.tb01577.x PMID:3991842

Deloitte. (2008). *Medical Tourism: Consumers in Search of Value*. Deloitte Centre for Health Solutions.

Deng, L., Jin, H., & Wu, S. (2013). Vmerger: Server consolidation in virtualized environment. *Proceedings of IEEE 11th International Conference on Dependable, Autonomic and Secure Computing*, *6844434*, 606-612.

Deonandan, R., Green, S., & Van Beinum, A. (2012). Ethical concerns for maternal surrogacy and reproductive tourism. *Journal of Medical Ethics*, *38*(12), 742–745. doi:10.1136/medethics-2012-100551 PMID:23047836

Dias, P., Oliveira, A., & Lopes, C. (2011). Social and behavioural determinants of alcohol consumption. *Annals of Human Biology*, *38*(3), 337–344. doi:10.3109/03014460.2010.548831 PMID:21434759

Díaz, A., Pons, J., & Solís, L. (2012). Improving healthcare services: Lean lessons from Aravind. *Int. J. Business Excellence*, *5*(4), 413–428. doi:10.1504/IJBEX.2012.047907

Dileep, M. R., Prathyash, V., & Jithin, J. (2019). Ayurtourism:A web based recommendation system for medical tourism. *ACM International Conference Proceeding Series*, 492-495.

Dominic, D. (2016). Medical tourism holds promising potential for UAE. *Middle East Economic Digest*, *60*(2), 1–5.

Dong, D., & Hu, Y. (2017). Study of System Dynamics for Health Care Housing Development in Panzhihua. *Proceedings of the International Conference on Construction and Real Estate Management*, 175-186. 10.1061/9780784481073.020

Dubai Health Authority. (2017). *Dubai Medical Tourism Industry Generated More than AED 1.4billion for the Emirate in 2016*. Retrieved from https://www.dha.gov.ae/

Dubai Health Authority. (2018). Retrieved from https://www.dxh.ae/about-us/about-dxh/

Dubai Health Investment Guide. (2019). A comprehensive guide on health investment in Dubai with a listing of investment needs and opportunities for health services- Towards a healthier & happier community. Dubai Health Authority, Government of Dubai.

Dubas-Jakóbczyk, K., Sowada, C., Domagała, A., & Więckowska, B. (2018). Building hospital capacity planning mechanisms in Poland: The impact of 2016/2017 regulatory changes. *The International Journal of Health Planning and Management*, *33*(2), e403–e415. doi:10.1002/hpm.2493 PMID:29417634

Dunets, A. N., & Zhogova, I. G. (2018). Significant changes of tourism industry in the altai-sayan mountainous region. *Journal of Environmental Management and Tourism*, *9*(4), 869–879. doi:10.14505//jemt.9.4(28).21

Dunn Ross, E. L., & Iso-Ahola, S. E. (1991). Sightseeing tourists' motivation and satisfaction. *Annals of Tourism Research*, *18*(2), 226–237. doi:10.1016/0160-7383(91)90006-W

Dunn, H. (1959). High-level wellness for man and society. *American Journal of Public Health and the Nation's Health*, *49*(6), 786–792. PMID:13661471

Easwaran, M., Bazroy, J., Jayaseelan, V., & Singh, Z. (2015). Prevalence and determinants of alcohol consumption among adult men in a coastal area of South India. *International Journal of Medical Science and Public Health*, *4*(3), 360–364. doi:10.5455/ijmsph.2015.1010201479

Edelhelt, J. (2008). Defining medical tourism or not? *Medical Tourism Magazine*, *5*, 9–10.

Edwards, M., & George, K. (2017). Tourism development in the State of Kerala, India: A study of destination attractiveness. *European Journal of Tourism Research*, *1*(1).

Ekuklu, G., Deveci, S., Eskiocak, M., Berberoglu, U., & Saltik, A. (2004). Alcoholism prevalence and some related factors in Edirne, Turkey. *Yonsei Medical Journal*, *45*(2), 207–214. doi:10.3349/ymj.2004.45.2.207 PMID:15118990

Elbert, R., & Knigge, J.-K. (2018). How order placement influences resource allocation and order processing times inside a multi-user warehouse. *Proceedings – Winter Simulation Conference*, *8632468*, 2921-2932. 10.1109/WSC.2018.8632468

Elias Ebrahimzadeh, E., Manuchehri, M. S., Amoozegar, S., Araabi, B. N., & Zadeh, H. S. (2018). A time local subset feature selection for prediction of sudden cardiac death from ECG signal. *Medical & Biological Engineering & Computing*, *56*(7), 1253–1270. doi:10.100711517-017-1764-1 PMID:29238903

Eom, T., Yu, J., & Han, H. (2019). Medical tourism in Korea – recent phenomena, emerging markets, potential threats, and challenge factors: A review. *Asia Pacific Journal of Tourism Research*, *24*(6), 563–573. doi:10.1080/10941665.2019.1610005

Essoussi, I. E. (2016) A performance evaluation of some collaborative inventory management practices in the healthcare supply chain. *Proceedings of International Conference on Industrial Engineering and Systems Management*, *7380171*, 277-284.

European Commission. (2019). *Cross-border healthcare*. Retrieved on July 8, 2019, from https://ec.europa.eu/health/cross_border_care/overview_en

Eva Ruka Pascal Garel. (2015). *HOPE*. European Hospital and Healthcare Federation.

Farmer, C. M., Hosek, S. D., & Adamson D. M. (2016). Balancing Demand and Supply for Veterans' Health Care. *RAND Health*.

Fatemian, S. Z. (2009). *A Wavelet based Approach to Electrocardiogram (ECG) and Phonocardiogram (PCG) Subject Recognition* (Master of Applied Science Thesis). University of Toronto, Toronto, Canada.

Federal Competitiveness and Statics Authority. (2018). *Sustainable Development Goals*. Retrieved from http://fcsa.gov.ae/en-us/Pages/SDGs/The-Global-Goals.aspx

Ferrer, M., & Medhekar, A. (2012). The factors impacting on the management of global medical tourism service supply chain. *Journal of GSTF Business Review*, *2*(2), 206–211.

Fetscherin, M., & Stephano, R.-M. (2016). The medical tourism index: Scale development and validation. *Tourism Management,* (52), 539-556.

Fetscherin, M., & Stephano, R. M. (2016). The medical tourism index: Scale development and validation. *Tourism Management*, *52*, 539–556. doi:10.1016/j.tourman.2015.08.010

FICCI. (2008). New Delhi: Fostering Quality Healthcare for All. Federation of Indian Chamber of Commerce & Ernst and Young.

Field, J. M., Victorino, L., Buell, R. W., Dixon, M. J., Meyer Goldstein, S., Menor, L. J., ... Zhang, J. J. (2017). Service operations: What's next? *Journal of Service Management*, *29*(1), 55–97. doi:10.1108/JOSM-08-2017-0191

Finch, S. (2014). Thailand top destination for medical tourists. *Canadian Medical Association Journal*, *186*(1), E1–E2. doi:10.1503/cmaj.109-4655 PMID:24246587

Finucane, P. M., Bourgeois-Law, G. A., Ineson, S. L., & Kaigas, T. M. (2003). A comparison of performance assessment programs for medical practitioners in Canada, Australia, New Zealand, and the United Kingdom. *Academic Medicine*, *78*(8), 837–884. doi:10.1097/00001888-200308000-00020 PMID:12915380

Fliedner, G. (2003). CPFR : An emerging supply chain tool. *Industrial Management & Data Systems*, *103*(1), 14–21. doi:10.1108/02635570310456850

Foley, R. (2010). *Healing Waters Therapeutic Landscapes in Historic and Contemporary Ireland* (1st ed.). London: Routledge.

Frederick, J. R., & Gan, L. L. (2015). East-West differences among medical tourism facilitators' websites. *Journal of Destination Marketing & Management*, *4*(2), 98–109. doi:10.1016/j.jdmm.2015.03.002

Freitas, H. (2010). *Turismo médico: A globalização da saúde* (Master Dissertation). University of Porto, Porto.

French, M. T., & Zarkin, G. A. (1995). Is moderate alcohol use related to wages? Evidence from four worksites. *Journal of Health Economics*, *14*(3), 319–344. doi:10.1016/0167-6296(95)90921-R PMID:10145138

Friedman, M. D., Bailit, M. H., & Michel, J. O. (1995). Vendor management: A model for collaboration and quality improvement. *The Joint Commission Journal on Quality Improvement*, *21*(11), 635–645. doi:10.1016/S1070-3241(16)30192-4 PMID:8608335

Gan, L. L., & Frederick, J. R. (2011). Medical tourism facilitators: Patterns of service differentiation. *Journal of Vacation Marketing*, *17*(3), 165–183. doi:10.1177/1356766711409181

Gan, L. L., & Frederick, J. R. (2018). The choice of facilitators in medical tourism. *Health Marketing Quarterly*, *35*(1), 65–83. doi:10.1080/07359683.2018.1434891 PMID:29474154

Gao, G. Q. (2003). *Computerised Detection and Classification of five Cardiac Conditions* (M. E. Thesis). Auckland University of Technology, Auckland, New Zealand.

Garcia-Altes, A. (2005). The development of health tourism services. *Annals of Tourism Research*, *32*(1), 262–266. doi:10.1016/j.annals.2004.05.007

Gauld, R., Al-wahaibi, S., Chisholm, J., Crabbe, R., Kwon, B., Oh, T., ... Sohn, S. (2011). Scorecards for health system performance assessment: The New Zealand example. *Health Policy (Amsterdam)*, *103*(2-3), 200–208. doi:10.1016/j.healthpol.2011.05.016 PMID:21723641

George, B. P., & Henthorne, T. L. (2009). The incorporation of telemedicine with medical tourism: A study of consequences. *Journal of Hospitality Marketing & Management*, *18*(5), 512–522. doi:10.1080/19368620902950097

Gepreel, M. A. H., & Niinomi, M. (2013). Biocompatibility of Ti-alloys for long-term implantation. *Journal of the Mechanical Behavior of Biomedical Materials*, *20*, 407–415. doi:10.1016/j.jmbbm.2012.11.014 PMID:23507261

Geweke, J., Keane, M., & Runkle, D. (1994). Alternative computational approaches to inference in the multinomial probit model. *The Review of Economics and Statistics*, *76*(4), 609–632. doi:10.2307/2109766

Ghose, K. (2010). Hospitality in and out of the hospitals. Creating and maintaining brand equity for medical tourism destination brands. *Romanian Journal of Marketing*, *5*(1), 114–131.

Gius, M. P. (2005). An estimate of the effects of age, taxes, and other socioeconomic variables on the alcoholic beverage demand of young adults. *The Social Science Journal*, *42*(1), 13–24. doi:10.1016/j.soscij.2004.11.002

Glinos, I., & Baeten, R. (2006). *A literature Review of Cross-Border Patient Mobility in the European Union*. Europe For Patients Project.

Global cancer diagnostics market 2018-2027: Prevalence of cancer cases, government initiatives for funding and awareness about cancer and growing medical tourism in Asia. (2018, Nov 26). NASDAQ OMX's News Release Distribution Channel.

Gobalakrishnan, C. (2015). *Sociology of Medical tourism* (1st ed.). Chennai: MJP Publishers.

Goodrich, J., & Goodrich, G. (1987). Health-care tourism- an exploratory study. *Tourism Management*, *8*(3), 217–222. doi:10.1016/0261-5177(87)90053-7

Gopinath, V. (2010, April-June). Oral hygiene practices and habits amongdental professionals in Chennai. *Indian Journal of Dental Research*, *21*(2), 195–200. doi:10.4103/0970-9290.66636 PMID:20657087

Government of India (GOI). (2003). *Health Sector in India, Government of India, 2003 Budget Papers*. New Delhi: GOI.

Government of India (GOI). (2003). *Health Sector in India*. New Delhi: GOI, Budget Papers.

Government of India (GOI). (2018a). *India: Healthcare Tourism*. Retrieved from http://www.indiahealthcaretourism.com/

Government of India (GOI). (2018b). *Wellness and Medial Tourism*. Retrieved from http://tourism.gov.in/wellness-medical-tourism

Graburn, N. (1989). Tourism: The Sacred Journey. In V. Smith (Ed.), *Hosts and Guests: The Anthropology of Tourism* (2nd ed.; pp. 21–36). Philadelphia, PA: University of Pennsylvania Press.

Greene, W. H. (2012). *Econometric analysis* (7th ed.). Boston: Pearson Education India.

Greger, M., Widomská, M., & Kander, L. (2010). Mechanical properties of ultra-fine grain titanium. *Journal of Achievements in Materials and Manufacturing Engineering*, *40*(1), 33–40.

Grénman, M., & Räikkönen, J. (2015). Well-being and wellness tourism – Same, same but different? Conceptual discussions and empirical evidence. *Matkailututkimus*, *11*(1), 7–25.

Griffin, R. W., & Moorhead, G. (2009). Organizational Behavior: Managing People and Organizations (9th ed.). Mason, OH: South-Western College Pub.

Grittner, U., Kuntsche, S., Gmel, G., & Bloomfield, K. (2012). Alcohol consumption and social inequality at the individual and country levels—Results from an international study. *European Journal of Public Health*, *23*(2), 332–339. doi:10.1093/eurpub/cks044 PMID:22562712

Gulf News. (2018). *Dubai Health Authority Focuses on Eye and Cancer Care Services*. Retrieved from https://gulfnews.com/

Gupta, A. (2008). Medical Tourism India: Winners & losers. *Indian Journal of Medical Ethics*, *5*(1), 4–5. PMID:18630244

Haarhoff, R., & Mokoena, L. G. (2017). The market place of medical tourism facilitators in South Africa. *African Journal of Hospitality, Tourism and Leisure*, *6*(3).

Hallab, Z. (2006). Catering to the healthy-living vacationer. *Journal of Vacation Marketing*, *12*(1), 71–91. doi:10.1177/1356766706059043

Hallem, Y., Barth, I., & Triki, A. (2010, September 1-3). *Customer perceived value of medical tourism: An exploratory study – The case of cosmetic surgery in Tunisia.* Article presented at the conference "Health, wellness and tourism: Healthy tourists, healthy business?", Dalarna.

Hamilton, V., & Hamilton, B. H. (1997). Alcohol and earnings: Does drinking yield a wage premium? *The Canadian Journal of Economics. Revue Canadienne d'Economique*, *30*(1), 135–151. doi:10.2307/136363

Hamlin, R. L., Smith, R. C., & Smetzer, D. L. (1966). Sinus arrhythmia in the dog. *The American Journal of Physiology*, *210*(2), 321–328. doi:10.1152/ajplegacy.1966.210.2.321 PMID:5901470

Han, M., Thiery, T., & Song, X. (2006). Managing Exceptions in the Medical Workflow Systems. ICSE'06, Shanghai, China.

Hanefeld, J., Smith, R., Horsfall, D., & Lunt, N. (2014). What do we know about medical tourism? A review of the literature with discussion of its implications for the UK national health service as an example of a public health care system. *Journal of Travel Medicine*, *6*(21), 410–417. doi:10.1111/jtm.12147 PMID:25156070

Han, H., & Hyun, S. (2015). Customer retention in the medical tourism industry: Impact of quality, satisfaction, trust, and price reasonableness. *Tourism Management*, *46*, 20–29. doi:10.1016/j.tourman.2014.06.003

Hansson-Sandsten, M., & Jonsson, P. (2007). Multiple window correlation analysis of HRV power and respiratory frequency. *IEEE Transactions on Biomedical Engineering*, *54*(10), 1770–1779. doi:10.1109/TBME.2007.904527 PMID:17926675

Haq, F., & Medhekar, A. (2015). Halal Branding of Medical Tourism: case of Indian hospitals. In H. El-Gohary & R. Eid (Eds.), *Emerging Research in Islamic Marketing and Tourism in the Global Economy* (pp. 160–189). IGI Global.

Hartmann, S. (2019). Mobilising patients towards transnational healthcare markets–insights into the mobilising work of medical travel facilitators in Delhi. *Mobilities*, *14*(1), 71–86. doi:10.1080/17450101.2018.1533694

Hartwell, H., Fyall, A., Willis, C., Page, S., Ladkin, A., & Hemingway, A. (2016). Progress in tourism and destination wellbeing research. *Current Issues in Tourism*, *21*(16), 1830–1892. doi:10.1080/13683500.2016.1223609

Harwood, H. J., Fountain, D., & Livermore, G. (1998). *The economic costs of alcohol and drug abuse in the United States, 1992.* Washington, DC: US Department of Health and Human Services.

Haseena, V. (2015). The Routes of Wellness in Tourism in Kerala and its Impacts. *Journal Of Tourism. Hospitality And Sports*, *5*(1), 21–26.

Health, D. (2019). *DXH Wellness.* Retrieved from https://dxh.ae/en-US/wellness-dubai

Heien, D. M. (1996). Do drinkers earn less? *Southern Economic Journal*, *63*(1), 60–68. doi:10.2307/1061303

Henama, U. (2014). Health tourism in South Africa: Opportunities and possibilities. *African Journal of Hospitality, Tourism and Leisure*, *3*(1), 1–9.

Henderson, J. (2003). Healthcare tourism in South- East Asia. *Tourism Review International*, *3*, 271–290.

Henderson, J. C. (2007). Destination Development. *Journal of Travel & Tourism Marketing*, *20*(3-4), 33–45. doi:10.1300/J073v20n03_03

Henderson, J. C. (2014). Global Gulf Cities and Tourism: A Review of Abu Dhabi, Doha and Dubai. *Tourism Recreation Research*, *39*(1), 107–114. doi:10.1080/02508281.2014.11081329

Hering, H. E. (1910). A functional test of heart vagi in man. *Men-schen München Medizinische Wochenschrift*, *57*, 1931–1933.

Heung, V., & Kucukusta, D. (2013). Wellness tourism in China, resources, development and marketing. *International Journal of Tourism Research*, *15*(4), 346–359. doi:10.1002/jtr.1880

Heung, V., Kucukusta, D., & Song, H. (2010). A Conceptual Model of Medical Tourism: Implications for Future Research. *Journal of Travel & Tourism Marketing*, *27*(3), 236–251. doi:10.1080/10548401003744677

Heung, V., Kucukusta, D., & Song, H. (2010). A conceptual model of medical Tourism: Implications for future research. *Journal of Travel & Tourism Marketing*, *3*(27), 1–30.

Hilton, M. F., Bates, R. A., Godfrey, K. R., Chappell, M. J., & Cayton, R. M. (1999). Evaluation of frequency and time frequency spectral analysis of heart rate variability as a diagnostic marker of the sleep apnea syndrome. *Medical & Biological Engineering & Computing*, *37*(6), 760–769. doi:10.1007/BF02513379 PMID:10723884

Hollmann, R. L., Scavarda, L. F., & Thomé, A. M. T. (2015). Collaborative planning, forecasting and replenishment: A literature review. *International Journal of Productivity and Performance Management*, *64*(7), 971–993. doi:10.1108/IJPPM-03-2014-0039

Hongnaphadol, W. (2010, September 1-3). *An exploratory study of consumer choice and motivation of medical tourism in Thailand: A case study of healthcare consumers visiting a private hospital in Pattaya*. Article presented at conference "Health, wellness and tourism: Healthy tourists, healthy business?", Dalarna.

Hopkins, L., Labonté, R., Runnels, V., & Packer, C. (2010). Medical tourism today: What is the state of existing knowledge? *Journal of Public Health Policy*, *2*(31), 185–198. doi:10.1057/jphp.2010.10 PMID:20535101

Horowitz, M. D., & Rosensweig, J. A. (2007). Medical Tourism-Health Care in the Global Economy. *Physician Executive*, *33*(6), 24–31. PMID:18092615

Horowitz, M. D., Rosensweig, J. A., & Jones, C. A. (2007). Medical tourism: Globalization of the healthcare marketplace. *Medscape General Medicine*, *9*(4), 33. PMID:18311383

Horowitz, M., & Rosensweig, J. (2007). Medical tourism - health care in the global economy. *Physician Executive*, *6*(33), 24–30. PMID:18092615

Hotelier Middle East. (2018). *Dubai on track to attract medical tourists*. Retrieved from http://www.hoteliermiddleeast.com/32871-dubai-on-track-to-attract-500000-medical-tourists-by-2020/

Hovav, S., & Tsadikovich, D. (2015). A network flow model for inventory management and distribution of influenza vaccines through a healthcare supply chain. *Operations Research for Health Care*, *5*, 49–62. doi:10.1016/j.orhc.2015.05.003

Hsu, H.-Y., Chang, M.-H., Ni, Y.-H., Jeng, Y.-M., Chiang, C.-L., Chen, H.-L., ... Chen, P.-J. (2013). Long-term follow-up of children with postnatal immunoprophylaxis failure who were infected with hepatitis B virus surface antigen gene mutant. *The Journal of Infectious Diseases*, *207*(7), 1047–1057. doi:10.1093/infdis/jis943 PMID:23300165

Hudson, S., & Li, X. (2012). Domestic medical tourism: A neglected dimension of medical tourism research. *Journal of Hospitality Marketing & Management*, *21*(3), 227–246. doi:10.1080/19368623.2011.615018

Huerta, M. C., & Borgonovi, F. (2010). Education, alcohol use and abuse among young adults in Britain. *Social Science & Medicine*, *71*(1), 143–151. doi:10.1016/j.socscimed.2010.03.022 PMID:20452109

Huikuri, H. V., Makikallio, T., Airaksinen, K. E., Mitrani, R., Castellanos, A., & Myerburg, R. J. (1999). Measurement of heart rate variability. A clinical tool or research toy? *Journal of the American College of Cardiology*, *34*(7), 1878–1883. doi:10.1016/S0735-1097(99)00468-4 PMID:10588197

Hunter-Jones, P. (2006). Managing Cancer: The Role of Holiday Taking. *Journal of Travel Medicine*, *10*(3), 170–176. doi:10.2310/7060.2003.35762 PMID:12757692

Hyndman, B. W., Kitney, R. I., & Sayers, B. M. (1971). Spontaneous rhythms in physiological control systems. *Nature*, *233*(5318), 339–341. doi:10.1038/233339a0 PMID:4940430

ICCCON. (2019). *ICCCON 2019 - 26th Annual Conference, Kochi*. Retrieved 27 July 2019, from http://www.icccon2019kochi.com/experience-kerala

Ilyas, M. (2008). Medical Tourism: India the Right Destination. *Southern Economist*, (1), 37-39.

IMTJ. (2017). Dubai Health Authority Partners to Drive Medical Tourism. *International Medical Travel Journal*. Retrieved from https://www.imtj.com/news/dubai-health-authority-partners-drive-medical-tourism/

Indian Hgh Commission Oman (IHCO). (2017). *Medical visas issued to Omani citizens*. Retrieved from https://www.morevisas.com/immigration-news-article/medical-visas-issued-to-omani-citizens-for-india-rise-100/4993/

Indian Medical Tourism (IMT). (2009). *India Ranks 2nd in Med-Tourism*. Available: www.medicaltourism.org/consortium.jsp?sect=con

Indian Medical Tourism (IMT). (2009). *India Ranks 2nd in Med-Tourism*. Retrieved from www.medicaltourism.org/consortium.jsp?sect=con

INE. (2012). *Anuário Estatístico da Região Centro 2011*. Lisboa: INE.

INE. (2018). *Conta Satélite do Turismo em Portugal: Destaque à comunicação social*. Retrieved on June 8, 2019, from https://www.ine.pt

Inhorn, M. C. (2016). Cosmopolitan conceptions in global Dubai? The Emiratization of IVF and its Consequences. *Reproductive Biomedicine Society*, *2*, 24–31. doi:10.1016/j.rbms.2016.04.004 PMID:29892713

Inhorn, M. C., Shrivastav, P., & Patrizio, P. (2012). Assisted reproductive technologies and fertility "tourism": Examples from global Dubai and the Ivy League. *Medical Anthropology*, *31*(3), 249–265. doi:10.1080/01459740.2011.596495 PMID:22540317

International Medical Tourism Journal (IMTJ). (2017a, May). *Medical & wellness tourism board for India*. Retrieved from https://www.imtj.com/news/medical-wellness-tourism-board-india/

International Medical Tourism Journal (IMTJ). (2017b, July). *India medical tourism statistics released.* Retrieved from https://www.imtj.com/news/india-medical-tourism-statistics-released

International, S. R. I. (2010). *Spas and the global wellness market: Synergies and opportunities*. Retrieved on July 25, 2019, from https://www.sri.com/sites/default/files/publications/gss_sri_spasandwellnessreport_rev_82010.pdf

International, I. P. K. (2012). *ITB world travel trends report 2012/2013*. Munich: IPK International.

Islam, N. (2012). New Age Orientation: Ayurvedic 'Wellness and Spa Culture'. Health Sociology Review, 21(2), 270-231.

Iso-Ahola, S. E. (1982). Toward a Social Psychological Theory of Tourism Motivation: A Rejoinder. *Annals of Tourism Research*, *9*(2), 256–262. doi:10.1016/0160-7383(82)90049-4

Jagyasi, P. (2019). *Medical tourism trends to watch*. Retrieved from: https://www.linkedin.com/pulse/medical-tourism-trends-watch-2019-dr-prem-jagyasi/

Jahan, A., & Edwards, K. L. (2013). Weighting of dependent and target-based criteria for optimal decision-making in materials selection process: Biomedical applications. *Materials & Design*, *49*, 1000–1008. doi:10.1016/j.matdes.2013.02.064

Jahanian, R., Tabatabaei, S. M., & Behdad, B. (2012). Stress management in the workplace. *International Journal of Academic Research in Economics and Management Sciences*, *1*(6), 1.

Jakšić- Stojanović, A., Janković, M., & Šerić, N. (2019). Montenegro as a high-quality health tourism destination: Trends and Perspectives. *African Journal of Hospitality, Tourism and Leisure*, *8*(3), 1–9.

Jaramillo, J., Goyal, D., & Lung, C. (2019). Birth tourism among Chinese women. *MCN. The American Journal of Maternal Child Nursing, 44*(2), 94–99. doi:10.1097/NMC.0000000000000500 PMID:30640727

Jasson, S., Medigue, C., Maison-Blanche, P., Montano, N., Meyer, L., Vermeiren, C., ... Swynghedauw, B. (1997). Instant power spectrum analysis of HRV during orthostatic tilt using a time/frequency domain method. *Circulation, 96*, 3521–3526. doi:10.1161/01.CIR.96.10.3521 PMID:9396450

JCI. (2019). *Joint Commission International Accreditation Standards for Hospitals*. Retrieved from http://www.jointcommissioninternational.org/about-jci/jci-accredited-or

JCI. (2019). *Joint Commission International Accreditation Standards for Hospitals*. Retrieved from https://www.jointcommissioninternational.org/about-jci/jci-accredited-organizations/?c=United%20Arab%20Emirates

JCI. (2019). *Joint Commission International Accredited Organizations List*. Retrieved from www.jointcommissioninternational.org/about-jci/jci-accredited-organizations/

Jindal, G. D. (1986). Impedance plethysmography for screening vascular diseases. *Journal of Postgraduate Medicine, 32*, 1–3. PMID:3746705

Jing, F., & Lim, C.-K. (2018). Advancement strategies toward the Chinese market in Korean medical tourism industry. *Asia Life Sciences Supplement, 15*(3), 2073–2081.

Johnson, T. J., & Garman, A. N. (2015). Demand for international medical travel to the USA. *Tourism Economics, 21*(5), 1061–1077. doi:10.5367/te.2014.0393

Johnston, R., Crooks, V. A., Adams, K., Snyder, J., & Kingsbury, P. (2011). An industry perspective on Canadian patients' involvement in Medical Tourism: Implications for public health. *BMC Public Health, 11*(1), 416. doi:10.1186/1471-2458-11-416 PMID:21627830

Johnston, R., Crooks, V., Snyder, J., & Kingsbury, P. (2010). What is known about the effects of medical tourism in destination and departure countries? A scoping review. *International Journal for Equity in Health, 9*(1), 24. doi:10.1186/1475-9276-9-24 PMID:21047433

Joint Commission International. (2019). *JCI accredited organizations*. Retrieved from https://www.jointcommissioninternational.org/about-jci/jci-accredited-organizations/?c=India&a=Hospital%20Program

Joint Commission International. (n.d.). *Joint Commission International*. Retrieved from http://www.jointcommissioninternational.org/

Joppe, M., & Choi, H. (2010, September 1-3). *The evolution of attitudes towards spa holidays in Canada*. Article presented at conference "Health, Wellness and tourism: Healthy tourists, healthy business?", Dalarna.

Kablan, A., & Ng, W. L. (2010). Enhancing High-Frequency Order Placement Strategies with Fuzzy Logic and Fuzzy Inference, *IAENG. International Journal of Computational Science, 37*(4).

Kahiya, E. T., & Dean, D. L. (2014). Export performance: Multiple predictors and multiple measures approach. *Asia Pacific Journal of Marketing and Logistics*, *26*(3), 378–407. doi:10.1108/APJML-11-2012-0119

Kajonborrirak, S. (n.d.). *The Importance of Professional Health Care and Spa Therapist Training in The Tourism Industry.* Retrieved from http://www.sarahorg.com/thaispa/Pata_Pattaya.pdf

Kana, M. (2010). *Mathematical Models of Cardiovascular Control by the Autonomic Nervous System* (Ph. D. Thesis). Czech Technical University in Prague, Prague, Czech Republic.

Kanittinsuttitong, N. (2015). Motivation and Decision on Medical Tourism Service in Thailand. *ASEAN Journal of Management & Innovation*, *2*(2), 24–36.

KannanP. (2014). Retrieved from http://www.thenational.ae/uae/tourism/dubai-reveals-master-plan-for-500-000-medical-tourists-a-year

Kannan, S., & Frenz, M. (2017). Seeking health under palm trees: Ayurveda in Kerala. *Global Public Health: An International Journal for Research, Policy and Practice*, *14*(3), 351–361. doi:10.1080/17441692.2017.1417458 PMID:29272989

Karthikeyan, P., Murugappan, M., & Yaacob, S. (2013). Multiple Physiological Signal-Based Human Stress identification Using Non-Linear Classifiers. *Electronics and Electrical Engineering*, *19*(7).

Kasper, H., & Reddy, S. (2017). Spaces of connectivity: The formation of medical travel destination in Delhi national capital region (India). *Asia Pacific Viewpoint*, *58*(2), 228–241. doi:10.1111/apv.12159

Kazemi, H. (2007). A Study of Unhealthy Behaviors and Stress Managment. *Journal of Psychology and Information*, 40-44.

Kerala Tourism Ministry. (2017). *Kerala tourism statistics 2017*. Retrieved 27 July 2019, from https://www.keralatourism.org/tourismstatistics/tourist_statistics_2017_book20181221073646.pdf

Keseslbrener, L., & Alselrod, S. (1996). Selective discrete Fourier transform algorithm for time frequency analysis: Method and application on simulated and cardiovascular signals. *IEEE Transactions on Biomedical Engineering*, *43*(8), 789–802. doi:10.1109/10.508542 PMID:9216151

Khaleej Times. (2017). *Dubai to promote medical tourism by easing visa procedures*. Retrieved from https://www.khaleejtimes.com/

Khan, M. J., Chelliah, S., Haron, M. S., & Ahmed, S. (2017). Push factors, risks, and types of visit intentions of international medical travellers-A conceptual model. *International Journal of Healthcare Management*, *10*(2), 115–121. doi:10.1080/20479700.2017.1304345

Khan, S., & Alam, S. (2014). Kingdom of Saudi Arabia: A potential destination for medical tourism. *Journal of Taibah University Medical Sciences*, *9*(4), 257–262. doi:10.1016/j.jtumed.2014.01.007

Khedder, G., Kachouri, A., Messouad, M. B., & Samet, M. (2004). Application of nonlinear dynamic method in the analysis of HRV towards clinical application: Tiresome diagnosis. In *Proceedings of the International conference on Information and Communication Technologies: From Theory to applications*, (*vol. 1*, pp. 177-182). Academic Press.

Khowaja, S. A., Prabono, A. B., Setiawan, F., Yahya, B. N., & Lee, S. L. (2018). Contextual activity based Healthcare Internet of Things, Services, and People (HIoTSP): An architectural framework for healthcare monitoring using wearable sensors. *Computer Networks*, *145*(9), 190–206. doi:10.1016/j.comnet.2018.09.003

Kim, J. H., Kim, S. Y., Yun, S.-J., Chung, J. I., Choi, H., Yu, H. S., ... Lee, J. Y. (2019). Medical travel among non-Seoul residents to seek prostate cancer treatment in medical facilities of Seoul. *Cancer Research and Treatment*, *51*(1), 53–64. doi:10.4143/crt.2017.468 PMID:29458236

Kim, J., & Lee, J. (2017). Particle swarm optimization based inventory policy for wholesale business in Devs-based medicine supply chain. *International Journal of Industrial Engineering: Theory Applications and Practice*, *24*(2), 146–161.

KO, T.G. (2011). Medical Tourism System Model. *International Journal of Tourism Sciences*, *11*(1), 18–51.

Koncul, N. (2012). Wellness: A New Mode of tourism. *Economic Research-Ekonomska Istraživanja*, *25*(2), 525–534. doi:10.1080/1331677X.2012.11517521

Kotton, C. N. (2013). Safe Travels! After Cancer Treatment. *Journal of Travel Medicine*, *20*(2), 69–70. doi:10.1111/jtm.12014 PMID:23464711

Kubota, M., Yanagita, M., Mori, K., Hasegawa, S., Yamashita, M., Yamada, S., ... Murakami, S. (2016, May). The effects of cigarettesmoke condensate and nicotine on periodontal tissue in a periodontitismodel mouse. *PLoS One*, *11*(5), e0155594. doi:10.1371/journal.pone.0155594 PMID:27203240

Kulkarni, A. (2008). Become healthy happy and balanced with Ayurveda. *Medical Tourism*, *2*(1), 38–39.

Kumar, A. (2017). Medical Tourism emerging as a next growth driver. *Travel Trends Today- T3 Magazine*. Retrieved from https://www.traveltrendstoday.in/news/india-tourism/item/5439-medical-tourism-emerging-as-a-next-growth-driver

Kumar, G.S., & Raj, R.K. (2015). Status, growth and impact of medical tourism in India. *International Journal of Pharmaceutical Sciences Review and Research, 34*, 284-91.

Kwon, I. G., Kim, S. H., & Martin, D. G. (2016). Healthcare supply chain management; strategic areas for quality and financial improvement. *Technological Forecasting and Social Change*, *113*, 422–428. doi:10.1016/j.techfore.2016.07.014

LaGanga, L. R. (2011). Lean service operations: Reflections and new directions for capacity expansion in outpatient clinics. *Journal of Operations Management*, *29*(5), 422–433. doi:10.1016/j.jom.2010.12.005

Laguna, P., Moody, G. B., & Mark, R. G. (1998). Power spectral density of unevenly sampled data by least square analysis: Performance and application to heart rate signals. *IEEE Transactions on Biomedical Engineering*, *45*(6), 698–715. doi:10.1109/10.678605 PMID:9609935

Lancaster, J. (2004). Surgeries, side trips for medical tourists. *Washington Post, 21.*

Laramée, P., Kusel, J., Leonard, S., Aubin, H.-J., François, C., & Daeppen, J.-B. (2013). The economic burden of alcohol dependence in Europe. *Alcohol and Alcoholism (Oxford, Oxfordshire)*, *48*(3), 259–269. doi:10.1093/alcalc/agt004 PMID:23371284

Lee, G. E. (2016). Factors Associated with Willingness to Participate in Clinical Trials among Diverse Asian Patients with Breast Cancer. *European Journal of Cancer*, *60*, 1–19. doi:10.1016/j.ejca.2016.03.030 PMID:27038842

Lee, G. E., Ow, M., Lie, D., & Dent, R. (2016). Barriers and Facilitators for Clinical Trial Participation among Diverse Asian Patients with Breast Cancer: A Qualitative Study. *BMC Women's Health*, *16*(43). doi:10.118612905-016-0319-1 PMID:27449505

Lee, H. K., & Fernando, Y. (2015). The antecedents and outcomes of the medical tourism supply chain. *Tourism Management*, *46*, 148–157. doi:10.1016/j.tourman.2014.06.014

Lenka, S. (2017). *Health tourism in Kerala: Relative perception study on the determinants of wellness tourism. In Millennial Workforce–A Contemplation* (1st ed.; pp. 180–187). Hyderabad, India: Zenon Academic Publishing.

Levin, S., & Berry, T. B. (2010). Next-generation vendor management: The experience of Centura Health. Healthcare Financial Management. *Journal of the Healthcare Financial Management Association.*, *64*(6), 106–116. PMID:20533685

Levkov, C., Micchov, G., Lyanov, R., & Daskalov, I. K. (1984). Subtraction of 50 Hz interference from the electrocardiogram. *Medical & Biological Engineering & Computing*, *22*(4), 371–373. doi:10.1007/BF02442109 PMID:6748774

Li, C., & Liu, S. (2013). A robust optimization approach to reduce the bullwhip Effect of supply chains with vendor order placement lead time delays in an uncertain environment. *Applied Mathematical Modelling*, *37*(3), 707–718. doi:10.1016/j.apm.2012.02.033

Lindblom, A., & Olkkonen, R. (2006). Category management tactics: An analysis of manufacturers' control. *International Journal of Retail & Distribution Management*, *34*(6), 482–496. doi:10.1108/09590550610667065

Linear Interpolation. (n.d.). Retrieved from the Linear Interpolation Wiki: http://en.wikipedia.org/wiki/Linear_interpolation

Lin, H. C. (2014). Assessment of the Partnership Quality between Travel Agencies and Health Care Organizations on the International Medical Tourism Market in Taiwan. *Journal of Quality Assurance in Hospitality & Tourism*, *15*(4), 356–381. doi:10.1080/1528008X.2014.921777

Lin, R.-H., & Pei-Yun, H. (2014). The study of CPFR implementation model in medical SCM of Taiwan. *Production Planning and Control*, *25*(3), 260–271. doi:10.1080/09537287.2012.673646

Liu, X., Chen, S., Tsoi, J. K., & Matinlinna, J. P. (2017). Binary titanium alloys as dental implant materials—a review. *Regenerative Biomaterials, 4*(5), 315-323.

Loevinsohn, B., & Harding, A. (2005). Buying results? Contracting for health service delivery in developing countries. *Lancet*, *366*(9486), 676–681. doi:10.1016/S0140-6736(05)67140-1 PMID:16112305

Lombardi, F. (1999). Heart rate variability: A contribution to better understanding of the clinical role of heart rate. *European Heart Journal Supplements*, *1*, H44–H51.

Lonely Planet. (2015). *Kerala*. Retrieved 20 July 2019, from http://media.lonelyplanet.com/shop/pdfs/india-15-kerala-preview.pdf

Lovoy Siem, K. V. (2007). *Modelling fibre orientation of the left ventricular human heart wall* (M. S. Thesis). Norwegian University of Science and Technology.

Lundborg, P. (2002). Young people and alcohol: An econometric analysis. *Addiction (Abingdon, England)*, *97*(12), 1573–1582. doi:10.1046/j.1360-0443.2002.00231.x PMID:12472641

Lunt, N., & Carrera, P. (2010). Medical tourism: Assessing the evidence on treatment abroad. *Maturitas*, *66*(1), 27–32. doi:10.1016/j.maturitas.2010.01.017 PMID:20185254

Lunt, N., & Carrera, P. (2011). Advice for prospective medical tourists: Systematic review of consumer sites. *Tourism Review*, (66): 57–67. doi:10.1108/16605371111127224

Lunt, N., Hardey, M., & Mannion, R. (2010). Nip, Tuck and Click: Medical Tourism and the Emergence of Web-Based Health Information. *The Open Medical Informatics Journal*, *4*(4), 1–11. doi:10.2174/1874431101004010001 PMID:20517465

Lunt, N., Horsfall, D., & Hanefeld, J. (2016). Medical tourism: A snapshot of evidence on treatment abroad. *Maturitas*, *88*, 37–44. doi:10.1016/j.maturitas.2016.03.001 PMID:27105695

Lunt, N., & Mannion, R. (2014). Patient mobility in the global marketplace: A multidisciplinary perspective. *International Journal of Health Policy and Management*, *2*(4), 155–157. doi:10.15171/ijhpm.2014.47 PMID:24847479

Lvanov, P. C., Rosenblum, M. G., Peng, C. K., Mietus, J., Havlin, S., Stanley, H. E., & Goldberger, A. L. (1996). Scaling behavior of heart beat intervals obtained by wavelet based time series analysis. *Nature*, *383*(6598), 323–327. doi:10.1038/383323a0 PMID:8848043

Madzingamiri, D., Schouten, M. A. C., & Blokland, M. (2015). Water, sanitation and hygiene partners collaborating to combat severe cholera outbreaks during the State of Emergency in Zimbabwe. *Water Policy*, *17*(2), 370–388. doi:10.2166/wp.2014.100

Majeed, S., & Lu, C. (2017). *Changing Preferences, Moving Places and Third-Party Administrators: A Scoping Review of Medical Tourism Trends (1990-2016)*. Almatourism. doi:10.6092/issn.2036-5195/6675

Majumdar, R., Yang, Y. Y., Li, H., Akçapinar, G., Flanagan, B., & Ogata, H. (2018). GOAL: Supporting learner's development of self-direction skills using health and learning data. *Proceedings 26th International Conference on Computers in Education, Main Conference*, 406-415.

Malik, M., & Camm Eds, A. J. (1995). *Heart Rate Variability*. Armonk, NY: Futura.

Malik, M., Cripps, T., Farrel, T., & Camm, A. J. (1989). Prognostic value of heart rate variability after myocardial infarction. A comparison of different data processing methods. *Medical & Biological Engineering & Computing*, *27*(6), 603–611. doi:10.1007/BF02441642

Malpas, S. C. (2002). Neural influences on cardiovascular variability: Posiibilities and pitfalls. *American Journal of Physiology. Heart and Circulatory Physiology*, *282*(1), H6–H20. doi:10.1152/ajpheart.2002.282.1.H6 PMID:11748042

Malpas, S. C., Leonard, B. L., Guild, S., Ringwood, J. V., Navakatikyan, M., Austin, P. C., ... Burgess, D. E. (2001). The sympathetic nervous system's role in regulating blood pressure variability: Understanding how SNA controls vascular tone is an important step in determining the pathogenesis of hypertension. *IEEE Engineering in Medicine and Biology*, *20*(2), 17–24. doi:10.1109/51.917720

Manaf, N. H. A., Hussain, H., Kassim, P. N. J., Alavi, R., & Dahari, Z. (2015). Medical tourism service quality: Finally, some empirical findings. *Total Quality Management & Business Excellence*, *26*(9/10), 1017–1028. doi:10.1080/14783363.2015.1068597

Mangeloja, E. (2005). Economic growth and religious production efficiency. *Applied Economics*, *37*(20), 2349–2359. doi:10.1080/00036840500217531

Mansfeld, Y., & Winckler, O. (2007). The tourism industry as an alternative for the GCC oil-based rentier economies. *Tourism Economics*, *13*(3), 333–360. doi:10.5367/000000007781497728

Marcus, A. G., Munoz, M., Olivares, R., Reboucas Filho, P. P., Ser, J. D., & Victor Hugo, C. (2020). Online heart monitoring systems on the internet of health things environments: A survey, a reference model and an outlook. *Information Fusion*, *53*, 222–239. doi:10.1016/j.inffus.2019.06.004

Marrella, A., & Mecella, M. (2017). Adaptive process management in cyber-physical domains. *Intelligent Systems Reference Library*, *123*, 15–48. doi:10.1007/978-3-319-52181-7_2

Martinez, P., Røislien, J., Naidoo, N., & Clausen, T. (2011). Alcohol abstinence and drinking among African women: Data from the World Health Surveys. *BMC Public Health*, *11*(1), 160. doi:10.1186/1471-2458-11-160 PMID:21392398

Martin, R. M., Sterne, J. A., Gunnell, D., Ebrahim, S., Smith, G. D., & Frankel, S. (2003). NHS waiting lists and evidence of national or local failure: Analysis of health service data. *BMJ (Clinical Research Ed.)*, *326*(7382), 188. doi:10.1136/bmj.326.7382.188 PMID:12543833

Martins, A., Lunt, N., Freitas, R., Ribeiro, S., & Klein, U. (2014). *Atlas de oportunidades para o turismo de saúde e bem-estar*. Leça da Palmeira: AEP – Câmara de Comércio e Indústria.

Massarweh, N. N., Chiang, Y.-J., Xing, Y., Chang, G. J., Haynes, A. B., You, Y. N., ... Cormier, J. N. (2014). Association Between Travel Distance and Metastatic Disease at Diagnosis Among Patients With Colon Cancer. *Journal of Clinical Oncology*, *32*(9), 942–948. doi:10.1200/JCO.2013.52.3845 PMID:24516014

Mathews, S. M., Kambhamettu, C., & Barner, K. (2018). A novel application of deep learning for single-lead ECG classification. *Computers in Biology and Medicine*, *99*(1), 53–62. doi:10.1016/j.compbiomed.2018.05.013 PMID:29886261

Mathon, D., Apparicio, P., & Lachapelle, U. (2018). Cross-border spatial accessibility of health care in the North-East Department of Haiti. *International Journal of Health Geographics*, *17*(1), 36. doi:10.118612942-018-0156-6 PMID:30359261

Mattoo, A., & Rathindran, R. (2006). How health insurance inhibits trade in health care. *Health Affairs*, *25*(2), 358–368. doi:10.1377/hlthaff.25.2.358 PMID:16522578

McCain, G. (1987). Black holes, cash pigs, and other hospital portfolio analysis problems. *Journal of Health Care Marketing*, *7*(2), 56–64. PMID:10301718

McGonagle, K. A., & Kessler, R. C. (1990). Chronic stress, acute stress, and depressive symptoms. *American Journal of Community Psychology*, *18*(5), 681–706. doi:10.1007/BF00931237 PMID:2075897

Medhekar, A. (2014). Government Policy Initiatives for Developing Sustainable Medical Tourism Industry. *GSTF- Journal on Business Review*, *3*(3), 95-105.

Medhekar, A. (2014). Public-Private Partnerships for Inclusive Development: Role of Private Corporate Sector in Provision of Healthcare Services. Procedia - Social and Behavioral Sciences Journal, 157, 33-44.

Medhekar, A., & Newby, L. (2013). Information Search to Travel Abroad for Medical Treatment: An Empirical Study. *Proceedings of International Conference on Healthcare Systems and Global Business Issues*, 77-96.

Medhekar, A. (2012). Managing the Growth of Medical Tourism in India by Public-Private-Partnerships. In K. Roy & S. Kar (Eds.), *Development Management in the 21st Century, Readings in World Development* (pp. 59–72). New York: Nova.

Medhekar, A. (2013). Indian Government Policy to Support Trade in Medical Tourism Services. In *Proceedings of the 7th International Conference on Healthcare Systems and Global Business Issues*, (pp. 205-218). Jaipur, India: JNU Press.

Medhekar, A. (2013). Maharashtra Medically Yours: A Global Player in Medical Tourism. *Bi-Annual Journal. Cosmos*, *3*(V), 38–53.

Medhekar, A. (2014). Government policy initiatives for developing sustainable medical tourism industry. *Journal on Business Review*, *3*(3), 267–283.

Medhekar, A., & Ali, M. M. (2012). A Cross-Border Trade in Healthcare services: Bangladesh to India. *The Business and Management Review*, *2*(1), 1–13.

Medhekar, A., & Haq, F. (2015). Halal Branding of medical Tourism: case of Indian hospitals. In H. El-Gohary & R. Eid (Eds.), *Emerging Research in Islamic Marketing and Tourism in the Global Economy* (pp. 160–189). IGI Global Publishing. doi:10.4018/978-1-4666-6272-8.ch008

Medhekar, A., & Haq, F. (2016). Medical Tourism Development in Dubai: Managing Challenges and Opportunities. *Global Journal of Business and Social Science Review*, *4*(4), 20–28.

Medhekar, A., & Newby, L. (2012). Information Search for Medical Treatment Abroad. *Journal of Applied Global Research*, *5*(3), 53–72.

Medhekar, A., Wong, H. Y., & Hall, J. (2014). Medical tourism: A theoretical framework for an innovation in global healthcare provision. In A. Goyal (Ed.), *Innovations in services marketing and management: Strategies for emerging economies* (pp. 148–169). Hershey, PA: IGI Global. doi:10.4018/978-1-4666-4671-1.ch009

Medhekar, A., Wong, H. Y., & Hall, J. (2019). Factors influencing inbound medical travel to India. *Journal of Health Organization and Management*, *33*(2), 155–172. doi:10.1108/JHOM-08-2018-0234 PMID:30950309

Medical Tourism Index (MTI). (2019). *Medical Tourism: Dubai Global Ranking*. Retrieved from https://www.medicaltourismindex.com/destination/dubai/

Medvedev, A. E., Molotnikov, A., Lapovok, R., Zeller, R., Berner, S., Habersetzer, P., & Dalla Torre, F. (2016). Microstructure and mechanical properties of Ti–15Zr alloy used as dental implant material. *Journal of the Mechanical Behavior of Biomedical Materials*, *62*, 384–398. doi:10.1016/j.jmbbm.2016.05.008 PMID:27258932

MEE. (2013). *Plano Estratégico Nacional do Turismo: Horizonte 2013-2015*. Lisboa: Ministério da Economia e do Emprego.

MEI. (2007). *Plano Estratégico Nacional do Turismo*. Lisboa: Ministério da Economia e da Inovação.

Merri, M., Areden, D. C., & Motley, J. G. (1990). Sampling frequency of the electrocardiogram for spectral analysis of heart rate variability. *IEEE Transactions on Biomedical Engineering*, *37*(1), 99–106. doi:10.1109/10.43621 PMID:2303276

Michael, I., Armstrong, A., Badran, B., & King, B. (2011). Dubai Outbound Tourism: An Exploratory Study of Emiratis and Expatriates. *Journal of Vacation Marketing*, *17*(1), 83–91. doi:10.1177/1356766710391448

Michael, N., Wien, C., & Reisinger, Y. (2017). Push and Pull Escape Travel Motivations of Emirati Nationals to Australia. *International Journal of Culture, Tourism and Hospitality Research, 11*(3), 274–296. doi:10.1108/IJCTHR-04-2016-0039

Mikati, T., Taur, Y., Seo, S. K., & Shah, M. K. (2010). International Travel Patterns for Patients Diagnosed with Cancer. *Abstracts of the 48th Annual Meeting of IDSA*. Retrieved from https://idsa.confex.com/

Mikati, T., Taur, Y., Seo, S. K., & Shah, M. K. (2013). International Travel Patterns and Travel Risks of Patients Diagnosed With Cancer. *Journal of Travel Medicine, 20*(2), 71–77. doi:10.1111/jtm.12013 PMID:23464712

Miller, E., & West, D. (2008). Characteristics associated with use of public and private web sites as sources of health care information. *Medical Care, 45*(3), 245–251. doi:10.1097/01.mlr.0000244509.60556.49 PMID:17304082

Miller, J. (2005). Wellness: The history and development of a concept. *Spektrum Freizeit, 1*, 84–102.

Ministry of Tourism (MOT). (2012). *Incredible India Theme Brochures- Government of India*. Retrieved from http://tourism.gov.in/tourism

Ministry of Tourism Government of India (MOT-GOI). (2018). *Wellness & Medical Tourism*. Retrieved from http://tourism.gov.in/wellness-medical-tourism

Miquel, L., Manthey, J., Rehm, J., Vela, E., Bustins, M., Segura, L., ... Gual, A. (2018). Risky alcohol use: The impact on health service use. *European Addiction Research, 24*(5), 234–244. doi:10.1159/000493884 PMID:30282079

Mirzaei, M., Aspin, C., Essue, B., Jeon, Y. H., Dugdale, P., Usherwood, T., & Leeder, S. (2013). A patient-centered approach to health service delivery: Improving health outcomes for people with chronic illness. *BMC Health Services Research, 13*(1), 251. doi:10.1186/1472-6963-13-251 PMID:23819721

Mochi, P., Shetty, N., & Vahoniya, D. (2013). Medical tourism-destination India. *Commerce and Management, 2*(3), 29–39.

Moghavvemi, S., Ormond, M., Musa, G., Isa, C. R., & Chandy, J. (2017). Connecting with prospective medical tourists online: A cross-sectional analysis of private hospital websites promoting medical tourism in India, Malaysia and Thailand. *Tourism Management, 58*(Feb), 154–163. doi:10.1016/j.tourman.2016.10.010

Mohamad, W. N., Omar, A., & Haron, M. S. (2012). The moderating effect of medical travel facilitators in medical tourism. *Procedia: Social and Behavioral Sciences, 65*, 358–363. doi:10.1016/j.sbspro.2012.11.134

Mohanlal, P. (2008). The Holistic Approach of Ayurveda. *Ayurveda &Health Tourism, 3*(1), 22–26.

Mohanty, D., & Madhav, T. P. (2006). Medical Tourism: India's Competitive Advantage. In *Health tourism an Introduction*. ICFAI University Press.

Mohsenzade, A. (2007). Stress Management. Journal of Management Advice (Industrial Development and Renovation Organization of Iran), 31-44.

Moorcraft, S. Y., Marriott, C., Peckitt, C., Cunningham, D., Chau, I., Starling, N., ... Rao, S. (2016). Patients' Willingness to Participate in Clinical Trials and Their Views on Aspects of Cancer Research: Results of a Prospective Patient Survey. *Trials*, *17*(17). doi:10.118613063-015-1105-3 PMID:26745891

Moore, A. A., Gould, R., Reuben, D. B., Greendale, G. A., Carter, M. K., Zhou, K., & Karlamangla, A. (2005). Longitudinal patterns and predictors of alcohol consumption in the United States. *American Journal of Public Health*, *95*(3), 458–464. doi:10.2105/AJPH.2003.019471 PMID:15727977

Mordor Intelligence. (2019). *Global Medical Tourism Market Report*. Author.

Morgan, M. A. (2007). Another view of "humanitarian ventures" and "fistula tourism". *International Urogynecology Journal and Pelvic Floor Dysfunction*, *18*(6), 705–707. doi:10.100700192-007-0309-9 PMID:17252312

Mossakowski, K. N. (2008). Is the duration of poverty and unemployment a risk factor for heavy drinking? *Social Science & Medicine*, *67*(6), 947–955. doi:10.1016/j.socscimed.2008.05.019 PMID:18573582

Mueller, H., & Kaufmann, E. (2001). Wellness tourism: Market analysis of a special health tourism segment and implications for the hotel industry. *Journal of Vacation Marketing*, *7*(1), 5–17.

Murray, M., & Berwick, D. M. (2003). Advanced Access Reducing Waiting and Delays in Primary Care. *Innovations in Primary Care.*, *289*(8), 1035–1040. PMID:12597760

Mutalip, M. H. B. A., Kamarudin, R. B., Manickam, M., Abd Hamid, H. A. B., & Saari, R. B. (2014). Alcohol consumption and risky drinking patterns in Malaysia: Findings from NHMS 2011. *Alcohol and Alcoholism (Oxford, Oxfordshire)*, *49*(5), 593–599. doi:10.1093/alcalc/agu042 PMID:25015981

Myers, G., Martin, G., Magid, N., Barnett, P., Wiess, J., Lesch, M., & Singer, D. H. (1986). Power spectral analysis of heart rate variability in sudden cardiac death: Comparison to other methods. *IEEE Transactions on Biomedical Engineering*, *BME-33*(12), 1149–1156. doi:10.1109/TBME.1986.325694 PMID:3817848

Naik, M. (2018). *Best Yoga Retreat in India*. Retrieved 27 July 2019, from https://medium.com/@medhan811/best-yoga-retreat-in-india-aafb1126d1df

Naik, N., & Lal, S. (2013). Economic Analysis of Indian Medical Tourism (International Healthcare Destination). *International Journal of Business Management, Economics and Information Technology*, *5*, 269–277.

Nakayama, M., Chen, C., & Ractham, P. (2018). Medical tourism for cosmetic procedures: Credibility assessment of service providers via online health forums. Handbook of Research on Emerging Perspectives on Healthcare Information Systems and Informatics, 498-514.

Nash, D. (2013). *Anthropology of tourism* (1st ed.). Oxford, UK: Pergamon.

National Geographical Traveller. (2012). *In search of serenity*. Retrieved 18 July 2019, from http://carolineeden.com/CarolineEden/Travel_features_files/NGT1012_104_kerala.pdf

Nekoranec, J., & Kmosena, M. (2015). Stress in the workplace-sources, effects and coping strategies. *Review of the Air Force Academy,* (1), 163.

Nelson, J. P. (2014). Gender differences in alcohol demand: A systematic review of the role of prices and taxes. *Health Economics*, *23*(10), 1260–1280. doi:10.1002/hec.2974 PMID:23868570

Netto, N. (2004). *Tourism development in Kerala* (1st ed.). New Delhi: Sage.

Newton, J. N., Henderson, J., & Goldacre, M. J. (1995). Waiting list dynamics and the impact of earmarked funding. *BMJ (Clinical Research Ed.)*, *311*(7008), 783–785. doi:10.1136/bmj.311.7008.783 PMID:7580440

Nino-Murcia, A., Pinto Ramirez, J. L., & Nino-Torres, L. (2018). Organ transplantation in Colombia. *Transplantation*, *102*(11), 1779–1783. doi:10.1097/TP.0000000000002409 PMID:30346371

Nollo, G., Del Greco, M., Ravelli, F., & Disertori, M. (1994). Evidence of low and high frequency oscillations in human AV interval variability: Evaluation with spectral analysis. *American Journal of Physiology. Heart and Circulatory Physiology*, *267*(4), H1410–h-1418. doi:10.1152/ajpheart.1994.267.4.H1410 PMID:7943386

Nordin, N., Norsyafawati, W., Radzi, W. M., Razak, R. C., Abdullah, S., Hamzah, M. R., ... Idrus, S. (2018). Complaints and compliments assessment in developing service delivery measurement. *Management Science Letters*, *8*, 293–304. doi:10.5267/j.msl.2018.4.018

Noree, T. (2015). *The impact of medical tourism on the domestic economy and private health system: A case study of Thailand* (PhD thesis). London School of Hygiene & Tropical Medicine. doi:10.17037/PUBS.02267963

Noree, T., Hanefelf, J., & Smith, R. (2014). UK medical tourists in Thailand: They are not who you think they are. *Globalization and Health*, *10*(29), 1–7. PMID:24885204

Novo, A. (2014). *Internacionalização na saúde: O cluster do turismo médico em Portugal* (Master dissertation). University of Minho, Braga.

Nwosu, B., & Onah, G. (2016). The role of government in driving human capital development in the tourism industry in Nigeria. *Worldwide Hospitality and Tourism Themes*, *8*(2), 221–234. doi:10.1108/WHATT-11-2015-0047

Nylén, U. (2007). Interagency collaboration in human services: Impact of formalization and intensity on effectiveness. *Public Administration*, *85*(1), 143–166. doi:10.1111/j.1467-9299.2007.00638.x

O'Hare, T., & Sherrer, M. V. (2006). Stress, Recent Changes in Alcohol Consumption Level, and Problem Drinking in FreshmanFirst Offenders. *Journal of Human Behavior in the Social Environment*, *13*(3), 33–50. doi:10.1300/J137v13n03_03

OECD. (2014). *Health at a glance: Europe 2014*. Paris: Organization for Economic Co-operation and Development.

OECD. (2015). *Tackling Harmful Alcohol Use: Economics and Public Health Policy*. OECD publishing.

Omar, F., Hassan, N., Hussain, H., Mana, S., & Awad, O. (2015). Travel Health, Gaps in Knowledge, Attitudes, and Practices among Dubai Travellers, Dubai, UAE. *International Journal of Preventive Medicine Research*, *1*(3), 126–131.

Ormond, M., & Sothern, M. (2012). You, too, can be an international medical traveler:reading medical travel guidebooks. *Health & Place*, *5*(18), 935–941. doi:10.1016/j.healthplace.2012.06.018 PMID:22809711

Osborne, B. (2000). Ayurveda: The Food Balancing Act (1st ed.). London: Janus Publishing Company Limited.

Osowski, S., Hoai, L. T., & Markiewicz, T. (2004). Support vector machine-based expert system for reliable heart beat recognition. *IEEE Transactions on Biomedical Engineering*, *51*(4), 582–589. doi:10.1109/TBME.2004.824138 PMID:15072212

Oxford Business Group. (2017). *Medical Tourism Grows in Dubai*. Retrieved from https://oxfordbusinessgroup.com/analysis/healthy-returns-medical-tourism-segment-

Pachanee, C-. (2009) Implications on Public Health from Mode 2 Trade in Health Services: Empirical Evidence [A Case of Thailand]. *Workshop on the Movement of Patients Across International Borders- Emerging Challenges and Opportunities for Health Care Systems.*

Panahifar, F., Ghadimi, P., Azadnia, A. H., Heavey, C., & Byrne, P. J. (2013). A Study on CPFR Implementation Critical Factors for the Automotive Spare Part Industry. *8th EUROSIM Congress on Modelling and Simulation*, 1-6. 10.1109/EUROSIM.2013.11

Pande, A. (2010). Commercial Surrogacy in India: Manufacturing the perfect mother worker. *Signs (Chicago, Ill.)*, *35*(4), 969–992. doi:10.1086/651043

Panigrahi, A. (2017). Managing Stress at Workplace. *Journal of Management Research and Analysis*, *3*, 154–160. doi:10.18231/2394-2770.2016.0001

Panzarasa, S., Maddé, S., Quaglini, S., Pistarini, C., & Stefanelli, M. (2002). Evidence-based careflow management systems: The case of post-stroke rehabilitation. *Journal of Biomedical Informatics*, *35*(2), 123–139. doi:10.1016/S1532-0464(02)00505-1 PMID:12474426

Pärna, K., Rahu, K., Helakorpi, S., & Tekkel, M. (2010). Alcohol consumption in Estonia and Finland: Finbalt survey 1994-2006. *BMC Public Health*, *10*(1), 261. doi:10.1186/1471-2458-10-261 PMID:20482852

Patel. (2011). Globalization of Ayurveda a global vision for the next decade. *International Ayurveda Facilitator*.

Pathak, N. K., & Kumar, P. (2016). Alcohol and tobacco use among male aged 15 year and above in urban area of Ghaziabad city, Uttar Pradesh, India: An epidemiological study. *International Journal Of Community Medicine And Public Health, 3*(11), 3026–3029. doi:10.18203/2394-6040.ijcmph20163904

Patients Beyond Borders. (2011). *Medical Tourism Statistics & Facts*. Retrieved from https://patientsbeyondborders.com/

Patients Beyond Borders. (2019). *Medical Tourism Statistics & Facts*. Retrieved from: https://patientsbeyondborders.com/medical-tourism-statistics-facts

Peltola, M. A. (2012). Role of Editing of R–R Intervals in the Analysis of Heart Rate Variability. *Frontiers in Physiology, 3*(148), 1–10. PMID:22654764

Peng, B.-L., & Ling, L. (2019). Association between rural-to-urban migrants' social medical insurance, social integration and their medical return in China: A nationally representative cross-sectional data analysis. *BMC Public Health, 19*(1), 86. doi:10.118612889-019-6416-y PMID:30658619

Perdue, C., & Noble, S. (2007). Foreign Travel for Advanced Cancer Patients: A Guide for Healthcare Professionals. *Postgraduate Medical Journal, 83*(981), 437–444. doi:10.1136/pgmj.2006.054593 PMID:17621611

Pereira, R. T., Malone, C. M., & Flaherty, G. T. (2018). Aesthetic journeys: A review of cosmetic surgery tourism. *Journal of Travel Medicine, 25*(1).

Peters, X., & Gangemi, A. (2018). An update on bariatric tourism: Time for a national registry? *Surgery for Obesity and Related Diseases, 14*(4), 528–532. doi:10.1016/j.soard.2017.12.018 PMID:29426706

Piccoli, L., Dubey, A., Simone, J. N., & Kowalkowlski, J. B. (2010). LQCD workflow execution framework: Models, provenance and fault-tolerance. *Journal of Physics: Conference Series, 219*(1 part 7), 072047. doi:10.1088/1742-6596/219/7/072047

Pocock, S. N., & Phua, H. K. (2011). Medical tourism and policy implications for health systems: A conceptual framework from a comparative study of Thailand, Singapore and Malaysia. *Globalization and Health, 7*(1), 12. doi:10.1186/1744-8603-7-12 PMID:21539751

Ponta, L., Scalas, E., Raberto, M., & Cincotti, S. (2012) Statistical analysis and agent-based microstructure modeling of high-frequency financial trading. *IEEE Journal on Selected Topics in Signal Processing, 6*(4), 381-387.

Pordié, L. (2013). Spaces of Connectivity, Shifting Temporality. Enquiries in Transnational Health. European Journal of Transnational Studies. *European Journal Of Transnational Studies, 5*(1), 6–26.

Portet, F., Hernanadez, A. I., & Carrault, G. (2005). Evaluation of real time QRS detection algorithm in variable contexts. *Medical & Biological Engineering & Computing, 43*(3), 379–385. doi:10.1007/BF02345816 PMID:16035227

Prasinos, M., Spanoudakis, G., & Koutsouris, D. (2017). Towards a model-driven platform for evidence-based public health policymaking. *Proceedings of the International Conference on Software Engineering and Knowledge Engineering*, 566-571. 10.18293/SEKE2017-180

Rafiee, J., Rafiee, M. A., Prause, N., & Schoen, M. P. (2011). Wavelet basis functions in biomedical signal processing Expert Systems with Applications. *Expert Systems with Applications*, *38*(5), 6190–6201. doi:10.1016/j.eswa.2010.11.050

Ramesh, U., & Joseph, K. (2012). The holistic approach of Ayurveda based wellness tourism in Kerala. International Journal of Advanced Research in Management, 29-39.

Ramesh, U., & Joseph, K. (2012). The holistic approach of ayurveda based wellness tourism in Kerala. *International Journal of Research in Management, 3*(2).

Ramesh, U., & Joseph, K. (2012). The holistic approach of Ayurveda based wellness tourism in Kerala. *The Holistic Approach of Ayurveda Based Wellness Tourism in Kerala, 3*(2), 29-39.

Rao, K. S., Nundy, M., & Dua, A. S. (2005). *Delivery of health services in the private sector." Financing and delivery of health care services in India. National Commission on Macroeconomics and Health–Background papers. Ministry of Health and Family Welfare*. Government of India.

Rath, S. P., Das, B., Mishra, S., & Puthan, P. (2012). New Avenue of Tourism & Revenue Generation in India-Medical Tourism. *International Journal of Business and Management Tomorrow*, *2*(1), 11–14.

Reddy, P. C. (2000). Healthcare Services in the New Millennium. *Management and Labour Studies*, 115.

Reddy, S., & Qadeer, I. (2010). Medical Tourism in India: Progress or Predicament? *Economic and Political Weekly*, *XLV*(20), 69–75.

Rehm, J., Baliunas, D., Brochu, S., Fischer, B., Gnam, W., Patra, J., & Adlaf, E. (2006). *The costs of substance abuse in Canada 2002*. Ottawa: Canadian Centre on Substance Abuse.

Reikkinen, H., & Rautaharju, P. (1976). Body position, electrode level and respiration effects on the Frank lead electrocardiogram. *Circulation*, *53*(1), 40–45. doi:10.1161/01.CIR.53.1.40 PMID:127674

Rekha Sahoo, S. (2016). Management of Stress at Workplace. *Global Journal of Management and Business Research.*

Reniers, G. (2011). Investigating the factors facilitating (a.o. safety and security) collaboration in the chemicals sector. *International Journal of Safety and Security Engineering*, *1*(1), 18–32. doi:10.2495/SAFE-V1-N1-18-32

Renu Madhavi, C. H. (2012). *Characterisation of Heart Rate Variability of Healthy, Cardiac and Non-cardiac Diseased Subjects using Nonlinear Techniques* (Ph. D. Thesis). Avinashilingam University for Women, Coimbatore, India.

Renu Madhavi, C. H., & Ananth, A. G. (2012). A Review of Heart Rate Variability and It's Association with Diseases. *International Journal of Soft Computing and Engineering*, *2*(3), 2231–2307.

Rerkrujipimol, J., & Assenov, I. (2011). Marketing Strategies for Promoting Medical Tourism in Thailand. *Journal of Tourism. Hospitality & Culinary Arts*, *3*(2), 95–105.

Revathi, A., Borrás, A. D., Muñoz, A. I., Richard, C., & Manivasagam, G. (2017). Degradation mechanisms and future challenges of titanium and its alloys for dental implant applications in oral environment. *Materials Science and Engineering C*, *76*, 1354–1368. doi:10.1016/j.msec.2017.02.159 PMID:28482503

Richmond, C. (1996). NHS waiting list have been a boon for private medicine in the UK. *CMAJ: Canadian Medical Association Journal*, *154*(3), 378. PMID:8564909

Ridderstaat, J., Singh, D., & DeMicco, F. (2019). The impact of major tourist markets on health tourism spending in the United States. *Journal of Destination Marketing & Management*, *11*, 270–280. doi:10.1016/j.jdmm.2018.05.003

RNCOS. (2010). *Booming Medical Tourism in India. Tourism Industry Research Solutions*. New Delhi: RNCOS E-Services.

RNCOS. (2010). *Tourism Industry: Booming Medical Tourism in India, Industry Research Solutions*. New Delhi: RNCOS E-Services Pvt Ltd.

Romero, D., & Molina, A. (2011). Collaborative networked organizations and customer communities: Value co-creation and co-innovation in the networking era. *Production Planning and Control*, *22*(5-6), 447–472. doi:10.1080/09537287.2010.536619

Rosales, C. R., Magazine, M., & Rao, U. (2015). The 2Bin system for controlling medical supplies at point-of-use. *European Journal of Operational Research*, *243*(1), 271–280. doi:10.1016/j.ejor.2014.10.041

Ross, K. (2001). *Health tourism: An overview by Kim Ross*. Retrieved on February 25, 2015, from http://www.hospitalitynet.org/news/4010521.html

Rossetti, M. D., Buyurgan, N., & Pohl, E. (2012). Medical Supply Logistics, *International Series in Operations Research &. Management Science*, *168*, 245–280.

Ruckert, R., & Labonté, R. (2014). Public-private-partnerships in global health: The good, the bad and the ugly. *Third World Quarterly*, *35*(9), 1598–1614. doi:10.1080/01436597.2014.970870

Runnels, V., & Turner, L. (2011). Bioethics and transnational medical travel: India, 'medical tourism', and the globalisation of healthcare. *Indian Journal of Medical Ethics*, *8*(1), 42–44. PMID:22106599

Runnels, V., & Turner, L. (2011). Bioethics and transnational medical travel: India, "medical tourism", and the globalisation of healthcare. *Indian Journal of Medical Ethics*, *8*(1), 42–44. PMID:22106599

Saadatnia, F., & Mehregan, M. R. (2014). Determining and prioritizing factors affecting to increase customers attraction of medical tourism from the perspective of Arabic countries. *International Journal of Marketing Studies*, *3*(6), 155.

Saavedra, K. P. (2015). Millennials as Travelers. *BusinessMirror*. Retrieved from https://businessmirror.com.ph/

Sag, I., & Zengul, F.D. (2018). Why do medical tourists choose Turkey as a medical tourism destination? *Journal of Hospitality and Tourism Insight*. doi:10.1108/JHTI-05-2018-0031

Saini, B. S. (2009). *Signal Processing of Heart Rate Variability* (Ph. D. Thesis). Dr. B. R. Ambedkar National Institute of Technology, Jalandhar, India.

Saini, M., Singh, Y., Arora, P., Arora, V., & Jain, K. (2015). Implant biomaterials: A comprehensive review. *World Journal of Clinical Cases: WJCC*, *3*(1), 52. doi:10.12998/wjcc.v3.i1.52 PMID:25610850

Salam, M. A., & Khan, S. A. (2016). Value creation through lean management: A case study of healthcare service operations. *International Journal of Services and Operations Management*, *25*(3), 275–293. doi:10.1504/IJSOM.2016.079513

Samaranayake, P., & Kiridena, S. (2011). *Patient Journey Modeling Using Integrated Data Structures in Healthcare Service Operations*. Penang: IEEE CHUSER. doi:10.1109/CHUSER.2011.6163802

Sandal, C. (2019). By the Way. the Last-Minute International Traveler. *Workplace Health & Safety*, *67*(2), 53–55. doi:10.1177/2165079918806535 PMID:30428770

Sandberg, D. S. (2017). Medical tourism: An emerging global healthcare industry. *International Journal of Healthcare Management*, *10*(4), 281–288. doi:10.1080/20479700.2017.1296213

Sanden, R., Everwijn, H., Rouwette, E., & Gubbels, J. (2005). Balancing supply and demand for dementia care in the Netherlands. *The Town Planning Review*, 1–23.

Savaşan, A., Yalvaç, M., Uzunboylu, H., & Tuncel, E. (2018). Article. *Quality & Quantity*, *52*(Suppl 1), 285–303. doi:10.100711135-017-0612-6

Sayers, B. M. (1973). Analysis of heart rate variability. *Ergonomics*, *16*(1), 17–32. doi:10.1080/00140137308924479 PMID:4702060

Schreibman, K. L., Thomas, C. W., & Levy, M. N. (1989). Spectral analysis of cardiac cycle length variations: Resampling overcomes effects of nonuniform spacing. In *Proceedings of the 11th Annual International Conference of the IEEE EMBS* (vol. 1, pp. 40-41). IEEE. 10.1109/IEMBS.1989.95561

Seaborn, G. (2010). *Changes in Autonomic Tone Resulting from Circumferential Pulmonary Vein Isolation* (M. S. Thesis). Queen's University, Kingston, Ontario, Canada.

Seifert, D. (2003). Collaborative planning, forecasting, and replenishment: How to create a supply chain advantage. American Management Association.

Şenyiğit, E., & Demirel, B. (2018). The selection of material in dental implant with entropy based simple additive weighting and analytic hierarchy process methods. *Sigma J Eng & Nat Sci*, *36*(3), 731–740.

Shah, M. K. (2016). The Immunocompromised Traveler. *Oncology*, *30*(2), 142–159. Retrieved from http://www.cancernetwork.com/oncology-journal/immunocompromised-traveler PMID:26888792

Shalini, P. (2017). Bridging Healthcare with Wellness Tourism in India. *Indian Journal Of Public Health Research & Development*, *8*(4), 345. doi:10.5958/0976-5506.2017.00367.9

Sharafuddin, M. A. (2015). Siddha and Wellness tourism: Opportunities and challenges for "Brand Tamilnadu". *Int. J. Res. Ayurveda Pharm.*, *6*(3), 387–394. doi:10.7897/2277-4343.06376

Sharpley, R. (2008). Planning for Tourism: The Case of Dubai. *Tourism and Hospitality Planning & Development*, *5*(1), 13–30. doi:10.1080/14790530801936429

Sheldon, P.J. & Park, S.Y. (2008). Sustainable wellness tourism: Governance and Entrepreneurship Issues. *Acta turis-tca, 20*(2), 151-172.

Shetty, P. (2010). Medical tourism booms in India, but at what cost? *Lancet*, *37*(6), 671–672. doi:10.1016/S0140-6736(10)61320-7 PMID:20879077

Sibthorpe, B., & Gardner, K. (2007). A conceptual framework for performance assessment in primary health care. *Australian Journal of Primary Health*, *13*(2), 96–103. doi:10.1071/PY07027

Silva, V. (2019). *Up and About: Etihad Offers Services to Passengers with Pre-Existing Medical Conditions*. Retrieved from https://apex.aero/2019/01/16/caring-passengers-preexisting-conditions

Simmons, J. (2013). *Autonomic Nervous System Response to Repeated Cold Exposure* (M. S. Thesis). Louisiana State University.

Singh, Y. N. (2007). *ECG Delineation and its Application in Individual Identification* (M. Tech Thesis). Indian Institute of Technology, Kanpur, India.

Singh, D., Vinod, K., Saxena, S. C., & Deepak, K. K. (2004). Effects of RR segment duration on HRV spectrum estimation. *Physiological Measurement*, *25*(3), 721–735. doi:10.1088/0967-3334/25/3/012 PMID:15253123

Singh, J., Cuttler, L., & Silvers, J. (2007). Toward understanding consumers' role in medical decisions for emerging treatments: Issues, framework and hypothesis. *Journal of Business Research*, (57): 1054–1065.

Singh, P. K. (2008). *Medical Tourism*. New Delhi, India: Kanishka Publishers.

Sjölund, S., Hemmingsson, T., & Allebeck, P. (2015). IQ and level of alcohol consumption—Findings from a national survey of Swedish conscripts. *Alcoholism, Clinical and Experimental Research*, *39*(3), 548–555. doi:10.1111/acer.12656 PMID:25702705

Smith, M. K., & Puczkó, L. (2016). The Routledge Handbook of Health Tourism. Routledge Publication.

Smith. (2015). *The brave approach to writing a joint business plan with a UK supermarket.* Retrieved from: www.makingbusinessmatter.co.uk

Smith, A. K., Shara, N. M., Zeymo, A., Harris, K., Estes, R., Johnson, L. B., & Al-Refaie, W. B. (2015). Travel Patterns of Cancer Surgery Patients in a Regionalized System. *The Journal of Surgical Research, 199*(1), 97–105. doi:10.1016/j.jss.2015.04.016 PMID:26076685

Smith, M., & Puczko, L. (2009). *Health and Wellness Tourism.* Oxford, UK: Elsevier.

Smith, M., & Puczkó, L. (2009). *Health and wellness tourism.* Oxford, UK: Elsevier.

Smith, M., & Puczko, L. (2014). *Spa, Wellness and Medical Travel (2nd ed.).* London: Routledge.

Smith, R., Álvarez, M. M., & Chanda, R. (2011). Medical tourism: A review of the literature and analysis of a role for bi-lateral trade. *Health Policy (Amsterdam), 103*(2-3), 276–282. doi:10.1016/j.healthpol.2011.06.009 PMID:21767892

Smith, R., Chanda, R., & Viroj, T. (2009). Trade in health-related services. *Lancet, 373*(9663), 593–601. doi:10.1016/S0140-6736(08)61778-X PMID:19167053

Snepenger, D., King, J., Marshall, E., & Uysal, M. (2006). Modeling Iso-Ahola's Motivation Theory in the Tourism Context. *Journal of Travel Research, 45*(2), 140–149. doi:10.1177/0047287506291592

Sohyeon, K., & Won, S. L. (2019). Network text analysis of medical tourism in newspapers using text mining: The South Korea case. *Tourism Management Perspectives, 31*, 332–339. doi:10.1016/j.tmp.2019.05.010

Soler-Vila, H., Galán, I., Donado-Campos, J., Sánchez-Alfonso, F., Valencia-Martín, J. L., Morilla, F., ... Rodríguez-Artalejo, F. (2014). Three-year changes in drinking patterns in Spain: A prospective population-based cohort study. *Drug and Alcohol Dependence, 140*, 123–129. doi:10.1016/j.drugalcdep.2014.04.006 PMID:24799288

Sornmo, L., & Laguna, P. (2005). *Bioelectrical Signal processing in cardiac and neurological applications.* Elsevier Academic Press.

Spline Interpolation. (n.d.). Retrieved from the Spline Interpolation Wiki: http://en.wikipedia.org/wiki/Spline_interpolation

Spline Mathematics. (n.d.). Retrieved from the Sline Mathematics. Wiki: http://en.wikipedia.org/wiki/Spline_%28mathematics%29

Stade, B., Ungar, W. J., Stevens, B., Beyene, J., & Koren, G. (2006). The burden of prenatal exposure to alcohol: Measurement of cost. *Journal of FAS International, 4*, e5.

Stephenson, M. L. (2014). Deciphering 'Islamic hospitality': Developments, Challenges and Opportunities. *Tourism Management, 40*, 155–164. doi:10.1016/j.tourman.2013.05.002

Stephenson, M. L. (2014). Tourism, development and 'destination Dubai: Cultural dilemmas and future challenges. *Current Issues in Tourism*, *17*(8), 723–738. doi:10.1080/13683500.2012.754411

Stolley, K., & Watson, S. (2012). Contemporary World Issue: Medical Tourism. *ABC-CLIO*, 3.

Stolley, K., & Watson, S. (2012). *Medical Tourism: A Reference Handbook -Contemporary world issues*. Retrieved from https://www.visitdubai.com

Subady, B. N., Assanangkornchai, S., & Chongsuvivatwong, V. (2013). Prevalence, patterns and predictors of alcohol consumption in a mountainous district of B hutan. *Drug and Alcohol Review*, *32*(4), 435–442. doi:10.1111/dar.12015 PMID:23231462

Sultana, S., Haque, A., Momen, A., & Yasmin, F. (2014). Factors affecting the attractiveness of medical tourism destination: An Empirical Study on India- Review Article. *Iranian Journal of Public Health*, *43*(7), 867–876. PMID:25909055

Sultana, S., Haque, A., Momen, A., & Yasmin, F. (2014). Factors affecting the attractiveness of medical tourism destination: An empirical study on India. *Iranian Journal of Public Health*, *43*(7), 867–876. PMID:25909055

Sungpo Yi, S., & Li, X. (2018). Hotel guests' perception of best green practices: A content analysis of online reviews. *Tourism and Hospitality Research*, *18*(2), 191–202. doi:10.1177/1467358416637251

T, S., & Mariswamy, H. (2016). The Role of Health Tourism on Tourism Development in Kerala State: An Evaluation. *IRA-International Journal of Management & Social Sciences*, *4*(2), 494-501.

Takahashi, A., & Hayashi, T. (2017). Collaborative quality framework: QoE-centric service operation in collaboration with users, service providers, and network operators. *EICE Transactions on Communications*, (9), 1554-1563.

Tang, C. F., & Lau, E. (2017). Modelling the demand for inbound medical tourism: The case of Malaysia. *International Journal of Tourism Research*, *19*(5), 584–593. doi:10.1002/jtr.2131

Tan, J., Wen, H. J., & Awad, N. (2005). Health care and services delivery systems as complex adaptive systems. *Communications of the ACM*, *48*(5), 36–44. doi:10.1145/1060710.1060737

Task force of the European society of cardiology and the North American society of pacing and electrophysiology Heart rate variability - standards of measurement. Physiological interpretation and clinical use (1996). *Circulation*, *93*(5), 1043–1065.

Telej, E., & Gamble, J. (2019). Yoga wellness tourism: a study of marketing strategies in India. *Journal of Consumer Marketing*, 1-12. doi:10.1108/jcm-07-2018-2788

Thakor, N. V., & Webster, J. G. (1980). Ground free ECG recording using two electrodes. *IEEE Transactions on Biomedical Engineering*, *27*(12), 699–704. doi:10.1109/TBME.1980.326595 PMID:7461645

Thanuskodi, A. (2016). A Webometric Analysis of Medical Tourism Websites in Kerala. *Library Philosophy And Practice*, *1*(1), 11–14.

The United Arab Emirates Healthcare Sector. (2014). Retrieved from http://usuaebusiness.org/content/up-loads/2014/06/HealthcareReport.pdf

Tomkins, S., Saburova, L., Kiryanov, N., Andreev, E., McKee, M., Shkolnikov, V., & Leon, D. A. (2007). Prevalence and socio-economic distribution of hazardous patterns of alcohol drinking: Study of alcohol consumption in men aged 25–54 years in Izhevsk, Russia. *Addiction (Abingdon, England), 102*(4), 544–553. doi:10.1111/j.1360-0443.2006.01693.x PMID:17362291

Tooman, H. (2013, May 24). *A framework for health tourism.* Article presented at conference "The future of health tourism: Creativity, innovation and sustainability", Parnu.

Touré, S. B., Kleiderman, E., & Knoppers, B. M. (2018). Bridging stem cell research and medicine: A learning health system. *Regenerative Medicine, 13*(6), 741–752. doi:10.2217/rme-2017-0129 PMID:30043682

Tourism Authority of Thailand. (2002). *Health Tourism – The Rising Star: Strategies for Success, Thailand as a Center of Excellent Health of Asia.* Available at: http://www.tatnews.org/common/print.asp?id=1983

Touvier, M., Druesne-Pecollo, N., Kesse-Guyot, E., Andreeva, V. A., Galan, P., Hercberg, S., & Latino-Martel, P. (2014). Demographic, socioeconomic, disease history, dietary and lifestyle cancer risk factors associated with alcohol consumption. *International Journal of Cancer, 134*(2), 445–459. doi:10.1002/ijc.28365 PMID:23824873

Trade Arabia Business News. (2019). *Zulekha opens extended facility in Dubai.* Retrieved from http://www.tradearabia.com/news/HEAL_350315.html

Tribe, J. (1997). The indiscipline of tourism. *Annals of Tourism Research, 3*(24), 638–657. doi:10.1016/S0160-7383(97)00020-0

Tribe, J. (2009). *Philosophical issues in tourism.* Bristol, UK: Channel View Publications.

Tripathi, V., Elneil, S., & Romanzi, L. (2018). Demand and capacity to integrate pelvic organ prolapse and genital fistula services in low-resource settings. *International Urogynecology Journal and Pelvic Floor Dysfunction, 29*(10), 1509–1515. doi:10.100700192-018-3561-2 PMID:29411073

Trivedi, M. (2013). *Medical Tourism in India.* Academic Press.

Turismo de Portugal. (2017). *Turismo em Portugal 2017.* Retrieved on August 14, 2019, from http://travelbi.turismodeportugal.pt/pt-pt/Documents/Turismo%20em%20Portugal/turismo-em-portugal-2017.pdf

TurkStat. (2010). Health Survey 2010. Ankara: Turkish Statistical Institute Publication Number: 3654.

TurkStat. (2012). Health Survey 2012. Ankara: Turkish Statistical Institute Publication Number: 4117.

Turner, L. (2007). First World Healthcare at Third World Prices: Globalisation, Bioethics and Medical Tourism. *Biosocieties*, *2*(3), 303–325. doi:10.1017/S1745855207005765

Turner, L. (2007). From Durham to Delhi: 'medical tourism' and the global economy. In J. Cohen-Kohler & M. Seaton (Eds.), *Comparative program on health and society* (pp. 109–131). Toronto: University of Toronto.

Turner, M., Fielding, S., Ong, Y., Dibben, C., Feng, Z., Brewster, D. H., ... Murchie, P. (2017). A Cancer Geography Paradox? Poorer Cancer Outcomes with Longer Travelling times to Healthcare Facilities despite Prompter Diagnosis and Treatment: A Data-linkage Study. *British Journal of Cancer*, *117*(3), 439–449. doi:10.1038/bjc.2017.180 PMID:28641316

Tze-Yeng Chang, E. (2013). *Towards understanding the Electrogram: Theoretical & experimental multiscale modelling of factors affecting action potential propagation in cardiac tissue* (Ph. D. Thesis). Imperial College, London, UK.

UAE Vision. (2018). *Vision 2021: National Agenda*. Retrieved from https://www.vision2021.ae/en/national-agenda-2021

UAE. (2019). *Fact Sheet*. Retrieved from https://www.government.ae/en/about-the-uae/fact-sheet

United Nations World Tourism Organization. (2018). *2017 International Tourism Results: The Highest in Seven Years.* Retrieved from http://media.unwto.org/press-release/2018-01-15/2017-international-tourism-results-highest-seven-years

UNWTO & ETC. (2018). *Exploring health tourism*. Madrid: World Tourism Organization.

Urbach, N., Ahlemann, F., & El Arbi, F. (2014). Towards a design theory for customer satisfaction-oriented it vendor management. *20th Americas Conference on Information Systems*, 1-14.

Vaeth, P. A., Caetano, R., & Durazo, E. M. (2014). Ethnicity and alcohol consumption among US adults with diabetes. *Annals of Epidemiology*, *24*(10), 720–726. doi:10.1016/j.annepidem.2014.07.007 PMID:25169682

Vanassche, S., Sodermans, A. K., Matthijs, K., & Swicegood, G. (2014). The effects of family type, family relationships and parental role models on delinquency and alcohol use among Flemish adolescents. *Journal of Child and Family Studies*, *23*(1), 128–143. doi:10.100710826-012-9699-5

Varier, P. (1986). The management of the problem of ageing, according to the Ayurvedic system of medicine. *Centenary Souvenir, Vasudeva Vilasam Ayurveda Pharmacy*, (1), 1-50.

Varol, M. (2011). *Alkol Raporu*. İstanbul: Türkiye Yeşilay Cemiyeti.

Varona, P., Chang, M., García, R. G., & Bonet, M. (2011). Tobacco and alcohol use in Cuban women. *MEDICC Review*, *13*(4), 38–44. doi:10.1590/S1555-79602011000400009 PMID:22143606

Venkatesan, C., Karthigaikumar, P., & Satheeskumaran, S. (2018). Mobile cloud computing for ECG telemonitoring and real-time coronary heart disease risk detection. *Biomedical Signal Processing and Control*, *44*, 138–145. doi:10.1016/j.bspc.2018.04.013

Vetitnev, A., Kopyirin, A., & Kiseleva, A. (2016). System dynamics modelling and forecasting health tourism demand: The case of Russian resorts. *Current Issues in Tourism, 19*(7), 618–623. doi:10.1080/13683500.2015.1076382

VICS. (1998). *Collaborative Planning Forecasting and Replenishment (CPFR).* Voluntary Interindustry Commerce Standards.

VICS. (2004). *Collaborative Planning Forecasting and Replenishment (CPFR): An overview.* Voluntary Interindustry Commerce Standards.

Vijayraghvan, G. (2013). Green Marketing – Issues Concerning Indian Organisations. *International Journal in Multidisciplinary and Academic Research, 2*(5).

Vilal, J., Barro, S., Presedo, J., Ruiz, R., & Palacios, F. (1992). Analysis of heart rate variability with evenly spaced time values. *IEEE Transactions on Engineering in Medicine and Biology, 2*, 575–576. doi:10.1109/IEMBS.1992.595719

Voigt, C., & Pforr, C. (2013). *Wellness Tourism: A Destination Perspective.* Routledge Publication.

Voigt, C., Laing, J., Wray, M., Brown, G., Howat, G., Weiler, B., & Trembath, R. (2010). *Health tourism in Australia: Supply, demand and opportunities.* Queensland: CRC for Sustainable Tourism Pty.

Voigt, C., & Laing, J. H. (2010). Journey into Parenthood: Commodification of Reproduction as a New Tourism Niche Market. *Journal of Travel & Tourism Marketing, 27*(3), 252–268. doi:10.1080/10548401003744685

Wachowiak, M. P., & Shah, G. S. (2000). Wavelet-based noise removal for biomedical signals: A comparative study. *IEEE Transactions on Biomedical Engineering, 47*(3), 360–368. doi:10.1109/10.827298 PMID:10743778

Wang, S. J., Shahidehpour, S. M., Mokhtari, S., Irisarri, G. D., & Kirschen, D. S. (1995). Short-term generation scheduling with transmission and environmental constraints using an augmented Lagrangian relaxation. *IEEE Transactions on Power Systems, 10*(3), 1294–1301. doi:10.1109/59.466524

Welcome, M. O., Razvodovsky, Y. E., & Pereverzev, V. A. (2011). Prevalence of alcohol-related problems among the Slavs and Arabs in Belarus: A University survey. *The American Journal of Drug and Alcohol Abuse, 37*(3), 189–195. doi:10.3109/00952990.2011.563334 PMID:21453193

Wellness and Medical Tourism & the Ministry of Tourism. (2015). Retrieved from http://tourism.gov.in/wellness-medical-tourism

White, A., & Hingson, R. (2013). The burden of alcohol use: Excessive alcohol consumption and related consequences among college students. *Alcohol Research: Current Reviews, 35*(2), 201–218. PMID:24881329

Whittaker, A., & Chee, H. L. (2016). 'Flexible bio-citizenship' and international medical travel: Transnational mobilities for care in Asia. *International Sociology, 31*(3), 286–304. doi:10.1177/0268580916629623

WHO. (2002). *Traditional Medical Strategy 2002-2005*. World Health Organisation. Retrieved from http://whqlibdoc.who.int/hq/2002/who_edm_trm_2002.1.pdf

WHO. (2011). *Medical visas mark growth of Indian medical tourism*. WHO.

WHO. (2014). *Global status report on alcohol and health, 2014*. Luxembourg: World Health Organization.

Wirtz, J. (2016). Balancing Capacity and Demand in Service Operations. *Winning in Service Markets,* 308 – 343.

Wongkit, M., & McKercher, B. (2013). Towards a typology of medical tourists: A case study of Thailand. *Tourism Management, 38*, 4–12. doi:10.1016/j.tourman.2013.02.003

Woodman, J. (2007). *Singapore: Patients Beyond Borders: Singapore Edition*. Singapore: Healthy Travel Media.

World Health Organisation (WHO). (2015). *UAE Health Strategy*. Retrieved from http://www.who.int/countryfocus/cooperation_strategy/_en.pdf

World Health Organisation. (2001). *Macroeconomics and Health: Investing in Health for Economic Development. Report of the Commission on Macroeconomics and Health*. Geneva: WHO.

Xu, E., Wermus, M., & Bauman, D. B. (2011). Development of an integrated medical supply information system. *Enterprise Information Systems, 5*(3), 385–399. doi:10.1080/17517575.2011.566630

Xu, Y., Prats, X., & Delahaye, D. (2018) Synchronization of traffic flow and sector opening for collaborative demand and capacity balancing. *Proceedings AIAA/IEEE Digital Avionics Systems Conference*. 10.1109/DASC.2018.8569789

Yamamoto, Y., Kiyono, K., & Struzik, Z. R. (2004). Measurement analysis, interpretation of long term heart rate variability. In *Proceedings of SICE Annual Conference*, (pp. 2598-2605). Academic Press.

Yaogo, A., Fombonne, E., Kouanda, S., Lert, F., & Melchior, M. (2013). Lifecourse socioeconomic position and alcohol use in young adulthood: Results from the French TEMPO cohort study. *Alcohol and Alcoholism (Oxford, Oxfordshire), 49*(1), 109–116. doi:10.1093/alcalc/agt128 PMID:23900495

Ye, B., Qiu, H., & Yuen, P. (2011). Motivations and experiences of mainland Chinese medical tourists in Hong Kong. *Tourism Management, 5*(32), 1125–1127. doi:10.1016/j.tourman.2010.09.018

Yeh, J., Fa, S., & Shieh, J. (2009). Human heart beat analysis using a modified algorithm of detrended fluctuation analysis based on empirical mode decomposition. *Medical Engineering & Physics*, *31*(1), 92–100. doi:10.1016/j.medengphy.2008.04.011 PMID:18547859

Yeoh, E., Othman, K., & Ahmad, H. (2013). Understanding medical tourists: Word-ofmouth and viral marketing as potent marketing tools. *Tourism Management*, *34*, 19–201. doi:10.1016/j.tourman.2012.04.010

Yoong, W., Sulaiman, N., & Baldry, D. (2013, December). *A framework development for promoting medical tourism (MT to Malaysia using Internet strategy for international patient tourists (IPT)*. Article present at FPTP Postgraduate Seminar, Johor.

Yousaf, A., Amin, I., & Santos, J. A. C. (2018). Tourists' Motivations To Travel: A Theoretical Perspective On The Existing Literature. *Tourism and Hospitality Management*, *24*(1), 197–211. doi:10.20867/thm.24.1.8

Zaidan, E. A. (2016). Tourism shopping and new urban entertainment: A case study of Dubai. *Journal of Vacation Marketing*, *22*(1), 29–41. doi:10.1177/1356766715589426

Zain, A. A. (2018). Over 4,500 new cancer cases in UAE this year. *Khaleej Times*. Retrieved from https://www.khaleejtimes.com/

Zallocco, R. L., & Joseph, W. B. (1991). Strategic Market Planning in Hospitals: Is It Done? Does It Work? *Journal of Health Care Marketing*, *11*(1), 5–11. PMID:10110082

Zhang, Y., Zhang, Q., & Wu, S. (2008). Biomedical signal detection based on fractional Fourier transform. In *Proceedings of 5th International Conference on Information Technology and Application in Biomedicine*, (pp. 349-352) Shenzhen, China: Academic Press.

Zhou, Q. S., & Olsen, T. L. (2018). Rotating the medical supplies for emergency response: A simulation-based approach. *International Journal of Production Economics*, *196*, 1–11. doi:10.1016/j.ijpe.2017.11.010

Zhou, X., Su, Z., Deng, H.; Xiang, X., Chen, H., & Hao, W. (2006). A comparative survey on alcohol and tobacco use in urban and rural populations in the Huaihua District of Hunan Province, China. *Alcohol (Fayetteville, N.Y.)*, *39*(2), 87–96. doi:10.1016/j.alcohol.2006.07.003 PMID:17134661

Zhu, L., Petersen, P. E., Wang, H. Y., Bian, J. Y., & Zhang, B. X. (2003, October). Oral healthknowledge, attitudes and behaviour of children and adolescentsin China. *International Dental Journal*, *53*(5), 289–298. doi:10.1111/j.1875-595X.2003.tb00762.x PMID:14560803

Zion Market Research. (2018). Retrieved on 30/04/2019 from https://www.globenewswire.com/news-release/2018/06/25/1528923/0/en/Global-Medical-Tourism-Market-Expected-to-Reach-USD-28-0-Billion-by-2024-Zion-Market-Research.html

About the Contributors

Sudip Paul is an Assistant Professor in the Department of Biomedical Engineering, School of Technology, North-Eastern Hill University, India since June 2012. He received his Ph.D degree from Indian Institute of Technology (Banaras Hindu University), Varanasi with specialization in Electrophysiology and brain signal analysis. He has also presented his research accomplishments in USA, Greece, France and South Africa. He has many credentials in his credit out of which his First Prize in Sushruta Innovation Award 2011 sponsored by Department of Science and Technology, Govt. of India and also he also organized co many workshops and conferences out of which most significant are the 29th Annual meeting of the Society for Neurochemistry, India and IRBO/APRC Associate School 2017. He was selected as Post Doc Fellow under Biotechnology Overseas Associateship 2017-18 supported by Department of Biotechnology, Government of India. He published more than 70 International journal and conference papers and also filled four patent. Recently he wrote two books published by LAP LAMBERT Academic Publishing, Germany and also published three book chapters in different international publishers.

* * *

Sunildro L. S. Akoijam is currently working as an Assistant Professor in the area of Marketing and Strategy at the Department of Management, North-Eastern Hill University (NEHU), Tura Campus, Tura, Meghalaya (India). He has more than 8 years of teaching experience at University level. He has presented research papers and case studies in various international and national seminars and conferences. He has also participated in various workshops, symposiums, Faculty Development Programmes, short term certificate courses and academic related activities organized by premier management institutes in different parts of the country and abroad. He has visited foreign countries like South Korea, Singapore, Thailand, Malaysia, United Arab Emirates (UAE), Sri Lanka, Nepal, Bhutan, Mauritius, Indonesia and Myanmar for various academic programmes. His research papers have been published in various refereed international and national journals. He has also organized various academic events like seminars, conferences, workshops, training courses, symposium, management fest etc. He is a member of esteemed management associations like All India Management Association (AIMA), Rural Marketing Association of India (RMAI), Delhi Management Association (DMA), International Society for Development & Sustainability, Japan, The Society for Management Education, Kurukshetra etc. He is associated as a reviewer and editorial board member with various International Journals like International Journal of Social Economics, Tourism Review (both Emerald Publication, UK), Standard International Journals, Coimbatore, Journal of Reviews on Global Economics, Canada, International Journal of Management and Development Studies etc. He has published seven books in various fields of management. Currently four research scholars are pursuing PhD under his supervision.

Ömer Alkan enrolled in Atatürk University Economics and Administrative Sciences Department of Economics in 2001 and graduated from there in 2005. He received her MS in Department of Business from the Atatürk University in 2008. In the same year, he enrolled in his PhD in Business of Atatürk University. In 2010 he started to work as an Research Assistant at the Department of Business. In 2013, he appointed as assistant professor in the Department of Econometrics. In 2018, he appointed as associate professor in the Department of Econometrics and is currently working in the same department. His main research interests are discrete choice modelling, categorical data analysis, count data, spline regression models, public health, health economics, and poverty.

Sachin Kumar Behera is currently working as Guest Lecturer as well as pursuing his Ph.D. from Department of Tourism and Hotel Management, North Eastern Hill University, Shillong. He has done his MBA (Tourism and Travel Management) from the Indian Institute of Tourism and Travel Management, Gwalior. He has presented several papers in many International and National Conferences. His area of interest is tourist behavior, adventure tourism, and nature-based tourism.

Zélia Breda holds a PhD in Tourism, an MA in Chinese Studies (Business and International Relations) and a BSc in Tourism Management and Planning from the University of Aveiro (Portugal), where she is Assistant Professor. She is also Director of the Master in Tourism Management and Planning, and member of the Research Unit 'Governance, Competitiveness and Public Policies'.

Jeconiah Louis Dreisbach is Senior Research Specialist at the Asian Institute of Management. He is an elected Fellow of the Royal Asiatic Society of Great Britain and Ireland. He was also elected as an Associate Member of the National Research Council of the Philippines' Anthropology and Linguistics cluster. He is currently sitting as Editor of *Southeast Asian Media Studies* and an editorial board member of *Studies in Ethnicity and Nationalism*. Jecon was an Instructor at the Department of Social Sciences, De La Salle Araneta University. He has a master's degree in Philippine Studies from De La Salle University where he specialized in Philippine cultural and linguistic studies.

Sheeba Hamid is Professor in the Department of Commerce, Aligarh Muslim University Aligarh. She has teaching experience of more than eighteen years and five Ph. D. and one Post Doc has been awarded under her supervision. Currently, one Post Doc Fellow and seven Ph. D. scholars are working under her supervision.

Farooq Haq is an Associate Professor and Coordinator for the BBA Program in Faculty of Management at the Canadian University Dubai. He received his PhD from Charles Darwin University in Australia in 2011. His research interests are in various types of special interest tourism such as spiritual and heritage tourism. He is also among the early researchers of Islamic Marketing, halal branding and marketing of Islamic products and services. He has several publications as journal articles, conference papers and book chapters in his areas of research.

Saliha Karadayi-Usta received the B.A. (Hons.) degree in industrial engineering from Dogus University, Istanbul, Turkey, in 2012, and the M.Sc. degree in industrial engineering in 2014 from Istanbul Technical University (ITU), Istanbul, where she is currently working toward the Ph.D. degree in medical tourism service supply chain management. She is currently a Research Assistant with ITU. Her main research interest includes service supply chain management.

Tabassum Khan is currently working as an Assistant Professor in Unity College, Dimapur, Nagaland, India. She is an MBA from Tezpur University, NET (UGC) qualified and PhD from Aligarh Muslim University. She has been teaching undergraduate and post graduates students for more than 13 years. She has also industry experience. Apart from HRM, which is her area of specialization, her area of interest includes subjects such as Commercial law, Financial Management and Organisational Behaviour. She has many research papers and books to her credit.

Sharad Kumar Kulshreshtha (b. 1978), is an Assistant Professor at the Department of Tourism and Hotel Management, North-Eastern Hill University, Shillong-Meghalaya (India). He has more than 15 years of teaching and research experience. He has acclaimed publications research papers in various books, journals of national and international repute. He has participated and presented many research papers in national and international Seminars and Conferences. Recently, he has presented a paper International Conference on Wine Market and Cultures of Consumption in School of Hotel and Tourism Management, the Hong Kong Polytechnic University, Hong Kong. He is supervising Ph.D research scholars in the areas of event tourism, wine tourism, and avi-tourism of north-east India. He has also invited as a resource person in various universities and business associations of India to deliver talks as subject experts. He has co-edited a book on 'Emerging Dynamics of India Tourism & Hospitality: Transformation and Innovation as well as also editing books on Event Tourism of Northeast India, Indigenous Food and Beverages of Northeast India with repute publisher of India.

Anita Medhekar is a senior lecturer in economics and holds a PhD from Deakin University, Australia. She has taught at undergraduate and post graduate levels in India, Indonesia and Australia. Currently, she is teaching at Central Queensland University, Rockhampton, Australia. Her research interest is in applied Micro and Macroeconomics, International Trade, Development Economics, Public Finance, South-Asia, Health Economics, Tourism Economics, Bilateral Trade and Development for Peace, Public Policy, and Public-Private Partnerships. She has presented papers at numerous international conferences and has numerous publications to her credit as refereed conference proceedings, book chapters, and journal articles.

Sharon Mendoza-Dreisbach is an Assistant Professor at the School of Business, Skyline University College. Her research interests include ecotourism, health tourism, and human resource management in public administration. Her services for the Filipino community and fellow cancer patients earned her features from leading publications and awards from the Philippines and the Middle East.

Bipithalal Balakrishnan Nair is based at the University of Bedfordshire, Luton, United Kingdom. She holds her PhD in Tourism Management from the Institute of Tourism Research (INTOUR), University of Bedfordshire, United Kingdom. Her research draws from the transdisciplinary research includes soft power and tourism, postcolonial tourism, colonial nostalgia and creative tourism.

Pinki Paul completed her MBA in Human resources management from SMU, India. She has sound knowledge about the managerial aspects, employee job role, HR Policies. She attended various conferences and workshops. Also Pinki published two international journal papers and two book chapters.

Kirti Rawal received her B.Tech degree in Electronics & Communication Engineering from IITT college of Engineering, Pojewal, India in 2005 and then obtained her M.Tech degree in Electronics & Communication Engineering from BBSBEC

Fatehgarh Sahib, Punjab. She has done her Ph.D. in the area of Biomedical Signal Processing from NIT Jalandhar. She is serving as Associate Professor in Lovely Professional University from last 3 years.

Vítor Rodrigues holds a Masters Degree in Tourism Management and Planning from the University of Aveiro. He is currently working as a Research Fellow at the ARTUR project "The impact of air quality on the competitiveness of the tourism destinations".

Barjinder Saini was born in Jalandhar, India, in 1970. He received his B.Tech degree in Electronics & Communication Engineering from Gulbarga University, India in 1994, M.Tech. degree in Electronics & Communication Engineering from Kurukshetra University, India in 1996 and Ph.D. degree in the area of Signal Processing of heart rate variability from NIT Jalandhar, India, in 2009. He is serving as Associate Professor in Electronics & Communication Engineering Department, NIT Jalandhar, India from last 15 years. His research interests include Biomedical Signal Processing, Image Processing, Microprocessors & Microcontrollers, and Soft Computing. He is a member of IEEE, IEEE EMBS, and Fellow IETE. He has guided more that 20 MTech students and guiding 06 PhD research scholars. He has published more that 20 research papers in International Journals of repute.

Indu Saini was born in Ferozepur, India, in 1971. She received her B.Tech degree in Electronics & Communication Engineering from Guru Nanak Dev University, India in 1994 and then obtained her M.Tech(by Research) degree in Electronics & Communication Engineering from National Institute of Technology Jalandhar. She has done her Ph.D. in the area of Biomedical Signal Processing from Dr B R Ambedkar National Institute of Technology Jalandhar, where she is also serving as Assistant Professor in Electronics & Communication Engineering Department since 2002.

Gonçalo Santinha is Assistant Professor at the Department of Social, Political and Territorial Sciences of the University of Aveiro, Director of the Master in Public Administration and Management, Member of the research units 'Governance, Competitiveness and Public Policies' (GOVCOPP) and 'Centre of Studies on Geography and Spatial Planning' (CEGOT).

Nitya Saxena completed her doctorate in Economics with health focused research. She is a healthcare enthusiast and has published papers in the domain of disease burden, health insurance and public private partnership in healthcare. Her research interest include cost effective analysis of interventions, disease burden estimation, insurance for poor and related fields. At present she is working in a UNICEF project as a consultant and analyst.

Şeyda SerdarAsan is an Assistant Professor of Industrial Engineering at the Istanbul Technical University since 2012. She received her BSc and MSc degrees from Istanbul Technical University in 1999 and 2001, and her Doctoral degree from Technische Universität Berlin in 2009. Her current research interests focus on service supply chain management and supply chain complexity management.

Gaurav Sethi received his B.Tech degree and M.Tech degree in Electronics & Communication Engineering. He has done his Ph.D. in the area of Biomedical Image Processing from NIT Jalandhar. He is serving as Professor in Lovely Professional University from last 13 years.

Umendra Shukla is a Professor and Head Dept. of Travel & Tourism management, Dr. Bhimrao Ambedkar University Agra. He is a former Dean in Faculty of Management and also former Director, Institute of Tourism & Hotel Management in Dr. Bhimrao Ambedkar University Agra. He has published many research articles in reputed national and international journals. He has contributed chapters in many books and also edited a book with Dr. Sharad Kumar Kulsreshtha, entitled "Emerging Dynamics of Indian Tourism and Hospitality" some more books are in process to come in the market. He has presented many research articles in national and international conferences at different part of the country, Sri Lanka, Malaysia, Indonesia and Italy.

Mohit Vij is an Associate Professor at the School of Business, Skyline University College, United Arab Emirates (UAE). With more than twenty years of experience, he is a recipient of academic scholarship from HEC Montreal, Canada. He has made significant contribution in tourism academia and his research work has been published in leading journals and books, national newspapers and tourism magazines. Dr Mohit has also been actively involved in tourism training projects for UAE Destination Management Organizations (DMO) such as SCTDA (Sharjah Commerce and Tourism Development Authority), RAKTDA (Ras Al Khaimah Tourism Development Authority) and ATDD (Ajman Tourism Development Department). He was awarded for Excellence in Teaching (AY 2011-12; 2017-18) and for Excellence in Services (AY 2014-15). Before joining Skyline University College, Dr Mohit served as Head of Tourism Department in the Institute of Integrated and Honors Studies, Kurukshetra University, India, where he led the development and launch of Bachelor in Tourism Management (BTM) program.

İkram Yusuf Yarbaşı enrolled in Atatürk University Economics and Administrative Sciences Department of Econometrics in 2009 and graduated from there in 2013. He fulfilled his Master's in Department of Econometrics from Atatürk University in 2015. In the same year, he enrolled in his PhD in Econometrics of Atatürk University and is currently a PhD student. In 2016 he started to work as a Research Assistant in Erzurum Technical University Economics and Administrative Sciences Department of Econometrics and is currently working in the same department. His main research interests are log-linear models, categorical data analysis, econometric analysis, time series analysis, and energy consumption.

Index

A

B

C

D

E

F

G

H

I

K

M

P

R

S

T

www.ingramcontent.com/pod-product-compliance
Lightning Source LLC
LaVergne TN
LVHW080559300926
849162LV00005B/996